HIT THE ROAD, JACK

Hit the Road, Jack

Essays on the Culture of the American Road

Edited by

GORDON E. SLETHAUG

STACILEE FORD

McGill-Queen's University Press

Montreal & Kingston · London · Ithaca

© McGill-Queen's University Press 2012

ISBN 978-0-7735-4075-0 (cloth)
ISBN 978-0-7735-4076-7 (paper)

Legal deposit fourth quarter 2012
Bibliothèque nationale du Québec

Printed in Canada on acid-free paper that is 100% ancient forest free
(100% post-consumer recycled), processed chlorine free

This book has been published with the help of a grant from the
University of Southern Denmark.

McGill-Queen's University Press acknowledges the support of the
Canada Council for the Arts for our publishing program. We also
acknowledge the financial support of the Government of Canada
through the Canada Book Fund for our publishing activities.

Library and Archives Canada Cataloguing in Publication

   Hit the road, Jack : essays on the culture of the American road /
edited by Gordon E. Slethaug, Stacilee Ford.

Includes bibliographical references and index.
ISBN 978-0-7735-4075-0 (bound). – ISBN 978-0-7735-4076-7 (pbk.)

   1. Travel – Social aspects – United States – History. 2. Migration,
Internal – Social aspects – United States – History. 3. Road films
– United States – History and criticism. 4. Travelers' writings,
American – History and criticism. I. Slethaug, Gordon II. Ford,
Stacilee

G155.U6H58 2012   306.4'8190973   C2012-905847-5

Typeset by Jay Tee Graphics Ltd. in 10.5/13 Sabon

Dedication

This book is dedicated to the hard-working, dedicated, and collegial team that specifically contributed to the Road in America course and made American Studies a success at the University of Hong Kong in the early days of the program. These include those who were under contract in the program, those co-opted from departments, and those who came as Fulbright scholars. At various times this team consisted of Iska Alter, Paul Attinello, Geeta Singh Chanda, Patricia Ehrens, Stacilee Ford, Eleanor Heginbotham, Susan Kuyper, Karen Jo Laidler, Gina Marchetti, Mano Mora, Carolyn Muir, Priscilla Roberts, Cotten Seiler, Max Skidmore, Gordon Slethaug, Tom Stanley, and Wendy Zierler.

Contents

Acknowledgments

We would like to acknowledge several people and agencies that have made this book possible. First, we would like to recognize the editorial staff at McGill-Queens University Press: Philip Cercone and Joanne Pisano who saw promise in the text; Lesley Andrassy who asked the right questions and helped to improve the text; and Ryan Van Huijstee who shepherded the manuscript through to publication. Next, we would like to thank the University of Southern Denmark (especially the Institute for Speech and Communication) for their financial support of this project and to the Department of History at the University of Hong Kong for hosting many of the Fulbright scholars as well as American Studies staff while the program was in transition to its present independent status. Then, we (especially Gordon Slethaug) would like to thank the Fulbright Foundation and Lingnan Foundation for their special support over a number of years. Dr Zierler would like to acknowledge her students in "Reel Theology" and "Modern Jewish Literature" at Hebrew University College for their insights into ideas for her chapter. Finally, we would like to thank the University of Chicago Press for their permission to include Dr Seiler's chapter.

HIT THE ROAD, JACK

Introduction

STACILEE FORD AND GORDON SLETHAUG

The essays in this anthology have different ideological and disciplinary perspectives on the road, but the authors all share a passion for an idea that is, in the important process of reconsidering notions of nation and national myth, surprisingly resilient. The inspiration for this book came from a course created in the late 1990s at the University of Hong Kong (HKU) by Gordon Slethaug, Stacilee Ford, Paul Attinello, Mario Mora, Patricia Erens, and Wendy Zierler. Since that time several other colleagues have participated in shaping the HKU course, and various versions have been taught in Guangzhou China, the USA, Canada, and Denmark.

Celebrating scholarly connections across the globe and building upon visiting Fulbright and Lingnan Foundation support for more than a decade, this collection reflects a journey that has nurtured collegiality, scholarship, and the building of American Studies in Hong Kong, and, to a certain extent, in the Chinese Mainland – a gathering of community on the road to knowledge. While we anticipate that professors, researchers, and undergraduate and graduate students across the globe will find this volume a helpful accompaniment to their work in American and cultural studies, US history, literature, and film, and global studies, we are confident that the volume has significant appeal for the general reader interested in the notion of the road in American culture.

Undeniably, the American road has captured global interest due to enhanced and ever-increasing links in transport, popular culture, and commerce. However, because of the importance of the road in the construction and critique of America and Americans, we focus on the road in the continental United States – albeit with theoretical perspectives that take note of critiques of more traditional

American studies and those with a more recent "New Americanist"/ post-national view. The construction and critique of America and the American dream that are *reflected and contested* in our study of the various media of the road include the importance of: individual and national freedom, independence, and mobility; democratic space in a simultaneously present and vanished frontier; self-reliance and liberal individualism; diversity in ethnicity, race, class, gender, and culture; communal and personal transformation; rebellious counter-cultural challenges to a complacent and conservative society; and the formation of a national identity posited on exceptionalism – the view that America has a special purpose, responsibility, and destiny that it must pursue nationally and internationally, materially, politically, and spiritually.

While we applaud the efforts of scholars deploying "New Americanist" transnational or post-exceptionalist perspectives to critically comment on the ethnocentric excesses and empire-building intellectual projects within American studies, we realize the need to understand how these dispositions and attitudes came into being and coalesced into a national identity. One need look no further than road genres to see not only how the myth of the journey to freedom, knowledge, and transformation continues to seduce travellers who set out to explore, escape, reinvent, and renew but also how they can contest those very values. Of course, we are not just speaking of actual highways but of the power of the road trope as it describes larger attitudes and values linked to the US political, social, and cultural landscape, past and present. This volume helps to parse the triumphalist rhetoric from the complex realities in a nation that can boast of a great deal but must also face deep internal inadequacies.

The special strength of our comparative and cross-cultural journey as teaching colleagues lies in our diversity of disciplinary and interdisciplinary approaches across genre and media as well as over time and geographic space. As a result, through a variety of cultural texts – literature, film, reality television, virtual reality sources (including video games and the internet), music, philosophy, and political rhetoric – this anthology digs deeply while casting a broad net in its approach to the road. Mindful of the classic road texts and films, this volume references and moves beyond them in a call and response that takes into account perspectives from history, literature, spatial relations, and material culture along the road, as well as postmodern theory, gender studies, and personal reminiscence/

narrative research. The essays, like their authors, take us on unique road trips that reflect experiences, scholarly expertise, and personality.

Another characteristic of this collection is its coupling of generational difference and the road. We have learned in our teaching – whether in Williamsburg, Virginia, or Guangzhou, China – that younger students are interested in the myth of the road, but they need to understand its contemporary resonance for each new age cohort. When Gordon Slethaug took our first group of HKU American Studies majors on the road, he was surprised at how little patience they had for sitting on a bus and looking out of windows at the rural landscape. We had assumed that our students – who were, in the classroom, quite captivated by the myth and mystique of the road – would embrace an honest-to-goodness road trip. What we had not anticipated was that Hong Kong students – with urban sensibilities and a desire to experience movement of a different sort – would have a different relationship to the road from that of Americans. Furthermore, their experience of being the "ethnic other" on the road shaped their experience, because in 1998 it felt as if we were a novelty: people seemed surprised to see a busload of Chinese students rolling down the highways of Virginia and North Carolina. As students saw the diversity of the USA, but also experienced being the targets of ethnic slights and racial slurs, they came to understand both the exploration and exploitation that has characterized the road over time. During the trip, we talked about the ways that this American journey reinscribed Jack Kerouac's accounts of trips across the United States and how it could help students to understand first-hand the issues raised by *Easy Rider*.

Most studies of the road have focused on literature, film, automobility, or history of the road, but singly rather than in an interdisciplinary combination. Among the earliest full studies were James Flink's important pieces discussing "The Three Stages of American Automobile Consciousness" (1972), *The Car Culture* (1975), and *The Automobile Age* (1988). These interconnected studies looked at the way the automobile, automotive industries, and the development of highways affected American culture during its development in the twentieth century. Many more automobility studies followed. Cotten Seiler's recent *Republic of Drivers* (2008) looks at "the *affect* generated by driving"[1] and relates automobility to various political (e.g., Workman's Compensation) and cultural initiatives (e.g.,

Taylorization) in the first part of the automobile phenomenon in the early twentieth century and during its high point in the fifties. This study explores the cultural, intellectual, racial, and social history of automobility, related "social and national identities and ideologies", and the development of an "expressive-individualist" automobile subjectivity based on self-realization and personal difference.[2]

Another group of critics focused on literary texts. Three key studies came out at about the same time: Ronald Primeau's *The Romance of the Road: the Literature of the American Highway* (1996); Kris Lackey's *Road Frames: the American Highway Narrative* (1997); and Roger Casey's *Textual Vehicles: the Automobile in American Literature* (1997). Primeau explores the structural history, generic configurations, self discovery, quest for national identity, social protest, and cultural diversity in fictional and non-fictional road narratives that combine "elements of pilgrimage, quest romance, *Bildungsroman*, and the picaresque."[3] Lackey also covers some of that ground in investigating fictive and non-fictive "shadow texts" that "ignored or repressed antithetical messages that lie beneath the authors' assertions."[4] Lackey's perceived road themes include freedom and automotive independence, discovery of the self and the virgin and pastoral land of the American West, the relationship between the essential self and technology, the personal and national past in relation to the present, and cynical and romantic highways. These literary themes carry over to the non-literary in twentieth-century highway books as well, and Lackey provides a taxonomy to explore them. Casey's dual exploration focuses on the automobile as well as its incarnations in the cultural matrix and especially in American literature. He observes that "the car is the driving machine of America, the machine that affects and has affected the lives of Americans more than any other" in society and in American literature. He notes the ongoing literary fascination with the automobile beginning in Broadway plays as early as 1893, well before Theodore Dreiser's *A Hoosier Holiday* in 1916, which is often considered the first American road novel.[5]

Other than those on automobility and literature, contemporary books on the road have focused on films, although, as recently as 2008, Devin Orgeron noted that "little sustained critical attention has been paid to the road movie, and still less to this much broader international and historical context."[6] The attention that has been paid began with Timothy Corrigan's *A Cinema without Walls: Movies and Culture after Vietnam* (1991), which noted that road films had been largely overlooked in film criticism, that the road genre did not really begin until after the Second World War, that it is a highly self-conscious genre, and that it is intrinsically tied to conflicted notions of the automobile.[7] More contemporary works on road movies include: *The Road Movie Book* (1997), edited by Steven Cohan and Ina Rae Hark; *Driving Visions: Exploring the Road Movie* (2002) by David Laderman; and *Road Movies: from Muybridge and Méliès to Lynch and Kiarostami* (2008) by Devin Orgeron. Another that has a bias towards film is Katie Mills's *The Road Story and the Rebel: Moving through Film, Fiction, and Television* (2006). Cohan and Hark's volume of sixteen separate essays discusses particular road films, mainly from the 1950s onward, from perspectives that include historical underpinnings, relevant technologies and film techniques, genre, gender, masculinities, feminism, existentialism, alienation, and the nation. Laderman's analysis was the first to provide a full view of road movies as they are attached to particular American historical developments. He notes that road films were already highly developed before the end of the Second World War and that other countries have been producing numbers of road films as well. Mills very specifically assesses only American road films following *Easy Rider*, while Orgeron is interested in international intersections that account for the flourishing of the genre, both past and present, in terms of realism and postmodernity.

Because we do not wish to assume that the reader has a certain "road quotient" or familiarity with the myth of the road in the US, we have tried to balance overviews of certain historical themes with contemporary and textured case studies. Various theoretical perspectives underpin the essays, but theoretical language has been kept to a minimum. Several chapters consider the impact of identity – particularly race, ethnicity, gender, and sexual orientation – on the way various road trips are taken.

Each contributor brings a unique perspective to the consideration of the road as symbol and reality. The first chapters explore the metaphorical and historical roots of the road culture and genre in the US, while the later ones focus on contemporary innovations. In "Mapping the Trope: A Historical and Cultural Journey," Gordon Slethaug opens the volume with an account of the ways that the trope – image, metaphor, symbol – of the road developed from Walt Whitman to the present. As he notes, the road was first used by

Whitman as a trope for adventure, camaraderie, and appreciation of the infinite variety of nature, culture, and humankind, but, especially with the accelerated settlement of the West through the Homestead Act, it took on a magnified sense of individualism, independence, and orientation to the West. As cars were introduced and roads developed more strategically, the road's relation to adventure continued, but became culturally embodied as an East to West journey that could be taken individually, with buddies, or with families. The essay notes that in the second half of the twentieth century the resistance to consumerism, middle-class values, and the Vietnam War helped to create a trope of the road focused on rebellion. Important fiction and film such as Kerouac's *On the Road* and Hopper's *Easy Rider* moulded the genres of road fiction and film by appealing not only to the young, adventurous, and rebellious but also to the disenchanted and cynical. Later, with multiculturalism, economic and social stability, and globalization, the road trope became increasingly ironic and self-contradictory, but also playful, soft, and romantic in self-consciously overturning "old hierarchies" and asserting "new meanings," which Katie Mills for one finds to be quintessentially postmodern.[8]

In "Politics, People Moving, and the American Myth of the Road," Max Skidmore, a political scientist and historian, demonstrates why the USA, which has been such a success in so many ways, fell behind in actual transportation infrastructure. He sees this lack as indicative of a larger national tendency to tolerate deficiencies in health care, retirement programs, and environmental protection measures. He notes the co-existence of both a community ethos and a Darwinian apathy in the public sphere. Providing an accessible but detailed historical overview of the development (and underdevelopment) of the highway system in the US, Skidmore explores the contradiction that is at the heart of the myth of the American road: American mobility is surprisingly limited despite the nation's wealth and technological prowess. Skidmore argues that America's Jeffersonian heritage created a spirit of independence, self-reliance, and wariness of oppression that served it well but also bequeathed resistance to government action and disregard of the public sphere.

Susan Kuyper's essay, "The Road in American Vernacular Music," turns from road-making to a consideration of the road and traveller in American folk songs from the earliest Puritan settlements to the present. This account reminds us that we all have tunes we associate with road trips, travelling, and movement, but the analysis suggests that "road folk songs" describe romantic, sad, nostalgic, and tragic moments; cover terrain from east to west and north to south; deal with spiritual and secular destinations; and treat different kinds of travellers, including the sailor, the soldier, the frontiersman, the cowboy, the lumberjack, the settler, the escaping slave, and the hungry migrants of the Great Depression. Kuyper manages to give a sense of the historical depth as well as the aesthetic variety of road music, reminding us that the sound track of America's road is at once personal, communal, and national.

Following on from themes raised by Slethaug, Skidmore, and Kuyper, Cotten Seiler's essay on "African-American Automobility and Cold-War Liberalism" turns our attention to the way racial identities have marked the ability to take advantage of the freedoms of the American road. In an essay drawn from one that appeared recently in *The Republic of Drivers*, Seiler provides a cultural analysis of guidebooks specifically written for African-American travellers on the American road in the mid-twentieth century. Seiler notes that the books "provided a multifaceted, often contradictory rhetoric of communal racial uplift and liberal individualism figured around driving." Seiler reminds us that the American road "was established under specific regimes of racialized inequality and limited access whose codes it reproduces." Yet, despite the discrimination that African-Americans faced on the road, publications such as *The Negro Motorist Green Book* and *Travelguide* expressed a surprising faith in "the equalizing mechanisms of American democracy and consumer capitalism."

In "Witnesses, Wanderers, and Writers: Women on the Road," Eleanor Heginbotham turns our attention to the women of the Beat Movement of the 1950s, many of whom appeared in, inspired, or wrote their own road stories. Doing the work of women's history/ gender studies on multiple levels, Heginbotham restores women to the historical landscape and shows how they claimed the space of the road and helped to shape a movement and a generation. Her essay adds to revisionist work on the women Beats. Yet more is at stake here than simply rendering women as visible actors on the road or in narrating the trope. Heginbotham reminds us that women have had a place – even in that most "male" of preserves – and illustrates how their experiences rupture earlier, more masculinist views, moving us towards a gendering and thus a reconceptualization of the road as place and symbol. Reminding us of the importance of the women, such as Gabrielle (Mamere) Kerouac and Edie Parker, who exercised a particular influence on Beat men, Heginbotham re-envisions the literary production – ranging from memoirs and letters to novels and biographical accounts of the Beat cohort/era – as more ensemble-like than solitary. She also foregrounds the work of several other prolific women of the Beat era, noting that, while they differed in their backgrounds, identities, and adventures, they shared in the literary/cultural revolution that served as a counterpoint to the rapidly developing American economic and military might.

While Heginbotham shows the complex gendering of an increasingly rebellious road in the 1950s, Paul Attinello in "Assassin in a Three-Piece Suit: *Slow Fire*, Minimalism, and the Eighties," demonstrates how cynical the road had become even in experimental, minimalist, and operatic musical traditions. He reinvents the journey to the West by describing a modern barbarian "gun for hire," a rigid, unrelenting paranoiac whose endlessly cycling memories are haunted by his father's rifle suicide, and who has solved the nightmare of that first gunshot by becoming a hired assassin who drives from place to place and job to job in a suit and wrap-around shades. In that context, he links the polished savagery of the 1980s' business warrior to ruthless right-wing capitalism and tropes of the road. In this study Attinello demonstrates how a child's fantasy of the road, based on images from the American collective consciousness, has turned into a paranoid nightmare world of the the post-Vietnam era when the United States' restless expansion westward turned into a murderous war that affected not only the Vietnamese but also the soldiers who returned and could not live with that burden but passed it on to their sons, who also could not live with it. In Attinello's account, showing how aspects of the road are tied to modernist music, there is no end of the road for the mass, only for the individual.

In "Complicating *The Simple Life*: Reality Television and the Road," Stacilee Ford shifts the focus from savage capitalist masculinity to the hyper-public road antics of Paris Hilton and Nicole Richie. Arguing that television road trips have helped to cement the myth of the road in American psyches, she compares *The Simple Life 2: Road Trip* to earlier American television shows focused on the road as a site of relaxation, comedy, and social critique via women's "sister acts" of encounter with the "other" at home. Linking the tropes of gender, nation, and class, Ford explores the way that even the frothiest of reality television shows force celebrities and viewers to confront contemporary realities. As reality television becomes more familiar in many cultural contexts, Ford connects themes within the Hilton/Richie series to larger debates about gender, generation, and the power of popular culture in an era of increasing globalization. Ford also explores some of the ways in which consumption, power, and national identity have been, and continue to be, intertwined in the production and reception of television programming.

In "Postmodern Masculinities in Recent Buddy and Solo Road Films," Gordon Slethaug offers a discussion of masculinities through the lens of Hollywood's late twentieth- and early twenty-first-century travellers, noting that the recent return to romanticism and the road connects the present to the past, as well as youth to the middle aged and elderly. He finds that it is especially age – with its accompanying exposure to life's experiences – that allows men in these films to connect with self, family, and society. This late postmodernism incorporates and harkens back to the social critiques and lessons of earlier road genres and acknowledges harsh economic realities, personal conflict and betrayal, dysfunctional family life, the difficulties of young love, and the ravages of age. But it also posits new masculinities that incorporate self-discovery, love, family and community, a resolution to the main complications, an evasion of threats and dangers, and a celebration of life.

In "*Transamerica*: Queer Cinema in the Middle of the Road," Gina Marchetti reminds us that "sexual minorities, the road, and the cinema share a long, complex, multifaceted history in American popular culture." Offering a brief but rich overview of various films and their representations of queer sexualities, Marchetti notes that the road was a space of possibility and danger for those whose identities placed them at odds with the hegemony of heterosexuality in claiming the road myth. She writes, "facing the constraints of the heterosexual norm or threats of violence at home, some LGBT people have found themselves on the road throughout American history as explorers, adventurers, prospectors, trappers, hobos, itinerant merchants or performers, hitchhikers, truckers, drifters, or cowboys." Marchetti's lively discussion of *Transamerica* historicizes the film and illustrates why it belongs to a venerable cinematic tradition of alternative sexuality and mobility in Hollywood as well as in independent film. Marchetti helps us understand that queer interpretations of the road are anything but marginal.

In "Fools on the American Road: 'Gimpel the Fool,' *The Frisco Kid,* and *Forrest Gump,*" Wendy Zierler looks at two films about the fool on the road, juxtaposing *The Frisco Kid* with *Forrest Gump* and relying on Isaac Bashevis Singer's short story "Gimpel the Fool" to underscore the importance of the Yiddish *schlemiel* – or holy fool – in seemingly disparate popular-culture comic texts. In arguing for a paradoxical mixing of meanings, Zierler's creative grouping of Forrest, Avram, and Gimpel models the arabesque that interdisciplinarity between film and fiction facilitates, even as she demonstrates the importance of the non-mechanized road in American culture.

Michael Truscello's essay, "Generically Mobile: the Projection of Protocol from the Road Movie to Virtual Reality and Video Games," compares the road movie with the virtual reality film. He notes that the road movie's concern with rebellion against traditional social and cultural norms persistently gives way to the very conservative cultural codes that the genre attempts to escape. Truscello challenges us to see manifestations of "the protocological road": we are free to move because of the rules and technology in place, yet our freedom is constrained by the same technological delimitations. This paradoxical freedom-constraint reading of these genres helps to articulate the constraints of technicity (the operations of technology at various times) in early road movies such as *The Wizard of Oz* (1939), the postmodern *Wild at Heart* (1990), the virtual reality film *TRON* (1982), and numerous current video games. Turning the metaphor of the freedom of travel inside out, Truscello notes that when we are travellers on the protocological road, the buoyant refrain "follow the Yellow Brick Road" becomes less the jubilant expression of deliverance from self-imposed exile and more the controlled imperative of industrialized wandering.

In their variety and scope, the essays bring together themes that connect past and present, challenge the fondest orthodoxies about the myth of the road, and open spaces to see how new myths may be created in a post-national world. The American road is indeed a trope, myth, and important symbol of an exceptionalist USA, but it is a vitally important idea to understand, unpack, and refashion. Like roads themselves in the USA, the metaphor of the road is always under construction.

1

Mapping the Trope: A Historical and Cultural Journey

GORDON E. SLETHAUG

I mean, man, whither goest thou? Whither goest thou, America, in thy
shiny car in the night.

Kerouac, *On the Road*

The popular expression and song, "Hit the Road, Jack," is as much
a part of American slang and culture as Jack Kerouac's best-selling
narrative of adolescent life, *On the Road*, but "the road" as a lure
and an icon predates these twentieth-century cultural productions.
European colonists went on transatlantic highways to settle the New
World; Americans pushed westward towards the ever-receding frontier in pursuit of the American Dream; and Chinese and Japanese
immigrants came to the West and gradually pushed toward the
East. Only well into the nineteenth century did men and women
go on the road to work or relax, be alone or enjoy companionship,
satisfy curiosity or follow dreams, and explore all those things that
we now identify with the road. From that time "the road" became
an increasingly complex image, metaphor, and icon – or trope – for
nation-based exploration and exploitation, the journeys of families
in pursuit of better living conditions and of individuals who hoped
to discover more about their identities, and, in the process, overcome
difficulties and limitations in transforming themselves.

Strictly speaking, the road is not confined to American culture,
but, as Laderman and Mills remark, in the USA it is inextricably
linked to claims of national identity, among them exceptionalism[1]
(the notion, albeit contested, that America from its inception has
had a special raison d'être and destiny based on religion, politics,

economy, and culture), because the development of the USA was so closely identified with innovative transportation and communications technology – ships, trains, planes, automobiles, and, of course, the media – that brought people together in diverse ways. The restlessness and ease with which large segments of the American population move and resettle characterizes many aspects of life in the USA, turning the road into one of the most powerful symbols in American history and culture. The road winds from past to present and encompasses all segments of society, regardless of appearance, ethnicity, age, gender, sexuality, or economic standing. For all of its risks, dangers, and disappointments, the road has held the promise of discovery and new occupations. It continues to do so today within and beyond the geographical confines of the USA.

In recent years, the road movie has been the primary artistic manifestation of the road trope, raising issues and building vocabulary, images, and ranges of meaning. As Bennet Schaber remarks, "the road film builds up its conceptual vocabulary by linking territory and memory, terrain and time, event and meaning, initiation and representation, narration and image."[2] What has been done in this area mainly begins with the Depression and the Second World War, but the process of "troping the road" across culture has been going on for centuries. This essay fills a textual and historical gap by looking at the development of the trope of the road through seminal periods and iconic texts that shaped this transformation in the USA from the mid-nineteenth century forward. When critics do try to situate the trope of the road or the requirements of the genre, it is usually in the context of a particular thematic feature such as rebellion. As Katie Mills says of her own study, "this project is less concerned with the question of auteurism – such as the specific contributions to the road genre made by John Steinbeck, Walt Whitman, Jack Kerouac, or Peter Fonda, for that matter – than it is with how these pioneers stimulated subsequent generations of rebels."[3]

To map the road trope historically, this essay begins with Whitman's "Song of the Open Road" and Romanticism; then explores Manifest Destiny, the frontier, and the movement westward as illustrated in John Ford's *Stagecoach*. Next it considers the imprint on the trope of the consequences of the development of automobiles and mechanized farming in John Steinbeck's/John Ford's *Grapes of Wrath;* then turns to the growth of trans-American travel after the Second World War and the counterculture as seen in Jack Kerouac's *On the Road*. The dystopian manifestation of that counterculture in Dennis Hopper's *Easy Rider* and other buddy outlaw films is then considered. Finally it looks at the confluence of multiculturalism, postmodernism, and the neo-Romantic in various films at the end of the twentieth century.

HISTORICAL AND CULTURAL BACKGROUND AND THE TYPOLOGY OF THE ROAD

The history of travel goes back thousands of years, but, with a few important exceptions, such as Roman roads, travel was largely restricted to paths, cart tracks, waterways, and open seas until the eighteenth century, and this was especially true in America. As the travel writer Bill Bryson notes, "until well after the time of the Revolution, America had virtually no highways worthy of the name. Such roads as existed were often little more than Indian trails, seldom more than fifteen inches wide and fraught with the obvious peril that you might at any time run into a party of Indians."[4] He further remarks, "Signposts, maps and other aids to the bewildered traveler were all but unknown. (The first book of road maps would not be published until 1789.)"[5] Just as tellingly, Bryson comments, "until well into the nineteenth century, it was as cheap to send a ton of goods across the Atlantic as it was to move it thirty miles overland,"[6] because only a couple of real roads existed around Philadelphia and Boston at the end of the eighteenth century.[7] The opening of the Erie Canal between New York City and the Great Lakes in 1825 was such an extraordinary success because there were few overland alternatives to move people and goods between the East Coast and the interior. As a result, the road as a reality and an important complex image and metaphor carried little freight until later in the nineteenth century.

Because there were so few roads, Walt Whitman's 1856 poem "Song of the Open Road" comes as a nice surprise. In the poem, he develops the trope of the road in pastoral, romantic, and transcendental ways that readers of culture might recognize in later fiction, film, and media – as Kris Lackey does in his study called "Transcendental Motoring."[8] In addition, as Ronald Primeau notes, "Walt Whitman contributed significantly to the modern road narrative in his synthesis of quest conventions and his expansion of the genre's protest against the status quo." He goes on: "'Song of the Open Road' is an epitome of the themes and concerns of later American road narratives which invite readers to move against the grain and to challenge dominant values."[9] Whitman's "Song of the Open Road" thus achieves a prominence in the road tradition that few other works can contest and it bears exploring in some detail.

Whitman divides the poem into two parts, the first an apostrophe or address to the road itself and the second an invitation (*Allons*! or "Let's go") from the narrator to the reader to travel the road together, share experiences, and mutually explore perceptions and insights. In this way, he creates the link between the road and the traveller that forms the foundation of the road trope. Not only that: he invests the road with a philosophical and religious aura that becomes a recognizable part of the image. Near the opening of the poem, the narrative persona apostrophizes the road, speaking in the language of a supplicant to a deity:

> You road I enter upon and look around, I believe you are not all
>   that is here,
> . I believe that much unseen is also here.
> Here the profound lesson of reception, nor preference nor denial
>   (2.16–18)

Having its own identity and open to interrogation, the road is the subject of meditation, a repository of wisdom, a participant in communication, and a social equalizer, allowing the narrator and reader access to the travellers' spirituality, physicality, and even sexuality.

The narrator's invitation to travellers is fully welcoming and extends into time indefinitely:

> Camerado, I give you my hand!
> I give you my love more precious than money,
> I give you myself before preaching or law;
> Will you give me yourself? Will you come travel with me?
> Shall we stick by each other as long as we live? (15.220–4)

The narrator's list of those he encounters on the road – "the black with his woolly head, the felon, the diseas'd, the illiterate person, are not denied" (2.19) – makes it clear that not all the walkers and riders are among the privileged; he includes those believed to comprise the underbelly of America at that time – those who were poor, black, sick, criminal, or uneducated. According to Kusmer in *Down and Out, On the Road: The Homeless in American History*, vagrants on the road included previous military men, former or escaped slaves, runaway servants or those who had completed their indenture, apprentices who had escaped their masters, and men expelled from small towns for laziness or irresponsible behaviour.[10] Whitman had the eye of a journalist in observing this diverse group but the mind of a romantic poet in turning their experiences on the road into a metaphor of democratic adventure and spiritual insight, because the narrator invites men and women equally and hopes to right some of the social wrongs through travel. Granted, this road poem celebrates social conscience, gender equality, and the "democratization of mobility"[11] rather than directly criticizing of the American cultural landscape, but it paved the way for those, such as Charlie Chaplin in *The Tramp* or John Steinbeck in *Grapes of Wrath*, who would be more critical of a society that failed to make equal allowance for all its people, particularly its marginalized underclass. Twentieth-century literature and film would have much to say about this underclass and the ways in which its members were scorned when they hit the road.

Those on Whitman's road, then, were a varied lot, and their journeys take on many forms and shape various messages as part of Whitman's inclusive and romantic vision: the road becomes a wild sea or wilderness path that creates unknown hazards for the traveller (10.124); it becomes a country road opening up endless vistas and fascinating opportunities for the autonomous traveller; and it cannot be entirely separated from the society, issues, and dependencies of the city street (12.151–4). As Ronald Primeau argues:

> The American road genre expresses this kind of emergence, reflecting in the road hero evolving social and cultural values and beliefs. Road narratives also express what Bakhtin calls "the spatial whole of the world." Space on the road is not a passive background or a completed scene travelers merely pass through, but is itself an evolving interaction of the pastoral landcape and cultural symbols.[12]

The road is more than just a means of going from one place to another; it is also a metaphorical path of life from past to present or youth to death and immortality, and, for Whitman's narrator, the universal way of spiritual progress. It is, then, the traveller's task

> To take the best of the farmer's farm and the rich man's elegant
> villa, and the chaste blessings of the well-married couple, and
> the fruits of orchards and flowers of gardens,
> To take to your use out of the compact cities as you pass
> through,
> To carry buildings and streets with you afterward wherever you
> go,
> To gather the minds of men out of their brains as you encounter
> them, to gather the love out of their hearts,
> To take your lovers on the road with you, for all that you leave
> them behind you,
> To know the universe itself as a road, as many roads, as roads
> for traveling souls.
>
> All parts away for the progress of souls,
> All religion, all solid things, arts, governments – all that was or
> is apparent upon this globe or any globe, falls into niches and
> corners before the procession of souls along the grand roads of
> the universe.
>
> Of the progress of the souls of men and women along the grand
> roads of the universe, all other progress is the needed emblem
> and sustenance. (13.175–83)

For Whitman, the road is more than a place for individual travel,
panoramic views of nature, and cultural observations, it is a locus
of community, the sustainer of life and instigator of change, and a
source of physical and spiritual energy. It is also a mark of progress.

Whitman's poem shapes the diverse elements into a romantic construction that has become critical to, and contested in, the trope of
the road in American culture:

· identification and participation between the narrative persona
  and the travellers
· the identity of the main travellers or subjects and their inherent
  relationship to the road
· the road itself
· leave-taking and reasons for going
· the mode of transportation or mobility (ship, walking, carriage)
· the physical journey and exploration

- the social community formed along the way
- the landscape and sights encountered
- the insights gathered
- the progress of the self, soul, and civilization as a result of this combination

To this Primeau would add protest, because "in some ways, all road trips are protests. People leave home to change the scene, to overcome being defined by custom, tradition, and circumstances back home, and – at least for a while – to construct an alternative way of living."[13] The trope of the road later undergoes important changes, though the elements and foundations remain so surprisingly in line with Whitman that Lackey can say of the automobile and motoring: "the automobile is a machine apart, good for autonomy and solitude, meditation and country escapes" and the Romantic or "Transcendental possibilities of motoring lie beneath most philosophical driving," especially in "the rolling examinations of self (as it relates to family, society, politics, aesthetics, and history)."[14]

What Whitman does not include is something that became increasingly critical in the culture of the road: the expansion of the American frontier. (Nor does he address the strong sense of the autonomous self that Katie Mills finds to be one of the most important parts of the trope of the road,[15] though there is plenty of self-celebration in other poems by Whitman.) Although Whitman is a New York City poet, he rarely confines himself to the city, so it is odd that nowhere in this poem does he specifically address westward expansion, for the "taming of the frontier" was already an important metaphor deployed by nineteenth-century elites in a rapidly developing market economy. With the Louisiana Purchase in 1803, Thomas Jefferson imagined he had "created an empire of liberty that stretched from sea to shining sea,"[16] and the explorers Meriwether Lewis and William Clark were deputized to justify and popularize this national purchase. Their much-vaunted expedition fired the American imagination and assured the expansion of travel and settlement well beyond the Eastern seaboard.

As the nineteenth century progressed, new paths were opened to the wide-open spaces of the Midwest and Far West and to multiple justifications of Manifest Destiny, a term first coined in 1845 by Whitman's friend John O'Sullivan of the *Democratic Review*. Advocating an American nation stretching from Atlantic to Pacific,

Manifest Destiny proclaimed the right and the duty of Americans to settle the vast North American continent, civilize and Christianize native peoples, and turn the wilderness into "productive" farms, ranches, and towns. For over 200 years America had considered itself exceptional and believed itself to have a unique calling or destiny, so Manifest Destiny as a cultural imperative provided a new instrument for reinforcing this belief. This was a political decision, which Whitman supported (though it does not specifically enter into "Song of the Open Road"), and others experienced as a form of colonization. Nevertheless, this notion of the territorial and spiritual destiny of America informed the travel and settlement of the West and ultimately attached itself to the trope of the road.

Related forms of cultural production linked mobility to Westward movement and increasingly rendered the trope of the road not only more "American" but specifically Western. For instance, the expansive Rocky Mountain landscapes of both Albert Bierstadt and Thomas Moran were direct products of the ideology of Manifest Destiny. Their visual representations accompany Whitman's words. Both Bierstadt and Moran were landscape painters identified with the Hudson River School in New York, but came to be identified with the Rocky Mountain School because of their magnificent paintings of the West.

A German-born American painter, Bierstadt went on an expedition across the United States in 1859 and, as a result, painted immense panoramic canvases capturing the power and majesty of the Rocky Mountains and Yosemite as well as the tranquility of Native Americans encampments. Moran was to make his journey to the West in 1871, slightly later than Bierstadt, but also with significant artistic and cultural consequences. Moran joined an expedition team led by Ferdinand Hayden, the director of the United States Geological Survey, to explore the Yellowstone region, which not only resulted in highly influential paintings of the dramatic beauty of the Rocky mountains, rivers, and Grand Canyon but also in the approval of Yellowstone as the country's first national park. Both painters broke from the more familiar vistas of upstate New York and landscapes of the Hudson River School to paint truly monumental "mountainscapes" of the "Rocky Mountain School" that glorified travel to the West. Bierstadt's and Moran's West is one of physical grandeur that intensifies Whitman's romantic evocation of the interaction between nature and the road, links the road to a spectacular Western landscape, and establishes the West as an ideal goal for Euro-American travel and settlement, but totally ignores the historical genocide imposed on the Native Americans that the men so romantically painted.

Although Bierstadt's canvases were not painted until four years after "Song of the Open Road," Whitman heartily supported a unified United States envisioned by "Manifest Destiny," and by 1860 began to write about the place of the West in his poetry. This new concern corresponded with the increasing importance of the frontier in the American vision and the imminent settlement of vast tracts of farmland.[17] For Whitman and many other Americans, the frontier and its topography increasingly would become part of the trope of the road.

Three things happened in short order that would alter the consciousness of the American public about the East and the West and the trope of the road: the Civil War, the Homesteading Act, and the transcontinental railroad. The Civil War began in 1861, and, while the immediate impetus was the escalating controversy over slavery that accompanied the accession to the Union of several states in the West and the South's subsequent decision to secede, the larger reasons involved a Northern/Southern cultural and economic divide over slavery, and between industrialization and agriculture. Not everyone agreed with the political position of either the North or the South, and many, especially new immigrants and Midwesterners, but even New Yorkers, thought that this was not their battle, though they were called to fight in it. When Abraham Lincoln signed the Homesteading Act on 20 May 1862 and set it officially in motion on 1 January 1863 in the middle of the war, many felt this was their opportunity to flee the problems of the East and South and head to new opportunities in the West and North. Thus began the great Conestoga wagon parade across the prairies of the Midwest as far as the ocean in the Far West, though similar treks by Mormons, the forty-niners, and other pioneers had preceded them. The excitement of this opportunity, recorded in the press and, as Kuyper notes, in song (see chapter 3 in this volume), gathered additional force with the passage of the Pacific Railway Act in July 1862, providing national assistance for a transcontinental railroad to stretch across the USA. A land united from sea to sea that was largely mythical in 1803 had become manifest with the completion of the transcontinental railroad in 1869. The frontier was accessible, if not "tamed,"

and hordes of Americans during and after the Civil War carved out
trails and roads and found their way there. Thus, the image of the
West and the frontier, as well as the difficulties of travelling there,
became ever more firmly embedded in the trope of the road. As the
nineteenth century tilted to the twentieth, the road was equated with
a magnified sense of space, great distance, fabled landscape, and
duress and heroism in taming the frontier. This, too, bears the strong
imprint of the Romantic, but it is not precisely Whitman's Romantic.

When immigration to the United States accelerated after the Civil
War, new arrivals from Europe and Asia began to think about a life
in the West instead of the East. So rapidly did Americans aim for
and settle the frontier that in 1893, a little more than thirty years
after the Homesteading Act, Frederick Jackson Turner delivered a
paper ("The Significance of the Frontier in American History") to
the American Historical Association in which, following the lead of
the 1890 declaration by the Census Department, he announced that
the frontier was effectively closed.[18] Turner argued that the "free
land" of the frontier was now occupied by miners earning good
wages, farmers plowing the land and building homes and barns, and
businessmen setting up shop. Whether early explorers or later shop-
keepers, these Westerners were, according to Turner, invariably characterized by energy, independence, bravery, heroism, and triumph
in carving out their places in this new land. Despite the closing of
the frontier, Turner believed that these qualities remained the most
important part of the fabric of the West as migration and mobility continued. As Deborah Madsen points out, Turner's exceptionalist notion of the frontier embodied a return to the primitive and
an "experience of perennial rebirth," "fluidity of social institutions,"
and "continual development."[19] Seiler adds that this primitive return
is predicated on mobility, "the genius of modernity and the signature
of the sovereign self";[20] in short, a wish to discover the primitive and
reinvent the self facilitated by modern mobility.

By the end of the twentieth century, a younger generation of
revisionist historians would challenge Turner's position, and the
metaphor of the frontier would serve as a conceptual site for re-
writing the history of the West as a multi-cultural encounter rather
than a noble conquest by Euro-Americans. Scholars, artists, students, and activists with ties to groups who had been marginalized
in earlier histories of the West – women, Native Americans, Latinos,
Asians, and African-Americans – had their own views of the West

and the road. Depictions of both in the post-Civil Rights era would challenge Turner's notions of the West and the elision of indigenous pasts, environmental waste, and misogyny.

Though critics have argued with Turner's view, it was immensely important in augmenting an ideology of the American West that came to dominate the trope of the road. The road thus became less about Whitman's romantic view of travelling souls and more about the personal, material, and national achievements and triumphs of the independent traveller seeking primal knowledge, understanding of life, and new opportunities in the West through the aid of freedom, civilization, and technology.

Excluded from this developing image of the road based on frontier growth and personal achievement, however, were the Native Americans that had inhabited the American space – both East and West – long before the Euro-American settlers came. In 1803 Jefferson stated that whites and Native Americans in the East could co-exist if the Native Americans gave up hunting and gathering, took on American customs, and settled down to an agricultural life or became skilled workers.[21] Many Indians did try to meet these requirements; some became farmers and craftsmen, but ultimately most lost their land to the settlers, were removed to reservations, or were annihilated. In 1830 under Andrew Jackson, the US Congress passed the "Indian Removal Act," that required the Native Americans to move to reservations that were not close to white settlers, and in 1838 the Cherokees, among others, suffered a forced march from Georgia to Oklahoma on what has become known as the "trail of tears" (see Marchetti, chapter 7). This, too, was a road journey to the West, but with none of the romance, heroism, or individualism attributed to the whites' movement. In fact, the depiction of the Native Americans in texts of the road was almost entirely negative, usually consisting of images of sneaky, hostile, and marauding bands that were intent on killing the white pioneers, as Tom Engelhardt has remarked.[22] Historically, of course, the opposite was true – the whites were the transgressers and marauders.

It comes as little surprise, then, that when a flourishing Hollywood began to produce road films, one of the most significant was John Ford's *Stagecoach* (1939).[23] This film moved away from the "pastoral vision of the West" and from the stagecoach trip as "an escape from all the cares and obligations of the contemporary world."[24] The filmic landscape is hostile, the stagecoach trip dangerous, and the action centred on the chase, calling for heroic action by the white travellers in the face of dangerously aggressive and hostile Indians.[25] Given that the automobile had already achieved great success, it may seem surprising that one of the relatively early great road films (if "road film" concerns mobility without automobility) depicted a vulnerable horse-drawn stagecoach in the West. But the frontier had so dominated the American imagination for almost a century and western fiction (begun, for example, by Owen Wister's 1902 *The Virginian*) had grown so quickly in popularity that a cowboy-and-Indians road film set in the Far West seemed natural, with its images of whites trying to create new settlements and Indians intent on annihilating them.

This film is not the usual cowboy-and-Indian story. Most of the action takes place inside the stagecoach, with the characters restricted to a small space and interacting much as they might in a car. *Stagecoach* undoubtedly enjoyed great commercial success because the audience would have consisted largely of those who owned or rode in cars. Such individuals fully understood the tensions and companionship that could arise in a small interior space, and had little or no experience with Native Americans. It is a very small leap in a little over a decade from *Stagecoach* to Jack Kerouac's *On the Road* and the hip conversations that would take place in the cars during his journeys across the country to California; nor is it much of a leap in Western imagery because *Stagecoach* created a repository of images (especially those of Monument Valley) that would dominate later road films (*Grapes of Wrath, Easy Rider, Thelma and Louise, City Slickers,* and *Boys on the Side*) as well as documentaries and docudramas (*Route 66*).[26] John Ford's productions reinforced the frontier in general and the West in particular as paramount to the process of troping the road – even if the frontier had officially disappeared years earlier. Orgeron thinks that Westerns (particularly Ford's) and film noir were the two most important influences on road movies.[27]

Though the real horse and the iron horse dominated overland travel in the nineteenth century and influenced fiction and films in the twentieth, ultimately the car became the mode of transport most clearly associated with the road trope.[28] Americans were slightly behind the Europeans in designing and manufacturing cars, but "by the time the Ford Motor Company was organized in 1903, the belief that the automobile would soon supersede the horse was commonplace."[29]

That belief was actualized almost overnight with exceptional and exceptionalist results. Americans took to the car quickly, dominated by the rich on weekend excursions near Eastern cities in the first few years, but then rapidly embraced by the middle class venturing further afield with the introduction of Henry Ford's Model N (1906–07) and Model T (1908–27).[30] Americans were enamoured of the car because it offered an effective form of transportation and could outpace the horse, because it represented the modernity and poetry of mechanization, and also because it spoke to the American psyche in some deep, psychological way. As James Flink argues,

> Individualism – defined in terms of privatism, freedom of choice, and the opportunity to extend one's control over his physical and social environment – was one of the important American core values that automobility promised to preserve and enhance in a changing urban-industrial society. Mobility was another. The automobile tremendously increased the individual's geographic mobility, which was closely associated with social mobility in the United States. It was certain to be prized by Americans. In our traditionally mobile society the motorcar was an ideal status symbol.[31]

Flink speaks of this status symbol as part of the "mass idolization of the motorcar" that grew as quickly as cars could be produced in the first decades of the twentieth century.[32] It is not surprising, then, that the automobile altered the trope of the road, making it less about pulling people together for a leisurely journey or the heroism of settling the frontier, and more about the rigours, excitement, and speed of autonomous long-distance mobility. The automobile coupled with the road and a self-conscious perception of their relationship within culture (i.e., automobility) links individualism, modern mechanical expertise, mobility, and "the reenactment of exploration and the willed illusion of discovery and conquest"[33] – a new and powerful reality and an equally powerful trope of the road that built upon noble images of Westward movement.

The car's popularity meant that adequate, hard-surfaced roads were needed, and it also meant that owners could drive conveniently from home to work, back again, and then out for the evening, thus facilitating the development of new suburbs across America (see Skidmore, chapter 2 in this volume). The car enabled long-distance travel for personal pleasure, work, or resettlement, and short-distance travel for daily activities and family life, but in both instances the lack of good roads early in the century posed a significant problem for easy transportation and economic development. Accordingly, towns and cities began to build more streets and roads within their jurisdictions, and sometimes towns joined together to build links between them. Nonetheless, it was not until 1913 that the Lincoln Highway – the first transcontinental highway in the United States and the world – was formally dedicated, followed in 1926 by the establishment of the even more celebrated Route 66, setting in motion the travel industry as we know it today, including gas stations, diners, cheap motels, and roadside attractions.[34] These new possibilities for long-distance travel and the reality that most of the real driving was from city to suburb created a paradox within the American psyche and the popular conception of the road. The image of short-distance suburban family travel, typical of most travel in America, was subordinated to and suppressed by the larger mythical stereotype of the individual on a long cross-country journey almost alone against the elements. Ironically, it was the story of the Joad family in John Steinbeck's 1939 novel *Grapes of Wrath* (filmed by John Ford in 1940) that best brought together and complicated these disparate images of individuality, family, and mobility.

The Joad family's escape from Depression poverty in Oklahoma to hoped-for opportunities in California on the most celebrated road in America, in a worn-out jalopy filled with family and neighbours, is pertinent to the developing myth and trope of the road, as almost all critics remark.[35] (Also, see Truscello, chapter 11 on the Depression and *The Wizard of Oz*.) For one thing, it is a "kin-trip" road narrative "in which the narrator's perspective is complicated by other family members who are often in some way along for the journey."[36] While kin-trips are not unusual narratives, they became dominated and replaced by the buddy narratives that Jack Kerouac popularized. For another, as Casey argues, Route 66 had become "the primary arterial system of American movement," representing the lure of hope, adventure, entrepreneurship, and good times, but at the same time resonating of hardship in leaving home and driving through the stark and hostile desert landscape.[37] *Grapes of Wrath* is not a journey for pleasure, and it is less about the discovery of individual identity or personal transformation than about survival and communal responsibility for an impoverished and distressed white family whose community collapses because of unforgiving wind storms, corporate farming, and irresponsible bankers. Steinbeck's renaming of Route 66 as the "Mother Road, the road of flight" suggests the need for care and comfort rather than business – as was encapsulated by "the Main Street of America," its first popular name, coined by Cyrus Avery – which was looked upon with suspicion by much of the American populace in the Depression era.

At the centre of this plight is the automotive technology that created many of the massive social problems, particularly for farmers: first, farmers needed the technology to farm larger plots of land, but equipment was expensive, leaving them with large debts for trucks, cars, and tractors; second, the way in which farm equipment was drawn by tractors created deep furrows and turned over large amounts of soil, making the land vulnerable to the dry winds of the Dust Bowl, ultimately driving farmers off the land; third, getting rid of the horses, farming more land, and trying to find substitute cash crops created a glut of grain, so that prices could not keep abreast of the costs; and, last, tractors made farming on a large scale possible, reducing the need for small, independent farmers and sharecroppers.[38] So, the technology of the "driving machine" itself bears a share of the blame for the Joads' dilemma, but it also helps them escape to California. As Roger Casey remarks, with Steinbeck,

> No longer is the automobile presented in an either/or fashion, but rather it is seen in all its cultural complexity. By the late Thirties the automobile was inexorably entrenched in the American way of life, for all its good and bad, and with *The Grapes of Wrath* we see one writer who predates what for most Americans was a post-1950's realization about the evils of motorized transport: that in spite of the negative realities of the automobile, it had achieved a condition of symbiosis with Americans and American life. Like a metastasized cancer, its effects had grown so deep that its excision would perhaps lead to social and economic fatality.[39]

The car then stands at the crux of dueling narratives and versions of the developing trope of the road: one strand of the narrative concerns the individual out to discover, transform himself (almost never herself at this early point), and find illumination or entertainment on

a Westward journey; and the other concerns the risks and dangers
of the road, rebellion against authority, and the consequent need
for personal generosity, social protest, and community action. This
second strand, which often combines personal revelation with group
effort and resistance, is based on "the attraction and repulsion" of
the car, for it could be seen as exalted and redemptive as well as
destructive and demonic.[40] As Mills writes, many images were associated with the development of automotive transportation and the
breakdown of the Depression-era communities, and these are best
illustrated by the well-known photographs of Dorothea Lange, especially the "Migrant Mother," depicting a desperate mother and her
half-starved children who migrate to survive.[41] Road novels, road
movies, road photographs, and road folk music thus were pulled
together to create a strong cultural critique during this period, ampli-
fying the relationship of mobility, rebellion, and social conscience –
important aspects of a revisionist road trope.

Following the privations of the Great Depression represented by
the Joads and the subsequent gas rationing of the Second World War,
Americans wanted mobility and freedom from duress. The ramping
up of industry during the war, followed by the consumption boom of
the late 1940s and early 1950s, bestowed jobs, money, and free time
on a large proportion of the American public, and many took to
the highway. Travel for recreation, adventure, business, and reloca-
tion accelerated across the United States. Gasoline as well as new
and used cars were all relatively cheap, young people could easily
find part-time and full-time jobs, and a new generation of youth
had the money to spend and the time to enjoy travel individually or
with friends. Jack Kerouac represents this new generation of individualistic wanderers who could leave conventions and responsibilities behind and search for a new identity. With just enough money
in their pockets to take buses, ride with friends, and/or hitchhike
across the country, these young adventurers could leave the "cor-
rupted" East Coast and follow their physical and spiritual desires
to what they considered the more innocent West, discovering something about America and transforming themselves in the process.
In this way, Kerouac, especially in *On the Road* (1957), leaves one
of the strongest impressions on the trope of the road. As Primeau
comments, with *On the Road*, "the road novel gained notoriety,
respect, and a sense of direction. The most famous account of Beat
travels gave the genre its name and brought the counterculture into

classrooms and the pages of literary reviews."[42] Laderman notes, too, that *On the Road* has been critical in shaping the road movie.[43]

To a considerable extent, Kerouac describes a spiritual journey in which "the soul journeys along the open highway of America, in search of permanence, of values that will endure and not collapse."[44] As the protagonist Sal Paradise says, he began his journey after he had split up with his wife and felt "that everything was dead," so getting away represented liberation and regeneration.[45] This regeneration is augmented by his heightened, even Biblical perception of the Western prelapsarian landscape: "all I had to do was lean back and roll on. Now I could see Denver looming ahead of me like the Promised Land, way out there beneath the stars, across the prairie of Iowa and plains of Nebraska, and I could see the greater vision of San Francisco beyond, like jewels in the night."[46] This truly is similar to the spiritual journey that Whitman describes in "Song of the Open Road," so one hundred years later the spiritual dimension is still intact, if distinctly reformed.

However, with the feeling of restlessness and resistance to middle-class values in the midst of American prosperity, consumerism, and national optimism, something distinctive in the American road story was born. Kerouac and his narrative avatar Sal were not just conventional seekers of philosophical and spiritual wisdom; they were part of the "Beat" counter-culture, rejecting mainstream cultural values and hoping to find new individual paths, personal identity, social liberation, and spiritual values. But, if they wanted spiritual insight, they also wanted "speed" – to "ball that jack," the emblem of their desires in going fast to press the machine to the limit, leave old vistas and ways quickly behind, reach new destinations, and take drugs to gain new psychological perceptions and spiritual insights.[47] (Also see Skidmore, chapter 2 in this volume.) These were the new "trips" of the rebellious young, as Mills notes.[48] Cars, speed, and drugs consequently became an important part of the trope of the road for the next thirty years, replacing more benign associations of leisurely travel in a variety of modes, the pioneering heroism of the western frontier, and family and community responsibility – or even the risks of travel brought on by the frontier and Great Depression. This, too, created another kind of American exceptionalism in which the young were perceived to launch out on their own and discover themselves, independent of family and cultural restrictions, to do what they wanted and go where they willed. The exceptionalist vision of personal freedom and self-transformation for young people in the fifties is deeply imprinted on the trope of the road.

Another part of the developing trope was the buddy aspect of *On the Road*. The main character Sal begins and ends his journeys across America mainly by himself, but in between he meets, bonds, and travels with friends, especially Dean Moriarty, whom he admires greatly as one freed from conventional moral restraints and family ties and personifying an unconventional and transgressive but universal beatific impulse. This transgressive buddy motif especially contributed to the road movie as exemplified by the male buddies of *Easy Rider* as well as those in *Butch Cassidy and the Sundance Kid* and the male-female buddy team in *Bonnie and Clyde* – all in the late 1960s – and later as the female buddies of *Thelma and Louise* in the 1990s.

Aligned with this culturally transgressive buddy motif is Sal Paradise's "social mingling" with the underclasses of America.[49] He is not drawn to the wealthy, educated, and socially approved but to those on the margins of society: the farmhands heading up to Montana, itinerant Latino farm labourers near Bakersfield, "bums and beat cowboys," "the sordid hipsters of America," "mad drunken Americans in the mighty land," dope addicts, hobos, thieves, and writers.[50] As Robert Holton notes, Sal is also drawn to the racially heterogeneous who assist in the development of his "alienation, rebelliousness, intensity and spontaneity."[51] Nancy Grace also finds that the character of Sal references one of the classic features of an American literary paradigm, consisting of "Emersonian or Whitmanian individualism by which one aligns one-self with the marginalized and self-reliant," psychic wholeness, and spiritual enlightenment.[52] This eclectic grouping in *On the Road*, however, is more inclusive than that of Whitman and Steinbeck, and insofar as it is seen through the eyes of a youthful, college-educated narrator, the mixture of education, class, and race adds significantly to the evolving complexity of the road trope.

Coupled with this narrative of liberation, spiritual regeneration, heightened perception, and inclusivity is one where everything sours and falls apart. Sal's expectations crescendo and then crash, sadness and loneliness take over, and he finds that he is not willing to, or cannot, hold things together. In this frame of mind, he grumbles about "the raggedy madness and riot of our actual lives, our actual night, the hell of it, the senseless nightmare road. All of it inside endless and beginningless emptiness."[53] As Tim Hunt remarks, "part one of *On the Road* is an extended confrontation between the 'sadder-but-wiser' hindsight of the narrator Sal and his earlier 'exuberances,'" but the entire structure of the book is built on "a series of road experiences that end in vision, exhaustion, and a return to the established order."[54] This oscillation between "building and collapsing"[55] and the sense of sadness and wretchedness wrapped together with cheerfulness, optimism, vitality, and youth gives the narrative its potency and establishes an altered and more complex trope of the road.

As with *Grapes of Wrath*, a key highway playing through *On the Road* is Route 66. Kerouac and others felt the need to travel this highway because of its vistas, cultural quirkiness, growing reputation as something people must see, and status as a national icon. The time just after the war was a very special moment in the history and development of this American road and others: only during this time did affordability, highway infrastructure, roadside accommodations, youth, individuality, and optimism come together, giving a unique sense of presence, possibility, and promise. As Michael Witzel notes, this is what people remember with nostalgia about the fifties,[56] though Kerouac's legacy novel and the buddy films of the sixties trouble that account even while they embrace it.[57]

As Brian Ladd finds, what had seemed liberating and promising about the road and mobility began to run into trouble from the government, citizens, and hipsters themselves from the late sixties. Improved highways and transportation networks developed under the Federal-Aid Highway Act of 1956 began to empty the cities of businesses and people as the roads cut through downtown and residential neighbourhoods and Americans increasingly moved to the suburbs. With this urban sprawl, the freeways, which were to make driving easier, became congested and hastened the death of cities even while they made the so-called blue highways obsolete. In addition, with the 1973 oil crisis, the automobile was singled out for consuming too many scarce resources and for increasing pollution within densely populated areas.[58] Kerouac's enthusiasm for the road was replaced by the "post 1960s fragmentation," an impending sense of despair, and the personal and social tragedies reflected in *Bonnie and Clyde, Easy Rider, Butch Cassidy and the Sundance Kid, Thelma and Louise*, and a host of other films that changed the way the counterculture saw the road.[59] These buddy films were often outlaw films in which the protagonists not only rebel against society but also directly break the law because they are alienated from, and harassed by, the dominant legal, economic, and (with *Thelma and Louise*) gender systems. These films responded to a growing disenchantment with, and cynicism about, the US government, the Cold War, the Vietnam War, and middle-class social and materialistic values, firmly linking the trope of the road to youth, rebellion, counterculture, and cynicism about social and governmental institutions.

These buddy films were buttressed by a string of outlaw biker films, including *The Wild One* (1953), *Scorpio Rising* (1963), and *Wild Angels* (1966), which intensified the counterculture images and complicated them by screening sexually taboo subjects such as casual sexuality, rape, and homosexuality – part of the portrayal of the sexual revolution that was well underway. Dennis Hopper's rebel-acid-biker road film *Easy Rider* reflected this social dis-ease, cynicism, and sexual revolution. As Peter Fonda, the lead actor of *Easy Rider,* remarked, "the time was right for a really good movie about motorcycles and drugs,"[60] – which were seen as anti-social and anti-familial symbols of rebellion.[61] Barbara Klinger qualifies, however, that this was "the road to dystopia"[62] that turned the freedom and autonomy of the rebellious young into dysfunctionalism and tragedy. The film itself consists of mingled images that suggest a rebellion gone wrong. It begins with the sale and smuggling of cocaine from Mexico to Los Angeles (considerably different in sentiment from the more innocent consumption of marijuana in the open-country part of the film) followed by a sequence of celebratory Western road shots as Billy (Dennis Hopper) and Wyatt (Peter Fonda) travel along Route 66 going East – not West – to New Orleans for Mardi Gras. However, the brutal killing of their companion George Hanson (Jack Nicholson), their LSD trip, and their confusing participation in and filming of Mardi Gras, a brothel, and a cemetery in New Orleans mark the strong bifurcation in this film between the initial almost innocent joy and beauty of travel in the American West (punctuated by Steppenwolf's legacy soundtrack) and the destruction caused by their infractions of the dominant culture's family and social codes. Their own subsequent murder by rednecks is the final stage of this dystopic vision as well as a condemnation of the prejudice and hate of that which does not conform to regular American social patterns.

Self-consciously evoking a sense of America, this film reels back the optimism that going West had created in previous novels (Tom

Wolfe's *The Electric Kool-Aid Acid Test* [1968]), travel narratives (John Steinbeck's *Travels with Charley* [1962]), TV series (Herbert Leonard and Stirling Silliphant's *Route 66* [1960–64]), TV documentaries (Charles Kuralt's *On the Road* and contributions to the CBS *Evening News* [1960s]), and films (Vincente Minnelli's *The Long, Long Trailer* [1954]). Through the Eastward movement, it instills wariness about the safety of travel on American highways for those who differ from mainstream middle-class sojourners or solid citizens of the towns. In this way it defines the alienation of those identified with the counter-culture in the 1960s, especially those who were young, black, oddly dressed, and against the war in Southeast Asia. Wyatt's "We blew it" references not only his own misplaced actions and values but the failure of the American Dream, a failure that translated itself into rock 'n roll, folk music, and even opera (as Attinello notes in chapter 6 of this volume).[63]

Although *Easy Rider* belonged specifically to the 60s and 70s, it reminds the viewer that the American road from Whitman to Hopper has always been about nation. It may have its roots in many different cultures and time periods, but it is especially identified with the USA. After all, Wyatt is also called Captain America and wears the American flag on his back and the colours of the flag on his bike. This road and this America differ wildly from those of Whitman, Turner, Steinbeck, Ford, or Kerouac because, even as the film embraces the landscape of Route 66 going eastward, it takes on, exaggerates, and protests against American racism, classism, and intolerance. Exceptionalism thus shifts from images of the United States as a positive example to the world to those of a negative example of arrogance, intolerance, and hatred of "the Other." As a result, the trope of the road for the following decades was inflected by a strong disrespect for normative American social behaviour, institutions, and government, which were seen by the counterculture as failed.[64]

Because the film created such a harsh image of the USA, the Republican administration was happy to see its legacy diminished some twenty years later. As Klinger notes:

In 1988 George Bush proudly noted that the United States had made a successful recovery from the excesses of the "Easy Rider society" of the 1960s ... In the Reagan-Bush era, reference to *Easy Rider* (1969) instantly conjured up demonic images of the hippie counter-culture with its long hair, experimentation with

drugs and sex, and violent social protests. For this more conservative political era, such images represented a permissive degeneracy and destructive militancy that had to be eradicated for the
nation to thrive.[65]

Klinger makes clear that this film marked the "serious rifts between
counter- and dominant cultures,"[66] so that it was cause for national
celebration when society no longer seemed to be so divided and
films no longer took such a cynical stance.

George Bush spoke too soon, however, for in 1991 Ridley Scott
brought out *Thelma and Louise*, which sustained the negative image
of a patriarchal American society that represses women, hunts down
the rebellious, and destroys the innocent. As Thelma and Louise go
flying over the cliffs of the Grand Canyon in their Thunderbird, they
are serving up a condemnation of a society that would first harness
them, then harass and pursue them to their death. More a cautionary tale than a testament to women's success in taking over the road,
Thelma and Louise, nonetheless, challenges certain established ways
of looking at the road tradition and notes the ways in which travel
and travellers were changing. It also reinforces the outlaw edge in
the growing tradition of female automobility begun a generation
earlier with Arthur Penn's *Bonnie and Clyde* (1967), Francis Ford
Coppola's *The Rain People* (1969), and Steven Spielberg's *Sugarland
Express* (1974), for example. *Thelma and Louise* not only put rebellious women on the same risky highway with men, but ensured
that issues of gender relations, femininity, and masculinity would
become dominant concerns in road films and contribute to an ever-
expanding and more complex trope of the road. The treatment of
women in *Thelma and Louise* also suggested a new kind of exceptionalism: that of American women, who were considered to be
stronger, more liberated, and more assertive than their sisters elsewhere. For many, this was a badge of honour, but for some it seemed
as if it would lead to the yawning abyss of the Grand Canyon.

Perhaps *Easy Rider*, *Thelma and Louise*, and their like were too
radical, rebellious, and cynical for mainstream audiences, because
David Laderman makes the point that, while "the road movie fiz-
zles out in the mid-1970s," it was revived in the 1980s by a mocking postmodernist impulse that continued countercultural and
existential *modernist* critiques but was repackaged, depoliticized,
redeployed, and "self-conscious of ... their own generic status and

modernist roots."[67] He finds these characterized by "stunning camera work, excessive violence, over-the-top performance, deadpan irony."[68] Films that he places in this category include Gus Van Sant's *Drugstore Cowboy* (1989), Jim Jarmusch's *Stranger than Paradise* (1984), Joel Coen's *Raising Arizona* (1987), and David Lynch's *Wild at Heart* (1990). These films carry on the traditions of the road, even while they challenge them, and the trope of the road in fiction and film becomes inflected by an ironic postmodern self-referential sensibility, which Mills for one finds too cynical, enigmatic, self-obscuring, and contemptuous.[69]

Mills notes, however, that in the 1980s the road film moves away from drug-filled rebellion and turns to issues of identity and the family: "the rebel in the 1980s is the one who works toward family unity rather than hitting the road in search of an elusive truth."[70] Moreover, this family "identity is relational, created in terms of position to others, rather than within rigid belief systems. Family identity evolved in different contexts rather than being fixed to one set of references or ideals."[71] This, too, is considered postmodern in revisiting previous aspects of the road, but is gentler and less ironic than what Laderman notes of the 1970s. This kind of postmodernism led a decade later to multiple and diverse road films, also centred on identity:

Into the 1990s, the road movie gathers considerable momentum, putting more miles on the cinematic highway than ever before – in a plethora of directions, through a diverse array of landscapes, with a multiplicity of multi-cultural drivers. It is perhaps no accident that this road movie boom coincides with the economic boom of the Clinton era, especially considering the administration's enthusiastic discourse about "crossing into" the next millennium, "bridging" the twenty-first century. According to Clintonian rhetoric, and most economic analysts, the primary "engine" for the economic prosperity of the 1990s was computer technology.[72]

These films reprise characteristics of earlier road narratives but situate them in a growing postmodern interrogation – including optimism and pride – of America's familial, gender, racial, and ethnic complexity. These attitudes changed the cultural landscape and trope of the road, luring audiences to reconsider who and what earlier road texts had ignored or suppressed. From commercial films (*Smoke Signals* [1998]; *Harold and Kumar Go to White Castle* [2004]; *Get on the Bus* [1996]) to documentaries (*My America, or Honk If You Love Buddha* [1997]), stories about families and ethnic and racial minorities on the road simultaneously critiqued earlier models while claiming that the road was self-consciously more egalitarian and diverse than many could have imagined when it was dominated by young white men.

Something else, however, was changing, which was not related directly to multiculturalism as such. As Mills notes, by the early 1990s, a few road films, such as *To Wong Foo, Thanks for Everything, Julie Newmar* (1996), used romance and comedy to situate their plots and messages, thereby breaking from adventure road films.[73] Attitudes toward the road began to soften, nullifying "transgression, rebellion, and cultural critique," gravitating to stability, and recuperating Whitman's Romantic trope of the road as postmodern pastiche.[74] But it was not until the transition from the twentieth to the twenty-first century that films and novels sought to restore some of the romance of the road while still paying attention to contemporary social and economic shifts, without letting them overpower the narrative. The psychological change in attitudes underlying genre changes in road texts may have resulted partly from the economic downturn in the stock market and technology sectors (the dot-com fizzle) in 2000 as well as the catastrophic terrorist events of 11 September. These factors chastened many Americans and led to a rethinking of youthful cynicism, national entitlement, and aggressive capitalism.

Road literature and studio films about the "other" (like *Smoke Signals*) emphasized the road, family, and communal responsibility, but they were not alone in embracing earlier and softer visions and tropes of the road. Mainstream Hollywood films about young white men and women on the road (*When Harry Met Sally* [1989] and *Elizabethtown* [2005]), as well as older white Americans on the road (*About Schmidt* [2002] and *The Straight Story* [1999]), reflected expanded thematic horizons and transformed identities (see Slethaug, chapter 8). These latter films broaden the cast of characters on the American road and expand the road metaphor for those seeking to establish a range of individual and social identities as well as psychological and spiritual healing.[75] This broadening could mean that the trope of the road has become postmodern in its simultaneous linkage to inclusivity, compassion, and commitment to family values (rather than self-referentiality or cynicism), or it could mean that the dystopic elements – so often supressed in the stories we tell, particularly road stories – are simply receding for the moment, like the landscape in a rearview mirror.[76] Alternatively, as Primeau maintains, this softening might only mean that the self-reliance and self-discovery of the road has "turned into a consumer-land of trendy conformity. Left with a realization that we have been uprooted with no sense of a future, the only adventure left involves ransacking the past. Hence, the myth still lives on – but as nostalgia rather than an ideal or a sense of achievement."[77] There are no simple answers to these questions, but it is clear that today the trope of the road is, as Laderman and Mills maintain, multiplicitous. It incorporates many communities, social attitudes, ethnicities, and ages. The road becomes a complex and highly unstable trope that can be used to describe the various experiences that people have or fantasize about in their quest for individual identity, personal transformation, and/or social unity.

The expanded trope of the road, and the new identities it articulates, challenge and reconfigure traditional boundaries, as two recent gender-bending examples illustrate. Annie Proulx's "Brokeback Mountain," the story of two young gay lovers, was turned into Ang Lee's instantly successful film. Similarly, *Transamerica*, a moving and somewhat sentimental film about a father seeking a sex change who rescues his son from hustling sex for a living, redefines the transgressive and healing power of the road. As with *On the Road*, these are stories of young men, but they revisit the buddy film, include women's stories, and take issue with conventional notions of masculinity and youth (see Slethaug in chapter 8 and Marchetti in chapter 9).

By the beginning of the twenty-first century, then, the road had extended beyond fiction, realistic film, and conventional TV programming. It has become an important part of cartoon films, reality TV, video games, and social media as Ford and Truscello note (see Ford in chapter 7 and Truscello in chapter 11). It embraces and has become an important part of the information highway. Road narratives have moved from postmodern to postnational and transnational. Today's road films address multiplicity, heterogeneity, self-contradiction, and self-difference – each establishing its own use with less dependence on conventional understandings of genre.[78]

The trope of the road, then, has undergone many permutations in the last hundred and fifty years and, though an enduring presence in American culture, it is never completely the same. Consisting of the road itself, the journeyer, the means of transportation, and the reasons for travelling, this image does have consistencies of approach. Still, culture attaches new meanings in each era, as do the individual sensitivities of each particular text so that Whitman's romanticism is not really the same as the new romanticism of the twenty-first-century road film.

2

Politics, People Moving, and the American Myth of the Road

MAX J. SKIDMORE

America entered the nineteenth century with a zeal for roads, but with disagreement about how to get them. It entered the twentieth century with a renewed zeal for roads – for good roads, that is; the few significant highways it had then still were rarely if ever as good as those that had graced the Roman Empire roughly two millennia before. "When the United States entered the twentieth century, its transportation system was confined largely to waterways and rail-roads. Roads, where they existed at all, were in most instances quite primitive. Often, especially in the West, they consisted of dust, or worse, mud."[1] Americans certainly needed – and most had come fervently to desire – good roads and the ability to move people quickly and efficiently, but they still had not agreed on what to do. One writer noted that there simply were no adequate American roads in the 1890s, and quoted a highway authority of the time as saying that the country's roads at that time were "inferior to those of any civilized country."[2]

By the first decade of the twenty-first century the country at last had its roads, but already it had outgrown them. They were clogged with traffic and deteriorating. America's overall transportation system remained inadequate, and to add to that it had become wasteful of natural resources while placing the country at the mercy of foreign powers to supply the energy that it consumed so voraciously.

American success is legendary. In many ways, the country had become the wonder of the world. Much that it did and had done was superb. What happened to cause it to be so inefficient with regard to the internal movement of its own people? What does that suggest about America as a culture?

It suggests that America's Jeffersonian heritage – a heritage that has contributed so much to personal liberty in America and in the world, and has encouraged self-government – has had mixed effects. On the one hand, it bequeathed to the culture a spirit of independence and self-reliance; a wariness of oppression that in many respects served it well. On the other hand, it bequeathed also a resistance to government action, however necessary, and a disregard of the public sphere.

Transportation is not the only way in which modern America, despite its dominance of the world, falls behind many other countries. The same dynamics may be seen elsewhere, such as in its systems of health care and retirement security.

The United States has chosen a system (or at least has allowed one to develop) that spends far more for health care, both in the aggregate and per capita, than does any other society in the world, yet it receives much less for what it spends; moreover, it does far too little to control expenses. Alone among advanced industrial countries, America has an enormous minority without access to quality health care (the Patient Protection and Affordable Care Act, passed belatedly in 2010, is now moving the country in the direction of universal coverage, with some curtailment of expenses, but one of the two major parties is so ideologically committed to "individualism," at least in matters of social justice, that it is doing all that it can to repeal the Act).

The retirement component of the US Social Security system was originally designed to be merely "one leg of a three-legged stool," not a complete program of income maintenance. Retirement income was to depend upon Social Security, personal savings and investment, and pensions from employers. Now, however, that stool has collapsed. With minimal savings or none, eliminating one leg, much of the workforce faces the future with only Social Security, as companies eliminate the other leg by ceasing to provide pensions. Although the last leg, Social Security – despite the attacks upon it – remains sound[3] it is not enough by itself to provide adequate retirement funding for American workers.

Throughout its existence, the country's choices in most cases have been beneficial. When its choices have been poor, however – when the nation has not given adequate thought to the manner in which it is developing, or when it has adhered rigidly to an ideology better suited for earlier times – troubles have emerged. In both its distribution of health care and its provision for retirement income, disaster is not too far distant. The same is true for America's systems of transportation.

Few things are more basic to a modern society than the ability of its people to move, to travel from one part of the land to another. Shortly after the adoption of the Constitution in 1789, there was wide recognition of the need for an infrastructure consisting of roads, canals, bridges, and the like. Many of the early efforts were private, or funded by states and localities. All, however, were piecemeal.

A member of the US House of Representatives from South Carolina, the young John C. Calhoun, introduced the "Bonus Bill," a popular measure that would have reserved for the construction of roads and canals all revenues that the government derived from the Bank of the United States. At the time, of course, Calhoun was still a nationalist. He had not yet devolved into the fierce sectionalist who was determined to protect slavery at all costs, even if that meant destruction of the country. Calhoun ably managed the bill's passage through the House. After Senate action, it went forward to President James Madison.

On 2 March 1817, two days before he left office, Madison sent a shock wave through the political community by casting a veto that killed the bill. A distinguished member of the House, the astonished Henry Clay, said that if an earthquake had destroyed Washington, DC, it would have been no greater a surprise than Madison's veto. Madison's biographer Drew McCoy, though, has argued that it should have been no surprise. The president had signalled his opposition to federal funding for "internal improvements" in numerous messages to Congress.[4]

Madison had acted upon his view of the Constitution, a view that reflected the Jeffersonian conviction that officials must interpret the document strictly ("strict construction," as opposed to "loose construction"). He favoured internal improvements, and recognized that they were vital for the new country, but thought the national government had no authority to fund them. Ironically, he did accept the national bank, about which the Constitution spoke no more directly than it did about internal improvements.

In the same year that Madison left the presidency and James Monroe succeeded him, 1817, the State of New York began construction of the Erie Canal, from Albany to Buffalo, a distance of more than 360 miles. New York officials had considered such a project since 1808. Although its critics derided it as "Clinton's Folly," or "Clinton's Big Ditch" (for Dewitt Clinton, New York's governor), the canal, upon its completion in 1825, became widely recognized as "the engineering marvel of its day."[5] It brought economic boom times, and quickly encouraged travel, including the westward movement. Its success also encouraged a flurry of canal building elsewhere.

Monroe, like Madison, recognized the importance of transportation. Also like Madison, however, he vetoed a bill that would have provided federal funding for internal improvements. Both he and Madison recommended a constitutional amendment that would have authorized such funding, but neither was successful.

Monroe's successor was John Quincy Adams, a visionary who proposed extensive and enlightened programs that in years to come – but under other presidents – would provide the foundation for much American policy. He was spectacularly unsuccessful, however, in securing action.[6] While both his predecessors received congressional enactments for internal improvements and vetoed them, Adams sought such bills, but failed. He would happily have supplied his signature, but Congress adamantly refused to give him the chance.

As the 1820s gave way to the 1830s, President Andrew Jackson followed the precedents of Madison and Monroe, and again caused a furor by vetoing a bill for internal improvements. Like his immediate predecessors, Jackson recognized the need for roads, and in fact did approve some projects. The 1830 bill to finance the Maysville Road, however, was too much for the "Old Hero." Jackson was sufficiently Jeffersonian that he was reluctant to support national funding for truly ambitious projects. He argued that the extensive road was solely in the state of Kentucky, and that the Constitution therefore did not authorize the national government to support it.[7] There likely was a political reason as well. Kentucky was the home state of Jackson's rival, Henry Clay, who was active in forming an anti-Jackson party that came to be called the Whigs. Jackson was hardly inclined to support measures that might strengthen a political enemy – especially one who also was from the West. He was more likely to approve measures proposed by Democrats.[8]

In any case, the strong sentiment for roads soon declined. A new marvel of technology was becoming the object of attention. Roads with their wagons and buggies no longer were exciting. Businesses, localities, and visionaries became champions of something faster and more comfortable. The railroad was quickly to become the state-of-the-art conveyance of the day, usually with considerable help from local and state governments.

Abraham Lincoln won the presidency in 1860 as the candidate of the new Republican Party. Lincoln was not only the great Civil War president who ultimately worked deftly to eliminate human chattel slavery but also a great partisan of railroads. With his enthusiastic support Congress began the program of extensive land grants to encourage the construction of a mighty transcontinental route.

Lincoln's experience on riverboats early in his life brought him views of the South's "peculiar institution," and helped to develop his fervent opposition to slavery. That riverboat experience also impressed him with the importance of transportation. With huge federal grants added to generous assistance from governments at other levels, railroads expanded throughout the century, and spread across America.[9]

Having captured Americans' imaginations, the railroads directed their attention away from roads, which languished. The westward movement could thrive without them. By the end of the nineteenth century, the railroad had become transcontinental, but roads had not. Well into the twentieth century, America was a "land mired in the mud," and the general opinion was that roads were purely a local matter.[10] The assumption was that anyone could build a road.[11] Outside cities, what roads there were tended at best to be sand, or even dirt. A traveller was considerably more likely to encounter roadways in which boulders rested and tree stumps – as much as three feet high – remained solidly rooted than to find a road of professional quality. "Hard surfaces were almost nonexistent, and even gravel was rare – especially in the west."[12]

As strange as it seems in modern America with its almost frenzied love affair with roads and automobiles, farmers at the time often were among the most ardent opponents of road building. Rather than seeing roads as advantageous, they were more likely to view them as intrusions into their lives, bringing outsiders and guaranteeing high taxes.[13] Some states had gone so far as to include prohibitions in their state constitutions against using state funds for "internal improvements." Michigan, for example, specifically banned state financing for the building or maintaining of roads. It did not remove the ban until 1905.[14]

Such a situation could not continue, as restless Americans sought better, faster, and more comfortable ways to roam around the continent. As the twentieth century drew near, a "Good Roads Movement" had begun, endeavouring to break down the old prejudices and to encourage states to eliminate their barriers to roads. This movement predated the automobile. A new sport, bicycling, had emerged. This, along with enthusiasm from some other groups, provided one of the first incentives for road building since early in the century. In 1880 sport cyclists founded the "League of American Wheelmen." Within a decade, it had become "the world's largest athletic association,"[15] and a significant pressure group.

Of course, the advent of the automobile made good roads absolutely essential. The production of the Model T Ford convinced farmers of the value of farm-to-market roads. Nevertheless, decades were to pass before the country's roads were adequate.[16] The new machine developed rapidly, far more quickly than did the roads it needed to fulfill its potential.

In the meantime, transportation inside cities was improving greatly. Streetcar lines (tram lines) evolved from earlier horse-drawn cars to new electric vehicles. They permitted orderly growth, as cities expanded along the rights of way. Commuters could travel considerable distances to work, school, and shopping. Automobiles were also becoming frequent on city streets. Interurban lines between communities also became common, and greatly enhanced Americans' ability to travel.

Autos still faced hostile territory, however, especially outside cities. The first transcontinental journey by automobile was a major undertaking. In 1903 Horatio Nelson Jackson's impulsive and arduous adventure from San Francisco to New York captivated a rapt country. It may well have laid the foundation for Americans' love affair with the automobile – even if that love affair did ultimately require some assistance from "motordom" (as Peter Norton felicitously termed it) in securing favourable treatment from local, state, and federal government.[17]

Jackson, later to become a successful entrepreneur, was a thirty-one-year-old former physician from Burlington, Vermont. His wife was quite wealthy, and after their marriage he had given up his medical practice. He undertook the harrowing trip following a friendly argument in San Francisco's University Club regarding the future of the automobile. He had been badly outnumbered by others in the group of comfortable young men who scoffed that the new machine was a mere novelty, a "rich man's toy," that would always prove to be too unreliable to be useful except perhaps for short distances. It would eventually fade away, they asserted confidently, and the horse would continue to reign supreme.

When someone bet fifty dollars that no one could drive to New York City in fewer than three months, Jackson accepted the challenge. Four days later, he was heading east across the continent with his mechanic, Sewell Crocker, and his bulldog, Bud. Jackson was driving a 1903 Winton that he had purchased used – he could not find a new one on the West Coast. He named his car "The Vermont," to honour his home state. These amateurs with no special equipment and little planning had begun to make history.[18]

Theirs was not, however, the first such attempt. That apparently was a journey that took place in the summer of 1899, when a journalist, Louisa Hitchcock Davis, and her mechanic husband, John D. Davis, set out from New York City, planning to reach San Francisco within a month. Three months later their ordeal ended as they struggled into Chicago and gave up the effort. Their progress had been so trouble-plagued, so "slow and tortuous that a one-armed bicyclist, who had left New York ten days after their departure, passed them before they reached Syracuse."[19]

A second attempt took place two years later, going in the other direction. Alexander Winton, the manufacturer of the popular Winton motorcar, had previously been widely heralded because he drove one of his own cars successfully from Cleveland to New York. In May 1901 he and his "publicity agent," Charles B. Shanks, attempted what was thought to be the greatest feat of all: crossing the continent. Driving a "Winton motor carriage," the two set off on what Winton anticipated would be a two-month journey. He chose to go from west to east in order to complete the most difficult part of the journey when his car would be in its best condition. Ten days later, 530 miles distant and stuck in sand in the Nevada desert, the hardy travellers admitted failure.[20]

Jackson, Croker, and Bud, on the other hand, demonstrated that the transcontinental automobile trip was possible. They had departed from San Francisco on 23 May 1903, and arrived in New York City on 26 July, well under the three-month period of the challenge. The actual time the trip required was 63 days, 12 hours, and 30 minutes.[21] According to an advertisement from the Winton Motor

Carriage Company, they had driven almost 6,000 miles (they had often detoured and even backtracked to find the most feasible route, thus accounting for the great distance), and had averaged more than 100 miles per day.[22]

Thus began America's fascination with mechanized individual travel.[23] A century later – in 2003 – the Public Broadcasting System chronicled that beginning with a documentary on the historic journey, "Horatio's Drive: America's First Road Trip," by Ken Burns and Dayton Duncan. Their excellent book by the same title was part of the same effort. It takes its place beside another, earlier, book on Jackson, Hill's *The Mad Doctor's Drive*.[24]

With the success of the first transcontinental excursion, other motorists quickly set out on their own journeys. They seized upon any new factor to claim as a first. For example, "In 1908, Jacob Murdock loaded his wife and children into his new Packard Model Thirty, and drove from Pasadena to New York City in 32 days – becoming the first family to drive across the country, and beginning a tradition of road trips that generations of American families would follow."[25] For a time, a ritual prevailed among many of the intrepid motorists who made the coast-to-coast drive. They would dip their tires in the ocean prior to departing, and dip them in the other ocean upon arriving. Never mind that they would almost assuredly have changed tires multiple times along the way, the symbolic meaning was clear. In fact, "if you were afraid of getting your car stuck on the beach, a variation was to fill a bottle with the brine of one ocean to carry across the continent to dump in the other."[26] Lester Whitman and Eugene Hammond, who carried a letter from the Mayor of San Francisco to the Mayor of New York in their Oldsmobile runabout, claimed to have inaugurated this tradition. They arrived in New York on 17 September and then drove on to Boston, where they became the "first true 'sea to sea' drivers."[27] Drake Hokanson remarked that drivers who performed this ritual must have felt a "vestige of Manifest Destiny, that great rationalization that allowed the nation to claim, buy, and steal all the miles of land to the Pacific, and beyond."[28]

The true excitement, though, as perhaps is characteristic of Americans, revolved around speed. In 1915, Henry B. Joy of the Packard Motor Car Company took twenty-one days to drive from Detroit to San Francisco. The next year, 1916, Bobby Hammond drove completely across the country in "an astonishing six days, ten hours, and fifty-nine minutes."[29] He held the record only briefly. The times kept shrinking over the next several years, and by 14 July 1925 the record stood at four days, fourteen hours.

On that date, Louis B. Miller – who sold X-ray equipment and who had no connection with the auto industry – left from the Western Union office in Jersey City, New Jersey, and set off for San Francisco. C.I. Hansen accompanied him to navigate and keep the driver awake. Miller drove a Wills Sainte Claire roadster that he had named "the Gray Goose." Breaking the previous record by seven hours, Miller and Hansen arrived in the Bay City after 102 hours, 45 minutes.

An improvement of seven hours, though, did not satisfy Miller. The next year he drove the route again, in the same car, alone. He reduced his time by nearly a day. Hokanson described the effect on Miller, who by then was well into his fifties. He was, Hokanson said, "never the same again; he couldn't forget the addictive effect of sleep deprivation, speed, and fame. In 1927 he was at it again." This time he was doing something no one had done. Rejecting a one-way trip as too tame, he created a new record, driving round-trip. "Miller drove nonstop from San Francisco to New York City, halted for exactly one minute in New York City ... then turned around and rushed back to San Francisco, taking just one minute less than a week."[30] Despite the existence of interstate highways and far superior automobiles, it would be a rare driver who could match his feat today.

Congestion and law enforcement – one might say progress, or even civilization – cut short the quest for speed on the ground. Since that time it is confined generally to racetracks and speedways. An even faster machine, the airplane, transferred preoccupation with speed to the sky.

In the meantime, the country struggled to improve its roads so that they could match automobile developments. Although road builders through the years had used many substances – with varying degrees of success – to provide hard surfaces, the use of concrete was relatively late in coming. Its first serious use on a public road came in 1909 when Wayne County, Michigan, paved a mile of Woodward Avenue just outside Detroit (it now is inside the city). In 1891 a small area in front of the Bellefontaine, Ohio, courthouse had been paved with concrete. One earlier use shortly before the Detroit street was for an eleven-mile segment of the Long Island

Motor Parkway in 1908. The parkway, though, was a private road. It served as the course for the Vanderbilt Cup races, and also as a toll road for motorists. "Likely the first concrete road ever built anywhere, it also was one of the earliest limited-access roads." The parkway was innovative in other ways as well. It was reinforced by wire mesh and had banked curves. No other road in America could equal it at the time of its construction.[31]

The parkway had no equals in quality for a very long time, but ambitious attempts were underway that were quickly to dwarf it in size. Initially, these, like the parkway, were private ventures.

The transcontinental routes America needed were in the offing. The first, or at least the first that was a reasonably realistic attempt, was the Lincoln Highway, the brainchild of Carl Fisher, who was famed for building the Indianapolis Motor Speedway.[32] Fisher accumulated pledges of one million dollars, but failed to gain support from the man he thought most important to the project, Henry Ford. Ford's view was uncharacteristically enlightened. "As long as private interests are willing to build good roads for the general public," Hokanson quoted Ford's secretary as replying on the auto mogul's behalf, "the general public will not be very much interested in building good roads for itself. I believe in spending money to educate the public to the necessity of building good roads, and let everybody contribute their share in proper taxes."[33]

Fisher ultimately gave up on Ford, and turned to Packard Motor Car Company President Henry B. Joy. With Joy's support, the Lincoln Highway got underway in 1913. It had become customary at the time for roads to bear names, and hundreds of named highways had sprung up throughout the country. Some even antedated the Lincoln, but they made no pretense to span the continent. By 1922 the Lincoln and eight others, according to Hokanson, deserved the title "transcontinental."[34] The two most significant were the Lincoln, the first, and the Theodore Roosevelt International Highway (TRIH). The TRIH was the only one with an international component. Running along the northern tier of the 48 states, close to the Canadian border, it had a modest segment that actually entered Canada and proceeded through Ontario.

The emergence of named – even presumably transcontinental – highways did not mean that auto travel in the early twentieth century had become easy. In 1915 a well-known writer, Emily Post – who later became for two or three generations of Americans the final word in etiquette – attempted to drive the Lincoln with her son Ned as chauffeur. *Collier's Magazine* eagerly published the articles that she supplied describing the group's travels – and travails.

Post had begun with absolutely no intention of roughing it. Not only was their huge, European car overloaded with steamer trunks, she demanded that they stop each night in acceptable hotels. Furthermore, she insisted that each afternoon, she, Ned, and their passenger (a cousin named Alice Beadleston), would stop by the side of the road for tea, which the women would brew and serve from a silver tea set.[35] They held more or less to Miss Post's standards until reaching Chicago. Beyond that greatest expression of Midwest urban culture, however, everything deteriorated. Proceeding west, the adventurers found conditions progressively worse. Wandering far from their intended course, they finally gave up, placed the huge, heavily loaded European travelling car onto a train, boarded the train themselves, and proceeded on in much more comfort to California. Clearly there had been much confusion. When they finally recognized and accepted defeat, they were at Winslow, deep in the Arizona desert![36]

Somewhat later, in 1919, the Lincoln Highway still proved a significant challenge, even for the US Army. In a severe test of their vehicles, the Army Transcontinental Motor Convoy set out from Washington, DC on 7 July to proceed north to the Lincoln, and then west to San Francisco. The convoy stretched two miles. It took sixty-two days – until 7 September – to reach its destination. Along the way, the heavy vehicles broke through 100 bridges, which the army's personnel repaired.

Although now largely forgotten, the trip was one of the major undertakings in American history. It was later to become even more significant to America's system of transportation, because included in the convoy was a young army captain (previously holding the temporary rank of Lt Colonel), Dwight D. Eisenhower. Eisenhower was appalled at the difficulties and dangers involved in transporting men, personnel, and equipment across the country, and concerned about the implications for national security.[37]

Figures are rarely adequate to convey more than a superficial understanding of the menace that hostile conditions offer, but knowing that 230 accidents occurred along the route[38] commands attention. It is difficult for Americans today to appreciate the hardships that those in the convoy had to endure. Having lived through them, however, Eisenhower knew intimately what had been involved. His memories of the harrowing experience influenced him, more than three decades later, to give his strong support to what became one of the most significant accomplishments of his presidency – and what arguably became the greatest public works program in world history – the Interstate Highway System.

By the 1920s both automobiles and paving techniques had advanced considerably. Many roads had been built, and their numbers increased dramatically throughout the decade. Some, although certainly not all, followed historic Indian paths and trails. Some followed the early settlers' routes westward.

The proliferation of named highways with no coordination became increasingly confusing, thus encouraging the federal government to increase its activities. It had already begun to participate with the Federal Road Act of 1916, during the Wilson administration, but the act was minimal, and the First World War hampered road construction.

Supported by pressure from farm groups and the increasingly powerful American Automobile Association, President Harding – who had long been a supporter of good roads – signed into law the Highway Act of 1921.[39] The act authorized the Bureau of Public Roads to assist states in constructing highways. The Bureau, incidentally, was a part of the Department of Agriculture, because so many roads were in National Forests, and the Forest Service was part of that department. With the creation of the Department of Transportation in 1966, the Bureau was transferred to the new department, and re-named the Federal Highway Administration (FHWA).

In 1924 the American Association of State Highway and Transportation Officials (AASHTO) officially recommended that the Secretary of Agriculture consider ways to increase standardization among American highways. AASHTO recommended a numbering system and, by 1927, highways began to receive numbers to replace the older system of names.

A prominent biographer of Calvin Coolidge wrote that "the single positive program of a social nature advocated by the Coolidge administration was road construction," and he suggested that the Harding administration's 1921 act "led almost immediately to the numbering of the new federal highways and the creation of a uniform system of road signs." Coolidge's Agriculture Secretary W.M.

Jardine approved a board of federal and state officials to undertake the task.⁴⁰

The result was the creation of US Highways, with even-numbered roads going east-west, and those with odd numbers going north-south. The most important east-west routes (those that were transcontinental or nearly so) were numbered in multiples of 10, beginning with US 10 across the north and progressing to US 90 across the south. (A partial exception – perhaps because of a large gap from Alburg, Vermont, across the Great Lakes to Michigan's Upper Peninsula – was the northernmost highway, US 2. It began in Maine and stayed near the Canadian border across the country, until its initial ending in Bonners Ferry, Idaho. Now, since the late 1940s, it continues west to Everett, Washington, making it transcontinental, except for the Great Lakes region.) North-south routes, similarly, began with US 1 in the east with numbers increasing toward the west, culminating in US 101.⁴¹ The scheme is not pure, of course, because of diagonal routes and others that do not exactly fit.

In any case, the numbering system led to the fading away of the named highways. The new system, Hokanson complained, "was a near-fatal blow to the Lincoln Highway and a death knell for all the other named highways of the country. Not only was the Lincoln broken up into several numbered roads, but the officials had ruled that all markers and signs for named highways would have to come down." He quoted Henry Joy as saying bitterly that the Lincoln Highway, "a memorial to the martyred Lincoln," by the government's authority had become known as "Federal Route 1, Federal Route 30, Federal Route 30N, Federal Route 30S, Federal Route 530, Federal Route 40, and Federal Route 50."⁴² Hokanson pointed out that evidence supported allegations that state and federal officials deliberately broke the named routes into separate designations to destroy their identity.

The Roosevelt Highway provides additional evidence. It had been a discrete unit. After the numbering of America's highways – in what must have been an effort to wipe it from memory – the Roosevelt became US 301 in Maine, NH 18 in New Hampshire, and Vermont 18 connecting with US 2 in Vermont. Then, through New York and (after its Canadian segment) Michigan's Lower Peninsula, officials assigned different segments a wide variety of numbers. It became US 2 in the Upper Peninsula and across Wisconsin, Minnesota, North Dakota, and Montana to Bonners Ferry, Idaho. From then on, as it progressed south and west through Spokane and Walla Walla, Washington, and on south into Oregon, it bore many different numbers. In Oregon, west through Pendleton, the Dalles, through the Columbia River Gorge, and on into Portland where it ended, it became US 30.

The demise of the more romantic highway (or "trail") names, though, did nothing to prevent America's romance with the road. In 1925 the creation of US 66 captured America's imagination as the "Mother Road," when it enabled motorists to drive on one road from Chicago, through Missouri and Oklahoma, and on into the exotic Southwest, all the way to Los Angeles. For more than half a century it was fabled in song and folklore. For a time, it was even the subject of a television action series, "Route 66," built around the experiences of two young men who continually roamed along the Mother Road in their powerful Corvette sports car finding new adventures each week – all apparently with no need for a paycheck or even for luggage in their two-seater car with no space for such mundane considerations.

Throughout the 1930s many Americans who had no work wandered the country's roads in search of jobs or more favourable locations. Ever since, the road has been a persistent theme in song and story, and in modern country music the truck driver often takes the role of a knight of the road. Americans welcomed the late Charles Kuralt's television specials and books chronicling his travels throughout the homeland.

The "road book" has become a staple of American literature. There have been travel stories for centuries, but the automobile and the American road together have created something different, and contributed a unique genre. The first of these was probably Theodore Dreiser's 1916 portrayal in *A Hoosier Holiday* of his automobile journey from New York City to his native Indiana. John Faris wrote *Roaming America's Highways* and a dozen or so popular books in the late 1920s and 1930s describing what he saw and experienced as he journeyed by auto around the country. Henry Miller's *An Air-Conditioned Nightmare* and Jack Kerouac's *On the Road* fit easily into the category, as do scores if not hundreds of other books – probably enough to form a respectable library.

Some road books are superb and likely will be read for generations, if not forever. The best-known are probably John Steinbeck's *Travels with Charley* – still in print after nearly a half century – and

William Least Heat-Moon's classic *Blue Highways*. Others deserve to be equally famous: works by such writers as Jonathan Raban, Dayton Duncan, Geoffrey O'Gara, and Howard Frank Mosher.

A sub-category of the road book genre deals primarily with specific highways: books about US 1 and Route 66, others about highways in certain states; rousing books by Hokanson and Davies about the Lincoln Highway (these are also scholarly resources, which I have cited here); and most recently (2007) my *Moose Crossing: Portland to Portland on the Theodore Roosevelt International Highway.*

When President Eisenhower signed the Interstate Highway Act into law in 1956, and even for some years later, some sections of roads designated US Highways were still unpaved and surfaced with gravel. The new interstate system developed rapidly. Interstates made it possible to drive from coast to coast without encountering a traffic light or a stop sign. The system was engineered to high standards, permitting smooth travel and high speeds. The highways were a vast improvement on anything that had preceded them.

This is not to say, though, that their effects were all salutary. Many communities dwindled when the interstates bypassed them, just as others had done a century earlier when railroads went elsewhere. The highways formed barriers that could be crossed only at widely spaced intervals, and sometimes cut large farms in two. They led to rapid movement of cars within cities that paradoxically helped destroy downtown sections. Above all, they continued to encourage America's reliance on the automobile to the exclusion of other, more efficient, forms of transportation.

Although it is disputed, evidence supports the widespread belief that electric inter-urban lines and mass transit systems in American cities fell victim to a conspiracy when certain companies – automobile and tire manufacturers, oil companies, etc. – worked over a period of decades to purchase street railway systems, trams, and streetcars, and switch to buses. Bradford Snell in testimony before the a committee of the US Senate described the process, which included, among other things, creating a dummy company, National City Lines, that destroyed one hundred or so such systems.[43] The purpose, of course, was to encourage the use of automobiles instead of other means of transportation. Snell does not allege an "evil plot," but rather as a shrewd business decision that had disastrous consequences. In any case, in 1949 a number of prominent American corporations were convicted of violating antitrust laws in the role they played in destroying urban rail systems. They included General Motors, Firestone, Mack Manufacturing, Phillips Petroleum, and Standard Oil of California. Neither the executives involved nor those reporting on the case seemed aware of the great damage that was done. The *New York Times* reported the conviction (which, incidentally, was upheld on appeal) on 13 March 1949. The newspaper buried the story, however, on page 79. The same dynamic – strong support for highways and airports – worked to benefit American trucking companies and air transit at the expense of railroads. The result of all this has been the near elimination of passenger rail in the United States. Some cities now have been forced by congestion to expend huge resources to develop mass-transit systems that could have evolved from their old streetcar lines, had those lines not vanished. In many cities, though, mass transit is so inadequate that for much of the population it may as well not exist.

In any case, America retains its myth of the road and its love of the automobile. There is little transportation available, except by auto or airplane. Traffic congestion is legendary in and around cities. Air travel for short and medium distances is wasteful and inefficient, and the United States – despite the renewed popularity of fuel-efficient vehicles – remains on a binge of oil consumption. Until very recently the most popular vehicles were enormous sport-utility vehicles that use resources voraciously – and the tax system encouraged their use.

The romance of the road prevails. For many Americans, the ideal in retirement is to roam America's highways in – often huge – recreational vehicles (RVs), stopping as they desire, and living in no fixed location. The call of the road is undeniable. Often, even critics feel it.

So the appeal remains and Americans continue to roam. They love their country, and often wish to experience it all, continually. Many of them will do so, so long as petroleum lasts, and so long as the climate permits it.

3

The Road in American Vernacular Music

SUSAN KUYPER

I'm just a poor wayfaring stranger
A-wandring through this world of woe.
Yet there's no sickness, toil or danger
In that bright land, to which I go.
>"Wayfaring Stranger," J. and A. Lomax, *Our Singing Country*

The singer of this haunting American folk song embodies the qualities of the many travellers in the new country: poor, plodding, visited by calamity, but hoping for the "bright land" of the future. The songs resonate with the weariness of travel, tell stories of terrible challenges, but also never lose hope. A rich vein of road songs is found in important folk collections of the nineteenth century that preserve the important legacy going back to the founding of America. Many of these road songs were revived in the middle of the twentieth century by folk singers such as Burl Ives, who used "Wayfaring Stranger" as the title of his 1944 album and his 1948 autobiography.[1]

This chapter focuses on the broad range of folk songs that have to do with travellers, the roads they travelled, the stories they told, and the horses and wagons, boats and schooners they rode – all of which become key components of the trope of the road. These wayfaring strangers tell an intimate story of the settling of the American frontier.

"Vernacular music" as a genre is difficult to define. Concepts used in definitions include "folk," "traditional," "oral," and "anonymous." Using the negative is helpful: vernacular music is *not* classical, *not* cultivated; it is for the "people," *not* the "elite." Pete Seeger, who sang folk music for pleasure and polemics, argues for a fluid definition to suit personal preferences in particular contexts. He claims folk music is really an age-old process of learning and singing mostly by ear, of formally untrained musicians singing for fun, not for pay, to friends and neighbours, and from time to time changing or creating verses or melodies as events move them.[2] James Leisy believes folk songs have a "certain sound – that ring of truth; songs of the people, by the people, and for the people."[3] John and Alan Lomax suggest that folk music "comes straight from the heart of the people and that its idioms reveal their daily habits of speech." The author/composer is invisible.[4] John Tasker Howard echoes these thoughts: "To be a true folk song it must be typical of the people who sing it ... the song itself must be more important than its composer."[5]

Defining *American* folk vernacular music is an even greater challenge. "There ain't no such animal," Alan Lomax bluntly claims, concluding that America's best songs and dances are hybrids of hybrids, mixtures of mixtures."[6] "What is it?" asks John Tasker Howard. "If Americanism is a matter of geography, or residence, the distinction is clear. But if sources and distinguishing traits are to be considered, the subject of American folk song offers a puzzle that is not easy to solve."[7]

American folk music, Howard concludes, does not have to be original, but it does have to align with the manner of speech and themes that are meaningful to Americans.[8] James F. Leisy quotes Bruno Nettl: "in folklore the most important works of music are probably those which are especially closely tied to the culture and which therefore are the most accurate expressions of its nature and character."[9] In this essay I use the broadest possible definition of "folk song," incorporating Seeger's process, Howard's anonymity, Leisy's ring of truth, and Lomax's daily habits of speech.

The common thread in these various definitions is the "heart of the people," for folk songs are meaningful to those who sing them as they work, play, love, and worship. They are sung for release from personal suffering and to ease the burden of work. They are sung to allow the voice of the people to be heard above the cacophony of political chaos. They are sung to bring spiritual understanding and comfort. Most importantly in this context, they are sung as the American people travel. There is a large subset of "road folk songs" in the history of the American vernacular music. Many were brought from Britain and sung by the colonists. The settlers in the Midwest, the cowboys of the west, and the "Forty Niners" created original songs of travel. Those travelling to a new life, those seeking a fortune, and those travelling for work all sang of their experiences. This chapter examines how such songs provide a "magical summing up of patterns" of the American way of life.

George O. Carney has written persuasively and analytically about the importance and discipline of the geography of music. He has isolated several "conceptual subdivisions" that can be studied, including spatial variation (country music is from the South, classical music is more common in the North) and spatial organization of music phenomena (such as the birthplaces of country musicians) useful in marketing music. This essay concentrates on his third concept, the origin and diffusion of music, with reference to how music and musicians travelled along the trails, rails, and roads of America from colonial times to the twentieth century. It also considered his fourth concept: "the psychological and symbolic elements of music pertinent to shaping the character of a place."[10] The main archive for this study is *Folk Songs of North America*, a compilation of 317 folk songs collected by the father and son duo John and Alan Lomax. The collection includes songs from three centuries of American development and is organized along broad geographic divisions. Of the 317 songs, approximately 95 include some reference to travel. This chapter examines the themes and stories of these American road song lyrics, listening to the individual voices to glean the stories of their journeys.

Devin Orgeron argues that road movies offer the viewer vicarious journeys, just as previous generations watched the landscape out of the train's window. The "viewer agrees to be 'transported.' Though the viewer is not on the physical journey, he is on an emotional journey 'out of himself.'"[11] Just as the road movie transports the viewer, road music transports the performer and the listener to an emotional plane "outside of him- or her-self." Road songs help one feel the journey. They come from the soul of the traveller and speak to the souls of the performer and the listener. Road music brings us to the character of the travellers and their inherent relationship to the road; to the road itself; to leave-taking and the reasons for going; to the mode of transportation or mobility (ship, walking, carriage); to the physical journey and exploration; to the social community formed along the way; to the landscape and sights encountered; to the insights gathered; and to the progress of self, soul, and civilization resulting from this combination (see Slethaug in chapter 1 of this book).

At the heart of all road songs are the travellers. The difficulties of their journeys, their hardships in love, and the loneliness of their life on the road, and also the revelry and entertainment they enjoy; all are remembered in American folk songs.

The road influenced American folk music in a unique way not included in Carney's concepts. The sheer increase in roads and automobiles in the early twentieth century made folk music accessible and recordable. Before 1900, before the radio and phonograph records, Americans as a collective community were not aware of their rich musical traditions. Walt Whitman rued the lack of quality of American songs and literature in his 1888 essay "Democratic Vistas,"[12] and it was not until 1944 that Paul Chancellor set right Whitman's lament: "What Whitman never learned, and what most Americans still don't know, is that folk song has flourished in America, and still does, with vitality and abundance to rival that of any nation of western Europe ... Today the case is different. We now know where our song is and what a wealth there is of it."[13]

Other twentieth-century commentators also celebrated the "discovery" of the folk music of America. John Tasker Howard wrote in the 1930s: "Throughout America there are sources of folk songs that have been appreciated by collectors only in recent years."[14] These collections are rich and varied. As Cecil Sharp[15] and George Malcolm Law[16] demonstrated in their respective collections of British ballads still sung in the hinterlands of the United States, music itself travels. "The map sings," Alan Lomax proclaims.[17] The colourful map in the front endpaper of his expansive collection *Folk Songs of North America* delineates families of song styles in swatches of bright colours: "Northern" is red, "Southern" yellow, "Border between Northern and Southern" is striped red and yellow, "Western" reflects its mixed heritage with orange, and the "Negro Song Style Family by Proportion of Negroes in Population" ranges from a green and yellow check to green stripes and yellow dots as the percentage decreases. Crossed and dotted black lines traverse the map, tracing the trails, wagon roads, canals, railroads, and cattle trails. Cities important to the history of folk music are carefully marked.

Alan Lomax's "Introduction" is a prose poem describing the "restless Americans" who took advantage of the mobility of the new country, "scattering" folk songs as they went.[18] George O. Carney, music geographer, has also written a comprehensive review of the movement of music and suggests that the road was not only the subject of many folk songs but the very means by which they were transmitted:

> From the British Isles came the sea chanteys heard along the Atlantic Coast and interior Great Lakes, and from France came the paddling songs from the French Canadians traveling along the St. Lawrence. European ballads transplanted in Newfoundland, Nova Scotia, and New England migrated West. Pilgrims and Puritans brought church music via the Bay Psalm Book, and the New England church singing-school concept diffused southward to other colonies. From West Africa through the Sea Islands, slave melodies spread across the Deep South from the Carolinas to Texas. As settlement moved westward into the Appalachians, new ballads and love songs were created and eventually were carried across the Upland South to the Ozarks of Missouri, Arkansas, and Oklahoma. Black workers chanted songs while building the South's railroads and levees, and from the cotton plantations of the Mississippi delta came the field hollers that, with the work chants, were the foundation for country blues. The country blues migrated up and down the Mississippi River. At the mouth of the "Big Muddy," New Orleans became a musical crossroads for African, Spanish and French sounds. The cultural mixture resulted in jazz. To the northern end of the Mississippi, blacks took the blues into the cities of the Midwest to produce ragtime in St. Louis and urban blues in Chicago ... As people spilled onto the Great Plains and Far West, songs and ballads depicted the culture of the miner, cowboy, and farmer ... The sounds of people and places have indeed become an important segment of North American culture.[19]

The first songs in America that celebrate roads appear in the early ballad tradition of the Puritan colony. They are "lane" songs and exhibit the hybridization that occurred as folk songs travelled from Britain to America. One set of "lane" songs has evolved from the ancient English ballad "Elfin Knight," in which a "maiden in her castle bower ... hears the faraway blast of the elfin horn and wishes the fairy knight were in her bed. The fairy (in ancient belief a man of medium stature) appears straightaway at her bedside, but he demands the answers to his riddles before he will consent to be her lover."[20]

The ancient ballad "Elfin Knight" has been adapted many times over the centuries and over the continents. It lives on in such folk ballads as "Petticoat Lane," "Scarborough Fair," "Cambric Shirt," and "Strawberry Lane." All are related by the set of impossible tasks demanded by the young girl of her lover,[21] and by the inclusion of a lane and a journey: "As I walked out in Petticoat Lane," "As I was a-walking up Strawberry Lane," and "Are you going to Scarborough Fair?"

The websites "The Traditional Ballad Index,"[22] a comprehensive and well-sourced compilation of folk songs and tunes, and the Mudcat Café Digital Traditional Folk Song Server[23] both identify another family of lane songs that includes the following titles: "Rosemary Lane," "Home, Dearie, Home," the "Servant of Rosemary Lane," "Raspberry Lane," "Ambletown," and "Bell Bottom Trousers" (a bawdy version). In each song, a forlorn maid rues her lot after she beds a sailor who leaves in the morning, throwing her coins for her unborn child. In "Rosemary Lane," the maid is in service on Rosemary Lane, but in "Raspberry Lane," the maid is a mistress of fame who walks upon Raspberry Lane. The ravishment in the latter occurs in "North Amerikee," and the sailor vows not to wed a foreign lady. The importance of the lane is significant: the lane imprisons the lady and provides escape for the errant lover.

Carney suggests that New England and the Mid-Atlantic colonies/states were "hearths" from which the ballads journeyed.[24] The lanes of the early colonies became trails into the wilderness. By the 1700s, new settlers had pushed into western Pennsylvania, and, when land became scarce there, they trundled into the Appalachian wilderness and eventually to the passage leading to the west. Alan Lomax imagines that the Cumberland Gap "witnessed some of the wildest jubilations," as poor white settlers walked over the pass and saw the rich land before them. The song "Cumberland Gap" is a fiddle tune, but if the settlers didn't have a fiddle in their saddlebags, they were "masters of the Celtic art of mouth music, those rhymed verses which precisely match the dance tunes and guide the feet of the dancers."[25] All of the versions of the folk song exhibit a strong rhythm.

CHORUS. Cumberland Gap, Cumberland Gap,
Mmmm (yelp), way down yonder in Cumberland Gap.

Me an' my wife an' my wife's pap,
We all live down in Cumberland Gap. CHORUS

Cumberland Gap is a noted place,
Three kinds of water to wash your face. CHORUS

The first white man in Cumberland Gap
Was Doctor Walker, an English chap. CHORUS

Daniel Boone on Pinnacle Rock,
He killed Injuns with his old flintlock. CHORUS

Lay down, boys, and take a little nap,
Fo' teen miles to the Cumberland Gap. CHORUS[26]

The lyrics describe the land (three kinds of water!), the life of its people (me, my wife, and my father-in-law), the history (first Boone and later Civil War events in the Cumberland Gap), and the weariness of travel (lay down, boys, and take a little nap). The music is rhythmic and quick; the melody meanders up and down the octave; and the singer will settle in the Gap – he is a wayfaring stranger on his way to the bright land. The importance of revelry and rest to the wayfaring stranger is reinforced in a myriad similar fiddle tunes, reels, and game songs of the American frontier.

The travelling motif takes on a religious significance as a result of the late eighteenth- and early nineteenth-century growth of Southern evangelism and camp meetings. At the end of the eighteenth century, influenced by reformists Lowell Mason and Thomas Hastings, itinerant singing masters and ministers travelled south, uncomfortable in the once-again strict northern religious environment.[27] As the fire-and-brimstone "religious leftist" ministers ("rural Baptists, chiefly, then Methodists, New Side Presbyterians, and others") preached to the southern frontier, the sedate psalm singing of the Northern tradition was replaced with the "folksy" hymns of Isaac Watts and Charles and John Wesley, and religious lyrics set to the old secular English ballads.[28] By 1800 the "all-denominational camp meetings took up these songs, livened them, filled out partially remembered texts with much repetition, refrains and choruses, and thus made them over into a rather roistering type of song ... and went under the various names – spiritual songs, camp meeting songs, revival songs, and chorus songs."[29]

As a result, the Great Revival of the late eighteenth and early nineteenth century "roared through the South-east like a forest fire."[30] Families and neighbours travelled to the nearest camp meetings, with poorer farmers bringing their black slaves with them.[31] Thus, two musical crossroads existed in these tent meetings: white Baptist hymnody met black spiritual, spawning the white spiritual: triadic harmony from the shape-note tradition gave the songs colour while African rhythms brought them to life.

The Christian journey to salvation, to heaven, to the "bright land," is a strong and prevalent theme in the frontier road folk song. The symbol of heaven as the reward for the earthly trials complements the vision of the frontier as the new future with riches and contentment. Howard calls some road themes in these songs "purely 'country' music," providing comfort and inspiration to the rural farmer and his wife singing in the tent in the heat of a summer night: "Let cares like a wild deluge come / And storms of sorrow fall; / May I but safely reach my home. / My God, my heaven, my all. / Chorus: I feel like, I feel like I'm on my journey home."[32]

In the South the white settlers and their ballads, fiddle tunes, and Sacred Harp music encountered the black slaves and their field hollers, call and response songs, community singing, and unique rhythms and dance, that contributed strongly to the development of an American road folk song with a spiritual destination. Alan Lomax includes a fascinating comparison of southern song "Roll, Jordan, Roll" as sung first in Sacred Harp square note singing in quarter note rhythms by the white congregation, with its belief in a "severe, patriarchal God," and then by the black slaves who added dotted rhythms to reflect the speech patterns of confession of a personal God. The Sacred Harp version awaits the judge severe:

He comes, He comes, the judge severe,
Roll, Jordan, roll,
The seventh trumpet speaks Him near,
Roll, Jordan, roll.
I want to go to Heav'n, I do,
Hallelujah, Lord,
We'll praise the Lord in Heav'n above,
Roll, Jordan, roll.

The black spiritual in its many verses invites all to share in the story:

O preacher (brother, sister, sinner), you oughta been there,
Yes, my Lord,
A-sittin' in the kingdom
To hear old Jordan roll.
Roll, Jordan, roll,
Roll, Jordan, roll,
I want to go to Heaven when I die
To hear old Jordan roll.[33]

The journey theme appears in many spirituals from the early eighteenth to the nineteenth century as gospel became the more common genre. The singer travels through "sickness, toil and danger" to the "bright" land in many 'black' spirituals. "Keep A-Inchin' Along" encourages the singer to inch along like a "po' inch worm," for Jesus "will come by'n'bye."

When I get to Heaven, ain't I gonna shout?
Nobody there to put me out ... CHORUS

Ever since my Lord set me free,
This old world's been a Hell to me. CHORUS

Sometimes I hang my head and cry,
But I'm gonna serve God till I die. CHORUS

There's a fire in the East, fire in the Wes',
There's a fire among us Methodes'. CHORUS

CHORUS: 'Twas inch by inch I saw the Lord,
Jesus will come by'n-bye,
'Twas inch by inch I saved my soul,
Jesus will come by'n'-bye.[34]

The journey to heaven can be by "Jacob's Ladder," by chariot ("Swing Low, Sweet Chariot"), by boat ("Hold the Wind"[35]), by ark ("The Old Ark's A-Moverin'"[36]), or by train ("This Train is Bound for Glory.")[37] The bittersweet irony of these journey songs is that the slaves were not allowed to travel. Congruent with the growth of slave labour, however, was the development of the underground railroad, which helped slaves escape from their desperate situations in the south through the free northern states to Canada. Slave owners, sensing the dangers of escape and rebellion, paid close attention to their chattel, severely curtailing any gatherings except religious meetings. The rhythmic, haunting black spirituals, often based on Old Testament stories, provided permissible musical comfort to the slaves, helping them sing of escape. But there was something more. Frederic Douglass discusses the hidden messages in various spirituals – all of them road songs: "Canaan" meant "north" in "I am bound for the land of Canaan"; "Run to Jesus" meant "shun the danger"; and "I don't expect to stay much longer here" meant "a speedy pilgrimage toward a free state."[38] Other coded spirituals include "Swing Low, Sweet Chariot" (the underground-railroad drivers will soon be here); "Steal Away" (we're preparing to leave); and "Wade in the Water, God's gonna trouble the water" (an escape by water will wash away the scent and the bloodhounds can't follow).[39]

During this same period of the early nineteenth century, settlers in the north travelled west from Pennsylvania and "crowded" New England, into the rich farmland and abundant waterways of what is now Tennessee and Ohio and eventually into the Great Lakes region. These settlers sang about the richness of their new homes in Ohio and Illinois, and the subsequent peace and pride of finding their "bright land." The matchmaker in "The Lovely Ohio" invites "all ye brisk young fellows who have a mind to roam," and "all you pretty fair maids" who can knit and sew to join him where "there are fishes in the river, just fitted for our use. / There's tall and lofty sugar cane that will give to us its juice, / There's every kind of game, my boys, also the buck and doe, / When we settle on the banks of the lovely Ohio."[40]

Pride of place is also found in El-a-noy, in which the land bordered by the Wabash and Ohio Rivers and the Great Lakes is compared to Eden, a land Solomon and the Queen of Sheba would have gladly ruled. And in Chicago, "men are all like Abelard, / her women like Heloise, / All honest virtuous people, / for they live in El-a-noy."[41]

Not everyone, however, thought the Midwest was Eden. "In Kansas" suggests that "all who want to roam in Kansas" need to be "contented with your doom" for potatoes grow small and the tobacco is thin. Life is also tough in Arkansas, where "they make polecat pie," and people "never wed, or so I've heard it said, they just tumble into bed in Arkansas."[42]

The journey was not only difficult and the destination unpromising in the lumberjacking areas of the Great Lakes, but tragedy was ever present. Moving cargo on the water was dangerous, heavy work, drowning was a constant danger, and grief for a parent or a young lover was ever present. In a nineteenth-century song telling of one of the "Beaver Island Boys," Johnny Gallegher, crossing Lake Michigan on the Lookout, the narrator begins with an invitation: "Come, all brother sailors, I hope you'll draw nigh/For to hear of the sad news" of the demise of Johnny Gallegher. He relates the conversation between Johnny's mother, who pleads with him not to go, and Johnny, who promises to return shortly. The narrator was on the fateful ship for he relates that "It was in October in '73, / We left Beaver harbor and had a calm sea / Bound away, Traverse City was our destination to go, / We were crossing Lake Michigan where the stormy winds blow." They finally reach Traverse City, but meet disaster upon their return:

We left Traverse City at nine the next day
And down to Elk Rapids we then bore away;
We took in our stores and to sea we did go,
For to cross o'er Lake Michigan
where the stormy winds blow ...

The Lookout she's a-running before a hard gale,
Upset went her rudder and overboard went her sail;
The billows were foaming like mountains of snow,
We shall ne'er cross Lake Michigan
where the stormy winds blow.

Siz own brother Johnny, "It grieves my heart sore
To think we will never return to the shore;
God help our poor parents,
their tears down will flow;
For we'll sleep in Lake Michigan
where the stormy winds blow."[43]

The lumberjacks who travelled into the north's remote forests also constantly teased death on the rushing rivers down which they travelled. "The Pinery Boy" begins with this caveat: "O, a rafts-man's life is a wearisome one, It causes many fair maids to weep and mourn ... For the loss of a true love that never can return."[44] Mary loses her river-running husband in "The River in the Pines:"

'Twas early in the morning
in Wisconsin's dreary clime,
When he rode the fatal rapids
for that last and fatal time.
They found his body lying on the rocky shore below
Where the silent water ripples
and the whispering cedars blow.

Now every raft of lumber
that comes down the Chippeway,
There's a lonely grave that's visited
by drivers on their way.
They plant wild flowers upon it
in the morning fair and fine,
'Tis the grave of two young lovers
from the River in the Pines.[45]

By the mid-nineteenth century, settlers had pushed west beyond the Great Lakes and the Mississippi, singing their journey songs as they went. Eden had moved from Ohio to Arkansas. "We're coming, Arkansas," sing the soon-to-be Arkansians on the road behind their "four horse team," eager for her healing crystal waters, easy hunting, good crops, strong girls, and good tobacco.[46] The contentment of the Ohio River dweller turns into a competitive, my-state-is-better-than-your-state set of songs as the settlers move west. In the early days, one fork of the big road west led to Arkansas, the other to Texas. A sign at the fork read, "This road to Texas." According to Texans, all who could read pressed on to the Lone Star State, while the others settled in Arkansas."[47]

Arkansas and Texas taunted each other in duelling road folk songs that were often about the sorrows (or joys) of parting rather than the anticipation of safe arrival or threat of tragedy. In "I'm Goin' Away to Texas," a lover reluctant to leave Arkansas sings "Oh, dear me," while his exasperated sweetheart can't wait to get rid of her bumpkin lover and replies "Just go on an' keep a-goin,'" "fa-la-diddle-la-la-day." In "The State of Arkansas," Charles Brennan, an Irish immigrant in Texas, tells of his horrible journey to Arkansas, after returning to Texas: "I never knew what misery was till I came to Arkansas."[48] Alan Lomax traces the route of parting songs very popular in the Ozarks back to a Scottish ballad, "The Girl I Left Behind:" "This song of parting ... has been cherished by the restless, footloose Anglo-American tribe for almost three centuries. The narrator leaves Ireland for Scotland, or sails from England bound for Amerikay, sets off on horseback from Virginia to Tennessee, turns west from Tennessee to Texas or old Missouri, or starts across the plains from Texas to Salt Lake City or California."[49]

The movement of these parting songs from the old country to the new and from the lanes of New England to the frontier of Texas speaks to the universality of its theme: leaving home and/or a lover. The potential problems include not only leaving behind a lover but also being sent away by a lover (as in "Hit the Road, Jack"), being jilted by the lover who travels, being jilted by the lover who stays, or finding love on the road. In the American version of "The Girl I Left Behind," a young man woos a farmer's daughter who vowed to be true to him while he was making his fortune in the "plains," but ended up leaving him before he returns:

As I was rambling around one day
all down on the public square,
The mailcoach had arrived
and I met the mailboy there,
He handed to me a letter that gave me to understand,
That the girl I left in old Texas
had married another man ...

Come all you ramblin', gamblin' boys,
and listen while I tell
Does you no good, kind friends,
I am sure it will do you no harm,
If ever you court a fair young maid,
just marry her while you can,
For if ever you cross over the plains,
she'll marry some other man.[50]

Other love stories in the road folk song genre are sung by the "freighters," men who drove wagons to carry goods from country to urban centres and back. As the settled country expanded, the need for transportation, cargo handling, and mail service became crucial. Bull-whackers drove oxcarts (known as "prairie schooners" because they "sailed" through the rugged terrain of the plains) and were renowned for their cursing and bragging, as that was the most effective way to control the stubborn animals. Alan Lomax designates "Root, Hog, or Die" as the "bull-whacker's most notable song."[51]

I'm a lonely bull-whacker
On the Red Cloud Line,
I can lick any son-of-a-gun
Can yoke an ox of mine.
If I can catch him
You bet I will or try,
I'll lick with him an ox-bow,
Root, hog, or die.

Well, it's out upon the road
With a very heavy load,
With a very awkward team
And a very muddy road,
You may whip and you may holler,
If you cuss it's on the sly,
Then it's whack the cattle on, boys,
Root, hog, or die. . .

There was good times in Salt Lake
I never can pass by,
That's where I met her,
My China girl called Wi.
She could smile, she could chuckle,
She could roll her hog-eye,
Then it's whack the cattle on, boys,
Root, hog, or die.[52]

The bull-whacker dreamed of love and a settled life with a "purdy gal." His ox-bow whacking with oxen is not great training for a lover! There was also the wagoner, who travelled the hinterland, transporting wares from Appalachian villages to eastern urban centres and back; he was a frontiersman with a strong, independent spirit.[53] "The Wagoner's Lad" is a dialogue between the farm girl and a wagon driver who had courted her relentlessly when he arrived; now that his wagon is loaded, he is leaving with no further ado.

> He: Your parents don't like me because I am poor,
> They say I'm not worthy of entering your door;
> I work for my living, my money's my own,
> And if they don't like me, they can leave me alone.
> She: Your horses are hungry, go feed them on hay,
> Come sit down here by me as long as you stay.
> He: My horses ain't hungry, they won't eat your hay,
> So fare you well, darling, I'll feed on the way.
> She: Your wagon needs greasing, your whip is to mend,
> Come sit down here by me as long as you can.
> He: My wagon is greasy, my whip's in my hand,
> So fare you well, darling, no longer to stand.[54]

Nostalgia for a loved one is a common, gentler theme for some travellers. By 1873 wagons were "freighting" in Arizona and California, and the older, experienced freighter in "From Wilcox to Globe" is frustrated by the bad conditions and low pay. His "best wheel horse" is stolen, and it took thirteen days to travel fourteen miles. He is not a youthful wanderer like the wagoner's lad, for he dreams of "home, dearest home; / And it's home you ought to be, / Over on the Gila / In the white man's country, / Where the poplar and the ash / And mesquite will ever be / Growing green down on the Gila; / There's a home for you and me."[55]

Another set of singers who bequeathed America a large repertoire of road folk songs was the nineteenth-century cowboys, who sang in the saddle as they herded the longhorn cattle from the ranges of Texas to the markets in Abilene, Kansas. Perhaps no other frontier group has been more romanticized than the cowboy. Bill C. Malone traces the development of the twentieth-century fascination with the cowboy, which is based on American exceptionalism and the promotion of mid-nineteenth century Manifest Destiny (see Slethaug, chapter 1 in this book). Jimmie Rodgers was a Mississippi railroad brakeman in the early twentieth century who spent a lot of time in North Carolina treating his tuberculosis: his singing persona was neither the railroad man nor the mountain hillbilly, for he fashioned his music and his stage persona after the cowboy: "In Rodgers's mind and songs, the cowboy may have meshed easily with the rambler, a figure traditionally venerated by the folk because of his bold assertion of freedom. But to a degree much stronger than the rootless rambler, the cowboy, unrestrained by the confining regimens of city life, but bound by a proper behavior and loyalty to friends, symbolized freedom and independence."[56]

John A. Lomax's collection *Cowboy Songs and Other Frontier Ballads* introduced America to "Home on the Range," arguably the national folk anthem. His "Collector's Notes" is a prose poem to the cowboy:

> That the cowboy was brave has come to be axiomatic. If his life of isolation made him taciturn, it at the same time created a spirit of hospitality, primitive and hearty as that found in the mead-halls of Beowulf. He faced the wind and the rain, the snow of winter, the fearful dust-storms of alkali desert wastes, with the same uncomplaining quiet ... To the cowboy, more than to the gold-seekers, more than to Uncle Sam's soldiers, is due the conquest of the West. Along his winding cattle trails the Forty-Niners found their way to California. The cowboy has fought back the Indians ever since ranching became a business and as long as Indians remained to be fought. He played his part in winning the great slice of territory that the United States took away from Mexico.[57]

John Lomax also provides two clues as to why the songs of the cowboy are so appealing: they are created and performed by "men who lived on terms of practical equality," and they are sung from the "impulses of the heart."

> The work of the men, their daily experiences, their thoughts, their interests, were all in common. Such a community had necessarily to turn to itself for entertainment. Songs sprang up naturally, some of them tender and familiar lays of childhood, others original compositions, all genuine, however crude and unpolished. Whatever the most gifted man could produce must bear the criticism of the entire camp, and agree with the ideas of a group of men. In this sense, therefore, any song that came from

such a group would be the joint product of a number of them, telling perhaps the story of some stampede they had all fought to turn, some crime in which they had all shared equally, some comrade's tragic death which they had all witnessed ... The broad sky under which he slept, the limitless plains over which he rode, the big, open, free life he lived near to Nature's breast, taught him simplicity, calm, directness.[58]

These cowboy songs still satisfy our hearts. The cowboy who sings "The Old Chizzum Trail" or "The Old Chisholm Trail"[59] (related lyrics, but different tunes) is soothing the cattle during his night shift with his "Coma-ti-yi-yippy, yippy yea, yippy yea." Simultaneously, he is soothing his own soul and the souls of his listeners with verses telling of his origins, his exploits against the elements, the difficult herding moments, and what his imagination can create ("The Old Chizzum Trail" version in *American Ballads and Folk Songs* continues for 39 verses[60]). In "The Old Chisholm Trail," the singer is a cow-puncher forever, for once he gets to the cattle market in Abilene he'll get drunk and repeat the journey all over again: "Oh, Abilene city is a dang fine town, / We'll all liquor up and twirl those heifers round; / Then back once more with my bridle and my hoss, / For old John Chisum is a damned fine boss. / I never hankered for to plough or to hoe, / And punching steers is all I know. / With my knees in the saddle and a-hanging to the sky, / Herding dogies up in Heaven in the sweet by-and-by."[61]

The cowboy in "The Old Chizzum Trail" sells his horse and saddle, hopping the train to go back to his gal and farm. He has no regrets and no great memories: "No more a cow-puncher to sleep at my ease, / 'Mid the crawlin' of the lice an the bitin' of the fleas."[62] This cowboy is in the minority. "I'm Bound to Follow the Longhorn Cows," sings another confident cowboy, who's proud of his skills and enamoured of the cowboy challenges. He ends with a whimsical salute to the girl who now has to find someone else, for he's a cowboy for life:

I'm bound to follow the longhorn cows
until I git too old,
It's well I work for wages, boys,
I git my pay in gold.
My bosses, they all like me well,

they say I'm hard to beat,
Because I give 'em the bold stand-off,
they know I've got the cheek ...

Now if I had a little stake, I soon would married be,
But another week and I must go,
the boss said so today.
My girl must cheer up courage
and choose some other one,
For I'm bound to follow the longhorn cows
until my race is run.[63]

The cowboy in "I'm A-Leavin' Cheyenne" is also committed to the
life on the trail: he is more attached to his horses Old Paint and Old
Fan than to any young girl. "I'm a ridin' Old Paint and I'm a-leadin'
Old Fan, / My foot's in my stirrup, my bridle's in my hand." "The
grass is a-risin' all over this land, / I'm sorry, young lady, I'm off to
Montan'."[64]

One young unemployed cowboy sings of his unpleasant journey
to New Mexico in "On the Trail to Mexico": he is fed up and will
never return. He was asked to join the trip by a drover, and he joined
a band of cowherds on a pleasant trip until they hit "old Boggy
Creek."

And there our pleasures ended
And our troubles they began,
The first hard storm that hit us,
Oh, how the cattle ran!
While running through thorns and stickers
We had but little show,
And the Indians watched to pick us off
In the hills of New Mexico.

After killing the drover who would not pay, they return to their
homes:

And now we've crossed old Boggy Creek
And homeward we are bound,
No more in that cursed country will ever we be found.
Go home to our wives and sweethearts,

Tell others not to go,
To that God-forsaken country
In the hills of Mexico.[65]

The cowboys of these various road folk songs are wanderers, poor in terms of home and pay but rich in commitment and experiences. For some of them, however, the pull of the trail and the magic of the longhorn is enough to keep them going until the "bright land" can be attained. The cowboy's journey is more rewarding than many of the nineteenth-century wayfarers. His songs of restlessness resonate with the Americans of all ages.

Two great migrations in the nineteenth century gave America more favourite road folk songs. The gold rush brought men first of all to California, and, later, flashes of gold lured them to Pike's Peak and Cripple Creek in Colorado, Virginia City in Nevada, and the Black Hills of both South Dakota and Wyoming.[66] The second push to the West was the Mormon trek from Illinois to their new home in Salt Lake City, Utah. The folk songs bring those migrations to life.

In "Sweet Betsy" and "Joe Bowers," the heroes of two ballads of the gold rush travellers, all hailed from Pike County, Missouri, which "was once as big as an ordinary state, and the men of Pike County, known as dead shots and fly sports, dominated the early plains period."[67] Joe Bowers, one such larger-than-life Piker, courted pretty Sally Black, but she wouldn't take him until he had a home. He went to California to make a fortune: "I said, 'Sally, O Sally, it's all for your sake, / I'll go out to California and try to raise a stake ... / I worked both late and early, in rainstorm and in snow, / It was all for my sweet Sally's sake, 'twas all the same to Joe." A letter arrives from his brother Ike that breaks his heart: Sally married a butcher and had a baby with red hair.[68] Like most gold rushers, he never makes his fortune and he also loses the girl he left behind. It may be the same luckless brother Ike who accompanies Sweet Betsy to California. The exaggerated exploits of this pair entertained the "Forty-Niners," lifting the drudge of the difficult travel to California, and the dreary conditions of mining once they got there. Sweet Betsy and Ike "swam the wide rivers and climbed the tall peaks, / And camped on the prairies for weeks upon weeks, / Starvation and cholera, hard work and slaughter, / They reached California spite of hell and high water." They fought off the Indians, she got drunk and "showed her bum to the whole wagon train," the wagon fell over, they crossed the Sierras, and she danced with another miner in California. Because the tale is told in the third person, Betsy and Ike are not present, and therefore they can easily be made fun of. The twist at the end, however, speaks to a more serious point, that of the lack of the female gender in the male-dominated frontier: "Long Ike and Sweet Betsy got married, of course, / But Ike, who was jealous, obtained a divorce, / And Betsy, well satisfied, said with a smile, / 'I've six good men waitin' within half a mile.'"[69]

Grim determination, or in reality, greed, drove the Forty-Niner. The balladeer in "Westward Ho" is very clear about his destination and purpose in travelling: not the Bourbon River of Colorado, the bowie-hunting in Montana, the pistol hunting of Wyoming, not "poker-haunted" Kansas, the roughs of Nevada, the "meek" Apache in Arizona, nor the New Mexico natives with "arrow-proof" insides – none of these attract him, but the fortune in California does:

Nay, tis where the grizzlies wander
And the lonely diggers roam,
And the grim Chinese from the squatter flees
That I'll make my humble home.

I'll chase the wild tarantula
And the fierce cayote I'll dare
And the locust grim, I'll battle him
In his native wildwood lair.

Or I'll seek the gulch deserted
And dream of the wild Red man,
And I'll build a cot on a corner lot
And get rich as soon as I can.[70]

Apparently, Custer spread the rumour about gold in the Black Hills around Cheyenne, Wyoming, in 1874. As the lands were in treaty to the Indians "a good many prospectors were well-feathered with Indian arrows."[71]

Kind friends, you must pity my horrible tale,
I'm an object of pity, I'm looking quite stale,
I gave up my trade, selling Right's Patent Pills,
To go hunting gold in the Dreary Black Hills.

The roundhouse in Cheyenne is filled every night,
With loafers and bummers of most every plight,
On their backs is no clothes, in their pockets, no bills,
Each day they keep starting for the Dreary Black Hills ...

I got to Cheyenne, no gold could I find,
I thought of the lunch route I'd left far behind,
Through rain, hail and snow, frozen plumb to the gills,
They call me the orphan of the Dreary Black Hills.

Oh, I wish the man that started this sell,
Was a captive, and Crazy Horse had him in Hell,
There's no use of grieving or swearing like pitch,
But the man that would stay here is a son-of-a-gun.

CHORUS: Don't go away, stay at home if you can,
Stay away from that city, they call it Cheyenne.
For big Wallipee or Comanche Bills,
They will lift up your hair on the Dreary Black Hills.[72]

The Forty-Niners as wayfarers were not romantics. Often luck-less farmers or labourers in the Midwest, they created a monstrous society once they got to the gold fields. Very few of them found gold. Their road songs reflect their earthiness and baseness.

The other migration was religious: the Mormons moved along the Oregon Trail on their way to religious and cultural freedom, and one charming travel song comes to us from this weary trek. A cheerful young Mormon encourages his team: "With a merry little jog and a gay little song, / Whoa! Ha! Buck and Jerry Boy, / We trudge our way the whole day long, / Whoa! Ha! Buck and Jerry Boy. / What though we're covered all over with dust, / It's better than staying back home to rust, / We'll reach Salt Lake some day or bust, / Whoa! Ha! Buck and Jerry Boy." He daydreams to while away the time driving his team, as the Arizona freighter did. Keeping his eye on the "pretty lit-tle girl in the outfit ahead," he wishes "she was by my side instead," and he anticipates evening camp: "O tonight we'll dance by the light of the moon, to the fiddler's best and only tune."[73] A serious and stirring road song also comes from the journey to Salt Lake City: in April of 1846, at a campsite in Iowa, William Clayton received the news that his son was born in Nauvoo, Illinois.[74] In his joy, he pens the words to a hymn of encouragement and reassurance that is still sung in the Mormon Church:

> Come, come, ye saints, no toil nor labor fear;
> But with joy, wend your way.
> Though hard to you this journey may appear,
> Grace shall be as your day.
> 'Tis better far for us to strive
> Our useless cares from us to drive;
> Do this, and joy your hearts will swell
> All is well! All is well! ...
>
> We'll find the place which God for us prepared,
> Far away in the West,
> Where none shall come to hurt or make afraid;
> There the Saints will be blessed.
> We'll make the air with music ring,
> Shout praises to our God and King;
> Above the rest these words we'll tell –
> All is well! All is well! ...
>
> And should we die before our journey's through,
> Happy day! All is well!
> We then are free from toil and sorrow, too;
> With the just we shall dwell!
> But if our lives are spared again
> To see the saints their rest obtain,
> O how we'll make this chorus swell,
> All is well! All is well!

The Mormons' journey was physical *and* spiritual. They will find the place that God has prepared "Far away in the West, / Where none shall come to hurt or make afraid," and like the poor wayfaring stranger, they will find freedom from sickness, toil, and danger, and they will find rest. Unlike the wayfaring stranger, there is now no sense of woe, for all is well.

To conclude, this chapter has taken a quick "backward glance o'er travel'd roads"[75] and broadly traced the road folk song's restless movement in the early days of the United States up to the twentieth century, while exploring some of the stories of the travellers themselves. The origins of these "road folk songs" are as rich and varied as those of the people who sang them. They have been diffused throughout America by social and economic upheaval as settlers found life unsustainable where they were and headed off to the promise of the frontier. The road folk songs explore content and discontent, grief, weariness, and love. They record the complaint of the freighter, the grief of Mary when her husband Charlie is lost in the Wisconsin rapids, the cowboy's lament over the campfire, and the young Mormon's crush on the pretty girl in the wagon ahead. Most song stories are told in the first person, more easily opening up the reservoir of empathy in the performer and the listener. Many begin with the invitation: "Come all my boys and listen,"[76] or "Come all ye railroad section men, / An' listen to my song,"[77] which brings the listener to the feet of the singer. Those sung in the third person are songs of death or caricature: the dead hero cannot sing his own tale, and those not present in the song become ready targets of humour. They are sung by men (only one girl appears in a dialogue), who are pulled into travel, into leaving home, into working on the trail. Carl Sandburg heard the voices in the folk songs he collected in *American Songbag*:

> Music and the human voice command this parade of melodies and lyrics. They speak, murmur, cry, yell, laugh, pray; they take roles; they play parts; in topics, scenes and "props" they range into anthropology, houses, machines, ships, railroad trains, churches, saloons, picnics, hayrack and steamboat parties, and human strugglers chanting farewell to the frail frameworks of earthly glory. There is patter and jabber of vulgarity, there are falsetto mockers and groaning blasphemies, there is moaning of prayers and tumult and shouting of faiths.[78]

Out of this cacophony, the traveller's voice can clearly be heard. The freighters, cowboys, and fortune seekers bring the listener on their journeys and share their inner thoughts on the long rides. The fiddle tunes capture their few moments of revelry, and the "come all ye's" bring everyone to the campfire to listen. The wayfaring stranger has wandered through this American world, singing his way to consolation and comfort. In each of these ways, the road folk songs transport listeners and readers "outside" of themselves, bringing meaning and comfort to personal journeys.

"So That We as a Race Might Have Something Authentic to Travel By": African-American Automobility and Cold-War Liberalism

COTTEN SEILER

Merging his Ford Model T with the traffic stream in E.L. Doctorow's 1974 novel *Ragtime*, the African-American pianist Coalhouse Walker is involved in a collision of sorts, one that will eventually prove fatal. En route to New York City after a visit with his fiancée on Long Island, Walker is humiliated by the Irish-American firemen of the Emerald Isle Engine brigade, to whom the sight of an urbane black man at the wheel of a new car is an intolerable affront. After denying Walker passage on the public road in front of the firehouse, the firemen vandalize and destroy his Model T. When his appeals for redress are dismissed by local authorities, and when his fiancée is killed while attempting to elicit aid from a politician, Walker responds with what we call, then as now, terrorism: he kills members of the brigade, bombs several firehouses, and later occupies and threatens to destroy New York's Morgan Library. Throughout the conflict, Walker's demand remains the same: that the fire chief restore the Model T ("black, with the custom pantasote top") to its prior condition. The police acquiesce, but then gun Walker down on 36th Street as he gives up his siege. The car, however, spirits away Walker's comrades-in-arms, one of whom is a white man, a young bourgeois-turned-revolutionary identified only as Younger Brother. Leaving the other members of Walker's gang in Harlem, he drives unmolested across the nation to the Mexican border, his whiteness licensing his flight. Walker's failed crusade will soon fade from official memory, just like the evanescent "trail of dust in the sky" kicked up by the southbound Model T.[1]

The fictional tragedy of Coalhouse Walker is a compelling illustration of the limited access that has governed the American road, and, by extension, the political culture the road reflects and constructs. Joining conversations among cultural historians (and literary scholars, not to mention artists and musicians) on the high stakes, pleasures, and perils of African-Americans' driving and car ownership, claims to the public space of the road, and general participation in an expanding culture of automobility, this essay focuses on the mid-century guidebooks *Travelguide (Vacation and Recreation Without Humiliation)* and *The Negro Motorist Green Book*.[2] These texts, which directed black drivers to hospitable roadside lodging, restaurants, and mechanical assistance, did more than offer helpful information. Through their images and editorial copy, they also provided a multifaceted, often contradictory rhetoric of communal racial uplift and liberal individualism figured around driving. Racial attitudes and policies shifted during these guidebooks' years of publication, 1936–57, as the Second World War and the Cold War made the national doctrine of white supremacy a global political liability. Within this historical context African-Americans' desire and fitness for citizenship were tethered to and divined in their participation in automobility, a practice that fused self-determination and self-representation, mobility, consumption, and social encounter. The rhetorical strategies of these guidebooks complemented a particular strain of liberal anti-racism necessitated by the Cold War, facilitated by the nationalization of post-war politics and economics, and acted out in increasingly standardized public spaces, such as the Interstate highway.

DRIVING WHILE BLACK

Mobility is a cardinal practice of modern society; and the spaces of the regnant mode of American mobility – the city streets, state and federal roads, and highways navigable by car – are where citizens performatively affirm their public identity.[3] Those who travel the public road without impediment are the implied citizens of what I call the "republic of drivers" – a political imaginary of anonymity and autonomy that finds expression in the practices and landscapes of automobility. The rhetoric of this republic holds that the driver enters the stream, as the citizen enters the public sphere, as a blank figure, divested of particularities, and thereby empowered to speak, act, and move. This self-abstraction of the citizen, as Michael Warner and others have argued, presumes a disembodied political agency while at the same time making clear that only those with specific attributes could assume it. Hence the crime of the public sphere, and of the road, consists in their "bad faith" – promises of universality and uniform access masking an ascriptive hierarchy.[4]

Philip Fisher has described vectors of movement such as the American road as democratic social space, "a universal and every-where similar medium in which rights and opportunities are iden-tical, a space in which the right and even the ability to move from place to place is assured." This space, the essential characteristics of which are "mobility (and) the right to enter or exit," provides a stage for the enactment of democratic, egalitarian citizenship.[5] Barbara Klinger has similarly noted the ways in which the road constitutes "a space by definition democratic since in theory no class systems or unfair hierarchies exist there; a space then where individual renewal, property relations, and industry can be achieved within a democratic framework."[6] The road thus stands as an ideal representation and product of what Charles W. Mills has called the "ideal nonracial pol-ity," in which "one's personhood is guaranteed, independent of race, and as such is stable, not subject to loss or gain."[7] These authors take various positions toward this idealized conception, but let mine be clear: the space of the American road, like the contours of citizen-ship, was established under specific regimes of racialized inequality and limited access, whose codes it reproduces. As Kathleen Franz asserts, "Although white travelers constructed the open road as a technological democracy, open to anyone who owned a car, they simultaneously limited access to automobility through a system of discrimination and representation that positioned nonwhites outside the new motor culture."[8]

Because spatial mobility has often been a means to or evidence of the social mobility of racial Others, regimes of white supremacy have sought to control or curtail those forms and moments of black mobility that they could not exploit for their own purposes. For example, in addition to imposing the Black Codes and Jim Crow in the decades between Emancipation and the First World War, south-ern legislatures attempted to limit the mobility of African-Americans, though such measures were generally piecemeal, and unable to pre-vent the migrations to the north during and after Reconstruction.

According to William Cohen, these years marked "a time when southern blacks lived at freedom's edge, suspended between the world of slavery that had once been theirs and a world of freedom that still belonged mostly to whites. The extent of black freedom varied with time and place, but always the right to move without hindrance was one of its most important features."[9] A chief effect of Jim Crow in the twentieth century was "a geography of thwarted action, of arrested motion" for African-Americans.[10] The Cold War offered a cruel new dimension to black immobility in the age of white flight, as shown in the civil-defence map of the fictional "River City" in Philip Wylie's 1954 doomsday novel *Tomorrow!*, with the "Negro District" at ground zero.[11]

Spatial forms, Manuel Castells has written, provide a "fundamental material dimension" of any given society, and will therefore express that society's relationships of dominance and subordination. Yet "spatial forms will also be marked by resistance from exploited classes (and) oppressed subjects. And the work of this contradictory historical process on space will be accomplished on an already inherited spatial form, the product of history and support of new interests, projects, protests, and dreams."[12] Ideal figurations of the road disintegrate when one contrasts Coalhouse Walker's capacities for self-determination and convenient self-erasure with those of Younger Brother. Yet African-Americans in the twentieth century, subject to whites' "extraordinary efforts to limit their freedom to occupy, use, or even move through space," nonetheless affirmed idealized spaces and moments of freedom. Consequently, the iconic road they crafted through imagery and narrative was both democratic social space and racial minefield.[13]

Automobility's promise was one of escape from Jim Crow: upward through socioeconomic strata and outward across geographical space. Yet Coalhouse Walker's tragedy synthesizes – and rewrites as revenge tragedy – countless stories of trouble on the road that have informed a black "highway consciousness" distinct from that of white drivers. From the earliest days of automobility, overlapping and mutually sustaining racist laws, social codes, and commercial practices have attenuated the mobility of the black driver: segregated roadside mechanical and medical aid, food, and shelter; the discriminatory membership policies of motoring organizations such as the American Automobile Association; profiling of minority drivers by law enforcement; the racial-spatial politics of highway planning and placement, especially in urban areas; the race-bound economics of auto financing and insurance underwriting; and the venerable practice of general police harassment for "driving while black."[14]

Moreover, since the advent of mass automobility in the 1920s, participation in the automotive market served to delineate the boundaries of republican personhood. As driving and car ownership were anchored by themes of competence and self-determination, the figures of the driver and the citizen were easily and often conflated, as they were established in racialized (and gendered) terms. A 1923 auto trade journal, for example, had designated "illiterate, immigrant, Negro and other families" aliens in the auto consumer's polity.[15] Myriad representations of non-whites and immigrants as physically graceless, technologically inept, and deservedly indigent served as reminders of the incapacity of racial Others to fulfill the obligations of citizenship in a modern and complex republic. Even the masterful prizefighter Jack Johnson was not immune from the stereotype of black driving incompetence. Johnson's unsuccessful 1910 challenge of the white driving champion Barney Oldfield led another white racer, "Wild Bob" Burman, to assert, "Just because Johnson has succeeded in reaching the top in pugilism, it does not alter the fact that he is a Negro and is not entitled to prestige in the cleaner and better sport of automobile racing."[16]

African-Americans challenged these representations, supplying counter-images and counter-narratives emphasizing mastery, elegance, self-possession, and decorum. Paul Gilroy has recently observed that blacks' "histories of confinement and coerced labour must have given them additional receptivity to the pleasures of auto-autonomy as a means of escape, transcendence and even resistance."[17] In 1922 the *Chicago Defender* chronicled A.L. Headen's journey from Chicago to Kansas City, celebrating "both the superior design of the car and Headen's technological expertise and physical prowess."[18] Charlie Wiggins, "The Negro Speed King," was held up as a model of guts and wits for his exploits on the segregated racing circuit.[19] Arna Bontemps's grim 1932 short story, "A Summer Tragedy," features an elderly black couple, worn down by years of sharecropping, using "the little rattletrap car (that) had been regarded as a peculiar treasure" as their implement of suicide. Like their decrepit Model T, the couple is "used up," no longer useful to the regime of production; yet their suicide – dressed in their Sunday best, they drive into a rushing river – testifies to self-possession and dignity even in despair.[20] "It's mighty good to be the skipper for a change," wrote Washington, DC schoolteacher Alfred Edgar Smith, "and pilot our craft whither and when we will ... it's good for the spirit to give the old railroad Jim Crow the laugh."[21] Smith's farewell wave to Jim Crow in the rearview mirror was, in 1933 (a year that saw at least 24 lynchings), a premature gesture. In Robert MacNeill's 1938 WPA photograph "New Car," a proud driver-owner stands with one foot on the running board, smiling cavalierly and surrounded by admirers.[22] Seven years later, Chester Himes's novel *If He Hollers Let Him Go* featured a protagonist to whom the roadscapes of Los Angeles offer a space for racial combat. The character, Bob Jones, notes that his Buick Roadmaster is "proof of something to me, a symbol"; the car is also his instrument in a score-settling campaign wherein he doles out "stare for stare, hate for hate" to whites in his peregrinations around the city. While the white drivers he challenges and overtakes may well enjoy their morning commute, Jones tells us, "to me it was racial ... all I wanted in the world was to push my Buick Roadmaster over some white peckerwood's face."[23] Whatever Jones's personal satisfactions, Jim Crow is diminished not in the slightest.

A disproportionate number of black road narratives impress upon the reader the traveller's near-constant anxiety on unfamiliar roads. Journalist Courtland Milloy recalled from his childhood a menacing environment in which "so many black travelers were just not making it to their destinations." More recently, writer Eddy Harris has recounted his motorcycle journey through a Southern landscape where he is "glared at, threatened, turned away, called names, and made afraid."[24] Given the racist harassment and violence that the automobile's signification of affluence and "a kind of mystically perceived total freedom" could prompt, it is unsurprising that, unlike their white-authored counterparts, black road narratives "do not concern the pursuit of the ideal self;" rather, they "reveal the fraudulence of space viewed as an essence, transcending class and color" and "resist all utopian fantasies predicated on the virtues of elsewhere."[25] And yet those narratives, such as the guidebooks examined here, engaged with a utopian fantasy peculiar to and animated by the political imaginary of corporate liberalism; that fantasy, glimpsed by bell hooks as a young girl, conjures a place "beyond the sign of race" just behind the horizon.[26]

BLACK AUTOMOBILITY AS COLD-WAR IMPERATIVE

The first in a long series of incidents on Route 40 on the way to
Washington occurred when a dark-skinned man, refused service at a
Howard Johnson restaurant at Dover, Delaware, in 1957, turned out to be
the Finance Minister of Ghana.

Harold Isaacs[27]

Travelguide and *The Negro Motorist Green Book* refract a historical moment of the early Cold War, when the political costs of
racial discrimination compelled American institutions to confront
it as a social problem of priority, and when American automobility was called upon to signify an important range of martial values
and ideals. "Few would debate," remarked the editors of *Fortune* in
1951, "the assertion that the greatest failure of American democracy
has been its failure to achieve a real emancipation of the Negro."[28]
Such acknowledgments of the racial situation were commonplace
in the middlebrow media and in the official transmissions of the
Truman and Eisenhower administrations; they were almost inevit-
ably followed by avowals of the problem's imminent resolution, as
in George Schuyler's claim, reprinted in a 1951 *Reader's Digest*, that
"the progressive improvement of race relations and the economic
rise of the Negro in the United States is a flattering example of democracy in action. The most 'exploited' Negroes in Mississippi are
better off than the citizens of Russia or her satellites."[29] Such comparisons, also typical of the era, indicated that racial equality – or
at least its appearance – was a matter of Cold-War expediency.[30]
A 1955 *Reader's Digest* article entitled "The Negroes Among Us,"
made explicit to a middlebrow audience the potential bitter harvest
of racial discrimination:

> Throughout much of the world, and especially in the Asian
> countries that have but recently emerged from colonial rule, the
> greatest single obstacle to friendship and cooperation is ignor-
> ance of great changes that have taken place in the status of the
> Negro. Typical is the question which Prime Minister Nehru of
> India says he is repeatedly asked: "What guarantee do we have
> that, if we side with the Western World instead of with Russia,
> that we won't eventually be treated as Negroes are in the United
> States?"[31]

By the early 1950s, Soviet propagandists were emphasizing racial injustice in the US in nearly half of their global output.

Though the 1954 *Brown* decision marked the beginning of genuine structural change to official hierarchies of race, political elites of the era saw as critical to actual melioration the dissemination of images and accounts of the "model Negro" moving forward in a racially enlightened nation.[32] The exigencies of the Cold War put a broad range of images and narratives of African-Americans as first-class citizens into circulation, however atypical these representations might have been.[33] Declarations of opportunity, equality, and colour-blindness (though few endorsements of integration) became standard components of the Cold War ethic developed in the middlebrow press and state propaganda. For example, in *Reader's Digest*, Adam Clayton Powell affirmed his and other black leaders' "delighted astonishment" at Eisenhower's feeble desegregation policy, citing the advances made in the most internationally visible and officially representative of cities, Washington, DC.[34] *The Saturday Evening Post* happily noted in 1955 that "Negroes Have Their Own Wall Street Firm," a development that posed "a challenge to many a preconception." "They Always Ask Me About Negroes," a *Post* article from the following year, related the experiences of a black cultural attaché in Italy as "a living refutation" of the charges of racism levelled by Communists, charges that non-white foreign nationals were inclined to believe. Activist Max Yergan's speech to Nigerian audiences occasioned a United States Information press release that announced, "Yergan Says Trend In U.S. Race Relations Is Toward Full Civil Rights For Negroes."[35]

Given Cold-War policy architects' antipathy toward collective and structural modes of social therapy, many of these images of the "model Negro" reflected the abiding liberal faith in a naturally egalitarian capitalist market, and in the notion that "freed individual achievement, and it alone, would dissolve caste."[36] Essential to the "vital center" consensus crystallizing in the post-war period was the belief that "the American free-enterprise system ... has a revolutionary potential for social justice."[37] An expanding, soberly regulated consumer economy, the rhetoric maintained, spurred progressive social change even in the most recalcitrant areas of American life, such as race relations. Such rhetoric echoed Booker T. Washington's 1895 assertion that "no race that has anything to contribute to the markets of the world is long in any degree ostracized," but updated

it for a Cold-War audience.[38] This rosy vision of naturally improving race relations was intended to flatter domestic audiences – who
could "be counted on to follow decent instincts without legislation"
– and to assuage international ones.[39]

The approach of full citizenship for African-Americans could be
divined, then, from the "vast new market with a purchasing power of
over 16 billion dollars a year – more than the annual value of all our
exports" announced by *Reader's Digest* in 1955.[40] One index of this
purchasing power was the increasing rate of car ownership among
African-Americans over the previous few decades. The car, as both
commodity and symbol, affected the American economy, landscape,
and social structure more than any other consumer product; and a
given group's level of automobile use and ownership could be taken
as an index of its participation in the "American way of life." In
1949 an *Ebony* editorial explained "Why Negroes Buy Cadillacs";
the editors' predictable conclusion, observed a skeptical Franklin
Frazier, was that "the Cadillac is a worthy symbol of their aspiration
to be a genuinely first-class American."[41] Two years later a piece in
the same magazine on an upscale African-American neighbourhood
in Queens, New York, noted with enthusiasm the number of two-
car households, and the frequency, moreover, of Cadillacs.[42] Chuck
Berry's 1950s "motorvatin'" rock and roll songs, which expressed
"a strong faith in mobility as a guarantee of dignity, democracy, pas-
toralism, and equal opportunity," and which also featured Cadillacs,
staked his and other African-Americans' claim to citizenship in the
republic of drivers.[43]

As Paul Gilroy notes, "it is difficult to resist the idea that the
special seductions of car culture have become an important part
of what binds the black populations of the overdeveloped countries to the most mainstream of dreams ... cars seem to have conferred or rather suggested dimensions of citizenship and status that
were blocked by formal politics and violently inhibited by informal
codes."[44] The power of the automobile to signify national membership was apparent to former president Herbert Hoover, writing in
a 1956 *Reader's Digest* article entitled "Let's Say Something Good
About Ourselves." "Much as I feel deeply the lag in giving a full equal
chance to our Negro population," he wrote, "yet I cannot refrain
from mentioning that our 14 million American Negroes own more
automobiles than all the 200 million Russians and the 300 million
Negroes in Africa put together."[45] African-American automobility,

considered in Hoover's terms, demonstrated a pair of triumphalist truths: first, that the American market of consumer goods had properly provided the natural fulcrum for the evolutionary movement of American society toward universal citizenship; and second, that the ownership and operation of an automobile bespoke membership in a fully modern and elite order of humanity housed exclusively in the "free world."

RESPONDING TO "NEGRO MOTORING CONDITIONS": THE RHETORICS OF *TRAVELGUIDE* AND THE *NEGRO MOTORIST GREEN BOOK*

So far as travel is concerned, Negroes are America's last pioneers.
> Lester B. Granger, National Urban League, 1947[46]

Would a Negro like to pursue a little happiness at a theatre, a beach, pool, hotel, restaurant, on a train, plane, or ship, a golf course, summer or winter resort? Would he like to stop overnight in a tourist camp while he motors about his native land "Seeing America First"? Well, just let him try!
> *The Crisis*, 1947[47]

Rising (though still low) rates of car ownership among African-Americans in the post-war era, as well as the plentiful images of joyous and footloose drivers in black publications and popular culture, suggested that automobility had ceased to be an exclusively white prerogative. As discussed above, these phenomena were held up by apologists as signs of African-Americans' ascent into the middle class and of racism's decline. Automobility expressed a forward-looking, individualistic, and emphatically modern sensibility; it provided practical and visible models of the social, political, and economic freedom of all Americans. Its promise to African-Americans, as bell hooks notes, lay in its perceived ability to enable escape from the racialized structures of American society and "find a world where there is no black or white."[48] Yet it was precisely in the act of driving through unfamiliar territory that the inescapability of race became, for so many African-Americans, so apparent. Whites' responses to black drivers generally ranged from the merely contemptuous – as in one writer's recalling of a policemen's plans for jailing an "uppity nigra" thwarted by her Cadillac-driving cousin's quick payment of an unjust fine – to the lethal, as in the 1948 case of Robert Mallard, attacked in his car by a Georgia mob (allegedly for being "too prosperous" and "not the right kind of negro") and murdered there in front of his wife and child. Occasionally whites could be solicitous, as in Charles Chesnutt's account of having his tire changed by a group of white men after he demonstrates his own ineptitude at the task. For black drivers, the road's only constant was uncertainty.[49]

Poised between the Jim Crow and Civil Rights eras, *Travelguide* and *The Negro Motorist Green Book* simultaneously protested the discrimination that confronted black motorists on American roads and proffered the hegemonic image of American freedom through driving. They articulated a collectivist racial politics, mobilizing their midcentury audiences for social change; yet they also rehearsed the individualistic, market-oriented strategies of black capitalism and the vital centre consensus, where, as Lizabeth Cohen notes, "the individual's access to the free market was a sacred concept."[50] This dualism was not so novel; many progressive publications by and for African-Americans, from *The Crisis* to *Ebony*, deployed rhetorics affirming black communal struggle in a society which "spoke individualism" to the exclusion of other social philosophies. The salient and novel element of *Travelguide* and *The Negro Motorist Green Book* was their focus on automobility as the practice through which African-Americans could reconcile, both in symbolic and practical terms, the competing values of individual agency and collective uplift.[51] Like other black business enterprises catering to black consumers in an era of eroding yet still-compelled deference, these guidebooks were rarely radical in their challenge to the legal segregation that circumscribed the mobility of touring black entertainers, athletes, business travellers, and other motorists; instead, they mounted a decorous campaign for racial reform informed by liberal principles of market agency, cross-racial "understanding," the prerogative of free mobility, and the assumption of human goodwill.

As the guidebooks rehabilitated automobility as something in which all who possessed the necessary means should and could take part, they simultaneously made claims about the republican "fitness" of their readership. From the first, then, these guidebooks emphasized the proximity, in matters of temperament and class, of black and white drivers. In the teeth of Jim Crow, they sounded a tone of aggrieved entitlement, mildly articulated, as when the *Negro*

Motorist Green Book reports that most of the better conveyances, hotels, resorts, and restaurants are "not available."

In 1936 Victor H. Green, the *Green Book*'s founder and namesake, began soliciting for his fledgling publication manuscripts describing road experiences comparable to those of white drivers. Green paid a dollar (by 1941, five dollars) to the writer for each accepted account "based on the Negro motoring conditions, scenic wonders in your travels, places visited of interest and short stories on one's motoring experience."

In subsequent years, Green included letters of testimonial and thanks from the guidebook's ideal subscribers. These letters functioned almost as a sort of ventriloquism by Green, who was silent in his editorial capacity, in terms of articulating the *Green Book*'s purpose. In the 1938 edition, a letter from William Smith of Hackensack, NJ, declared,

> It is a great pleasure for me to give credit where credit is due. Many of my friends have joined me in admitting *The Negro Motorist Green Book* is a credit to the Negro Race. It is a book badly needed among our Race since the advance of the motor age. Realizing the only way we knew where and how to reach our pleasure resorts was in a way of speaking, by word of mouth, until the publication of *The Negro Motorist Green Book* ... We earnestly believe that (the guidebook) will mean as much if not more to us as the A.A.A. means to the white race.

In 1941, a similar letter from William H. Denkins Jr, of Trenton, read,

> I am proud of your *Green Book*, and consider it a great little motorist guide. After receiving a copy I only wished that I had one with me on a recent trip I had made, as I am sure it would have made the entire vacation perfect. *The Green Book* not only serves the Negro motorist well, but does a splendid job for its advertisers.

When the publisher did speak, it was to thank the publication's sponsors and influential supporters, among them the *Cleveland Call and Post*, the Louisville *Leader*, and pioneering African-American marketing representative for Standard Oil James "Billboard"

Jackson. In 1940 Green made it clear that by sponsoring the guide-book these organizations and individuals were doing extremely necessary and valuable work.

> The Publishers of this guide wish to publically (sic) thank the following people and newspapers who have contributed and worked to bring this travel guide before the public and up to date, so that we as a race might have something authentic to travel by and to make traveling better for the Negro.[52]

Travelguide, which began publication in 1947, updated Green's tactics and language for an era informed by the official, if super-ficial, anti-racist stance of the nation emerging out of the Second World War and the Cold War, and awakening to the integrationist sensibilities of the nascent Civil Rights movement. The guidebook's founder and publisher, William H. "Billy" Butler (1903-1981), had been a jazz musician and bandleader in the 1930s and 1940s, and had borne his share of indignity and privation while on tour. At Butler's funeral in 1981, a friend eulogized him with a telling anecdote:

> I am reminded of the time back in the early days, when racial dif-ferences still kept many Americans apart. And Billy was traveling with his fellow musicians in the South. They were tired and hun-gry. But there was no place is this town that would let them all eat together. So, Billy got the idea to go to the wardrobe mistress to get some capes and turbans. Newly attired, they entered the restaurant of their choice, and had a most enjoyable evening as visiting foreign dignitaries.[53]

The *Pittsburgh Courier* heralded *Travelguide*'s arrival in 1947, and, in subsequent years, ran columns and articles by Butler, includ-ing a 1954 six-part series entitled "Travel vs. Discrimination." The *Crisis* routinely ran advertisements for Butler's publication, and sold it through the *Crisis* Book Shop in midtown Manhattan. The mainly white daily, the *New York Post* profiled Butler in 1947, describing him as "Musician and Guide to His Bedeviled Race."[54] *Travelguide*'s usefulness to itinerant black entertainers and athletes was emphasized in a back-cover testimonial by Mabel A. Roane of the Negro Actors Guild, who stated,

TRAVELGUIDE should create confidence for the traveler in the acting profession as well as those in the entire field of entertainment. Its orderly and authentic information covers necessary news and eventually should eliminate sitting-up-all-night in railroad stations, hotel lobbies, and lunchrooms. Often unemployment of Negroes results because placement while traveling is such a problem.[55]

Though this audience remained an important one, *Travelguide*, like its predecessor *The Negro Motorist Green Book*, was more ambitious. These guides depicted, even in the context of Jim Crow's all-too-evident circumscription of mobility, African-Americans as upwardly and outwardly mobile vacationers, habitually mobile business travellers, and blithely gallivanting consumers. And, however pernicious and widespread the discrimination that black drivers met on the American road, it was crucial that *The Negro Motorist Green Book* and *Travelguide* aver their continuing faith in the equalizing mechanisms of American democracy and consumer capitalism.

According to classical free-market doctrine, all who possessed the appropriate values and engaged in the right practices could compete in an arena in which they were rewarded (or penalized) for their ability (or lack of) as individuals and not for their categorical status. Black intellectuals in the early twentieth century, intent on countering the myriad and increasingly vicious stereotypes that saturated all manner of media, fashioned positive and even heroic images of "a new class of colored people, the 'New Negro' ... who [has] arisen since the (Civil) war, with education, refinement, and money."[56] By midcentury, this "black bourgeoisie" had expanded sufficiently to make possible publications, such as *Travelguide* and the *Green Book*, which offered images of the good life through consumption to African-Americans living under Jim Crow.[57] The 1937 issue of the *Green Book* featured, in addition to national listings for lodgings hospitable to black travellers, advertisements for top-shelf liquor and New York-area auto repair shops, beauty salons, restaurants, nightclubs and country clubs, including the Harris Tea Room, "Westchester's sepia rendezvous," and Harlem-on-the-Hudson, "featuring a talented cast of sepia beauties."[58] *Travelguide* also featured profiles of prominent African-American personages (e.g., Jackie Robinson, George Schuyler, and Langston Hughes) and racially progressive companies.[59] These features complemented the publication's attribution of racism to whites' ignorance of black achievement, respectability, and economic vitality.

In their depictions of mobile, affluent, benignant, and generally decorous black travellers, *The Negro Motorist Green Book* and *Travelguide* implied the economic, if not the moral, costs of discrimination. Deploying a rhetoric of anti-discrimination increasingly common in what Cohen has called the post-war "consumer's republic," the guidebooks asserted that, however one evaluated the ethics of segregation, in the long run it was bad for white-owned businesses.[60] As one of *Travelguide*'s editors, Marguerite Cartwright, wrote in the inaugural 1947 edition,

> Hundreds of millions of dollars are spent annually by discerning members of minority groups in the course of their travels throughout the U.S. Many worthy enterprises, unaware of the tremendous potentialities, deny themselves of this revenue. It is the purpose of TRAVELGUIDE to assist in bringing these two groups together for the benefit of ALL.

The increasingly affluent, numerous, and mobile black members of the middle class, the guidebook editors suggested, were more identifiable by their status as consumers than by their race.[61] Hotels, restaurants, nightclubs, service stations, and other enterprises that discriminated on the basis of race would be won over by the purchasing power of these travellers of colour. The guidebooks' covers accented the gentility of their readership. *Travelguide* depicted no men on its covers; these were usually graced by well-dressed and light-skinned women, who almost always carried golf clubs with them.[62] These seemingly trivial but highly symbolic objects were the exclamation points on *Travelguide*'s declaration of African-American arrival into the middle class, at a time when the overwhelming majority of golf courses remained barred to black players. If the links to which these visibly affluent golfers were heading did not discriminate, *Travelguide* implied, how could any business not follow their example? The placement of Mark Twain's dictum "Travel is fatal to prejudice" on the cover of the 1949 *Green Book* shifted its usual meaning: here it was the visited, rather than the visitors, who would find themselves enriched by the encounter.

Yet vital-centre liberalism conceded that the market alone would not resolve social problems; rather, an institutionally cultivated will to humanitarianism (in this case, anti-racism) expressed through market transactions would produce conditions of equality. The admixture of consumer and political sensibilities in *Travelguide* and *The Negro Motorist Green Book* – their simultaneous pitches for the NAACP and, say, *Field & Stream* – typified the vital-centre strategy for racial harmony. Organizations such as the NAACP were conducive to the proliferation of the anti-racist sensibility, as was the Cold-War propaganda of the United States Information Agency, *Life*, and *Reader's Digest*. But much of the real advance in civil rights and national unity, the guidebooks and like publications suggested, would be made through the quasi-intimate realm of transactional encounter. "I should like to urge Negroes to visit North Dakota," wrote an ostensibly white *Green Book* reader in the small town of Dickinson, "not only for the tourist attractions, not only because of the friendliness of her people, but also because of [sic] these visitations would enable North Dakotans to better know and understand a great part of our national citizenry."[63]

The guidebooks articulated their own role as sacrificial. "It is perhaps a significant barometer of the progress we have made in our democracy that such a listing is even required," Cartwright archly noted.

> However, we have faith that the day is not long distant when such a booklet will be outmoded and considered unnecessary. Racial distinctions and creedal "restrictions" (or "church nearby"), whether through openly cruel barriers or hypocritical evasions, are contrary to the American ideal and repugnant to people of good-will. We think that such persons will show their displeasure in the manner in which it hurts most – through economic boycott – and TRAVELGUIDE will in this way hasten the day when considerations such as these artificial and subject distinctions will be a thing of the past. We pledge to do all in our power to hasten the day when we "can put ourselves out of business."[64]

The Green Book editors expressed their hope in nearly identical language:

There will be a day sometime in the near future when this guide
will not have to be published. That is when we as a race will
have equal opportunities and privileges in the United States. It
will be a great day for us to suspend this publication for then we
can go wherever we please, and without embarrassment.[65]

One would be hard-pressed to hear such a wish for self-annihilation
coming from, say, a handgun manufacturer, or another commercial
enterprise dependent upon fear and sadism. Yet perhaps such rhetoric did not indicate a martyr sensibility amongst the editors of the
guidebooks; perhaps they anticipated the evolution of their publications with the onset of integration, and with it a jump in circulation.
In 1955 *Travelguide* declared,

The time is rapidly approaching when TRAVELGUIDE will cease
to be a "specialized" publication, but as long as racial prejudice
exists, we will continue to cope with the news of a changing situation, working toward the day when all established directories
will serve EVERYONE.[66]

This rhetoric paid lip service to, even as it undercut, the gradual-
ist language of the state and most institutions: given the current gla-
cial pace of racial reform in the United States, the guidebooks were
under no immediate threat of losing their utility. Recalling his 1955
move from Chicago to California with the aid of the *Green Book*,
Earl Hutchinson Sr, writes in his autobiography that "you literally
didn't leave home without it."[67]
Anyway, there would be no place for these publications after their
specialization was no longer necessary. Though African-American
guidebooks exist today, directing travellers to sites of significance
in black history, *Travelguide* and *The Negro Motorist Green Book*
would suffer the fate of Negro League baseball and other Jim Crow
institutions: absorption by larger, richer, white-controlled entities.
They would be crippled, ironically, by the successes of a Civil Rights
Movement "premised on claiming the power to move, and in so
doing to remap space."[68] Although the power to move with the heed-
lessness of whites remains an ideal for African-Americans, aggrieved
black drivers of the present era have at their disposal a formal set
of legal and political tools for the redress of grievance of which the
readers and editors of the Jim Crow guidebooks could only dream.

Travelguide closed up shop in 1957; the *Green Book* would drop the Negro from its title and limp along until 1964. These publications had articulated a link between a driving subjectivity and a national identity, and had pressed that deeply problematic ideal into worthy service.

LIMITED ACCESS HIGHWAYS AND THE DECLINE OF JIM CROW

There was some truth to automobility's promise in what we might call its high-modern moment, during the era that conferred a commonsense legitimacy on the nationally transformational Interstate highway project. Despite the violence and intimidation directed toward black drivers, the road, even in its earlier iteration, had to some degree provided a space upon which the everyday discrimination and coercion African-Americans faced in other public spaces – in stores, theatres, public buildings, and restaurants, for example, or on sidewalks and public transportation – could be blunted, circumvented, and even avenged. "Only in automobiles on public roads," one commentator wrote in 1936, "do landlords and tenants and white people and Negroes of the Black Belt meet on a basis of equality." Another noted the procedural equality mandated by the "rules of the road" even in the rural South of the early 1900s. "The geographic mobility and equality on the road of automobile travel," historian Cory Lesseig writes of the early twentieth century, "helped usher in a new age of political, social, and economic opportunity for Mississippi."[69] "I wasn't particularly happy about driving in the South," Chester Himes wrote in his autobiography, *The Quality of Hurt*. "I had a bad temper and wanted to avoid trouble. But it was like driving anywhere else – priorities were controlled by the traffic laws. They don't discriminate against cars, just people."[70]

These instances of formal equality on the road no doubt proliferated after 1956, with the coming of the National System of Interstate and Defense Highways. The highways of the post-war era were more than simply better roads. Fundamental to the Interstate project was the extraction of the highways out of their geographical and social context; this elevation minimized their contact with the surrounding countryside or cityscape and created an enclosed and standardized zone to which access could be limited. This limited-access space devitalized what we would call "place," in terms of the traumatic reconfiguring of a range of landscapes and communities by the Interstate highways and their ancillary built environment. Nowhere was the obliteration of local spaces of value and the disruption of patterns of everyday life more apparent than in the nation's urban centres, where highway planners sought to facilitate (white) suburban commuters' blithe mobility over the defunded and deteriorating (black and brown) city. The destruction of the main African-American commercial and residential districts of Miami, Detroit, Nashville, and Birmingham provides particularly stark examples of a more wholesale "negro removal" component to the post-war schemes of "urban renewal" for which expressway construction was imperative.[71]

At the same time, the Interstate highway as a new, temporarily inhabitable space enabled an emancipatory levelling of the status-oriented social relations that characterized premodernity. Driving on – or, more accurately, within – the more self-contained space of the Interstates diminished the risk of humiliation of and violence against "marked" drivers, especially when compared to the state roads, which, passing through every town and accessible at myriad crossroads, exposed those drivers to the casual racism of white citizens and the various prejudices and predilections of local businesses and law enforcement. It was the limited-access, fast-moving highway, rather than the automobile, that effected the divestiture of the status of the driver.

"Once you were on the Interstate," Tom Lewis observes, "you could be anywhere; an Interstate in the Deep South felt much like an Interstate in the North." Lewis's claim that, "At last, African Americans enjoyed the right to move where and when they wanted" is egregious; but the neutral space of the Interstate and its standardized gas-food-lodging environs did indeed afford black motorists "a measure of protection ... however thin a veneer as that protection might be."[72] The Interstate highway, set apart from and above the landscape and local culture through which it cut, provided the spatial opportunity for obscuring one's identity from the scrutiny of others. The self-obscuring speed and procedural regulation of highway driving provides a metaphor for the abstraction of the liberal subject in the political public sphere.

It is important to see the deterritorialized and standardized space of the Interstate Highway System in the context of a more overarching federal presence – and with it a progressive enervation of parochialism – effected by the Second World War and its aftermath, the Cold War. Virginia Scharff notes that post-war America saw "[n]ew political and economic connections [that] penetrated and disrupted settled patterns of locale and of region, offering unprecedented opportunities and risks. People and places often suffered in the change, but the breaching of local isolation by nationalizing forces also carried the power to upset local tyrannies and offer open horizons."[73] Certainly, Miami's black Overtown neighbourhood, decimated by the building of I-395, was one place that suffered in the change; but by contrast rural Florida was rendered less menacing to African-American drivers, who were offered mobility by the highway and were sustained by increasingly national "McDonaldized" amenities at the interchanges.[74]

This new national public space of which the Interstate was but one example would be the ground on which the Civil Rights Movement would expand, and in which Jim Crow would be buried. This was the space of and from which Chuck Berry sang in his "motorvatin'" songs "Maybellene" (1955) and "No Particular Place to Go" (1956), as he seized the independence promised by the automobile and hurtled down the highway, bound only by the gas gauge and the limits of the pavement. This space would also render superfluous the guidebooks that had served the black drivers of the previous decades. "20 years of Service to the Negro Traveler," the cover of 1957 edition of the *Green Book* reminded readers. But the cover depicted no black travellers, no golf clubs, no Cadillacs; just an overhead view of the sleek, deracinated space of the Interstate Highway.

Yet highway automobility did not, and does not, inspire a genuinely democratic political imaginary beyond liberalism. Rather, the new Interstate highway enabled the African-American driver to pass as the anonymous liberal subject, and to effect, under certain circumstances, the privatist withdrawal that has been such an extravagant and problematic characteristic of American citizenship. "Liberalism," Christopher Newfield has written, "is a transitional ideology, midway between authoritarian and democratic structures."[75] The limits of highway automobility as an emancipatory practice are coterminous with those of liberalism as a democratic political sensibility: both obscure or negate, in order to manage, racial difference; both offer their subjects only procedural participation in already established regimes. Whatever citizenship under the democratic structures of the future will look like, it won't look like driving. But the assumption of the figure of the driver by the readers of *Travelguide* and *The Negro Motorist Green Book* corresponded to Martin Luther King's invocation of the Declaration of Independence and various foundational myths in his rhetoric: both explicitly tethered the quest for civil rights to a national narrative of exceptionalism, progress, and individual freedom.

5

Witnesses, Wanderers, and Writers: Women on the "Beat" Road

ELEANOR ELSON HEGINBOTHAM

I believed then and still do, that Democracy can never be fully accomplished without the leadership of hip, happy, active women.

Ted Johns in Knight, *Women of the Beat Generation*

Along with all else that it represented, the "Beatnikdom" that erupted in American culture in February 1958 seemed a male construct. Almost all the reviews and parodies that followed the publication of *On the Road* and the works in that decade of Jack Kerouac, Gregory Corso, and Allen Ginsberg privileged the aggressive, some thought almost nasty, masculinity of its characters. And almost all those characters "hit the road." Although Stacilee Ford and Gordon Slethaug describe that road as "a locus of community, the sustainer of life and instigator of change, and a source of spiritual energy" (Introduction to this book), not all were equally included in the "community." For African-Americans, for example, as Cotten Seiler argues (chapter 4 in this book), "the road's only constant was uncertainty." According to sociological studies of the Beats, women, too, were unwelcome on the road. One such study claims that they "were seen by the Tormented Rebels as 'encumbrances,' a 'source of problems for man.' Few of these men expected anything but sex out of relationships with women."[1]

That said, when Joyce Johnson, Jack Kerouac's lover of that period, was asked whether Kerouac could include a woman on his road, she declared, "I didn't altogether see why not."[2] She and a score of other women proved their value as road companions, figuratively and also literally. However much the characters of Kerouac and his Beat brothers exploited women for sex, and however much the female characters seemed complicit, the women behind those characters were powerful and self-constructing women who would carve out their own careers in writing, art, drama, and, in almost all cases, in political activism as well. They have attracted their own critical community, and this chapter is indebted to such scholars as those cited below. They and the female memoirists give testimony to the women of what turned out to be one of the most important American cultural movements of the twentieth century, one that defines a new, radically rebellious exceptionalism in the USA. They shine in retrospect through their memoirs, collected letters, latter-day interviews, and creative work, as well as their talent, courage, fortitude, and sense of the history of which they were so much a part. A survey of some of them answers roundly Allen Ginsberg's question: "But then, among the group of people we knew at the time, who were the [women] writers of such power as Kerouac or Burroughs? Were there any? I don't think so."[3]

Although or perhaps *because*, as Stacilee Ford says (chapter 7 in this book), "women who claim the space of the road are still, sadly, seen as engaging in a somewhat subversive, or at least novel art," the women at the core of this essay – Carolyn Cassady, Diane di Prima, Brenda Frazer (Bremer), Hettie (Cohen) Jones, and Joyce (Glassman) Johnson – shared the road and its subversive possibilities, and produced a range of artistic contributions of their own from their sometimes terrifying rides.

By now, says one columnist, "anyone familiar with the Beat canon [knows that] 'Kicks and chicks' connect the dots from ocean to gulf to river to other ocean ... Beat men built elaborate pedestals only to upset them, taking to the ribbon of asphalt again. The Lee Anns, Marylous, Camilles, Mardous, Tristesses of Kerouac's most famous disclosures hover like perfumed ghosts on the page."[4] Johnson, however, knew that women were not mere pedestal decorations. From her vantage point, women "were part of his [Kerouac's] 'road,' the infinite range of experience that always had to remain open to fuel his work."[5] Kerouac himself responded to his print critics in an unpublished letter saying that *On the Road* "was about tenderness," and that the Neal Cassady/Dean Moriarity character "was not a knife-wielding hoodlum but 'spiteless.'"[6] This book is witness to Kerouac's (and his characters') yearning for, potential tenderness toward, and sometimes even respect for, women. As the letters between Cassady, Kerouac, and Ginsberg, reveal, the search for a girl – and with the words to describe her – is one of the journey's refrains: "Oh where is the girl I love? I thought, and looked everywhere, as I had looked everywhere in the little world below,"[7] says Sal.

Kerouac's novels before and after *On the Road* all included interesting women based on those he knew. Nancy Grace, to whom I am much indebted for this chapter, details Kerouac's use of some of the women in his life in "A White Man in Love"; she has detailed Kerouac's use of some of the women in his life in his "FictoAutobiography."[8] The range of romantic/sexual moods in Kerouac's novels is wide and reveal what Grace describes as the conflict in Kerouac between his "tendency toward the Romantic lyricism of spiritual fulfillment" and his "special repugnance" at his sexuality.[9]

Although the women of considerable achievements who are the focus of this essay transcend the simply "romantic" or "sexual," Kerouac's fictional characters owe much to them. First – and for almost his whole life – there was his formidable mother, Gabrielle (Mamere) Kerouac, who by all accounts, shaped her son's empathy with working people.[10] Religious, hard-working, and domineering, Mamere did little to ease the confusion of the growing Jean/Jack; instead she became his lifelong concern. He bought her houses, saw to her companions, and spent as much time with her as one travelling the road could manage. In the 1940s Jack's then-good-friend Bill Burroughs was familiar enough with the mother-son situation to offer some pop-Freudian psychology. According to Dennis McNally, Kerouac "spoke at length, building a detailed, frightening picture of Gabrielle's starched white apron strings turned snake, guilt works coiled ever tighter ... around him."[11] However, as McNally continues, Kerouac did not buy the malignant metaphor, maintaining a "stubborn loyalty" to his parents. In fact, Kerouac's journal is full of grudging admiration for his mother, particularly for her native wisdom. For example, one Thanksgiving in the forties he records having learned so much from her: "She speaks of the fat, happy Russian women, the peasant women, and how, if Russia is ruined by Communist Politburos ... all that 'planned' scientific coldness of the system, Russia might yet be saved when *the women bring the men down to their knees.*"[12]

Outside his family, Kerouac was nurtured, nourished, and sometimes bedevilled by a number of women, many of whom appeared in his autobiographical novels. One of the earliest, junior-high English teacher Helen Mansfield was, according to McNally, "a sort of secular nun, an aging spinster whose life was directed toward her pupils."[13] Miss Mansfield "shared dreams, spells, and enchantment; Jean/Jack shared his tentative experimental writing with her – a short story about a policeman – and his first attempt at a novel, *Jack Kerouac Explores the Merrimack*."[14] Not many years later, he had fallen in love with a girl who would turn up in a more sophisticated novel. Mary Carney, a neighbour who rejected Jack's marriage proposal, became the sweet Maggie Cassidy in the book that bears her thinly veiled last name.[15]

Women continued to exasperate, inspire, and often support Kerouac all his life. This is made clear in the biographies by McNally and Ann Charters, both published in the seventies, and in Kerouac's own journal, edited and published in 2004 by Douglas Brinkley – although the journal is primarily Kerouac's ruminations and reports on his professional progress as a writer. Not all the women were bedded, but Stella Sampas's brother Jim, who knew Kerouac in Lowell, told me that he actually numbered those who were. In addition to the innocent Mary Carney and the drug-addicted Esperanza (the "hope" of Esperanza having become the "sadness" of *Tristessa*[16]), they included a variety of females: "a perfect, queenly girl" he saw in the library and noted in his journal;[17] a woman identified in his journal only as "Dark eyes," who came to his house one night, with whom he "danced all night long and into the morning";[18] a girl named Peggy Grasse, "perhaps more beautiful, older (22), graver, more eloquent, and perhaps more *exacting*";[19] and an unnamed "little princess ... a child ... a wise, patient child," who is perhaps the girl whose picture looks like Shirley MacLaine; and more.[20]

A number of women were traded back and forth between Cassady and Kerouac. For example, Kerouac introduced one lover, model Diana (Di) Hansen, to pal Neal with heavy consequences (Neal had to divorce Carolyn to marry the pregnant Di). In turn, LuAnne Cassady became another Kerouac road companion after a "manic" Neal Cassady "dumped" her,[21] and a woman named only "Jackie" (by Ann Charters) preferred Neal but "settled for Jack."[22] Perhaps the most doomed was Natalie Jackson, whose horrifying suicide[23] because of Neal Cassady's bad behaviour put both Cassady and Kerouac, who had been designated by Cassady to care for her, into some of their darkest moods.[24] The beautiful Carolyn Cassady wrote most prolifically and touchingly about the triangle of which she was the nexus.

Most important in Kerouac's personal life were the women to whom he was related through marriage. Each wife gave Kerouac something necessary. First and briefly (but with lingering consequences) was Edie Parker, Kerouac's first wife, on whom he depended for comfort in his sexual anxieties and for bail money in a bizarre case for which he was a witness.[25] The second, Joan Haverty, also provided sustenance – and his only child; the third, Stella Sampas, offered help with Mamere and with his own aging and fatally intoxicated last years; the duties of executor of the estate fell to her brother when she died. His second and third wives and the daughter he barely acknowledged provide insights into the difficult problems created when Jack Kerouac tried to share a life with women.

Tall, dark-haired, model-slim, and newly widowed, young Joan Haverty married Kerouac almost immediately after they met. She worked to support the couple as he withdrew to write in "mad compulsive long days and nights on the long rolls of paper he fashioned."[26] Her support made *On the Road* possible, though another woman would share the dubious pleasures of its success, and her other great accomplishment – giving birth to and raising the remarkable Jan Kerouac – also produced bittersweet results.[27] Jan not only looked so much like Kerouac that Allen Ginsberg was convinced she was Jack's daughter on first sight,[28] but she also apparently inherited some of his strengths and failings. For a time after her mother's death on Mother's Day 1990, she "turned to the ultimate form of degradation, working as a stripper in a cheap bar."[29] If her father's dark side appeared to be part of her DNA, so was his drive to record a risky, conflicted life. She was on the road most of her short life, too, and, as Brenda Knight points out, she published novels much earlier in her life than had her father. She also challenged him in *Trainsong*.[30] Sadly, Jan was excluded from her father's life and from his death; she was not asked to the ceremonies honouring him in Lowell that were arranged by the Sampas family.[31] That exclusion is the more poignant because she was a literary woman with an experimental bent, who appreciated her father even after all the sadness. As she told Dianne Jones in 1996, "I would like to help in leaving the legacy to them and to all people who appreciate the Beat Generation and what it signifies, and the wild, spontaneous prose that my father started."[32]

"Wild, spontaneous prose" also marked the many memoirs by women; like the novels of Jan Kerouac, most experimented with the form as did the men in their novels and memoirs.[33] Joan and daughter Jan both produced important memoirs: Joan's *Nobody's Wife* and Jan's *Trainsong* belong to a genre that Ronna C. Johnson finds "connected to but distinct from the domestic sphere of their eclipse."[34] Johnson's discussion, which includes texts by Brenda Frazer (Bremser), Diane di Prima, Joyce Johnson, Hettie Jones, Carolyn Cassady, and Janine Pommy Vega, maintains that in their memoirs – records most often of self-invention – "women Beat writers work a new instrumentality into the dominant Beat movement representations and gender assumptions."[35] For example, when Diane di Prima writes with such startling frankness of women's experience with lusty sex; when Carolyn Cassady records tension between a desire for an ordered household and a desire for the houseguest (Jack Kerouac) without diminishing desire for her husband; when Brenda Frazer (Bremser) uses understatement for a harrowing tale of travels and tenuous child-rearing techniques; and when all of them celebrate themselves along with the men who (often) seemed to exploit them, they were "introducing further heterogeneity into the discourse of beat."[36] Although some of the stories seem to be cases of domestic abuse or at least exploitation of woman as objects, the act of writing the story enabled these women to triumph over the objectification. Beyond their own stories, the women became influential in the creative arts and in political movements, they engaged with the world beyond themselves, and, some might say, beyond the self-involved, existentialist isolation of the men.

For all that, they are still barely visible. For example, in the collection of photographs taken by Allen Ginsberg (they filled four rooms at Washington's National Gallery of Art in 2010) only two or three show women. Similarly, the pictures of Fred and Timothy McDarrah's memorial to their Beat friends are full of crowds in coffee houses, on the steps of city streets, and in cars; most are men. However, though women are identified in only about 35 of the 200-some pictures, the text acknowledges them as editors, patrons, poets; in other words, as women who go far beyond the role of groupie or girlfriend.[37] McDarrah's volume also names women who have entered the mainstream of literary studies: Anaïs Nin, Barbara Guest, Denise Levertov, Grace Paley, Susan Sontag, May Swenson, and Diana Trilling. Perhaps not all of them were "happy," "hip," or even "active," but most of them (as with the two dozen women anthologized by Brenda Knight, wildly different as they are from each other) aspired to an ideal of democracy privileged by the "Beat" movement.

Perhaps not all of them were always "sober," but each was a witness to the manifestation of the movement in her particular city or household. Unsung as they were for most of the forties through to the sixties, they *were* part of – even essential to – the "Road" made famous by Kerouac, Cassady, Ginsberg, Corso, Orlovsky, and all the others. In the decades since their most astonishing feats, they have earned the attention of a number of chroniclers. Brenda Knight's *Women of the Beat Generation*, organized them into "The Muses," "The Writers," "The Precursors," and "The Artists."[38] The collected interviews of nine prominent "Beat" women conducted by Nancy M. Grace and Ronna C. Johnson concludes with a bibliography of six pages of tightly packed entries, most of which are primary materials from these remarkable women. The list makes the more ironic the words of Allen Ginsberg with which the Grace and Johnson book begins: "Were there any? I don't think so."[39]

From among so many personalities who happened to be "the most observant and sober witnesses of this historic period"[40] and so many writing styles and genres, this chapter focuses on five of the most prolific and powerful: Diane di Prima, Carolyn Cassady, Brenda Frazer (Bonnie Bremser then), Hettie (Cohen) Jones, and Joyce (Glassman) Johnson. Along with some dozen others who could also stake this claim, these women challenged the hegemony of the often smug and conservative character of post-war America. As different as they are in family and educational background and in their sexual and political adventures, they share a pride of place that deserves to be noted in the literary/cultural revolution that existed in counterpoint to the comfort and order of the veterans and their wives who energized the American economy and made the nation, for better or worse, the acknowledged leader of the world. Not only did each set out on her own road trip, often dangerous and difficult, but each wrote about her journey with a vividness that warrants broader readership in the context of a collection of road studies.

DIANE DI PRIMA

Diane had "impeccable beatnik credentials." So said Sam Kashner, whose idiosyncratic memoir *When I Was Cool* includes few women. In fact, said Kashner, Diane di Prima was "one of the women Allen

Ginsberg could *see*."[41] Although he had been intrigued by her "erotic" look in pictures, when Kashner met her at Allen Ginsberg's flat, all he asked her for was help in playwriting.[42] Kashner's story, recollected fifty years after that meeting, suggests the two ways in which di Prima is so representative of the period she vividly memorializes (frequently too explicitly to quote with comfort) in autobiography, poetry, and essays: the sex adventures that she details in *Memoirs of a Beatnik* (1969);[43] and the progress toward becoming an artist and critic that she describes in her later and fuller *Recollections of my Life as a Woman* (2001).

In the latter book, she remembers her mother and grandmother, who taught the young, bright child that "women had to learn to bear more pain than man."[44] The world she describes as she attended Hunter, then a typing school, and then for two years, Swarthmore, was one of "safety we made together within the circle of our mutual sight."[45] Keats, Byron, Shakespeare, and Millay helped her to question that drive for safety: "Something fills my belly and rises to my throat. It is the taste of possibility." Perhaps it was "Life lived in the vision of art to be achieved. Lived in possibility."[46] Leaving Swarthmore, she began a new life in 1953 as a "bhikshuni." Though she didn't "then know the word," she became one "dedicated to art and to the life of art." As she told Tony Moffeit, she would like to pass on the need to "realize that you can't value too highly your own curiosity, inquisitiveness ... about everything."[47] For Diane di Prima that meant curiosity toward everyone from her befuddled parents to her contemporary Ginsberg. As she points out, she had already published a daring work before his *Howl* hit the nation's consciousness: "we've always had a lot to learn from each other and talk about."[48] "Bhikshuni" also meant curiosity toward Ezra Pound, whom she visited in his Saint Elizabeth confinement, and curiosity toward the books he recommended, even to the difficult extent of learning some Greek so that she could read Homer. It meant curiosity toward the many uses of language, colloquial and formal, and it meant straining far beyond the expected – even in the world of the modernists she came to read deeply – and stretching beyond the bounds of the acceptable "THE ONLY WAR THAT MATTERS," she yells typographically in "Rant" is "THE WAR AGAINST THE IMAGINATION." She repeats the line two times – all capped.[49]

The curiosity, talent, passion, and imagination created poems like "Ave," a sort of road anthem "to all women, especially the pregnant aboriginal": "pregnant you wander / barefoot you wander / battered by drunk men you wander," assuring her sister that "I move within you, light the evening fire / I dip my hand in you and eat your flesh / you disappear like smoke on misty hills."[50] For the child there is another poem: "Song for Baby-O, Unborn," in which the poet cannot promise that "you'll never go hungry / or that you won't be sad on this gutted / breaking / globe / but I can slow you / baby / enough to love / to break your heart forever."[51]

Di Prima's decision to move to the city alone – and "to be an artist – writer, dancer, painter, musician" – was a brave choice in the world of the forties and early fifties. In *Recollections* (2001) she looks back on "those first years in Manhattan ... full of bravado and playfulness. Learning the rules of survival or making them up,"[52] she survived through many partners, cramped terrible apartments, a problem pregnancy, and illness. She looks back on that playful girl who "made what I thought of as my decision not to be beautiful ... and so I began to clunk and barge through the world."[53] The self-reflective humour of the mature book is at odds with the not-ironic soberness of her earlier *Memoirs of a Beatnik* (1969), in which she mainly reports on her own early sexual exploits and dawning realization that "a new era had begun."[54] Although it is worth remembering that the fifties also produced a rebel book, *Peyton Place*, by another rebel woman, such writing was far from the norm for those years. In explicit language, di Prima speaks of losing her virginity;[55] she itemizes in a long riff the varieties of kissing styles;[56] she reacts to reading Hesse and listening to "Carmina Burana"; she describes mixed, almost choreographed, couplings with lots of candles, firelight, hair, and food. From a communal farm on the Hudson, in a mood more of braggadocio than confessional, she says, "yes it was good, being a chick to three men, and each of them on his own trip."[57] Most interesting to the literary historian is her discovery of *Howl*, of being "caught up immediately in that sad, powerful opening" and her recognition that she was not alone, that "if there was one Allen there must be more."[58]

In *Memoirs* di Prima spoke disparagingly of "our code, our eternal tiresome rule of Cool." She was not "cool"; she was passionate. Comparing the picture of the downward-looking, deadpan, beatnik child/woman on the cover of *Memoirs* with the outward-looking, smiling, comfortable older woman at work in the world of arts and politics in the Grace and Johnson book is to see the way the movement as a whole, and those who lived through it, matured. Called "the major female poet to emerge from the Beats," Diane di Prima has produced at least eight books of poetry and two memoirs, reviewed through the years in quite different ways;[59] in the early days of the movement, she helped LeRoi Jones/Amiri Baraka, with whom she had a two-and-a-half-year affair and a child, edit an important journal; and she still plays a leading role in helping younger writers and artists to publish. She travelled on a bus celebrating living revolutionary art. She had affairs with famous men of letters and had (at least) three marriages and five children. The sheer energy involved in all of that seems at odds with the word "cool."

CAROLYN CASSADY

Diane di Prima was propelled by passion, particularly, as she put it in her 1989 interview with Tony Moffeit, "a big energy of anger."[60] That is just one of the ways she differed radically from another memoirist of the Beat Generation – a beautiful, serene-looking, and apparently entirely pleasing Carolyn Cassady. Diane di Prima gave herself to many men. Later she told Ann Charters, "You do understand, don't you, that I never felt anything for any of these people";[61] what she privileged was her role as an independent artist – above all and always an artist. Carolyn Cassady was almost the opposite. Cool blonde Carolyn Cassady (di Prima was an intense – looking brunette) left her artistic training to devote herself almost totally to the prototype of the Beat Movement, Neal Cassady – aka Dean Moriarity. In spite of his constant womanizing (and his homoerotic escapades), his inability to hold a job, his depressions, and who knows what else, Carolyn struggled to create a more or less normal life with their three children. Although she had taken a huge risk in her marriage, she seems, in contrast to di Prima and others of the movement, to privilege nesting and domestic solidity.

Although Cassady's title, *Off the Road: My Years with Cassady, Kerouac, and Ginsberg,* suggests the opposite, hers is indeed another road book. Appropriately it begins with Dante: "In the middle of the journey of our life I / came to myself in a dark wood where the straight way was lost." The passage ends with "I will relate the other things I found," and she does. Unlike di Prima, whose *Memoir* only suggests but does not specify dates, Cassady begins her narrative precisely with a date: March 1947, when she met the zoot-suit clad

Columbia University student Neal. "Beneath his subtle charm," she remembers, "I sensed a taut energy that was subdued ... like a drawn bow."[62] Also unlike di Prima, whose *Recollections* begins with her own family background and childhood, Cassady begins her story with a focus on the man who was to be perhaps the single most influential member of the Beat generation – not because of his own writing but because he modelled the whole notion of hipsterism for Jack Kerouac. In fact, Carolyn Cassady begins her memoir with a symbol of that relationship. She describes the famous snapshot of student Neal with his two friends, Jack Kerouac and Allen Ginsberg, "the one a famous football player, the other a poet."[63]

Both of the other figures in that picture would play a large part in Carolyn's life with (and without) Neal. Although she seemed shocked by the physical relationship between Ginsberg and Cassady, she "grew increasingly fond of" the poet. Perhaps alluding to how much she missed these qualities in Neal, she says Ginsberg "was open and frank, yet quiet and thoughtful. And always kind. He took a sincere interest in my stories."[64] As for Jack, she would take up enthusiastically her own physical relationship with him later in her marriage to Neal. When he came to Denver to see Carolyn and Neal, she recognized "here was the warm physical attraction Neal lacked."[65] A reader may wish to yell at the young Carolyn "don't go there," when, even though she knew of Neal's youthful jail term, his failed marriage to LuAnne (not yet finally finished when she met him), and more, Carolyn "saw Neal nearly every day," finding his company "far more satisfactory than any other."[66] She recognized his lying and rationalizing, but felt "vibrant, brilliant, witty" in his presence.[67] Appropriately, they were married on April Fools' Day, 1948, after she had spurned a more suitable match in San Francisco.

The pattern for their lives together and apart seemed clear from the beginning. A three-page letter from her to him in the midst of some of his philandering begins, "First know that I love you. All I want in life is to be your wife and the mother of your children – but I want all that this implies. Foremost it means I want you as a husband and father – and all that implies."[68] In the letter she alluded to two problems with her desire for so stable a life: his womanizing and the contents of his library. His answer: "Love has nothing to do with it."[69] She responded, again with something that makes the post-*Feminine Mystique* woman squirm: "When you are away and when you write as you did, I am left with the feeling only of pride to have been a Mrs. Cassady, even such a one, to have been accepted briefly for whatever reason, and to have two precious lives as a result. You have not destroyed me."[70]

Nevertheless, because of Neal, the talented, well-educated artist Carolyn Cassady joined her husband in taking drugs. Because of him, the three children became almost entirely her responsibility, except (horrifyingly) when she went to work, leaving the baby with Neal. Later, pregnant herself, she acceded to the demand of one of Neal's girlfriends, Diana Hansen, also pregnant, to divorce Neal so that they could marry.[71] Still later, a woman took even greater advantage of the couple. When in 1954 the Cassadys had finally accumulated a bit of money in a lawsuit in which they were plaintiffs, a young woman named Natalie Jackson not only stole Neal (for a time), but she also forged Carolyn's signature and stole all the money. After Natalie's suicide, Neal returned, but the money was gone. Finally, when the oldest child was eight, Carolyn was completely on her own: Neal had gone to jail for selling marijuana. By the time he was released in 1960, Carolyn had found a life without him and the drugs which he continued to take. For all the disturbing details she offers of their life together and apart, Carolyn called Cassady, "the only man I wanted," and he who had been married three times and slept with many more women called her "Dear Wife, my only one" and "My one and only family, my sweet Carolyn."[72]

She was not without her own great resources: Carolyn Cassady was an accomplished woman before she met Cassady. She was an actress, trained in the Stanislavsky method, an artist who had studied sculpture, ceramics, architecture, painting, and drawing. She had worked with Martha Graham in dance and with Erich Fromm in psychology.[73] Thus she was able to draw on these talents when her life with Neal Cassady played out (after seventeen years of marriage); she returned to art and turned her experiences into history through the memoir, through helping on a film (starring Sissy Spacek) of the book, and through editing letter collections. From her home in England, she continued to fight for the old road show. When Kerouac's scrolled draft of *On the Road* was for sale (at $1.5 million), Cassady was outraged: she believed the book, which she said had been typed on her sister's typewriter, should have gone to the New York Public Library.[74]

Off the Road seems part soap opera (about the narrator/ primary character's unsparing honesty) and part documentary (about the generation and movement, the patterns of which she sees in her retrospective voice). Although she is deeply personally connected with them, her voice is remarkably reportorial as she assesses Allen Ginsberg on the brink of *Howl*; as she tells the terrible (but darkly comic) story of Helen Hinkel[75] and the tragic story of Joan Burroughs; and as she offers a glimpse of a young Gregory Corso,[76] a young Lawrence Ferlinghetti,[77] and an old Henry Miller.[78] Perhaps most importantly, she reports on her part in the creation of *On the Road*. Although it was to be another woman who would share the effect of that book on Jack Kerouac, Carolyn Cassady's insights into Jack and into Allen Ginsberg are sufficient reason in themselves to read her memoir.

She records, for example, bits of letters between Jack and Neal and Allen on the new book. Allen tells Neal: "I read it [*On the Road*] with great wonder, stopping and laughing out loud every few paragraphs, so much clarity and grace and vigor seemed to shine in the writing,"[79] but as Jack's agent, Allen, also says, "He was not experimenting and exploring in new deep form; he was purposely just screwing around."[80] Depressed, presumably by the distance between his expectation for *On the Road* and such comments as Ginsberg's, Kerouac wrote to Carolyn Cassady, "Your life would have been impossible with me – I'm very unlucky – and doomed to be robbed by all the cheap litterateurs of my time."[81] Although the tone of both the memoir *Off the Road* and her introduction to the Neal Cassady letters edited by Dave Moore is eerily calm and objective, she does not negate the high personal stake she had in the writers themselves.

By the time Jack Kerouac was deeply into the writing of *On the Road,* he and Carolyn Cassady had become lovers. She tells the story in frank detail, beginning with his visit to the Cassady home in 1952. Invited to do so by both Cassadys, Kerouac slept in a tiny attic space over the rest of the household which then included little girls, four and three years old, and the baby, John Allen (named, of course, for the two foremost writers of the Beat Generation). Carolyn admits to having set a sort of trap for Jack, into which he fell easily. Though she claims to have enjoyed the physical relationship, she also enjoyed the company. While Neal worked at his railroad job, Carolyn performed her chores while Jack read excerpts from work in progress or from Proust or Shakespeare.[82] He sang her praises: "Ideal Mother Image, Madwoman, Chick, Ingenue." He went along on family trips – to Minnesota to see Carolyn's family and to Nogales in New Mexico.[83] He asked for an open ménage a trois (six with children): "I am at your beck and call to come and go, in other words I accept loss and death, and if you offer me some of your life I'm very grateful."[84] Later that year in a bigger house outside San Francisco, Kerouac returned to live in the ménage that seemed to suit them all. As Carolyn remembered, "Jack read to us from *Dr. Sax* in a great booming voice, spiced with W C Fields or Major Hoople imitations ... Sometimes we were high and hilarious, other times sentimental and romantic."[85] When news of Neal Cassady's[86] death reached Carolyn in 1968 – long after he had joined the Kesey Pranksters and she had made a new life for herself – Jack called her to say, that he would be "joining him soon."[87] Years later, she and Diane di Prima and others would remember these days unchastened, but soberly, and their children would have their own strong, often judgmental memories.

BRENDA FRAZER (BONNIE BREMSER)

Although Brenda Frazer's soft smile gazes out from her arbor background with a kind of quiet modesty in the collection of essays by Grace and Johnson, her story is perhaps the most frightening of any in this small sample of the women of the Beat Movement. Nancy Grace describes her life as balancing on and off "a fault line of American writing, the point at which confession borders salacious entertainment."[88] Grace's summary of Frazer's young life is almost unbelievable. She describes the woman whose picture is on the same page as emerging from her Sweet Briar college life to marry poet Ray Bremser three weeks after she met him. They avoided the law, which sought him for parole violation, by travelling in Mexico, where she gave up her daughter Rachel for adoption in order to earn money as a prostitute. Rachel was not part of the article by Daniel Pinchbeck introducing the children of Beatniks on their reactions to their parents' heterodox lives, but her very survival seems a miracle.

The gentle woman in the picture, who by then was retired from the new life she made after her hipster days, that of a governmental soil surveyor and the mother of other children, seems an altogether different person from the hostile narrator of her own early story. That 1969 memoir, *Troia: Mexican Memoirs* begins with this inscription: "Damn the pain: it must be written."[89] Anne Waldman singled out the book as "an extraordinarily brave book" in her interview with

Nancy Grace, but she also explained why that courage has not been more broadly known. Bremser, says Waldman, was shy; she was married to a problematic partner (poet Ray Bremser), and she had a "philosophical/melancholic cast of mind."[90] Narrator and subject Bonnie/Brenda introduces herself in the paradoxical way that some of the men – Kerouac and Cassady certainly – appear to their readers: part romantic ("all my life my heart knew that Ray was on his way to me") and part sexual adventurer ("I have a dirty mind").

Her road story makes Kerouac's *On the Road* seem provincial; her anger out-howls *Howl. Her* road story is also a far cry from the hijinks of recent televised women buddies described by Stacilee Ford (see Chapter 5 in this volume). This Washington, DC-bred, private-schooled young woman travelled from Mexico City to Veracruz to Texas, back to Mexico City, and on to New York. Dependent on drugs and alcohol for much of that time, she dragged her child on grimy buses with drunken Indians, acknowledging with part of her mind the danger to her child: "Rachel, your story will come out as you awake into next month's mud puddles," she writes.[91] As she becomes a hooker in "a very short corduroy skirt" and "a blouse of limp rayon,"[92] she remembers musing: "All day my mind shrinks from the undesirability of what I have to do at night,"[93] but by the earthy (and unquotable) ending of the book the shrinking appears to have become bravado. The reader, aghast, wonders how she could have left her baby in Veracruz to get her husband out of jail in Laredo and how, after all she had gone through to do so, she could still tell Nancy Grace in her 1999 College of Wooster interview that

> We were a married couple and had our own life. Ray was in this poetic process all the time, so my total focus was on Ray. I was watching him write. I learned his opinions. I looked at the books he looked at. We were inspired by the same things. We experienced all the things that he wrote about together.[94]

This pre-feminist spousal loyalty, much like that of Carolyn toward Neal, appears to be at odds with the illegal and risky adventures of her road trip. So is the style of much of *Troia*. Frazer's subject matter is radical, her "behaviors violating long-held patriarchal constraints."[95] However, her *style* is often remarkably traditional and hauntingly vivid. Each of the women cited in this essay, of course, has a distinctive style; hers is a strange blend of knockout hostility and the lyricism of the long-distance runner. As Nancy Grace and others note, that style reflects the style of the man whose work she was reading while writing. She declared her debt to Kerouac in her interview with Grace, particularly his "knack of the long sentence which is carried by emotional weight fueled by transcendent flashes of realization."[96] What emerges, while carrying its own emotional weight through right-branching sentences like those of Kerouac, is nevertheless distinctive and – though sometimes indeed hostile and even ugly – often beautiful as a fugue: "Look across to the Gulf, and nothing looks back, save the mesquite bushes, a mangy dog chases a couple of not promising cows across a landscape you would not expect to carry even that much vision of life."[97]

If *On the Road* was "about being lost in America with Neal,"[98] Bonnie Bremser's/Brenda Frazer's book was about being lost in Mexico with (and without) Ray. Bremser is expansive about Kerouac in talking to Nancy Grace, admiring "the sweetness of it [*On the Road*], the way things expand when you look at it." She spoke of trying "to keep those things in mind, if I try to keep the transcendent quality in mind when I'm writing."[99] In some sense, *Troia* is similar to McNally's description of Kerouac's style ("dewlike" but also bursting with energy, with a feeling of life struggling inside a deathly society."[100]

HETTIE JONES

Much better known politically and culturally is the woman who created an entirely new identity out of a conforming Jewish background, but even she is cheated of the fame that has been granted for forty years to her ex-husband and one time editing companion. Although Hettie [Cohen] Jones worked side by side with the man who became her husband, LeRoi Jones aka Amiri Baraka, and although she is the mother of the child in his most famous and poignant poem ("Suicide Note"), she is not even mentioned in the small biography of Jones/Amiri Baraka in Waldman's major anthology.

Grace and Johnson call their interview with Hettie Jones "Drive" and that with Bremser/Frazer "Artista" (Brenda Knight titles her inclusion of Bremser "Transformed Genius"). While Grace and Johnson show a picture of Hettie Jones, smiling with energy, on a city street, Bonnie Bremser's recent picture is set in an arbor. The contrast between the two women is stark, but the comparisons and intersections are just as interesting. Akin to their sister members of the Beat generation, both transformed themselves by their own will and by the accidents of their male bondings; both took those transformed selves to impressive achievements beyond their roles as supporters of more famous and notorious husband/writers and as friends of other focal figures in the Beat movement. Both women leapt from Southern colleges for women – Hettie Cohen's Mary Washington College and Bremser's Sweet Briar – to begin their rugged, strange, risky adventures on separate roads.

Both also anticipated interracial movements. For Bonnie Bremser, "blackness" was a metaphoric choice. Clearly Caucasian, she explained to Nancy Grace what she meant when in *Troia* she speaks of being Mexican and of being Black:

> What I was doing was identifying in a way, my psychology, my make-up ... Much of that [dying her hair black, for example, as she did after she had given up her child] may have been just a sort of despair, sort of a feeling. It was almost as though the people in Mexico are so open to their poverty, or so open to the oppression of being down trodden or something like that. That's what I was identifying with, that darkness in myself.[101]

For Hettie Jones the identification was not metaphoric; it was, though not without difficulty, something she embraced consciously and, as she implies in her 2001 memoir, most often joyously. She had biracial children with LeRoi Jones, something that even on the East Coast was not an ordinary sight. In *How I Became Hettie Jones,* she writes a frank account of fending off the rudeness she encountered.[102] She mentions meeting Jimmie Baldwin. She participates with Jones ("Roi" in her book) in writing political protests about American policy regarding Cuba.[103] And, sadly, she describes how Roi, apparently feeling tainted by his association with her in Black liberation circles, would not take her, his wife, to an event at Howard University: "You're white," he explained.[104] Bremser takes up a false racial identification as a sort of self-flagellation; Jones accepts a future of blended children with some scorn but mostly with the same matter-of-fact directness with which she writes the whole memoir.

Described by Russell Banks as "possibly the best account yet written of what it was like to be at the center of New York Bohemianism in the 1950s and 1960s," *How I Became Hettie Jones* differs from Bremser's book – and from the other memoirs described in this article – in its crisp, direct, spare, and sometimes funny style. Appropriate to one who is also an accomplished fiction writer, poet, teacher (including prison settings), and editor, Jones begins with a specific scene, that of a twenty-two-year-old "Queens Jew" reading Kafka at an ancient rolltop desk when LeRoi Jones met her. She records the impression he made at their second meeting: "And, at that moment, as he appeared to me, in all his dapper, young, familiar self, all my last doubts disappeared. At the Five Spot the music had spoken, and now here were the words. The signs were clear. I would follow the language with this man and find the tunes."[105] Thus began Hettie Cohen's figurative road trip toward becoming "Hettie Jones."

By the time she made this decision, she had already been published and was already an editor. She was also something of a woman of the world: "I [had] dated a Pakistani, an African who lived at International House, and a Jewish-Lutheran lawyer from Washington Heights."[106] Hettie's story is a personal one: her first visit to the Jones family ("more middle class than mine");[107] her search for and landing of the great job on the *Partisan Review*; and – straight out of Lucy and Desi – her frantic trip, accompanied by six "Beat" artists, to the hospital for the birth of Kellie, the child to whom she dedicates her memoir.

It is also a remarkable account of the flowering of the arts – Beat and otherwise – from the 1950s on. Her marriage, her work on the *Partisan Review*, her ambition, and her appreciation for the work of others make *How I Became Hettie Jones* an account of how American letters turned many corners in the second half of the twentieth century. Here she writes of one of the books that created change: "I've just finished reading the new, hot book, *On the Road*. I love Jack Kerouac's footloose heroes who've upset complacent America simply by driving through."[108] In the coffee house, Jazz on the Wagon, she and Roi met "a small but provocative literary group sometimes gathered at the squeezed-up, wobbly tables. They even had a name – the 'Beats.'" This group, Hettie reports, shared, along with B-movie glamour, "a saintly disaffection" and "a wild head of hair"; among these were writers Lawrence Ferlinghetti, Allen Ginsberg, Gregory Corso, Diane de Prima, Frank O'Hara; artists such as Larry Rivers; and musicians such as John Coltrane.[109] Publishing the *Partisan Review* with Philip Rahv, she worked with literary figures on the brink of fame.[110] *Yugen,* the journal Hettie helped Roi publish, offered less well-known writers a chance to publish. The story of how Hettie Cohen became Hettie Jones is also the story of how American letters changed through, among other influences, the works of the Beats. What, asked Nancy Grace, does Hettie Jones mean by "Beat or bohemian?" "I guess," said Hettie Jones, "it's a looser approach to life ... Bohemians are people who live outside conventions, as most artists do, who are loose. And I don't just mean people who are loose sexually. But e-e-e-easy. Easy with their emotions. More emotionally available."[111] Two women important to this discussion might fit that description. One is Diane di Prima, who entered the life of Hettie Jones shortly after the birth of her daughter Kellie. She lived with LeRoi Jones for two years and had a baby with him. She even lived with LeRoi and Hettie for a time.[112] Di Prima recalled Hettie as "brightly cheerful, having worked all day, and come home and cooked."[113] Apparently the quadrille-like games of changing partners did not rule out continuing connections between competing women or men.

Perhaps more than in any other literary/cultural period the characters in the Beat generation couple up in intricate, dizzying ways. Just as di Prima moved in on the Jones marriage and included her views of the man and the marriage in her *Recollection,* so the beautiful, properly raised, multi-talented Joyce Glassman moved into the life of Jack Kerouac. Their relationships form complex quadrilles. To review: Cassady had travelled with and married LuAnne Henderson in 1945; they divorced so that Cassady could marry the pregnant Carolyn in 1948; by 1949 LuAnne had become a friend and travel companion of Kerouac, who had been married briefly to Edie Parker in 1944. In 1950 several women after LuAnne and Edie, Kerouac married Joan Haverty, who had been married to his friend Bill Cannastra (whose beheading in a subway accident was the stuff of horrible legend). In 1951, supported by Haverty, Kerouac wrote the first draft of *On the Road* at great speed on the rolls of white paper, also now famous in legend. In 1952 he stayed with the Cassadys and shared the sexual favours of Carolyn. That was also the year that Joan gave birth to Jan Kerouac, and Jack, denying any responsibility for that birth, completed the version of *On the Road* that would be published in 1957. Meanwhile Hettie and LeRoi Jones were entertaining Ray and Bonnie Bremser after their Mexican adventure, and Diane di Prima was about to begin her affair with Roi. Hettie praised Kerouac's new book. That brings us to Joyce Glassman's youthful expedition to a party at the house of Lucien Carr, who had figured in the marriage of Jack Kerouac to Edie Parker in 1944.[114]

JOYCE (GLASSMAN) JOHNSON

That party at Lucien Carr's, when Kerouac was on the brink of fame and Joyce Glassman (Johnson) was on the brink of her remarkable life, becomes the turning point for the young woman who had grown up as a privileged only child of a New York City Jewish family. In her memoir *Minor Characters* (which pursues a year-by-year comparison of her life with Kerouac's), she comments on her obsessive mother, who wanted to freeze her family "into a Victor Herbert operetta in which the furnishings and music were vaguely 'classical,' the values sentimental, post Victorian."[115] In the autobiographical novel she would write in 1962, Johnson further hints at the character of that family. The father of the fictional Susan believes that "a man should not be timid; a father should not be weak," so when his daughter misbehaves, he chastises her in unimaginative words: "You've done something foolish and you know you've done something foolish."[116] In high school, the real-life talented musician Joyce thwarted the Victor Herbert ideal of her mother by sneaking off, donning "a pair of long copper earrings" that 'constitute my downtown disguise,"[117] and hanging out in coffee houses, posing as an older girl/ woman. In 1951 at sixteen she had entered Barnard; she would stop just one class short of graduation. She had already fallen in love at least twice and had already undergone an ugly illegal abortion.

During those years she had become familiar with J. Alfred Prufrock, reflecting ruefully on the depiction of a Silent Generation type: "'Do I dare to eat a peach?' had an especial poignancy," she says. She had *not* read, however, *The Town and the City* by an unknown writer – but then no one else had either. By contrast, during her Barnard years she had met Elise Cowen, who becomes a major character in *Minor Characters* – and an inspiration. Through Elise she had come to understand "the Beats." Elise had read John Clellon Holmes's *Go* (he had helped to name the era), and had fallen in love with Allen Ginsberg. Canny and epigrammatically inclined, Johnson reflects on that friendship: "Elise was a moment in Allen's life. In Elise's life, Allen was an eternity."[118] Cowen may have prompted Ginsberg to make his first famous shout of "Moloch" to an "unshockable audience" the year of the San Francisco Renaissance.[119] Elise, however, was doomed to kill herself. The friendship of the beautiful, brave fugitive from the make-believe conformity of a Victor Herbert world with the sad and odd Elise Cowen was one of the first evidences of Joyce Glassman's readiness to choose another way to live in the middle of the twentieth century. She said, "I *was* attracted to decadence ... I had little respect for respectability. I was sure only cowardice kept me on the straight and narrow."[120] Another way she had diverged from parental expectations was that she had literary aspirations. She did not tell her mother when she published in the Barnard literary magazine, because "I came to think writing was like sex – an illicit and transgressive act."[121]

She was ready for Kerouac, with whom she would have a symbolic "road trip." As was true of Hettie Jones, Johnson's road story is that of a sensitive witness, one who, because of enforced distances, fortunately wrote and kept letters and journals. The parallel lines she has drawn between Kerouac's and Johnson's road trips in her sharply focused and deeply etched memoir come together in Joyce Glassman Johnson's book at the New Year's Eve party at Lucien Carr's the last day of 1956. By that time Joan Haverty, who had enabled the first draft of *On the Road,* was struggling to raise a daughter, now four, on little support; Carolyn Cassady, who inspired a re-write in an upstairs room in California, was also struggling to raise her children, who were then five, six, and eight. Neal Cassady, who had provided the model for the book, had met Edgar Cayce and would soon be serving two years in prison before he joined the Merry Pranksters of Ken Kesey. Joyce Glassman had written her first novel and had the contract for its publication with her when she met the about-to-be famous Kerouac. *She* was already a professional – if unaccomplished – writer. As it turned out, Kerouac had skipped Lucien Carr's party, but Allen Ginsberg arranged a meeting for the two at a Howard Johnson's in the Village shortly thereafter. They began the new year together. With the understanding that they would "Fly Now; Pay Later," Kerouac moved in with Glassman, reminding her of "a sailor with his few belongings pared down."[122] Although in some ways she felt herself to be a character in a novel, she wistfully reported on the distance between herself and the females (like Esmeralda/ Tristessa, the "whore and saint, so beautiful and lost") in Kerouac's fiction. Glassman/Johnson describes herself as "unprimeval and distinctly of the city ... everydayness."[123]

The affair between Joyce Glassman and Jack Kerouac lasted only a year and ten months. It was a crucial period for American letters as the world was reading *On the Road* for the first time. In spite of a prolific output of other writings, Joyce Glassman Johnson is perhaps best known for her connections with Kerouac and other Beat writers, and, because she wrote so well about them, she became one of the most identifiable women of the Beat movement. Jack was, after all, always "on the road," during these years – to California, Florida, Mexico, and Tangiers – which is one reason for the fascinating paper trail. As a complement to the published journal (that ends before the meeting with Glassman) and the letters from Kerouac included in Cassady materials, the letters between Joyce and Jack written in 1957-58 provide a rich glimpse into the vocabulary and vision of these two frank and articulate people and into others in their world.[124] Joyce reports that her agent wants her not to accompany Jack to Mexico but to go to New England "and pretend I'm Sarah Orne Jewett or someone."[125] Jack compares himself to Twain.[126] In *Minor Characters*, which fills in the gaps between the letters – and much more – Johnson remarks that Jack's jaunts at sea aligned him with the greatest of American novelists, but one with a twist: "*On the Road* would bring them [American readers] the voice of a supreme outlaw, validated by his art ... pure and sparkling."[127] In fact, the whole book places these writers in the mainstream of American literature.

In her introduction to *Door Wide Open*, Johnson, who went on to have two interesting marriages and many literary successes, looks back on her twenty-one-year old self, who, she said, "learned to write by writing to [Kerouac]."[128] She recalls her expectations of the man she had seen on the cover of earlier novels: "tender, half melancholy, half proud, dressed like an impoverished young college instructor."[129] The man she met was restless and unhappy. Paraphrasing Hawthorne on Melville, she said he "could neither be alone [n]or with people, much less sustain a love affair,"[130] but she describes herself as deeply in love with *him* "in all the embarrassingly conventional ways." Through letters, she says, they became "more than lovers – we became friends."[131] As a friend she could tell him, "I just wish you'd find some place in the world where there's some comfort for you and whatever demon it is that pursues you from city to city can't find you."[132] Much of the correspondence is darkly yearning.

Some of the letters, however, are larks. Both pose. He writes from Tangiers: "lonely here, don't like whores anyway and no girls speak English ... have had everything in the books, smoked opium, ate hasheesh, don't want any of it, just musing in my room."[133] He sends menus from cheap restaurants. He begs for her company; she resists in the name of her own work (she had a good editorial job she needed to keep), but when he telegraphs that he will see her at the end of April, she sends back a one-line telegram that could be a description of the mindset of any member of the Beat Generation: "DOOR WIDE OPEN."[134]

The door was certainly wide open to the careers of both correspondents. Joyce's refrain is that she needed sustained time for her own writing. She already had a contract for a novel when she met Kerouac. What would turn out to be the first Beat novel written by and about a woman, *Come and Join the Dance*, would not be published until 1962, but Johnson's yearning to get on with the work comes through in many of her letters. As for Jack, his most famous book was already written and about to explode on the world. What he talked about in these letters was "a perfect play" with Allen Ginsberg. The play later became *Pull My Daisy*, also a film. It would be the product, as he told Joyce, of bits of *Visions of Cody* and *Desolation Angels*.[135] In a manic mood, he writes that "I'm going to write the funniest comedy in the history of American Theater."[136] Followers of the Beat movement would be interested in any of these letters, but what makes them most interesting is the dawning reality of what has happened with the publication of *On the Road*. "I got a review copy of *On the Road*, read it and think it's a great beautiful book," Joyce wrote in July 1957.[137] In August Jack cancelled his trip to Mexico, and by September 2 he returned from Florida, passed through that "wide open" door, and moved in with Joyce just in time for the "extraordinary review" by Gilbert Millstein in the *New York Times*. A heady time followed Millstein's declaration that the book was "the most beautifully executed, the clearest, the most important utterance yet made by [the Beat Generation]." It was, remembered Joyce Glassman Johnson, "all very thrilling – but frightening too."[138]

It had been quite a year. In Tangiers, Jack and Burroughs had been working on *Naked Lunch*. In San Francisco, the US Customs Office had confiscated 520 copies of Ginsberg's *Howl* for "obscenity." In New York, Norman Mailer published "The White Negro:

Superficial Reflections on the Hipster." With Millstein's review and word of mouth (through college students and through the city writing community), Kerouac's book shot to number seven on the best seller list. The pendulum turned. The popularity of *Road* elicited Truman Capote's famous snide comment, "That's not writing. That's typewriting." Johnson's response was to defend "Jack's true literary achievement – his breakthrough into spontaneous prose" by quoting Gertrude Stein on Picasso: "Anything truly new and innovative in art is initially considered ugly."[139] Johnson lists other cruel reviews, including Norman Podhoretz's remark that Kerouac wanted "to replace civilization by the street gang."[140] And Johnson, wise beyond her years then, already realized that Jack could not handle fame, much less notoriety. He drank too much and said "stupid things" on late-night television. "Fame was as foreign a country as Mexico, and I was his sole companion in its unknown territories," said Joyce.[141] By the next spring, she realized that their affair was over; she also recognized that Jack "never would learn how to be a public figure. He was still an awful failure as an egomaniac."[142] In one of his last letters, written in 1958, Jack tells Joyce that he has "lost all interest in literature."[143]

Of course he had not. *Dharma Bums* (1958); *The Subterraneans* (1958); *Doctor Sax* (1959); *Vanity of Duluoz* (1967), "a heartbreaking last effort as an author";[144] and *Visions of Cody*, published posthumously with Johnson's assistance, followed. To the end of his life, according to his brother-in-law Jim Sampas, even in the little house in Florida, the orderly arrangement of manuscripts and correspondence, at odds with the disorderly arrangements of his life, attests to his interest in the work itself. In the next years, he attempted to renew connections with Carolyn Cassady and with Joyce Johnson with no success. By the time he called Johnson, she was married. "Bring your little husband," he said.[145] That husband, John Johnson, subject of much of *Minor Characters,* would soon die in an accident, leaving her a young widow at 27. Johnson would later marry Peter Pinchbeck, who would be the father of the son who would one day write the next chapter. She grew into an editing job at *Dial,* where her boss was E.L. Doctorow and where she fostered the publication of Abbie Hoffman's work and other "publishing rebels who want to turn the prevailing order upside down."[146] The world turned its attention to fighting over the war in Vietnam and to the Civil Rights and Women's Movements.

A case could well be made that the rebel honesty of the Beat writers invited and modelled ways of fighting inertia and conformity. Johnson claims that they did, particularly that the women did. Looking back to 1957 in her introduction forty plus years later, she says,

> The Beats – now routinely castigated by doctrinaire feminists for their macho behavior and attitudes – ushered in sexual liberation, which would not only bring a new and permanent openness to American art and literature but transform life for everyone ... Ginsberg and Kerouac would give powerful, irresistible voices to these subversive longings; they'd release us from our weirdness, our isolation, tell us we were not alone.[147]

The role of the women in all of that varied. This chapter has only sampled the work they left behind, their views as witnesses, as hecklers, as encouragers, as enablers, and as writers in their own rights. It has not included Pommy Vega and Eileen Kaufman, for example, or others in the Knight anthology or the Grace and Johnson collection of interviews. It has not included Joan Haverty's *Nobody's Wife*. According to Haverty, *she* was the one who urged Kerouac to write *On the Road:* "And I wanted him to write it all down, or better yet, record it. No matter how faithful the reproduction."[148] She was not included in the discussion organized by Ann Charters at the time of the publication of Brenda Knight's book, but the "chicks" who were there, looking back forty years, answered a question that lies, perhaps, at the heart of this chapter. Did they consider themselves "victims"? Ann Charters, Carrolyn Cassady, Joyce Johnson, Hettie Jones, Eileen Kaufman, and Joanna McClure were of one voice: "no." Carolyn Cassady insisted that "I always felt I had a choice"; Hettie Jones said, "No – never: it wasn't until I found myself there among these people that I could make as much noise as I wanted, and no one gave a shit"; Eileen Kaufman said, "I never considered myself a victim. I considered myself quite fortunate to sit at a poet's feet that was a genius [sic]"; and Joyce Johnson said that the period was "the really formative experience of my life."[149]

From such big questions the six women turned to their memories of their own versions of "the road show," particularly of having shocked their parents. Joyce Johnson (she of the Victor Herbert musical lover mother) remembered that "There were terrible, terrible rifts between the women who got involved with the Beats and their parents."[150] But what of these women and *their* children? It happened that Cathy Cassady (she who had been a tiny child when Jack Kerouac moved in with the household and slept with her mother) said, "I would say that it was not a childhood that I would recommend to everybody, but it was definitely interesting."[151]

In fact, it was so interesting that Johnson's son, Daniel Pinchbeck, caused a stir with a *New York Times Magazine* article reporting on his visits with a number of the children of the Beat writers. When the article appeared, the kicker to the title was "Their parents lived for art and left them a bitter legacy." Pinchbeck introduces his pastiche of the experiences of others with his own memory of ransacking his mother's library for scraps and fragments of her past. His mother had Kerouac's words "mad to live, mad to love, mad to be saved, desirous of everything at the same moment" inscribed on his high-school yearbook. Pinchbeck ends the article with the good-natured John Allen Cassady, named for the giants of the movement, and the son of Diana Hansen and Cassady, who said, "They [the Beats] offered some kind of antidote to the repression of the Cold War period." These children showed an ability, perhaps fostered by their years with those "on the road," to dilute their anger at difficult childhoods with pride at the willingness to take risks and pave the way for changes in American culture that was their parents' legacy.

Joyce Johnson anticipated the remarks of the children in her son's story. She quotes Keith Jennison's wry remark that the Beat Generation "sold books, sold black turtleneck sweaters and bongos, berets, and dark glasses – sold a way of life that seemed like dangerous fun."[152] Indeed, it was dangerous fun – for the men on the road and the women who were sometimes on the road but mainly off the road caring for the children who would, forty years later, criticize them. But then, as Johnson pointed out, they had aspirations of their own, and "no one had taught us how to be women artists or writers." "Naturally, we fell in love with men who were rebels," she continues. "We fell very quickly, believing they would take us along on their journeys and adventures. We did not expect to be rebels by ourselves, and we did not count on loneliness."[153] For all the bravado of some of the accounts of these brave (perhaps foolhardy also) women, they do have an undercurrent of exactly that: loneliness. Each thought herself to be fighting the hegemony alone.

Whether they were writing poetry, fiction, or the all-important (for the purposes of this chapter and feminist studies generally) memoir, the women of the Beat Generation survived because of art. Di Prima's capitalized demand to fight those who would fight the IMAGINA-TION is a thread that runs through almost all the work. How they carried on, each in her own way, and then adapted to post-hipster-ism lives and writing careers might be answered by Brenda Frazer who mused to Nancy Grace: "Maybe there was an advantage to the fact that we [women of the Beat generation] didn't hang together all the time, the way the guys did, [the way they] would travel from coast-to-coast together in a car or something like that. Maybe we had some advantage – the isolation that all of us experienced as women. Maybe in some ways it [the isolation?] was formative."[154] Whether they were fearful for a child in the unknown territory of Mexico as was Bonnie Bremser; experiencing racial slurs from both black and white strangers as was Hettie Jones; or trying to run a satisfactory household in the midst of drugs, unemployment, and constant houseguests as was Carolyn Cassady, these women shared something profound. These remarkable and diverse women were in the centre of the revolution. But because of their own memories, tal-ents, outrage, and humour, they were able to *document* the opening and growth of a remarkable movement in American history. They did much more than go along for the ride.

6

Assassin in a Three-Piece Suit: *Slow Fire,* Minimalism, and the Eighties

PAUL ATTINELLO

The road once represented the vastness of space and all its result-ant possibilities in America, especially in the West. But things have, of course, changed – and changed a great deal: literatures of rebel-lion, freedom, and emptiness (of land, of values) have become more cluttered, just as the vast stretch of suburban pseudo-cities that make up greater San Francisco has become more crowded, more filled with cars; as the endless suburbs of Los Angeles and San Diego have joined into one vast, seemingly inescapable conurbation. In a world where open spaces have shrunk or vanished, the frontiersmen of those spaces and heroes of the road – machos, rebels and heroes, cowboys and gunslingers, free thinkers and motorcycle gangs – have found themselves intolerably crowded.

And, of course, when you crowd a macho man too much, what you usually get is some kind of fight: competition, hostility, violence. As traditionally depicted in American popular culture of the twen-tieth century, violence accompanied by this crowding of men has been linked to the Western and the road movie. As Shari Roberts has noted, "frontier symbolism is propelled by masculinity and a particular conception of American national identity that revolves around individualism and aggression." She adds that "as the Western condensed further into ... the road film these characteristics become concentrated and codified" in an "ideal of masculinity" linked to "underlying conceptualizations of American national identity."[1] While this concept of an individualist and aggressive frontier mascu-linity is clearly part of the Western and Western-looking road film, Michael Kimmel believes that it has its roots in a nineteenth-century "marketplace" masculinity related to wealth, power, and status, which is carried over into the twentieth century.[2] Taken together, Roberts's and Kimmel's views help to explain this individualist and aggressive masculinity of the 1980s that, fresh from the abyss of the Vietnam War, aligns itself with a harsh Darwinian economic environment. These political and economic changes, which transformed the late twentieth-century America into a land more ruthless and more unforgiving than it once was, were accompanied by a new feminization of culture that provided the basis for other possible conflicts.

For anyone who grew up from the 1950s onward, the 1980s mark a time when all this competition and hostility was suddenly on the increase – initially in an economic and political context, but ultimately across many aspects of Anglophone culture. Paradoxically, the experimental performing arts during the same period were opening out in a very different direction: new contemporary opera, performance art, minimalism, expanded electronic technologies, all tended to move beyond the "masculine" control-oriented obsessions of the 1950s and 1960s to focus on more "feminine" or androgynous aspects of culture (thus the work of Laurie Anderson, operas by Philip Glass and John Adams, performance works by Diamanda Galás and Meredith Monk and Pina Bausch, et al.). These experiments often created free space, not along physical roads, but in spaces of personal experience, memory, and imagination – perhaps pointing out that new frontiers could only be internal, as it has become harder to drive across the fenced-in lands.

However, one notable solo opera, *Slow Fire* (1985), written by two artists – Paul Dresher and Rinde Eckert – living in the distinctly gender-flexible cultures of San Francisco's Bay Area (as it happens, and as makes particular sense in this context, both heterosexual men), reveals, examines, and critiques a more intense view of cultural transformation: that "masculine" men, feeling left behind in that vast and multi-staged wash of change, might react with a testosterone-poisoned paranoia that would become increasingly dangerous. But the dominant musical idioms of the 1980s were not expressive of tension and conflict – in fact, they suggested the reverse: all of which opportunities and limitations coalesced into an opera that shimmers with the sensually repetitive tonal pleasures typical of the time, but that gradually reveals its own brutal underside. That underside could be seen as a forecast of a then-nascent Americas: Bush's America of terrorism, economic banditry, war, and insanely polarized political oppositions; but, of course, no one anticipated any of that.

INTRODUCTION TO THE OPERA

Paul Dresher's monodrama *Slow Fire*, composed on texts by virtuoso performance artist Rinde Eckert, is one of the more famous of their collaborative opera/performance works. Influenced by their previous work with radically imaginative Bay Area theatre director George Coates, the piece plays with numerous techniques that appear in other works by Dresher and Eckert: puns and wordplay over slightly changing repetitions; live electronics that transform musical and verbal phrases extracted from the stage performance; and a range of pop- and world-influenced minimalist tropes.

Aside from the evident influences and trends represented in the work, it is an arresting piece of theatre – not only because of its brilliant musical, verbal, visual, and performative moments but also because of its sheer intensity. That intensity is somewhat different from the many comparable works from the eighties; rather than representing the emergence of half-erased identities or excluded traditions, it gradually reveals a return of the (unexpected and deadly) repressed – the testosterone-poisoned male in an era that ignores him at its peril, a relic from a time of guns, frontiers, marketplace mentalities, and repressed feelings. In the sense of this critique of a society over-ridden with violence, it is also reminiscent of a road film much closer in time than the Westerns and road films set in the nineteenth century: *Easy Rider* (1969), which shows the violence of "fascistic and bigoted"[3] Americans in the grotesque shootings of Wyatt/Captain America and Billy. This haunting image of aggressive rednecks in a truck gunning down mildly rebellious riders on bikes encapsulates a pervasive feeling of despair among the youth that all of the innocence of the road had been sacrificed by the brutality of the American military-industrial war machine in the late sixties and continuing through the escalation of the Vietnam War in the seventies. This period marked a low point in American personal and national esteem.

Part of the mechanism for Dresher's depiction of aggressive and violent masculinity is the complex, witty text, which gives a socially laconic and paranoid character an extraordinarily wide-ranging and flexible poetry of expression – all of which, however, seems to be locked inside a secret dream world of memory and imagination. The real events – both past (remembered) and present – are few and simple; but the verbal pyrotechnics that surround the characters like rivers, and the vivid and energetic music that conveys them, take us into the head of a man whom we would normally find entirely obscure, incomprehensible – and ultimately monstrous. Our ability to penetrate his memory and imagination differs from many Westerns and road films where it is the action and accounts outside the mind that capture our attention, so this internal narrative and the accompanying postmodern, operatic musical score add a unique dimension to this treatment of the road.

MUSIC IN THE EIGHTIES

It may be useful to go through some of the basic trends of music in the 1980s, and how they fit into the broad spectrum of ideas and experiences associated with the shift from modernism to postmodernism and with this treatment of masculinity on the road. First of all, musical postmodernism is generally regarded as appearing later than postmodernism in literature and the other arts – this is, incidentally, typical of the history of Western music, where major cultural shifts (the Renaissance, Baroque, Romantic, etc.) appear in musical rhetoric some years after they appear in other artistic media. Thus, the crucial breaks in twentieth-century music appear around 1912–13, 1945–50, and 1968. Although there is not a consistent agreement on how to label these, my own approach is to identify the phases approximately starting at each of these breaks as modernism (or early modernism), "high" modernism (a more developed and refined style, somewhat like the "High Renaissance"), and postmodernism.

The postmodern break in 1968 was associated with many stylistic changes – increased attention to tonality, popular music styles, women's identities, world music, and a definite shift away from the thorny, atonal complexities of musical high modernism. This led to extensive experiment and innovation in the 1970s, but its emergence into fame and influence was brought into focus in the 1980s, when minimalism, new popular opera, performance art, and cross-influences between genres became accepted as valid and even fashionable, and women composers went from peripheral and occasional appearances in music history to positions of real strength. This was the era in which Meredith Monk, Laurie Anderson, Diamanda Galás, and many others created a firmly established place for women composers, often in what must be called the avant-garde (partly because "classical" music power structures were still slow to encourage women as composers).

This is not a new narrative, as the general story of increased visibil-ity and power for women throughout the 1970s and 1980s is com-monplace. But we do not often enough notice the counterbalancing story – that, although some men accepted more ambiguous gender/power positions during that time, others responded with confusion and resentment. The metropolitan arts communities of New York, London, San Francisco, and other cities thought they could ignore this resentment, as it seemed to be someone else's problem, but that, of course, turned into a cultural and political mistake. This growing resentment finds an important place in the depiction of the mascu-linity of the postmodern road in *Slow Fire*.

DRESHER AND ECKERT

As *Slow Fire* was created at the centre of a productive period of col-laboration for the two artists, the surrounding context and related works have a bearing on this postmodern music of the road. This is also especially interesting because the work represents a time of lively experimentation in minimalism, performance art, and new technologies across the urban West Coast, centred on the Bay Area, the California Institute of the Arts in southern California, and the Cornish School in Seattle. Recent books documenting these styles have tended to ignore California (with the significant exception of John Adams), not least because the withdrawal of government arts funding in the mid-1980s, combined with a paucity of the kind of funding from wealthy individuals and private organizations that maintained New York arts communities, demolished many arts careers and organizations in the Bay Area. All this suggests that the opera's road narrative and its artistic/cultural/political contexts are even more closely related than one might expect.

Dresher, born in Los Angeles in 1951, played guitar and wrote songs when young; he interrupted a degree at Berkeley to play with Steve Reich's ensemble and engage in studio work, including (in a way that parallels the early experiences of many of the minimal-ists) training in Indian, African, and Balinese music. He studied with Terry Riley, and, after graduating from Berkeley with Roger Reynolds, Pauline Oliveros, and Robert Erickson at UC San Diego, he travelled through India and Indonesia in 1979–80, taping environ-mental sounds for tape works and experiencing the musical cultures. His studies at Berkeley with Janice Giteck introduced him to her husband, operatic tenor John Duykers (who has been, like Eckert, the centre of several of Dresher's stage works, in addition to famously creating the role of Mao for Adams' *Nixon in China*), which led him to work with George Coates in San Francisco.[4] Dresher's career thus developed among a rich group of innovative artists, and his ability to bring people together for a variety of projects engendered a wide range of works from 1980 onward.

Eckert grew up in the Midwest, the son of two opera singers; he studied voice and theatre at Iowa and Yale. He began creating works with The New Performance Group in Seattle, which led him to George Coates's Performance Works in San Francisco and his meeting with Dresher, which resulted in ten years of collaboration. Connections with dance companies allowed him to expand from performing and writing libretti to composing his own music theatre works; in the two decades since, he has developed a wide-ranging career in performing, composing, writing, directing, and teaching a variety of workshops. Eckert now lives in New York, and his international career continues to engage all of these activities in various combinations.

Dresher and Eckert created a number of stage and concert works beginning in the early 1980s, often in conjunction with other artists, notably Duykers, Coates, and choreographer Margaret Jenkins. Coates was always enthusiastic about playful and illusory stage transformations; Eckert is especially interested in doing something similar with everyday objects, and the development of these staging ideas are scattered throughout *Slow Fire* (for instance, the three boards that fall to the ground to reveal the performers holding them; the Road whose median strips become squares that can be picked up, where the protagonist can climb with heroic, frontier-conquering steps; and most strikingly the energetic kneeling choreography with two lit work lights).[5]

Dresher and Eckert continued to collaborate on performances after the 1980s; especially notable was Steve Mackey's opera *Ravenshead* (1998), which had a text by Eckert and was performed by Dresher and his ensemble. Eckert's text uses techniques comparable to those of his works with Dresher, and the topic is similarly about a man in crisis; Mackey's music uses some similar materials, though very different techniques from those in Dresher's works, including more sounds from popular music. The whole opera is essentially about a world-spanning sailing race, indeed about being, as it were, "A

Man" – evidently as Eckert the actor and writer is particularly good at such situations. Other modern, postmodern, and minimalist/postminimalist works could be related to the work of Dresher and Eckert, and some focus specifically on the roads of the Midwest and West as well as on the problems of masculinity: for example, Robert Ashley's *Perfect Lives* (1979–80) and *Improvement* (1985), and even such antecedents as Harry Partch's *Barstow* (1941).

SLOW FIRE

Dresher and Eckert's solo opera *Slow Fire* seems at first energetic and fairly humorous, a recognizably enjoyable example of mid-1980s minimalist performance art showcasing the digital sampling and live electronics that were new and exciting at that time. However, as we are introduced to the inside of the protagonist's mind, we gradually realize that frightening things are living there – things that will explode into the outside world in the opera's final moments. These involve images of driving and death, suicide at the side of the Road, the urge to own and control the frontier, and thereby the world – all intricately combined with reflections on fathers and sons, guns and possessions, advertisements and technology, business and murder, paranoia and civilization, ultimately suggesting that contemporary American men are already poisoned by testosterone and its urgings. All of these are strong reminders of the Western/road films that lie behind this construction of masculinity, the frontier, possession, and mobility.

In the course of this dazzlingly flexible work of theatre, juggling as it does verbal and visual puns and surreal metaphors, we enter the mind of a modern barbarian – a rigid, unrelenting paranoiac whose endlessly cycling memories are haunted by his father's rifle suicide in a truck on the road in California, and who has solved the nightmare of that first gunshot by repeating it – he has become a hired assassin in a suit and wrap-around shades. In that context, he suggests the polished savagery of the 1980s business warrior, linking the reality of violence and death to metaphors of right-wing brutality and the rise of ruthless capitalism.

The opera is a monodrama, performed through the late 1980s and early 1990s by a trio that included the author as vocal soloist, the composer on keyboards and electronics, and percussionist Gene Reffkin playing a variety of instruments and objects. All productions were directed by Richard White. Commissioned by the New Music America festival when it was held in Los Angeles in 1985, its first performance was of a partial work, though it met with great success; an expansion to two singers was temporary, leading back to a shortening and reduction of forces, and a twentieth anniversary performance of this final version was successful in 2007.

MATERIALS, VERSIONS, PROBLEMS

Materials available for analysis include the commercial CD and the commercial video; I will also compare some of the unpublished materials given to me by the composer.[6]

The order of the ten scenes in this opera underwent some changes over the years following the first productions, as can be seen in the commercial video and in an unpublished 1992 performance; the commercial CD established yet another order of the opera's sections. Comparison of the changes, all of which appear to be made to clarify the central points for different media and stages of development, helps to illuminate the intended thrust of the work. The contrast of this sharply disturbing work with the gentler content of other minimalist operas of the 1980s also suggests some of the later darkening that overtook the theatre of post-minimalism, including Adams's later operas or the work of Louis Andriessen and his followers, including David Lang's concert work *Cheating, Lying, Stealing* (1993).

A more substantial set of changes was made for the "two-act version," which the creators finally decided did not work as well. This version, about an hour and twenty-five minutes in length, added a second act with a woman singer who functions as Bob's mother and foil. Much of the second act focuses on her, with both characters brought together for the final scene. Although this version allows more room to expand on the story, the focused drive of the one-act version seemed somewhat dissipated. Of course, what is particularly interesting about this version is the possibility of altering my interpretation: if this is a man and a woman, is it really an opera about the plight of men in crisis? But this expanded two-act version does not really bring in a new point of view for the female character – although she sings a great deal, she functions so exclusively as a reflection of Bob that the result is only a dilution of the original.

Like the first opera, the second and third operas in "The American Trilogy," which starts with *Slow Fire* – *Power Failure* and *Pioneer* –

emphasize male crises in culture, and the titles themselves suggest the centrality of the road and the frontier in this crisis.

Significant dates in the history of *Slow Fire* include:

1985 – first incomplete solo version, created for the New Music America festival, performed at the Mark Taper Forum in Los Angeles.

1986 – commercial videotape of incomplete version by Target Video.

1986, October – two-act/two-voice version, performed in Philadelphia at the American Music Theater Festival.

1986, November – final performances of two-act/two-voice version in La Jolla and Seattle.

Following these performances Dresher and Eckert decide that this version doesn't work, whereupon they consider changes for a year; they then go back to a format with one vocalist playing Bob and his father, and expand their relationship.

1988, March – two more months of rehearsal and performance result in final version.

1989, May – *Power Failure*, the second opera in "The American Trilogy," premieres in Philadelphia.

1990, May – *Pioneer*, the second opera in "The American Trilogy," premieres at the Spoleto Festival.

2005–07 – twentieth anniversary revival tour of *Slow Fire*.

THE MAP

I will briefly go through the scenes in the order followed in the stage versions, although the most widely available version is unquestionably the CD. As is made clear in Table 1 at the end of this chapter, two tracks of the CD are presented in a different order from any other version – perhaps because in the absence of a dramatic staging, and given the normal fragmentation of a stage work reduced to CD tracks, a listener may be more engaged by "Sleeping with the Light On" than by the more complicated, expository "Magazine Dream." The fact that the scenes are also defined as CD tracks – or nearly so, in most cases – is yet another pointer to the manifold nature of the work, which skims across the borders of avant-garde, classical, and popular cultures.

When teaching the opera, I combine explaining it through its own narrative, pointing up its technical innovations, and mentioning works and trends that refract various elements – thus tying the opera to its context, predecessors, and followers. I offer here a brief version of this to highlight the impact of the road on this piece – justified not only by the work's position during a time rich in innovation but also because there is still insufficient written history of postmodern opera and theatre.

1. *Magazine Dream*

"Magazine Dream," the opera's densely energetic exposition, opens with a composite of flickering percussive, plucked, and brass sounds that parallel a cloud of phonemes resembling concrete or surrealist poetry, or even the Language poets who became important in Northern California during the 1970s.

The first stage image is disturbingly blank – a white facade, a clock ticking; after some moments of tension, this splits into three panels that fall forward, revealing three prone performers. The two musicians retreat to their instruments to play strong, dark chords that introduce us to Bob's world: then there is a flickering brightness as Bob looks up, energetic as a child, spinning on his back, bare feet in the air. A dark green jumpsuit emphasizes his size and sensual energy (Eckert is built like a bouncer, which always gives his stage movements an extra impact) and suggests the military images that float across the background of the opera. Shifting spotlights pick out the angles of his arms, linking the stage action to visual art in a way typical of much performance art and experimental theatre. The sounds combine into a complex multi-tracked mixture of live and prerecorded vocal samples, which are transformed into sirens that recall the dangers of the outside world.

As for the content – which proceeds in a complex, overlapping manner under all this spectacle, so that the audience responds to it almost subliminally – Bob combines a mechanical world of cars, technology, and guns, a shimmering dream landscape of cowboy hats and land and the Road, plus an ambiguous shadow from a dark past ("just before he died, his Dad said"). Bob is young and eager in his dream, wonderfully played by Eckert alternately looking up as a boy, then looking down as his Dad; adroit timbral and registral shifts articulate the difference between a light, high-overtone boy's voice and a darker, gruffer tone for his father. These shifts are definite enough that both Eckert and Dresher consider this a two-character opera, even though it is performed by one person (the version that adds a female singer is thus the "three-character version"). Of course, Bob and his father are also very different emotionally – we can already see the barely controlled despair that characterizes Dad ("you can't fall asleep one second, or you lose"), which reminds us of a tougher, more taciturn Willy Loman.

"What state are we in now, Dad?" Bob and his father seem to be driving west through Nebraska, Wyoming, Nevada – and there is a sharp break and a pause as we reach California, where the world ends. But we are not finished ("keep driving, keep driving"): this is a road that cannot end – it must continue if it is to support the dreams of the desperate man, the cowboy, the man on the Road, anyone who wants to be free of civilization and its responsibilities. A fluidly melismatic arioso pulls us into the ecstatic, hallucinatory world of the Road, and it is broken up by grand chords of the kind that suggest an assertively male film score, as in Westerns and road movies. The Road is also invoked through spotlights overhead that flicker on and off as disturbingly hypnotic warnings, suggesting open freeways and traffic lights.

"Close your eyes: the car will take you where you're going." The white rectangles on a stage ramp that seem to be painted lane separators are picked up and revealed as white cards that can be shuffled and collected, and they become a new and disturbing group of states to pass through. We fall into a tone that is more dreamlike, more malevolent: "This state is Vietnam – this state is Cambodia – real estate, real estate! ... Don't be fooled by the decoys, boy: get yourself some land – anybody's land." and the music evaporates. This is the dream of the conquerable frontier, which becomes a commodity for those who move Westward in America and extend that mobility into Vietnam and Cambodia, viewing that transgression as an American right.

In the silence evoked by this dream, the telephone rings: Bob, awake, is suddenly adult and businesslike, answering a terse business proposal: his next job is scheduled for Monday at 10:00.

2. *Sleeping with the Light On*

"Sleeping with the Light On" walks us through Bob's home, life, and interests, all splashed with a loony, amusing paranoia (at least, at this point it is amusing). This is Bob's conscious mind, as he comes

home on a Friday evening – we'll return to nearly this level of consciousness when he reads "The Sunday Paper," and at the end of the
opera (and his weekend) with "Eyes Open," where he will actually
prepare to face the world – on, of course, his own terms.

"Sleeping" is an energetic tour de force of aggressive guitar licks
and sampled fragments, manic but focused; it mixes Bob's obsessive attachment to his belongings with control issues, his father, and
fragments of their "last trip." He reads magazines – *Popular Mech-
anics*, *National Geographic*, and *Soldier of Fortune* – a mixture of
technology, the road, and war; in the last, he sees an article on "slow
fire" – converting a submachine gun to 800 rounds per minute. The
humour and illusion of the staging is at its best here, for he opens a
briefcase on stage, and pulls out a bathrobe that he ties around him,
sunglasses that he puts on, a combat/work vest over the whole, and
two work lights, both astonishingly already switched on, which he
will wave in a loony pseudo-choreography while dancing about on
his knees. At the same time a shimmering network of live voice samples will give Bob all the schizoid dreaming energy he needs.

But Bob interrupts himself with an explosion of minor paranoia:
"Did I lock the car?" He lists the things that are in his car, remembering what they cost in a rising panic of loss and obsessive control
issues; he finally goes out to check, but it is of course locked, and he
returns relieved though still energetic.

The music for this scene overlaps circling guitar licks, which are
sampled (along with fragments of percussion and vocal lines) to
become the background for ecstatic live guitar solos that rise into
an energetic, prismatic delirium. (This scene is always a particular
favourite with my students, who are enchanted at the possibilities of
combining rock guitar and drums, electronics, and intense theatric-
ality.) As the music falls away at the end of the scene, Bob points out
that he "might as well be dreaming": he turns out the work lights,
removes the vest, sunglasses, robe, and falls to the floor as everything fades into silence.

3. Swimming

At the end of this tour de force, the lights dim to an underwater blue,
and Bob relaxes over synthesized gongs. Making swimming movements across the floor, he pulls a sheet over himself and drifts into
sleep on the Friday night of the opera's timeline. The shimmering

music is matched by a hallucinatory wash of live, then recorded, concrete poetry: Eckert repeats a number of proverbs, then breaks them in half, scrambling subjects and predicates to form a cloud of stern but nonsensical warnings. The same text appeared in a concert work by the creators from the early 1980s; its reappearance here transforms an earlier text experiment into an exploration of the deep roots of Bob's dreams, and also his anxiety over the dangers and traps of the world.

4. Duck Blind

"Duck Blind" introduces Bob's father through a memory Bob recalls on Saturday morning. Although Eckert performs as both Bob and as Dad, always with a sense of a remembering or translating his father's words, both Dresher and Eckert speak of the solo opera as performed by Eckert as the "two-character" version, meaning Bob and Dad. (They also tend to talk about the rejected version performed by two singers as the "three-character" version, which emphasizes the extent to which Dad is perceived as present in the opera.) As Bob builds in his workroom, he remembers Dad teaching him – explicitly about tools, but implicitly about courage and wariness in an uncertain world – and about achieving certainty with a gun, which will end up becoming a central motif.

Bob was taught to use his hands, and to do it right – "nail it home, boy" – and instructed on how to survive in a threatening world – "if you don't weigh 'em down they'll blow away like a house of cards." The grand, long vocal lines of Bob's arioso have the tonal nobility that Americans hear as a reference to their own confident history – to music by Copland and Barber, which recalls the yearning grandeur of the distant horizons of the Midwestern plains. But this memory is dangerous, because ducks, of course, get shot: and that leads Bob's memory into places where he doesn't want to go – "one clean hit – blam!" – and there is a blackout that ends the first half of the opera.

5. Dad's Letter

Act Two starts in a delicate world of circling gamelan-like sounds, interrupted by guitar glissandi that recall a soft, hallucinatory acid rock out of the late 1960s and 1970s – that time when the Road, freedom, sensuality, the West, and everything associated with them were tied to new hopes and pleasures; a time irreparably poisoned and destroyed by the mid-1980s.

Dad's letter is presented in a dream memory, with no present frame. Because of its loose moorings, the letter might be real – or it might be distorted by imagination: his father's assertions become more anxious, more frantic, more paranoid. There is an eerie sense that Dad's world is falling to pieces as his desperate attempts to connect with his son, and to protect both of them, disintegrate into the frightened delusions of a terrified failure.

6. Sunday Paper

Then Bob wakes, optimistic energy pulling him out of the nightmares of the past into an entertaining Sunday morning. There is a noise at the door, a bang. Bob has his predictably paranoid response, invoking a number of possibilities: it could be a Jehovah's Witness, it could be a big man, an angry woman with a Smith and Wesson, or the wrong address.[7] But it is just the Sunday paper – "no hard men, no angry women." Cheerful and confident at the pleasure of reading the paper, he runs through the sections – News in Brief, Living, the Funny Pages – seeing familiar trivia as an antidote to existential dread.

The lively guitar licks and percussion backbeats give a background to a Bob's cheerful enjoyment; but unexpected details drag him in a direction he doesn't want to go – guns, right-wing groups. Elements of masculine violence float past – "boys will be boys," "*Johnny Got his Gun* ... my kind of movie." He is brought up short as he reads a headline, "Eyewitness to Roadside Killing," – and he pulls away to "turn to the living, the section on Living." The fragmentation and silences that end this scene climax in his reading a final, disturbing passage: "First Aid for the Nuclear Family – Rule no. 1: Never expose your face."

The allusion to the roadside killing and the necessity to hide one's face suggests that the road itself, once a beacon of hope for the promise of new beginnings and redolent life, in fact has become the scene of killing, death, and the abandonment of hope. Bob's mental confusion, paranoia, and likely culpability in the murder go hand in hand with this bleak view of a destructive road.

7. *Match Stick Empire*

Shimmering, delicate music returns us to a quieter, more introverted Bob, sunk in reverie; but we have already seen that reverie is as dangerous for him as memory. On Sunday afternoon, Bob "opens" two large stage panels which thereby become a book: it is a scrapbook of photos of him and his dad, memories of happy times. We begin with a sense of comfort, of a world where safety reigns and all of his father's promises seem true and dependable; Bob brings himself into focus by practising self-defence exercises.

But sad melodies shimmer over the irregular circling of instrumental lines – we wander through an endless round of memories, reflections of love and security that went terribly wrong. Bob builds a "dream house" with the panels as his father reassures him about the future: there will be a house, a place Dad will build, a place of safety for both of them. Dad wants to build a matchstick city, an empire that emphasizes its own fantastic impossibility, though he remains filled with dreams – "we're the builders now, we're the pioneers." This is an Eden and a dream city of the West that never came to pass – Eckert's face flickers through Dad's expressions of optimism and the adult Bob's feelings of loss. These emotions are, of course, that are closely tied to the Road, where the next thing over the horizon is exactly what you want – until you get there, and there is only more road stretching out before you.

8. *Riding Shotgun*

As Dad's dream disintegrates, we enter into a memory etched in blood. As he becomes increasingly disoriented, we are torn by recorded fragments of broken glass, guitar wails, mercilessly repetitive percussion, and stories of tornadoes and other disasters. It seems to be Sunday night, and Bob "remembers what his Dad said." Dad's moments of hope and despair threaten to pull his son down with him. He seems to think that the way to freedom is to get back into the truck and onto the Road; but of course we know that the Road is not a source of stability, it's just a way to keep running.

As fragments of Dad's voice are taken away into looping, overlapping samples, Bob is left watching his own mind, his memories, and his losses. Dad tells Bob to get out the map, an act that promises direction on the road; and as Bob pulls out the white panels that are now the roadmap, he lays them down and they become the road itself – and in fact that particular stretch of road where his father died. "Late night, due west; Bob is riding shotgun ... Dad is on his last cigarette" ... the car runs out of gas, Dad sees ducks everywhere; falling into hallucination and terror, he shoots himself after calling out a last command: "get yourself some land."

Dad's suicide ties up all Bob's memories and hopes into a deadly knot of ducks, death, Dad, guns, maps, a truck, the Road – and glues them into a nightmare that will haunt the rest of his life. As we hear the final gunshot, Bob passes out.

9. Interlude: Without a Word

Decompression follows this revelation of the central tragedy of Bob's life, filled with wordless, florid melismas. This scene is both inside and outside the larger dramatic frame of the entire opera, as it could be Bob's sleeping relaxation after the dream; or it could be a sense of grief that is beyond words – sorrow that can't be put into words, especially by men. However, it could also be beyond time and place, a reflection of our reaction to the tragedy, where words don't make sense any more. If it is the latter, it resembles the famous orchestral interlude before the final scene of Berg's *Wozzeck*, where a purely musical invocation of grief mirrors our own response to the tragedy we are watching.

In a transition to the final scene, Bob finally removes his jumpsuit, revealing the white shirt and underwear from which he will rebuild himself. A second phone call, an echo of the first, drags Bob out of silence into the world of things that he needs to do.

10. Eyes Open

The weekend is over: it is Monday morning, and Bob prepares to face the world, completing a large frame of recapitulation from scene 1. Bob glances through his possessions, including his expensive watch, and brushes his teeth, giving himself disciplined instructions on doing it correctly – almost as though he is still a child, following rules and trying to keep up with the world, trying to be good enough for ... something. Bob's preparations are military in their discipline: he eats, rapidly puts himself together, plans for traffic, and negotiates bits of home technology and instant food. However, something is wrong about these preparations – he dresses for work, but his clothes, beginning with a tie, are made of camouflage fabric.

Driving to work, he seems perfectly normal, a businessman negotiating a California freeway: "time for coffee," "55 all the way" – there is a shadow of the memory of his father driving the truck. He responds coldly to a flash of the memory of his father's suicide: "real heroes die of old age." The phrase "got the business end where I want it," which his father said of the rifle he used to kill himself, recurs as one of a series of disturbing echoes.

In the last minute of the entire opera, there is a sudden increase in the speed of Bob's actions: this is the punch line for the entire opera, revealed rapidly enough to raise the tension up to the final, functionally "frozen," soaring chords, creating a surgically precise shock for the audience that doesn't let up even after the piece has ended. Because Bob is actually going into an office building, shooting someone at his 10:00 deadline, and walking out in the doubtlessly resulting though unmentioned confusion: he is a professional assassin, and sirens and a tangle of allusively garbled sentences accompany the malevolently soaring final vocal lines.

Bob's life is deeply entwined with Dad's Westward trajectory that turned to suicide and death. What Bob has learned from that death is not that he should abandon the kind of distorted and perverted masculinity that gave rise to it, but that he should use that masculinity as a weapon against others instead of turning it on himself. By extension, this is the lesson of the movement into that Asia in which the wasted opportunity of the settlement of the American West has now been turned as a smoking gun into Vietnam and Cambodia.

CALIFORNIA AND THE ROAD

It is fascinating, if disturbing, to compare this opera with other California minimalism. Compared to the aggressive abstraction of New York process music, California has frequently offered a sweeter, gentler tone, as in the works of John Adams or the students who followed Harold Budd at the California Institute of the Arts. But, as both the state's inhabitants and its critics have pointed out from time to·time, success in California can be twisted by the darkness that lies beneath it.

Bob's car, his belongings, his memories – at first they seem pleasantly normal, even common. But they are connected with the dark side of the Road, especially its end – the realization that when one reaches the Pacific one can go no further in the United States, and one is reduced to fighting over what one already has, what one already is, or turning that weaponry against others on another continent. And so, a world hedged around with guns, paranoia, war, and death: gangs and riots in Watts and Oakland, and the transcendental death by earthquake that seems to be the only imaginable way of getting off the end of that road. As we are led from Bob's road trip with his father to the broad canvas of American political and military imperialism, the opera takes us to a place of violence and death. Which is, perhaps, the ultimate Road Trip.

THE ENDING
(ENCORE)

After circling around so many memories, so many dreams – so many nightmares – Bob has finally revealed his real task, his true nature. We are horrified, of course, because it is unexpected, although we have had clues scattered throughout the obsessive chaos of his mental journey. And in the last few lines, he repeats to himself with military precision the plan for his actions: but the words splinter into other words, and Eckert uses verbal transformations to recall all the disturbing resonances of Bob's mind, and of the culture that helped to create it:

> *Through the glass double doors, in and out in no time: no suspects, still clean.*

The opera brings up the abject terror of the 1980s, which so many of us who were Reagan's children or Thatcher's children can hardly articulate, even now: three-piece suits, dark ties, mirrored sunglasses, eyes like slits. The homeless, AIDS, poverty, crack houses, terrorism, arms deals, conspiracies: mercy doesn't pay, those who can't survive deserve to fall, and, as Laurie Anderson reminds us, "there is no parachute."[8] The beautifully machined, civilized despotism of the boardroom, and the transformation of those of us who could not become predators into prey.

> *Through the vast troubled wars, in and out in no time. No suspects, still clean.*

Police sirens, guns, and slow fire: we realize in these fearful repetitions that he is, indeed, a hired assassin. Not metaphorically, but actually: he drives to a building, goes through the glass double doors, and fires a real and deadly shot.

Through the vast troubled wars, in and out in no time. No suspects, still free.

This powerfully built man, this confident businessman: but also this traumatized child, this psychotic killer. Trapped in a cage of memory, endlessly revolving around that shot, the one that killed his father: and every carefully placed bullet that makes his living conceals a desperate wish to shoot the lock off the door of his own life. But it can't be done, because that lock is the only thing that keeps him from imploding in catatonic despair.

Still free. Still free. Still free.

Slow Fire: Table 1
Dresher, *Slow Fire* - version/scene structure

1992 CD track titles	1986 Video Order	1986 Video Start	1986 Video Length	1988 (Final) Script other section titles	1988 Script Order	1992 CD Order	1992 CD Length	1992 Video Order	1992 Video Start	1992 Video Length	Average Lengths	
The Magazine Dream	1	0:30	14:15	Magazine Dream	I - 1	4	11:04	1	0:15	15:15	16:00	
Phone Call I	2	14:45	1:15		I - 1a	–	–	2	15:30	1:00		
Sleeping with the Light On	3	16:00	9:20		I - 2	1	06:07	3	16:30	10:00	10:00	
Swimming	4	25:20	6:10	[continuation]	I - 2a	5	06:09	4	26:30	5:30	6:00	
Duck Blind	–	-			I - 3	2	06:38	5	32:00	8:30	9:00	40:00
Dad's Letter	–	-			II - 1	3	04:37	6	40:30	5:00	5:00	
The Sunday Paper	–			Sunday Papers	II - 2	6	04:15	7	45:30	7:00	7:00	
Match Stick Empire	–			Postcards	II - 3	7	05:12	8	52:30	7:45	8:00	
Riding Shotgun	–			[continuation]	II - 3a	8	05:17	9	60:15	6:45	6:00	
				Suicide	II - 4							
Without a Word	–	-		Wordless Aria of Pain / Without a Word	II - 5	9	02:47	10	67:00	2:20	3:00	
Phone Call II	–	-				–		11	69:20	0:20		
Eyes Open [ends]	5	31:30 / 38:10	6:40 / 37:40	*Act II divided variously*	II - 6	10 / 4 & 5 out of order	05:00	12	69:40 / 75:20	5:40 / 75:05	6:00	35:00 / 75:00

Slow Fire: Table 2
Dresher, Slow Fire - dramatic/temporal/psychological structures

1992 version (CD titles)			"Real" time	Average Lengths	
The Magazine Dream	Present Frame	Memory/reverie: nonlinear memory, as boy remembering Dad	Real world; introduction to Bob's thoughts	(Friday afternoon)	16:00	
Phone Call I	Present	Reality/external contact	Reality Frame	(Friday afternoon)	
Sleeping with the Light On	Present	Coming home; conscousness; paranoia/obsession/guns	Gateway to memory/dream	(Friday evening)	10:00
Swimming	Present Frame	Fantasy/dream	Sinking from conscousness	(Friday night)	6:00
Duck Blind	Present Frame	Memory: father/son, masculinity; tools, courage, wariness, guns	Past experience that organizes Bob's present	Saturday morning	9:00	40:00
Dad's Letter		Memory/fantasy (no present or frame)	The past made more real	Saturday night	5:00
The Sunday Paper	Present	Reading newspapers: paranoia, violence, masculinity, danger	Present consciousness with symptoms	Sunday morning	7:00
Match Stick Empire	Present Frame	Memory: men as builders, frontiersmen	The past is justified as valid/sane	(Sunday afternoon)	8:00
Riding Shotgun		Memory: Dad's final monologue & suicide (no present or frame)	Deepest memory & dramatic climax; roots of trauma	(Sunday evening)	6:00
Without a Word		Interlude: sleep, silence, retreat	Deep unconsciousness; trauma/ memory contained/silenced	(Sunday night)	3:00
Phone Call II	Present	Reality/external contact	Reality Frame	Monday morning	
Eyes Open	Present	Preparation to leave house (external world) & for assassination	Real (brutal) world; implicit response to inner world	Monday morning	6:00	35:00
TOTAL					75:00

7

Complicating *The Simple Life*: Reality Television and the Road

STACILEE FORD

Let's take two girls, both filthy rich, from the bright lights into the sticks.
From velvet ropes, to cattle pulls;
Let's take away their limousines, their credit cards and shopping sprees.
Well, they're both spoiled rotten, will they cry when they hit bottom?
Heaven knows if they'll survive this simple road trip kinda life.

Theme from *The Simple Life*

Media coverage of the lives and exploits of Paris Hilton and Nicole Richie, co-stars of the reality television series *The Simple Life*, bears witness to an existence that is anything but simple. Both women belong to a cohort of privileged celebrity progeny who sport the latest fashions and travel to a range of exotic locales, partying with abandon. Yet they also cope with media exposés of their relationships, addictions and eating disorders, arrest records and jail sentences, as well as their red-carpet couture and personal triumphs. (As of this writing, Richie's life seems "simpler" than Hilton's.) Although there is some academic work concerning the series, most critics and cultural-studies scholars dismiss it altogether or (in keeping with the theme of this book) dub it little more than a roadside stand perched along the highway to the decline of Western, particularly American, civilization. Yet *The Simple Life* is not so simply dismissed. Undeniably banal, the show nonetheless merits consideration here for its connection to the early history of television as well as to present anxieties and preoccupations in the US and beyond.

Deftly mixing comedic and girl-power metaphors with pranks and snide comments, the show began in 2003 with Hilton and Richie temporarily relinquishing their Hollywood lifestyles and trust funds to live like ordinary folk. A twenty-first-century reality TV reprisal of the twentieth-century situation comedy *Green Acres* (1965–71), *The Simple Life* was, originally, a Fox Studios production that straddled first-generation reality television series such as MTV's *The Real World* and *Road Rules*, and the still popular CBS high-adventure game show *Survivor*. More recent spawn such as *Keeping Up with the Kardashians* (and various spinoffs), *Jersey Shore*, and the seemingly endless iterations of the *Real Housewives* series, take many of their cues from *The Simple Life*. Hilton and Richie captured viewer interest by living and working with/for "average Americans" in various states across the US. The duo performed "fish out of water" antics simply by being their celebrity selves deigning to act with "real people" in ordinary situations.

The two heiresses (Hilton is linked to her family's hotel dynasty, and Richie is the daughter of singer/producer Lionel Richie) go from town to town throughout the United States, relying on the kindness of strangers while trying to earn enough money to pay for their expenses as they move along the road. Although the entire series is, arguably, a journey of sorts, during the 2004 season, the road metaphor was invoked with even more intensity in *The Simple Life 2: Road Trip*. Driving a pink pick-up truck pulling a silver Airstream trailer (full of designer clothes, shoes, accessories, and cosmetics) from Palm Beach, Florida, to Los Angeles, California, the two-pop culture princesses embarked on a series of encounters with American families and temporary employers.

As many scholars have remarked, the notion of the road as a democratic public space is more ideal than reality. This becomes patently clear in many of the interactions between Hilton and Richie and those they meet along the way. While *The Simple Life 2: Road Trip* plays on the sentiment that "hitting the road" is the birthright of every American, and the tabloid queens forgo the anonymity most sojourners take for granted, they know that, as Hilton tells one toll booth operator, "In our real life, we have money." On a more immediate level, they know there is a host family waiting for them each night, and, although we do not see the camera crew filming their journey, we know that the two are rarely, if ever, truly on their own. Yet despite their wealth and celebrity status, they are, like all

travellers on US highways, subject to bad weather, tolls, unpredict-
able drivers, construction work, and the uncertainty that comes with
putting oneself behind the wheel of an automobile.

The people who interact with Hilton and Richie are the real stars
of the show. Fluff it may be, but it is fluff that points to certain realities of contemporary American life. As Ronald Primeau reminds us,
television facilitates a situation where "'serious' reading is occurring
during all the road fun and the significance of the genre rests in no
small measure on its broad-based appeal."[1] Moreover, as reality television becomes standard fare in many countries – not just in the USA
but across the globe – it is one more type of cultural production that
simultaneously reproduces and contests diverse notions of national
identity, race, ethnicity, and class.

As popular culture crosses borders, other nations "read" the USA
as well as their own societies, reflecting back what they have learned
about what they observe. The process works in reverse as well. Certain US programs are patterned on predecessors in earlier historical
eras and in non-American settings. Television – for all of its distor-
tion of reality – can also reflect (and interrogate) the micro "pursuit
of happiness" within a larger national/transnational frame. Reality television particularly, albeit scripted and heavily edited, often
offers clues into what twenty-first-century Americans value and fear.
It thrives on voyeurism, but it also instructs, critiques, and reconfig-
ures certain conventions.

In addition to telescoping current preoccupations, *The Simple Life
2: Road Trip*, converses with historical antecedents. Television has
helped perpetuate the myth of the American road as a place where
sojourners bond with one another (or those they meet along the
way), engage in a range of comic encounters, learn life lessons, invert
and/or reaffirm socio-cultural hierarchy, or reinvent themselves.
Hilton and Richie are just two of many individuals who have used
the small screen as a forum for exploiting the drama, humour, and
mystery of the open road in ways that invite those sitting in their living rooms along for the ride.

As we pay attention to what came before *The Simple Life*, a range
of connections and continuities between genres, characters, plots,
and punch lines can be seen. What follows is a brief historical con-
textualization of the series, in terms of both the history of television
and the current reality television landscape. Next, I consider the
ways in which Richie and Hilton are simultaneously in and out of

synch with early twenty-first-century preoccupations about women and power in popular culture. Finally, I discuss how *The Simple Life* – and by association a range of other reality television shows – addresses, often unintentionally, a range of very real inequality and power imbalances in the US today.

THE SMALL SCREEN AND THE OPEN ROAD: A VERY BRIEF HISTORY

The myth and mystique of the road has been perpetuated through many types of popular culture. As this volume affirms, there is substantial scholarship on the trope of the road in film, literature, and music. However, in comparison to film studies, scholarly analysis of television and the road remains rather thin. This is somewhat surprising given that storylines about road trips – in both situation comedies and dramas – date to the earliest days of the medium. As Max Skidmore has noted (see chapter 2 in this volume), the 1960 debut of *Route 66* is often cited as the earliest example of the television road series. However, one could argue that Lucille Ball's 1950s television shows were another important precursor to *The Simple Life*. In many respects, Lucy and Ethel are Paris and Nicole's TV godmothers. Their friendship, their self-deprecating physical comedy, and their proclivity for getting into and out of mischief form an important model for the twenty-first-century reality TV duo.

Nascent roots of such connections are particularly evident in episodes filmed in the early 1950s. Although the original series aired from 1951 to 1960, over two dozen episodes of *I Love Lucy* centred on a road trip from New York to California. Later packaged and distributed as a film titled *I Love Lucy's Zany Road Trip: California Here We Come*, the episodes followed Lucy and her husband, Ricky Ricardo (played by her real-life spouse at the time, Desi Arnaz), and their friends Fred and Ethel Mertz (William Frawley and Vivian Vance) making their way across the country and encountering everyday folk as well as celebrities such as William Holden and John Wayne.

While the Ricardo marriage is the primary relational focus of the show, from the earliest episodes, various subplots highlighted Lucy and Ethel sharing adventures, and forging their own sisterly bond. Most "I Love Lucy" viewers can easily spot the ways in which Hilton and Richie reprise several "Lucy and Ethel" moments. During *The Simple Life: Road Trip,* Hilton and Richie wreak havoc in various episodes, à la Lucy and Ethel, whether they are disrupting a sausage-making assembly line, driving their truck/trailer into ditches, or stuffing their mouths full of fast food they do not have the cash to purchase. The difference is that what seemed simply wacky in *I Love Lucy*, now seems wasteful or self-indulgent by virtue of what we know about Hilton and Richie in their off-camera lives. This is compounded by a certain global social fatigue with young media-seeking celebrities squandering their privileges in tough economic times. It is uncomfortable to witness the way Hilton and Richie exit the scene of their various dust-ups, cavalierly leaving the host families and employers, who have opened their homes and workplaces to them, to clean up the messes they leave behind.

There are other early television antecedents besides *I Love Lucy*. *The Simple Life 2: Road Trip* is on the contemporary end of a continuum that has its beginnings in the Cold War era. While the automobile is the vehicle for most television road trips, the peripatetic traveller on cross-country sojourns could be on foot, on a horse, or in a stagecoach. Dramas like *Route 66* (1960–64) and *The Fugitive* (1963–67) were, to a certain extent, the offspring of earlier television westerns such as *Wagon Train* (1957–65), *Rawhide* (1959–66), *Maverick* (1957–62) and *Have Gun – Will Travel* (1957–63). The themes of encounter, mobility, and adventure were reprised in multiple storylines, featuring travel via varied forms of transport, including feet, bicycles, cars, motorcycles, and spaceships. The best-known examples include: *Then Came Bronson* (1969–70), *Three for the Road* (1975–76),[2] *Kung Fu* (1972–75), the original *Star Trek* series (1966–69), *Lost in Space* (1965–68), and *The Time Tunnel* (1966–67). In each case, episodes combined elements of the Western and the road trip, often projecting and/or addressing certain social issues and contemporary preoccupations, particularly Cold War anxieties. The "foreign other" could be a trusted travel companion or dangerous nemesis depending on the geopolitical situation and the mood of the country at the time a particular show was produced. While *The Simple Life 2* resurrects certain tropes of the West, the frontier, and the cowboy, it also inverts the trope of the other, painting white southerners as the new aliens in a world where hunting and meat-eating are (in Hilton and Richie's eyes at least) deemed barbaric.

Seeing television history as women's history reminds us that while Lucy and Ethel were among the most prominent women on the small screen during the Cold War period, they were not alone. More women claimed the space of the television road (and television in general) as the twentieth century concluded, although they had been there all along. Katie Mills has shown that women were never the post-war TV pariahs that many critics have rendered them.[3] However, after the early success of Lucille Ball, women as narrators or central characters on the road were, indeed, atypical. The mostly male-centred adventures that captured the nation's imagination often ignored television's most loyal viewer, the American housewife. That began to change in the wake of the second-wave women's movement.

Women played a number of leading roles in the television world of the 1970s and 1980s. The situation comedy *Alice* (based on the 1974 road film *Alice Doesn't Live Here Anymore*) aired from 1976 to 1985. The title character was a single mother supporting herself and her son by waiting tables in a roadside diner. *The Partridge Family* was, primarily, a vehicle for pop idol David Cassidy, but it featured a strong and independent widow (played by Cassidy's stepmother Shirley Jones) taking her brood on the road in a refurbished psychedelic bus to perform their music. As second-wave feminism paved the way for third-wave girl power genres, women hit the road in special "one off" or "sweeps week" episodes featuring "all-girl" journeys or women as partners with men on the road in popular comedies and dramas ranging from *Family Ties* (1982–89) and *One Day at a Time* (1975–84) to *Buffy the Vampire Slayer* (1997–2003) and *Sex in the City* (1998–2004). In the twenty-first century, women are frequent road trippers.

This brief backward glance at road-centred television texts views television as a repository of the same road tropes (metaphors, images, and vocabularies) of travel and transport that Gordon Slethaug has noted (see chapter 1). In multiple ways, television shows have, from the beginning, reconfigured or reaffirmed cultural and national myths of self-made manhood/womanhood, Manifest Destiny, class mobility, the frontier mentality, and American exceptionalism. Although we think of iconic films such as *Easy Rider* or *Thelma and Louise* as defining the road genre in popular culture, television has also played its part in searing the road trip and the road trope into our collective national consciousness. Thanks to its quotidian reach, the frequency and familiarity of re-runs and DVD franchising, television memorializes and mythologizes the road in deep and diverse ways. Today, the romance with the road continues, as reality television combines many of the aforementioned components with new elements that reflect current perspectives and desires.

THE SIMPLE LIFE 2 AND ITS REALITY RELATIONS

Reality television's love affair with the American road is evident in several of the earliest exemplars of the genre. The most popular examples include MTV's *The Real World* (1992–), the spin-off series *Road Rules* (1995–2007), and *The Amazing Race* (2001–). In these reality road trips, the path leads well beyond the continental United States. In *The Amazing Race* series, which is also franchised in several other national media markets, automobiles are swapped interchangeably with airplanes, trains, bicycles, or other modes of transport, and the road stretches across the globe rather than across the country. The principle of survival and competition among other sojourners, and the importance of the twin themes of enlightenment and escape are central to all of these shows.

Certain familiar elements are embedded in the aforementioned road reality series, but there are important differences as well. Katie Mills argues that reality television moved in a different direction from other 1990s media projects and societal trends. While the end of the twentieth century introduced "audiences to new concepts of community, shaking up social views of gender, sexuality, and race" and returning to the 1960s' notion of "the road as a space of rebellion," in the early twenty-first century the pendulum shifted to a focus on commodity rather than creativity.[4] Mills asserts that not only does MTV cater to the "short attention spans of the reality generation" but also the production team of Mary-Ellis Bunim (who died of cancer in 2004) and Jonathan Murray exploited two themes of interest, the road and the celebrity. Mills writes:

> These days, the television medium attracts viewers by showing people doing shocking things, things that people do not do everyday, like working in a nudist camp or eating worms. Reality shows have fostered the Horatio Alger myth that anyone can succeed on reality TV (well, anyone who is good looking and garrulous, or conniving and bad, or willing to eat worms). For most of the participants of these shows, money and fame seem to be

the driving forces. Once heiress Paris Hilton and wealthy Nicole
Richie entered into the reality TV road genre, however, an entirely
new class discourse could be seen – the dream of social mobility is flattened somewhat when the very rich are the stars of a
reality road series ... Bunim-Murray switched premises entirely
when creating *The Simple Life* franchise for Fox TV in 2003. (It
is worth keeping in mind that Paris Hilton is the age of viewers
who started watching *Road Rules* back in 1995 as adolescents.
In that sense, *The Simple Life* 2 is already next-generation reality
road TV.)[5]

I agree with many of Mills's observations about reality television
generally and *The Simple Life* specifically. Still, I see certain redemptive aspects in the show and the genre. Most episodes offer moments
of rare and unrehearsed human connection: a fleeting reward for
living-room voyeurs. What follows is a brief consideration of a few
such moments in *The Simple Life* 2, an American studies text that
features Hilton and Richie serving (unwittingly at times) as foils for
the "average folks" they encounter in the course of their travels.

CLAIMING THE SPACE: GENDER AND *THE SIMPLE LIFE*

Part of what makes the Hilton/Richie *Simple Life* television road
trip noteworthy is that in reality, as well as in reality television,
women who claim the space of the road are still, arguably, engaging
in a somewhat subversive, or at least novel act. Stories by and about
women on the road in film, television, or popular literature are
nowhere near as popular as men's stories, and those that exist are
not, for the most part, narratives of liberation or empowerment.
Even the most revered of road "chick flicks," *Thelma and Louise*,
sent an ambivalent message about women and independence. (This
may help to explain why there has been no attempt to resurrect the
film in an era when revivals and remakes are a Hollywood staple.)
Hilton and Richie are as close as we get to Thelma and Louise on TV.
This is somewhat surprising given the explosion of "girl power" television series and plots. While some may cringe at the comparison of
Hilton and Richie and Susan Sarandon and Geena Davis, Paris and
Nicole are ahead of cinema's female road icons simply by virtue of
the fact that they are still alive and driving!

Perhaps the paucity of road-tripping women in popular culture mirrors a larger reality. Despite the real influence of the women's movement on women's mobility and the increase in the numbers of women who travel alone, women are still considered "at risk" on US roads in daily life. Various media reports of women being kidnapped and assaulted testify to the strong societal caution women receive to think twice before they hit the road without the protection of a man (or a dog or a gun). On highways throughout the nation, it is still much more common to see men hitchhiking than women – and those women who do hitchhike are more subject to negative assumptions and stereotyping as well as real danger. So while more and more women may be attempting to break the glass ceiling in higher education or the workplace, on the road it is a different story.

In the light of this anxiety about women travelling without male companions, *The Simple Life* represents a triumph, albeit small, of sorts. On camera, Hilton and Richie come across as spoiled and silly, but they are striking out on their own for an adventure without their fathers, boyfriends, or credit cards. It is a gimmick, but one that puts women behind the wheel and grants them a modicum of control about where they stop, sleep, and work.

It is surprising that there are not more women on the road in popular culture, as they can be seen taking to the screen, if not the road, in many roles. On television, women wield power and challenge male hierarchies in hospitals (*Grey's Anatomy*, *Private Practice*), politics (*The West Wing*, *Commander in Chief*), or the urban jungle (*Sex and the City*, *Caroline in the City*, *Felicity*). Since the 1990s, women have occupied more leading roles in television series (witness girl power staples from *Buffy the Vampire Slayer* to *Alias*, *Tru Calling*, *The Ghost Whisperer*, and *Heroes*), but the contemporary television road trip (as fantasy or reality) is still the province of men. Charles Kuralt can take his trailer *On the Road*, but even well-established media icons such as Barbara Walters and Whoopi Goldberg stay indoors and sip coffee around the cozy kitchen-like table on *The View*. (To be fair, Goldberg did go "on the road" with Drew Barrymore and Mary-Louise Parker in the 1995 road film *Boys on the Side*.) Popular culture has, for the most part, mirrored reality in that road trips are for women as members of a couple, a family, or a co-ed tour group. Regardless of what one thinks of the inane Hilton and Richie road antics, the two are, in many respects, pioneers.

THE SIMPLE LIFE 2: ROAD TRIP: CLASS CRITIQUE AND CONSUMPTION

In the 1990s, a handful of American-based, American-owned, multinational multi-media corporations began amassing increased global power and influence. The continual merging of media institutions, accompanied by the increasing turn towards global cultural exchange and international cultural flows – much of it aided by the rise of the practically borderless World Wide Web – ushered in an era in which cultural texts and their representations of American teen culture became even more accessible to international audiences. With that came the opportunity for the enhanced economic exploitation of an expanding worldwide market. These developments suggest that we are on our way to witnessing the rise of a global teen culture that embraces and shares a host of similar media products.[6]

Pioneers they may be, but Hilton and Richie are not promoting any sort of feminist (or post-feminist) agenda, nor does either appear to be thoughtful or deliberate about paving the way for women of their own generation or any other. The pair are canny about their marketability as a commodity in the realm of youth media culture. Although "average Americans" lampoon them for the clothes they wear and the vacuous phrases they use (Hilton: "That's hot!" Richie: "Do you love it?"), they have millions of fans around the world, and they play to them and their wallets via the promotion of their fashion, fragrances, and other consumer products. Because both women are objects of relentless media attention, the narrative within the television series parallels and at times collides with stories about the two in the news and infotainment sector.

Poster children for conspicuous consumption and unabashed about their own economic privilege, Hilton and Richie's reality road trip provides opportunities for reflection on youth culture, consumption, and social class in the contemporary United States. Both young women are constantly applying make-up, checking hairstyles, and commenting on attire (theirs or others). Viewers have no idea when or where the two will decide to stop, but we can be sure that they will be primping when they arrive. Hilton and Richie "play" at work, and much of the comic effect of The Simple Life is achieved as a result of their refusal to conform to the expectations of those who host them. At times this refusal is somewhat galling and borders on thinly veiled contempt for many of those they meet along the road. But the contempt – or at least suspicion – flows both ways and that is where reality television informs as well as entertains.

At each stop along their road trip Hilton and Richie are greeted by a family primed and ready for their stay. All host families appear to be comfortably middle class although some homes are larger and more elaborate than others. A few families appear rather apprehensive about welcoming the celebrities into their lives. Others express a sense of mission about their participation in the television spectacle and they frankly declare their desire to instill a greater sense of responsibility in the party girls from LA. In addition to performing chores in the homes that they visit, Hilton and Richie are employed in a range of temporary jobs. The work varies from cleaning fish to making beds in hotel rooms, but, regardless of the task, the attitude is the same. The celebrity road trippers do not want to work; they want to have fun. They look for ways to freeload and they coax food, gas, and cash from those (usually men of various ages who stare, stutter, and fawn) who are willing to open their hearts and homes. They trade on their looks and their celebrity, and they repeatedly express their glee at what they are able to "get away with" time and time again.

Hilton and Richie rarely express much interest in the simple life. They may be the stars of the show but their wealth, status, and class privilege renders them downright alien in Middle America. The pair's "fish out of water" antics elicit a range of reactions in others, from amusement to horror. It is funny when the two try to kill a moth with Nicole's Chanel bag. It is less so when they lose track of a young girl they are responsible for babysitting. As Mills writes, "Role reversal is the essence of comedy," and the series makes the most of the premise of rich girls who are placed in dramatically different circumstances from those which are familiar.[7] Yet the comedy is shot through with subtle (and not so subtle) reminders of how wealth feeds difference and how privilege divides and disempowers.

Mills adds that "reversal" is a key historical motif and source of humour. Citing its use in Frank Capra's films, particularly *It Happened One Night*, she argues that *The Simple Life* "offers a measure of the changes in moral values between the Depression era of *It Happened One Night* and the George W. Bush administration, which has been working to dismantle the social security system set up during the economic crisis of the 1930s." Mills also believes that "all consideration of the common folk is gone in *The Simple Life 2* ... Richie and Hilton live up to their reputation as spoiled rich girls, and in the process, they provide some public catharsis of contempt at these wealthy characters who offer so little."[8]

It is, perhaps, unfair to level all blame for the consequences of Hilton and Richie's antics directly on them. The show's producers are in on the gag as well. It is difficult to know what is scripted and what is improvised and who determines what viewers will ultimately see. What is clear is that the road trip follows an odd path that ignores most of the country. The "coast-to-coast" road trip is really a drive through the southern part of the US with the majority of stops taking place in Florida and Texas. (It strains credulity to believe that all Hilton and Richie seem to know about Mississippi is that "it's the place where Forrest Gump came from.") There are moments when the pair exhibit genuine appreciation for the hospitality they receive and a grudging engagement in the activities in which they participate. Ultimately, however, they are most at home with male peers who are roughly their same age (or younger) and can show them where to find the best clubs and nightlife. In these encounters, pop culture references serve as common ground and icebreakers to bridge class differences.

In his analysis of *The Simple Life,* Judge Brett Cullum writes scathingly of the series even as he acknowledges its connections to more "respectable" predecessors:

> *The Simple Life 2: Road Trip* owes a lot to some grand traditions in comedy – and no, I am not kidding. If you look at Depression-era comedies, and films like *My Man Godfrey,* you'll find an underlying fascination with cinema and making rich people look foolish. Consider the legacy of Lucy and Ethel's botched jobs in *I Love Lucy,* as well. Anyone remember *Green Acres?* (Ironically, Paris is actually related to the Gabors!) This is just a staged reality television show that borrows from the best sources it could possibly find. Please don't tell me you believed *any* of this had to do with reality. Paris and Nicole both burst that bubble when they made endless talk show appearances chatting about their "characters." They were promoting this sequel, and freely admitted they were acting the way producers wanted them to act. I

know a lot of people debate how 'real' reality television is, but in this case, you have no need to wonder.[9]

Yet while Cullum sees the interactions on *The Simple Life* as staged rather than authentic, I would take issue with the assertion that there is nothing "real" about this reality television show.

In addition to tapping into a venerable American comic tradition, Hilton and Richie are part of another television sorority that began to form in the Cold War period. Bill Osgerby argues that young women became more central to TV plots in the 1950s and 1960s in both the United States and the United Kingdom:

> In Britain and America gender inequalities remained pronounced, but in both countries women – and *young* women especially – were beginning to benefit from higher levels of disposable income and wider opportunities in employment and public culture. In media representations, therefore, it was hardly surprising that young women were frequently configured as being at the sharp end of social and cultural transformation – teenage girls often constructed as the living, breathing embodiment of post-war affluence and the widening horizons of commodity consumption.

Osgerby shows that in the post-war period, television's teenage girls were exhibiting a type of "consumerist hedonism" and "using the products and resources of commercial youth culture to carve out a space for self-expression and personal pleasure that was independent of parental (and often masculine) authority."[10]

Teen television, particularly shows featuring independent young women, experienced a renaissance in the 1990s, and, by the year 2000, the US teenage population had reached 31.6 million – higher than the baby boom peak of 29.9 million in 1976. Hilton and Richie were perfectly poised to tap into this new sub-culture of consumer-minded girls. An important cohort at mid-century, young women continued to feature in the growth of a commercial youth wave up to the end of the twentieth century and into the present.[11] Hilton and Richie are, then, two of many women in a line of female icons helping to sustain the well-established legacy of consumer hedonism in the twenty-first century.

Osgerby argues that the girls in main roles in contemporary shows, such as *Sister, Sister, Moesha*, and *Beverly Hills 90210* are not very different from starlets belonging to the Patty Duke/Gidget genre. "Such programs are better understood as developing out of a longer 'teen girl' TV tradition whose accent on freedom and fun *always* gestured towards a femininity that was independent and active."[12] The question is, how do young women in the reality television world differ from women in other television programs? The answer is found not only in *The Simple Life* series, but also in shows such as *America's Next Top Model* and, more recently, *The Girls Next Door, The Kendra Show* (based on the lives of *Playboy* "Bunnies"), and *Keeping Up with the Kardashians* and its spinoffs. These shows do little to encourage girls to focus on anything other than partying, backbiting, and obsessing about appearance. They may exhibit "fun and independent" femininity, but reality television's femmes fall short of their fictional sisters' attempts to integrate beauty and brains. Thelma and Louise may have driven over a cliff to their deaths, but they were, after all, taking a stand against domestic violence and the objectification of women. Hilton and Richie (as well as the reality heroines that have now eclipsed them) seem – at times – to be raising objectification to an art. One cannot help but ask what good it does a young woman to be active and independent if she becomes such in order merely to shop and consume rather than to improve herself or the world around her?

There are, of course, moments in *The Simple Life 2: Road Trip* when Paris Hilton and Nicole Richie are doing more than primping and trying to avoid work. Sometimes they break certain rules to genuinely reach out to others. For example, when they work in a prison cafeteria, Hilton and Richie are told not to talk to prisoners while delivering meals. Yet the two decide to ignore this rule. They talk to several of the men they serve, attempting to comfort one prisoner by letting him know that he should not feel too bad being incarcerated because, after all, the weather outside is lousy. Exhibiting a type of schizophrenia that Susan Douglas argues is a byproduct of "growing up female with the mass media" in America, Hilton and Richie manifest a variety of attitudes and behaviours on the road, and they are often contradictory.[13] In one episode, the two "make over" a 13-year-old girl prior to her first date. As they help her apply make-up, they joke that it's time to "get slutty." A few minutes later, however, they negate their previous frivolity as they discuss dating "dos and don'ts." They remind the young girl: "Do be cute, but don't be a slut." They may push limits everywhere they go, but they speak out frequently against sexism, mistreatment of animals, and other perceived social injustices they encounter on their journey.

Some moments are truly painful to watch in episodes where the arrogance of class privilege reveals itself. In one, when the two complain that they are hungry, they convince people they meet along the road to share their homemade meals with them. Yet after eating what they consider to be "greasy food," the two complain about what they have been served. In another, the duo exploits a woman from Colombia who works as a maid in a motel where Hilton and Richie are supposedly employed as maids themselves. They change out of their uniforms and in to their street clothes, pretending to be guests at the motel. They then order room service while the woman cleans the room they were assigned to clean. In these moments the "real" meets the artifice of "reality" television. The "real" people in *The Simple Life* construct, intentionally and unintentionally, a counter narrative to Hilton and Richie's antics. In these moments reality television becomes particularly compelling.

RACE, REAL PEOPLE, AND *THE SIMPLE LIFE*

As Alessandra Stanley has noted, "Reality shows are staged, scripted and heavily edited, but for some reason there is still a frisson of authenticity behind the artifice: real people seem to have more staying power than established celebrities who are cast in reality shows."[14] Hilton and Richie are, at times, dismissive of many people they meet. Yet there are plenty of examples throughout the series of "average Americans" thumbing their noses right back at the two celebrities. This aspect of the show is, for me, the most interesting and, dare I say it? Real. In one episode, members of the James family express surprise that Hilton is able to cook for herself, and they are determined to teach both of the California girls the importance of adhering to standards of southern etiquette. Clearly, it is difficult to know when interactions between various individuals are staged and whether the sentiments expressed are genuine or manufactured for the camera. But there are plenty of examples of the "average folks" talking back to the celebrities and their milieu. In fact, the families exhibit a fair amount of self-righteousness about *their* own ways of doing things.

As previously mentioned, many believe that they can (and should) try to bring the girls down to earth, develop a work ethic, and change their ways. So even though the premise is laughable, many of those who are cast to play bit parts along the way seem to take the Hilton/Richie reality road trip quite seriously. Occasionally, some light is shed – if only briefly and in caricatured form – on the way the "haves" and "have-nots" see each other in the US; and on how gender, regional, and religious identities intersect and morph with various formations of class and racial identity. Red State meets Blue State on *The Simple Life,* and the encounter is both amusing and enlightening.

RACIAL IDENTITY AND THE CASH FAMILY

In one of the most simultaneously bizarre and touching moments in the season, Hilton and Richie meet the Reverend Dr J.L. Cash and his family. In a season full of Caucasian faces, the Cashes are the one black family who house Hilton and Richie. Among the most outspoken of the patriarchs of the host families featured in this season's episodes, Dr Cash appears dogged in his determination to teach Hilton and Richie how to behave in a more understated manner and how to think critically about class, race, and ethnicity.

In the Cash home, Richie speaks openly of her African-American paternal heritage, something she does not do in any of the other homes. One night during dinner, as Dr Cash is discussing the history of his family and of many of the black people in the town where they live, Richie proudly announces, "I'm a black folk too." Hilton seems a bit taken aback by Richie's sudden desire to be associated with blackness, but Richie is emphatic in her declaration of connection with the Cashes. Meanwhile, Mrs Cash reminds Hilton that everybody "belongs" at the Cash home, where there are no outsiders, regardless of skin colour. The exchange between Richie, the Cashes, and Hilton ruptures and inverts the insider/outsider dynamic of white privilege that Hilton typically takes for granted. It also reminds viewers of Richie's bi-racial identity and of the differences between the two celebrities rather than how alike they are.

More generally, interactions between Hilton, Richie, and the Cashes signal the ways in which the politics of identity are evident in daily life. *The Simple Life* is an example of the intersectionality of race, gender, class, and generational differences. That Richie can "pass" as white does not mean that she experiences life in America in the same way that Hilton does. However, for most of the season, class (or at least economic privilege) and gender bond rather than separate Hilton and Richie. They are also the more salient identities – at least on screen – for most of those who come in contact with the young women. Clearly, Richie is in a privileged cohort of African-American entertainers and icons. She is, arguably, spared the more blatant forms of racism present for many people of colour in the US. However, in the Cash home, moments of difference are apparent. One such moment is in the kitchen while the entire family is preparing breakfast under Richie's supervision. They all begin singing and dancing together, and Hilton must be drawn in from the side of the kitchen where she is standing and observing. She is gently encouraged to "join the family," which now symbolically includes Richie.

In the end, however, the Reverend Cash and his family see Hilton and Richie as more alike than different. The two young women are linked by their behaviour and, in the eyes of Reverend Cash, their misuse of the privilege that comes with fame and celebrity. In his comments to the camera before the young women arrive as well as in a "heart to heart" session with the two of them prior to their departure, Dr Cash speaks for all of his family when he makes it clear that they are out to save the Hollywood duo from themselves. The Cash children say things such as "We've seen the news; we've read the magazines; we believe we can help them;" or "They're really sweet girls. They just need some discipline." Dr Cash is modest in his expectations. He looks into the camera and flatly declares, "I don't expect for them to be Jesus tomorrow. I'll just try to help point 'em in the right direction." Mrs Cash makes the rules of the house clear to the young women when they sit down for their first meal. She explains: "We have some rules, ok? We don't speak profanity. We don't wear halter-tops, short shorts, and showing all of your stomach. Just pitch in and help. Mess up, clean up. Let's eat."

But it is clear that the two are not following all of the house rules and, although he is clearly fond of the girls, Dr Cash feels compelled to sit them down and "talk to them about respect." He begins by declaring that he wants "people to see you as very beautiful women inside and out." He acknowledges that their celebrity status will bring them instant recognition, but he encourages them to try to "leave something in folks' lives or hearts that'll kind of go along with 'em." Prodding them to use their looks and fame to make the world a better place, he reminds them that there is "something special" about them, but that they could diminish that sense of specialness by their "language and other little stuff." Nonetheless, he reassures them, "If you clean that part up (the language) I think they'll see the jewel that's in there." Cash then tells the two that he'll be watching them. (Of course we know that he actually will be able to watch them, as they are television stars and tabloid celebrities.) As Hilton and Richie drive away from the Cash home, they are sent off with a final hymn of praise and thanks for their visit. Ironically, the reverent mood is shattered the minute Hilton and Richie pull out of the driveway. Their use of profanity renders their expression of gratitude rather pointless. As they drive away the voice-over declares that in spite of the collective effort of the Cash family, nothing has changed.

References to racial, gender, and class identities in *The Simple Life 2: Road Trip* remind us of the role television plays in larger discussions of what is acceptable/off limits to say and do in public. Reality television is in a particular zone of ambiguity, it seems. Because people are supposedly acting on the impulses of the moment, without carefully scripted lines, they are more able to surprise and shock the viewing audience. Not surprisingly, this comedic device either impoverishes or entertains depending on one's point of view. In his book, *Cracking Up: American Humor in a Time of Conflict,* Paul Lewis argues that Americans need to think more carefully about what it is that makes them laugh.[15] Lewis worries that we are attuned to bad humour that offends our own sensibilities, but rather careless when it comes to offending others.

Watching one episode of *The Simple Life* seems innocuous – and diverting – enough. However, watching episode after episode for purposes of writing this chapter has made me more sympathetic to Lewis when he asserts that while humour is a "potent force for good," it has an underside as well. "Humor can help us cope with problems or deny them, inform or misinform, express our most loving and most hateful feelings, embrace and attack, draw us to other people who share our values or fallaciously convince us that they do when they don't."[16]

Asking us to pay attention to the ways humour is deployed, and to take "note of boundaries crossed, highlighting moments of comic contestation, and speculating about the needs and values buried in banter," Lewis would suggest we construct standards of humour that enhance the quality of public discourse. However, such a manoeuvre will, of course, open up new and even more contentious discussions of freedom of speech.[17]

CONCLUSION: THE TRANSNATIONAL CACHET OF REALITY TELEVISION

The final episode of *The Simple Life 2: Road Trip* concludes with Hilton and Richie back home in Beverly Hills, sipping drinks by the pool at the Hilton estate. Hilton blandly announces that: "It was kind of neat to see, like, all of America." Although it is clear that the two did not, by any measure, see all of America, Hilton's words are worth pondering. *The Simple Life* series is broadcast on television stations in many countries, and available on DVD (legitimate and pirated) or on the Internet in many others. Thus, while Hilton has not seen all of America, millions of people have witnessed all or part of Hilton's (and Richie's) road trip. There are doubtless better ambassadors for the USA, but at this point, Hilton and Ritchie are more familiar faces than most US leaders and politicians. For many, including this author, that's a rather sobering thought, but Alessandra Stanley helps put things in perspective. In her discussion of next-generation reality television shows such as *Jersey Shore* and *Keeping Up with the Kardashians,* Stanley reminds us of a longer history of anxiety about popular culture and offers a fitting conclusion to this discussion of *The Simple Life*:

> Reality shows that exalt indolent, loud-mouthed exhibitionists may seem like almost biblical retribution for our materialistic, celebrity-obsessed age. But actually, these kinds of series are an extension of a time-honored form of entertainment, one that reaches back to the era of landed gentry, debutantes and social seasons in places like Newport, R.I., or the French Riviera ... News judgment, even then, skewed toward entertainment. *The New York Herald* was the first American newspaper to use the wireless telegraph in 1899 – inventor Guglielmo Marconi was invited to New York to report not the conclusion of the Dreyfus affair or the start of the second Boer War, but the results of a high-society sailing regatta, America's Cup.[18]

8

Postmodern Masculinities in Recent Buddy and Solo Road Films

GORDON E. SLETHAUG

In an article called "Remember the Cicadas and the Stars," the well-known travel writer Paul Theroux reminisces about a less populated, quieter America, noting that "nowhere was solitude more available than on a long drive especially at night; and it seems to me that my generation was defined by the open road, and the accompanying hope that a promise lay at the end of it. The almost trance-like experience of driving down the soft tunnel of a dark highway at night was something I relished."[1] He goes on to say:

> Late at night, in most places I knew, there was almost no traffic and driving, a meditative activity, could cast a spell. Behind the wheel, gliding along, I was keenly aware of being an American in America, on a road that was also metaphorical, making my way through life, unhindered, developing ideas, making decisions, liberated by the flight through this darkness and silence. With less light pollution, the night sky was different, too – starrier, more daunting, more beautiful.[2]

He sums up: "I have not seen roads or night skies like that for many years."[3] The highway he nostalgically describes is one of quiet, solitary wonder and great beauty leading to personal insights, individual growth, and social well being – all part of a comic and romantic construction of the road.

Theroux's reflections on the road are among the most recent of numerous accounts, but a self-conscious, romantic awareness of the road in the USA arguably begins with Walt Whitman's "Song of the Open Road" (see Slethaug, chapter 1). The poet opens this poem by proclaiming:

Afoot and light-hearted I take to the open road
Healthy, free, the world before me,
The long brown path before me leading wherever I choose.
(ll. 1–3, 149)

By the end of the poem, he invites the reader to join him, proclaiming:

Allons! The road is before us!
It is safe – I have tried it – my own feet have tried it well – be not
detain'd!
...
Will you give me yourself? Will you come travel with me?
Shall we stick by each other as long as we live? (ll.214–24,
158–9)[4]

Although Whitman is acutely aware of, and excited about, the effects of technology on the lives of travelling Americans in the mid-nineteenth century, he focuses mainly on those who walk, including the homeless that Kenneth Kusmer later documents in *Down and Out, On the Road*, but also those out for the sheer physical pleasure, wonder of discovery, and spiritual contemplation that Theroux mentions.

In this poem, Whitman envisions countless beginnings, personal achievements, and individual growth, and, in that respect, creates a template for the comic and romantic road that Theroux describes. In literature, the comic and romantic include: an emphasis on self-discovery, friendship, and love; an assertion of the value of family and community; a resolution of serious complications; an evasion of threats and dangers that endanger peace and harmony; and a celebration of life. To these features of the romantic road Lackey would add that in many road narratives: "the highway serves the domestic ideal by schooling and refining men and women to make them fit for their spouses."[5] In the late twentieth-century road romance, this incorporation into society is not exclusive to heterosexual relationships but includes buddies, friends, family, and social community.

Since Whitman other road works have reified such possibilities, including Jack Kerouac's *On the Road* (see Slethaug, chapter 1), but gritty *noir* films such as *Detour* (1945) and *They Live By Night* (1948) and counterculture films such as *Easy Rider, Butch Cassidy and the Sundance Kid*, and *Thelma and Louise* from the 1960s to the

1990s invested the road movie genre with a cynicism and paranoia[6] that seemed to leave little space for personal fulfillment, affectionate relationships, and familial and social reconciliation. Devin Orgeron argues that road movies posit "a hopeless and lamentable mobility in an effort to eulogize or find *stability*."[7] Certainly Orgeron is right about the hopeless mobility in what Laderman thinks of as the formative road film, *Easy Rider*. This film also confirms the conventions of the buddy road film – a pairing of personalities based on complementary opposites ("active/passive, intellectual/sensual, straight/wild," etc.) along with a "compulsive thrill-seeking drive" and "a reflective, spiritual search."[8] The links between hopeless mobility and the buddy films of the young and restless are, however, tenuous.

Recent American buddy and solo road movies interrogate hopeless mobility and rebellion as pre-requisites of the road by emphasizing how boys and men of all ages can use various kinds of, and attitudes toward, mobility to affirm themselves, their partners, fathers, and places in the broader American culture, and therefore to overturn some of the assumptions of the countercultural road narratives. They do so on foot and in cars, vans, buses, RVs, trucks, trains, and airplanes; even on lawn tractors – any form of transportation capable of moving them to their geographical and emotional destinations where "interconnections"[9] can take place. As Katie Mills mentions, these new road narratives have "been jacked up, dropped down, ripped apart, and recombined – in other words, substantially re-envisioned for a multimedia and multicultural age."[10] Yet there is a return to a romantic vision, though with an awareness of how odd, unusual, and unrealistic this may be. This is part of the more general postmodern phenomenon of pastiche that re-views and refashions older forms and attitudes toward art, literature, film, and general culture to create new awareness and understanding. It is also part of new postmodern understandings of masculinity.

Postmodernism is, of course, many things, including the continuation of the modernism that Laderman notes, but, as Joseph Natoli and Linda Hutcheon state, "the one thing it usually connotes is change."[11] Change can hardly comprise a cultural movement in itself, but has given rise to the simultaneous incorporation and transgression of previous forms, modes, and characteristics leading to new kinds of personal, social, and artistic awareness. As Hutcheon remarks, "postmodernism is a fundamentally contradictory response: its art forms (and its theory) at once use and abuse, install and then destabilize convention."[12] In the road genre, it is not altogether possible to restore the pre-*Easy Rider* naïve wonder of Whitman's romantic celebration (though Theroux is convincing), but it is possible to use and abuse the romantic in reconfiguring the masculinity of the road and thereby upset old patriarchal paradigms of the road while also wresting personal victory and social harmony from the difficulties of late twentieth- and early twenty-first-century life. This chapter explores this postmodern recuperation of romance linked to a reconstruction of masculinity in film narratives at the end of the twentieth century.

Georges Van Den Abbeele comments that travel has been perceived as a male enterprise based on "patriarchal values and ideology."[13] Laderman notes that "the bulk of the road movie genre seems to presuppose a focus on masculinity," and, referencing Jane Tompkins, Shari Roberts finds this kind of hegemonic masculinity firmly embedded in the Western novels and road movies.[14] For Roberts this masculinity of aggression, individualism, independence, and control is tied to "American national identity."[15] Mary Carden remarks that, though road heroes such as Neal Cassady and Jack Kerouac in the 1950s do reinvent certain aspects of masculinity, they "tap into the mythology that conflates the male-identified dynamics of travel – the 'imperial eye' of the self-contained adventurer, the bracing challenge of the unknown, the empowering erotics of discovery and conquest – with the male-identified dynamics of American origin stories – exploration, self-determination, and of course, conquest."[16] Stuart Aitken and Christopher Lukinbeal argue that this characterizes buddy films as well, and Ina Rae Hark finds that, even when these films fell out of fashion in the eighties and nineties, the few anti-buddy road films that did appear still adhered to patriarchal capitalism and hegemonic masculinity.[17]

Timothy Corrigan, one of the first to study the road film, noted, however, that road movies were never so conventionally hegemonic but concern the "destabilization of male subjectivity and masculine empowerment," which have been linked to escapism and technology. In any case, a revision of masculinity in this new era reverses the customary road trajectory and turns social hierarchies and value systems upside-down.

As Bob Pease urges in his book *Recreating Men: Postmodern Masculinity Politics*, changing masculinity may not be easy, but it is necessary:

One of the most central issues for women's prospects for equal-ity is whether men can and will change. I believe that men's sub-jectivity is crucial to gender domination and that changing the social relations of gender will necessitate the transforming of men's subjectivities as well as changing their daily practices.[18]

To focus on changes in masculine identity in road literature and acknowledge stress between male buddies, lost fathers and dysfunc-tional families, repressed personal desires, suppressed social emo-tional needs, suicidal impulses, and the ravages of age – and still to celebrate friendship, reconciliation of fathers and sons, and other romantic possibilities and triumphs – is to re-examine identity, gender, and the construction of family, and to reconfigure buddy- and solo-film narratives in a postmodern way.[19] Others such as Orgeron think of "the disconnected and the arbitrary" as the criteria defining the postmodern road film, and Laderman thinks of it as ironic self-consciousness,[20] but my position is that the reconfigured buddy and solo road film offers a postmodern combination of the romance and pluralistic masculinities of reconciliation and recon-struction. Cohan and Hark find that pre-sixties' road films generally concern the "reintegration of road travelers into the dominant cul-ture," and this is true of those at the turn of this century, though in a postmodern, partly ironic sense.[21]

Michael Kimmel notes that "our definitions of manhood are constantly changing, being played out on the political and social terrain," and at present consist of both normative "hegemonic mas-culinity" and "alternative masculinities."[22] He equates hegemonic masculinity with the "marketplace masculinity" that emerged in the nineteenth century and was linked to the accumulation of wealth, power, status, and a flight from femininity. Kim Dolgin finds this masculinity characterized by "specialized, activity-based friendships filled with impersonal talk and competition and lacking in expressed affection (and perhaps intimacy)."[23] To that view Theodore Cohen adds that these hegemonic men are "competitive, rational, and uncomfortable with revealing their innermost feelings."[24]

Scott Swain calls hegemonic masculinity a *"deficit approach* to men's intimate capabilities" and assumes that men are capable of emotional support, self-disclosure, and deep intimacy but often covertly rather than overtly.[25] Jon Morgan agrees, saying that "fem-inist men" "reject the old definitions of masculinity and femininity ...

behave in more realistic, non-sexist ways than our traditional brethren [and] don't feel any need to act aggressively or hide our emotions to prove that we are men."[26] Bob Pease prefers to call this a "postmodern feminist framework,"[27] and Ronald Levant prefers "reconstructed" masculinity, but the sentiment is much the same between the two views.[28] I prefer "postmodern masculinities" as the operative term to encapsulate the diverse and "inherently unstable"[29] "multiplicity of masculinities"[30] that confront hegemonic masculinity in this current period. Kimmel flippantly refers to some of these masculinites as "wimps, whiners, and weekend warriors," but they are more varied than that, not so negative, and perhaps even ultimately unnameable.[31]

Sharon Willis (1997), however, is not persuaded that buddy films or road movies in general continue to maintain that hegemonic masculinity, as evidenced by films like *To Wong Foo, Thanks for Everything! Julie Newmar* and *Boys on the Side*, both produced in 1995.[32] I would agree with Cohen (2001) that considering the "permissible masculinity" (here of new buddy and solo road films) can help interrogate traditional patriarchal capitalism, hegemonic masculinity, and exclusive heterosexuality and embrace pluralistic postmodern masculinities that promote the value of reconciliation.[33]

Great numbers of male-dominated buddy and solo road movies have come out since the mid-nineties, focusing on a conjunction of postmodern masculinity and the comic/romantic. Significant films that incorporate postmodern masculinity and engage the romantic road include, in order of the ascending ages of the principal male characters: Chris Eyre's *Smoke Signals* (1998); Ang Lee's *Brokeback Mountain* (2005); Cameron Crowe's *Elizabethtown* (2005); Alexander Payne's *Sideways* (2004); Jim Jarmusch's *Broken Flowers* (2005); Alexander Payne's *About Schmidt* (2002); and David Lynch's *The Straight Story* (1999). The major characters in all of these films are male. The first three films are concerned with young men, the fourth (*Sideways*) with newly minted middle-agers, and the last three with retired men, even geezers – in the language of Lynch's *The Straight Story*.

Contemporary road movies about young men are, by and large, buddy films about male bonding that focus on special friendship and love between young men, and the relationships are often, but not always, successful. The young men's prominent relationships with their fathers, however, often require more work to be successful, and, according to masculine crisis theory, that is the most significant component. As Arthur Brittan argues, "a healthy gender identity requires a proper identification with some kind of father-figure," for the "child's mental and physical health is now seen to be crucially dependent on the father's participation in nurturing activities."[34] How these father-sons relationships are constructed and what they mean is not a given in society generally or in road films specifically, and the field of masculinity studies does an uneven job of addressing the issue. Levant, however, thinks that physically absent or emotionally unavailable fathers, coupled with their high demands for the sons when they are present, create a "wound," "manifested in myriad direct and disguised forms of [a son's] desperately seeking some contact, some closeness, with his father (or his surrogate) or in being furious at him for his failures."[35] In considering *On the Road*, John Leland argues that the "lament for lost fathers" is one of the strongest themes in Kerouac's life and novel and American culture: "For Kerouac it reflected an American rupture that began with the Gold Rush, but it really came home with the death of his father, Leo, a year before Sal's first journey. To salve the nation's wound, Sal has to heal his own, and vice versa."[36] Neither Kerouac nor Sal could restore his father, and Sal closes his narrative with a tribute to his friend Dean's missing father, so this wound in the prototypical road narrative remains. I would argue, however, that postmodern romantic buddy films frequently postulate a repair in the son's wound that permits restoration and comic redemption. This, however, is more likely to be seen in road narratives about young men than old men (whose fathers are long dead). In the case of narratives about older men, the repair is with their own sons, siblings, and partners.

Of the three films about young men, *Smoke Signals* focuses on male friendship, and *Brokeback Mountain* and *Elizabethtown* are structured mainly around love – the gay love of one and the heterosexual love of the other – but all three also concern the young protagonists' relations with their fathers. The young men's ability to resolve (or not) the problems of their buddy/love relationships is closely tied to their coming to terms with fathers and community, and the road is central in each of these films in working out issues of masculinity.

In the first two of these road films, *Smoke Signals* and *Brokeback Mountain*, the setting is clearly the West (rural Washington state and Arizona for the first and the Rocky Mountains of Wyoming for the second), and this West is closely related to that of classical Western movies. As Shari Roberts notes, this putting together of the road and Western movie genres is fairly common, going back at least to *Stagecoach*, and is specifically designed to depict "silent male heroes" with strong and aggressive masculinities: "As portrayed in the western and alluded to in the road movie, frontier symbolism is propelled by masculinity and a particular conception of American national identity that revolves around individualism and aggression."[37] The depiction of strong and silent males and aggressive masculinity, however, is taken up as a postmodern enterprise in both *Smoke Signals and Brokeback Mountain*, not to maintain a traditional John Wayne sensibility, but to interrogate it. While *Elizabethtown*, for all practical narrative purposes, begins in the East, it also ends up in the West (Oregon), but is even further removed from the traditional Western movie in its representation of masculinity.

SMOKE SIGNALS: EMERGENT POSTMODERN MASCULINITIES

The youngest of these men on this road are the Native Americans Victor Joseph (Adam Beach) and Thomas Builds-the-Fire (Evan Adams) of Chris Eyre's *Smoke Signals*, a film constructed on the multiculturalism and identity politics that emerged in the 1990s.[38] These young men are barely out of high school, though in *The Lone Ranger and Tonto Fistfight in Heaven*, the volume of Sherman Alexie's short stories that gave rise to the film, Victor has just lost his job with the Bureau of Indian Affairs, a post he had taken up after high school.[39] The road trip in this film centres on Victor's retrieving the ashes and possessions of his father, Arnold, who had previously abandoned him and his mother and has now died alone in a mobile home in Arizona. Victor and his companion Thomas decide to travel to Phoenix from Spokane, Washington, to clear out the trailer and return with the father's truck. Victor's special issue is his resentment and anger over his father's physical abuse and abandonment of him when he was a little boy, while his chatty, story-telling companion Thomas, who provides the financial resources for the trip, goads Victor into identifying with his father. Thomas himself could have a reason to dislike Victor's father as well, because Arnold inadvertently started the New Year's Eve fire that killed Thomas's own parents on 4 July 1976, but he bears no grudges. Although this particular fire and the Bicentennial date are personal for Thomas

and Victor, as Slethaug and Laderman have noted, these also reference the cultural conflagration of Native Americans as a result of the
massive American intrusion into the West following independence.[40]
Symbolically, this is a nationally transgressive father.

This loss of, and attempt to regain, the transgressive father has
been a prominent theme in road literature and film at least since
Kerouac's *On the Road* where Sal Paradise's buddy Dean Moriarty
drove crazily across the country looking for, but not finding, his
father on the skid rows of Western American cities. The last line of
On the Road ends: "I think of Dean Moriarty, I even think of Old
Dean Moriarty the father we never found, I think of Dean Moriarty,"
and, as an echo of Kerouac's conclusion, *Smoke Signals* ends with
the final song/poem – "Do we forgive our fathers?"[41] In both, seeking and forgiving the fathers is a prerequisite for the positive male
friendship that the road can foster.

Although Victor in *Smoke Signals* remained close to his mother,
Arlene, both parents lived in a chaotic alcoholic haze when he was a
child, and his father subjected him to drunken physical abuse. Constantly pained over his father's abusive behaviour, Victor withheld his
affection, though he was distressed when his mother kicked Arnold
out of the house and doubly distressed when he heard nothing more
from him before his death. Without a father, his identity "wound" is
visible: he remains partially unassimilated in his family and, ultimately, on the reservation. Because of the Bicentennial references, this
is also a visible national wound, causing the lack of assimilation for
the entire Native American population. Consequently, the central
problem of this film is Victor's antagonism toward his father, need
for reconciliation, and integration into his Coeur d'Alene Indian
tribe and the American nation – but only through the intervention
of his geeky companion Thomas. This is about postmodern masculine self-discovery as well as the "comic" maintenance of familial,
tribal, and national identity.

Typically, in the American road genre, the vehicle for this kind of
discovery of self, friendship, family, and community is a car or truck
that moves across the United States from East to West, as is the case
in Jack Kerouac's novel *On the Road* and John Ford's film *Grapes
of Wrath*. Vehicles moving in other directions usually represent
more complicated and often difficult social and cultural relationships. Victor's process of self-discovery in *Smoke Signals*, however,
takes place on an Intermountain bus that moves from Northwest to

Southwest and that comes to serve as a symbol of male friendship and communal identity – what Laderman calls a "traveling community" that appears in only a very few other places in American film (*Midnight Cowboy* [1969]) and literature (Tom Wolfe's *The Electric Kool-Aid Acid Test* and Douglas Brinkley's *The Majic Bus*).[42] This bus brings Victor and Thomas into dialogue with each other and with the American culture outside the reservation and prepares Victor to accept his own weaknesses and those of his father. Like the bus in Spike Lee's *Get on the Bus* (1996) or even the coach in John Ford's much earlier *Stagecoach* (1939), this vehicle engages in cultural critique and puts strangers in connection with each other, highlighting questions about differences, prejudices, stereotypes, and social roles but also about commonalities.

Victor's and Thomas's bus trip to Phoenix makes their interwoven identities quite clear. They have a history of playing together as children and standing aloof from each other as adolescents, mainly because Victor hates his absent father and Thomas goads him with positive accounts of him. With limited funds, however, Victor depends on Thomas's financial resources in picking up his father's effects after Arnold dies from a heart attack in Arizona, so he has to tolerate him. The two youths are pulled together by their goal to retrieve the belongings, Thomas's aim to restore Arnold's image in Victor's eyes, their status as the only Native Americans on the bus, and ultimately their position as a small minority in the USA because of the injustices of the past.

Though the boys are in many respects mismatched in appearance and sensibility – Victor is a good-looking, athletic, hegemonic masculinist and Thomas a geeky, sensitive postmodern masculinist – their differences become complementary, as is frequently the case in buddy films. In possession of better social skills than Thomas and more attuned to dealing with the world off the reservation, Victor sizes up the other passengers on the bus and figures out how to deal with them and also teaches Thomas how to dress and fit in better. Thomas, however, is the articulate one and is able to put into words affections and memories that Victor can only glimpse subconsciously. For the most part, the other passengers leave the two alone though they look at them suspiciously, but, when two obnoxious racists take their seats, Victor and Thomas are forced to relocate but respond by singing "John Wayne's teeth," a comic reflection on this actor who not only portrayed the frontiersman's conquering of Native Americans but physically embodied hegemonic masculinist ideology. (It also pushes the viewer to think of a similar sing-along on *Get on the Bus* that is both celebrative and highly political, but there it is communal, while here it is restricted to the Native American pair – though the accompanying tribal chanting and drums suggest a communal force.) So the song celebrates a double triumph: an emergent adaptative postmodern masculinity and the continuation of Native Americans, despite the white man's attempts at their annihilation. For his part, Thomas continues to tell celebratory stories about Arnold Joseph, forcing Victor to reassess his anger toward his father, so that when they arrive at the trailer, Victor can begin to participate in a healing process that could symbolically restore his father, stitch up the psychic wound, and allow him to take the ashes back to his mother, thus closing the gap in the family circle.

Victor's journey to Phoenix in itself does not complete his task, and he must finish the loop by returning home – not on the bus but in Arnold Joseph's pickup truck (trucks in themselves usually signifying traditional hegemonic masculinity). In driving his father's truck, Victor begins to assume the mantle of manhood, but before successfully taking on that role, he crashes the vehicle while in an argument with Thomas over his family relationships. This accident, in the midst of yet another car crash, results in his running miles for help, magically assisted by his father's spiritual intervention, thus enabling the final phase of their reconciliation. Symbolically, he ends up recuperating in the hospital overnight.

When Victor successfully achieves that magical reconciliation with his father and begins the transformation of his own masculinity, he is truly ready to drive the truck home to his mother and to life on the reservation. He fully understands why Thomas goaded him and accepts the gift of forgiveness that his questions and stories bring. More than that, he is able to take his father's ashes and spread them on the water of the Spokane Falls, affirming his father's life, confirming his own links to an ancestral home and way of life, and asserting his own newly discovered masculinity. The film's final song/poem, "Do we forgive our fathers?," sums up Victor's masculinist enterprise: his road trip to Phoenix and back, his personal journey to forgive his father, his recognition of the importance of his tribe, and his ability to accept the larger American society that has let him and his people down over the ages. In this way, the road journey leads to a reconciliation of self, family. tribe, and nation, giving rise to an emergent postmodern masculinity and a comic vision.

BROKEBACK MOUNTAIN: PRIVATE POSTMODERN GAY MASCULINITIES

Ang Lee's *Brokeback Mountain* is not typically considered a road film, and it is not exactly a Western either, though its establishing shots make it clear that vehicles and journeys are inherently connected to the buddies' identity and destiny and that these take place in the rural mountainous West inhabited by cowboys. Roger Ebert notes that many called it a gay cowboy movie, but he finds that a "cruel simplification" because it is such a timeless narrative of "forbidden" and thwarted love and "crippled" egos;[43] it is also a simplification because the combined representation of the West, the road, and masculinities makes this film particularly engaging, complex, and enlightening.

This film is part of a developing tradition in the movie industry. As Robert Lang, Gina Marchetti, and others note, there is a strong tradition of gay road movies, gay Westerns, and combinations of the two. In his analysis of Gus Van Sant's *My Own Private Idaho* (1991) Robert Lang identifies the following as among the most interesting gay road films: are Gregg Araki's *The Living End* (1992), Steve McLean's *Postcards from America* (1994), *The Adventures of Priscilla, Queen of the Desert* (1994), *Boys on the Side* (1995), and *To Wong Foo Thanks for Everything! Julie Newmar* (1995).[44] To these should be added Philip Kaufman's *Henry & June* (1990). In her analysis of the recent transvestite road film *Transamerica* (2005), Marchetti notes that "the road, the cowboy, and the queer come together in a string of films, including *Johnny Guitar* (1954), *The Ballad of Little Jo* (1993), and *Even Cowgirls Get the Blues* (1993)" (chapter 9 in this volume). For many in the gay community, the beautifully photographed and nicely articulated *Brokeback Mountain* was the *pièce de résistance* that established once and for all the value of their community and civil rights battles,[45] and the complex layering of the film especially achieves this.

The opening scene of *Brokeback Mountain* at once picks up on the road, the West/Western, and the strong, silent heroes by showing Ennis Del Mar (Heath Ledger) and Jack Twist (Jake Gyllenhaal) in their cowhand gear leaning against their pickup trucks in front of the employment agency, eyeing one another without being obvious. Affordable relics of another day, the trucks signal their lack of money, their need for subsistence-level jobs, the parallel journeys they will take, and their ties to traditional codes of masculinity, but they also help to mask and facilitate the boys' curiosity and desire for each other. Their upcoming experiences on Brokeback Mountain are, of course, not inextricably tied to these pickup trucks, but the horseback journeys that take them there are part-and-parcel of the road and Western movie traditions (see Slethaug in chapter 1 and Zierler in chapter 10), and their subsequent relationship off the mountain can only be facilitated by their vehicles because Ennis stays in Wyoming and Jack ends up in Texas.

Neither Ennis nor Jack has finished high school, and both struggle to compete in the late twentieth-century US with its rapid changes from subsistence farming and ranching to the growth of agribusiness and the related collapse of small country towns. These are also young men who, without having recognized their latent homosexuality, have falsely assumed that they are comfortably heterosexual and will be happily married. Because they have not taken their personal masculinities and social identities sufficiently on board, they are ripe for failure. Both end up marrying and having children, but, having recognized their homosexual inclinations on Brokeback Mountain, neither is happy with family life. (When the film was first released, their self-divided sexual identity created a great stir among critics who contested whether the young men were gay, bisexual, or even straight.)[46] Moreover, neither has a fulfilling career: while they love the rodeo circuit, it cannot sustain them. Ennis goes from one low-paying job to another, and, although Jack does reasonably well in farm equipment sales by marrying the boss's daughter, he hates the job and is under the financial and family rule of his wife and father-in-law.

Although the film celebrates the physical passion of Ennis and Jack in the Wyoming Rockies, their discovery of this gay identity and new masculinity is ambiguous. Like the mountains and road trips themselves, their relationship and intertwined identities are simultaneously beautiful and dangerous. David Bell points out that forests can "evoke nature as an erotic topography" for gay men, but Jo Little notes that "wilderness and untamed landscapes" are more commonly coded as "constructions of hegemonic rural masculinity."[47] Thus, Manohla Dargis's assertion that the Rockies of

Brokeback Mountain suggest an unlimited homoerotic freedom that stands in juxtaposition to the hidden quality of closeted desires in the valley must be closely interrogated.[48] While these high and beautiful mountains may not be the forbidding pillars of Monument Valley portrayed in road films ranging from *Stagecoach* and *Grapes of Wrath* to *Thelma and Louise*, they are neither idyllic in reality nor uncomplicated metaphors of free male passion. Accompanying the stunning alpine scenery are treacherous storms and fearsome wolves and bears, and the boys' consuming passion must be hidden from equally treacherous people on or off the mountain or it will destroy them – as it finally does Jack. Ennis's own guardedness and ambivalence about his sexual identity and his wife's discovery of his attraction to Jack result in alienation, divorce, and a more-or-less permanent dysfunctionality. Jack dreams of the two buddies starting life together on his father's ranch, but Ennis is not comfortable enough with his sexual identity, their relationship, or public reaction to entertain that possibility. Instead, he is forced to stay alone in a bare-bones mobile home that lacks comfort and permanence and to see Jack only occasionally. Their masculinity is postmodern gay/bisexual but is not continuously romantic and celebrative because it cannot be played out in public spaces.[49] Theirs is the conflict between the hegemonic masculinity expected of them (and is part of conventional road and Western movie narratives) and an alternative and subverted postmodern gay/bisexual masculinity that remains closeted.

The use of the road subsequent to the young men's mountain-top experience highlights this ambiguity. Culturally, trucks are associated with a macho masculinity, but, historically, in rural America they "gave men access to gay spaces both local and distant, became a gay space itself, and helped shape stationary gay spaces as they evolved."[50] In this film it is only through their trucks that the buddies can join each other on fishing trips/liaisons, but their mobility does not symbolize happiness or transformation; rather, it marks their inability to settle down and make a life together. In one scene, as Ennis and Jack meet on the side of the road, with Ennis's daughters in the car, a truck drives by on the highway and both men look at it uneasily, suggesting that trucks connect them and form part of their alibis, but also stand in the way of domestic bliss, either with their own families or between them as a couple. Ironically, Jack is beaten and killed in 1983 by tire-iron wielding homophobics, who fabricate the story that his tire exploded and killed him while he was changing it. The automobile/truck, then, functions as a lure in bringing the boys together, a conveyance in accommodating their annual fishing trips, and an alibi for their sexual liaisons. It also becomes the weapon in Jack's murder. The automobile both enables and subverts postmodern gay/bisexual masculinity.

Brokeback Mountain, then, is a gripping story of deep but conflicted love between male lovers, who on occasion and in private enjoy a postmodern gay masculinity, and this is the way that many moviegoers want to remember it, even down to the detail of Ennis discovering and cherishing his old shirt wrapped in his lover's in – tellingly – Jack's closet after his death. However, it also serves as a warning to those who veer away from hegemonic masculinity and familial and social norms. Judging from Jack's father's stern and hostile looks at Ennis and his refusal to allow Ennis to scatter Jack's ashes on Brokeback Mountain, Jack's homosexuality alienated him from his father, and this wound was never repaired. Those who violate these familial and socio-cultural sanctions, even when following their deepest instincts, frequently are alienated and victimized. As Annie Proulx, the Wyoming author of the story, would have known only too well, the year before she published her volume containing "Brokeback Mountain" (1999), Matthew Shepard, a gay college student, died after having been kidnapped, beaten, and tied to a fence by gay-bashers in near freezing temperatures in Laramie, Wyoming. Few reading this story at the time of its publication could have avoided the painful memory of that nationally documented tragedy.

Nonetheless, a partly redemptive historical allegory may be buried in the tale. Ang Lee's movie is set between 1960 and 1983, as gay culture emerged from the closet. Born in 1940, Jack begins his relationship with Ennis around 1960 and is killed in 1983. This is the time of the Stonewall Riots (1969) that launched the gay-rights movement; the first gay rodeo (1976); and the 100,000 strong Gay and Lesbian March on Washington (1979). These celebratory moments correspond to the flourishing of Jack and Ennis's relationship. However, the identification of AIDS in 1982, its acknowledged links to gay culture, and a sombre awareness of the rising death tally brought a new homophobia to the fore in American society. It was not until new AIDS drugs were introduced that this hysteria abated, allowing for greater acceptance of gay lifestyles, rights, and even marriage – truly an indication of the acceptance of a new kind of postmodern masculinity. The initial passion and the resultant love of the buddies Jack and Ennis, as well as the improvement in the ways gay individuals are received in American culture, establish the basis of a new less homophobic masculinity and a romantic highway in this film, but the pain of their conflicted lives and Jack's tragic death provides a strong cautionary note that there are many, not wholly compatible, masculinities in this postmodern period and that the private postmodern gay masculinity that cannot go public – or even one that does go public – is still at risk. Thus this film simultaneously looks forward to an age of complete acceptance for gay identitiess and backward to the time of *Easy Rider*, when those who deviate from social norms pay with their lives. Its postmodernity mixes the romantic and the tragic.

ELIZABETHTOWN: POSTMODERN MASCULINITY OF EXPRESSION AND AFFECTION

Another tale of a young man on the road is a much less complicated and conflicted romantic buddy film but an equally compelling account of restructuring masculinity. This is Cameron Crowe's *Elizabethtown*, the story of Drew Baylor (Orlando Bloom), who is laid off after losing US$972,000,000 for his company as a result of poorly designed and marketed shoes and who is so distraught that he contemplates suicide. Clearly his "marketplace masculinity" cannot sustain him, but his suicide plan is interrupted by news of his own father's heart attack and death and his need to represent the family at the funeral and memorial service. It seems he must do that because his mother (Susan Sarandon) has caused stress in the family by moving her husband to California and is not sufficiently welcome at this event to take a responsible role. On the flight from Oregon to Louisville, Kentucky, close to where the memorial is to take place, Drew meets the flight attendant Clare Coleburn (Kirsten Dunst), who not only takes him under her wing during the flight but provides him with road directions to Elizabethtown and forms a friendship and then romantic attachment afterwards. This is an unabashedly romantic account of a male/female buddy relationship that turns to love but, nonetheless, arises from Drew's having to come to terms with being fired after his poor investment, the death of his father and ambivalent feelings about him, and a problematic extended-family relationship. Although he recognizes at the memorial that his father's death did bring the family together, it takes the intervention of Clare before he can shed tears and acknowledge his "wound" and love for him.

The conflict with his real father is one of several that Drew experiences: another concerns Phil (Alec Baldwin), his boss within the shoe company, who acted like a supportive father while he was doing well in the company and then fired him without remorse when he performed poorly. A third is less personal but nationally symbolic: as part of his road trip, Drew visits the place where Martin Luther King Jr was shot, depriving America of one of its most important late-twentieth-century fathers. Drew, then, is triply wounded by fathers who abandon him on family, corporate, and national levels. This film, which mainly concerns private relationships, embraces American national history and issues typical of other buddy films.

The road is the avenue and a sporty car the vehicle that draws Drew to his real father, Clare, and national fathers and helps him cope with his wounds. Increasingly, air travel has become part of the road trip and genre, but for the most part it only serves to get the highway trip underway. Likely, airplanes (and trains) lack the freedom, randomness, and spontaneity that asphalt roads, cars, and choices of destinations are thought to bring (see Truscello in chapter 10). The plane first establishes a comfort zone and cocoon for Drew and Clare's developing relationship, but it is the car that allows it to mature.

The drive from the Louisville airport to the father's ancestral home in Elizabethtown, Kentucky, is largely inconsequential, though Drew's failure to follow Clare's careful directions gets him lost and confirms her as a good friend, buddy, and reliable guide. It also makes him realize that she is there to catch him in his needy moments: she is, after all, the only person to listen to him when he desperately pleads to his cell phone, "Somebody, call me back"; she also follows him to Louisville to help him through his painful ordeal, even though she herself is going through a difficult time with her boyfriend. This is every bit as much about friendship as *Smoke Signals* and *Brokeback Mountain* and indicates that within postmodern masculinities, buddies who share things emotionally can be mixed or same-sex gender. The new mixed-gender romantic relationships transgress the old same-sex buddy relationships and transform the outlaw mixed-sex buddy relationship of *Bonnie and Clyde*.

Drew's developing friendship with Clare, his unexpectedly pleasant encounter with his father's family, his stay-over at the Brown Hotel (where a wedding celebration is in progress that thematically serves as a foil for the funeral – "life and death and life and a hair between them"), and the crazily exuberant memorial service where his mother tap-dances and tells inappropriately comic stories help him to put aside his despair and sense of failure and affirm his relationship to his father, family, and community. This is the most confirming scene of his repaired wound as he overcomes the physical and emotional distance from his family and embraces a new masculinity and family circle.

Otherwise, it is the road trip home from Elizabethtown to Oregon that allows Drew especially to mourn his father and consolidate his relationship with Clare. After the memorial celebration and funeral service, Clare gives him a minute-by-minute and mile-by-mile itinerary, including carefully chosen music, detailed maps, specific sites to see, and things to do. Drew has these to guide his every mile from Kentucky to Oregon, accompanied by his father's ashes in an urn placed in the passenger seat. His hegemonic masculinity is no longer in the driver's seat for he responds in every detail to the journey planned by Clare and has the urn with his father's ashes quite literally sitting by his side, so, although this is a solo road trip, it paradoxically functions as a buddy trip. Because Clare maps out and manages Drew's every move on the highway, the traditional freedom and abandon of the road trip disappear, along with expected gender roles.

The road from Kentucky through the Midwest and out to the Pacific coast is critical for this kind of postmodern film, even as it was in earlier generations of films where protagonists had to battle the dust-covered plains and western deserts as symptoms of their internal demons and social struggles, but here the imagery is symbolically soft and verdant. In leaving Elizabethtown, Drew drives first to Frankfort, Kentucky, and on to Memphis, Tennessee, through miles of lush, green countryside, interacting with friendly people and coming to terms with the death of his father through private time in the car. In Memphis, he also comes to terms with the death of Martin Luther King Jr, who was assassinated at the Lorraine Motel, now the site of a national memorial. Even when he comes to Oklahoma City – the site of a memorial commemorating the deaths caused by the terrorist Timothy McVeigh and the heart of the dust-bowl that sent so many sojourners on the road in search of food and jobs during the Great Depression – the city is soft and verdant, suggesting forgiveness and a new beginning. As well, Route 66, the mother road that took the hungry and homeless Westward, now fallen into disrepair, offers off-freeway comfort and beauty as he travels through Kansas and Nebraska to California, where he is destined to meet Clare at the nation's "Second Largest Farmer's Market." In other films, many of these places and even the folk music associated with them served to highlight the difficulty of life and the paucity of alternatives for travellers (see Kuyper in chapter 3). Here, the landscape is green and lovely, the sites charming, and the music soft and rhythmic, allowing Drew to come to terms with his own failures, the death of his real and symbolic fathers, and, by extension, the difficulty of family relationships and the tragic moments in American culture and history. His reconciliation to his various familial, business, and national fathers represents the sway of a new romantic postmodern masculinity.

The final carnivalesque scene at the farmer's market brings Drew and Clare together in the midst of lively youthful activity and an abundance of summer fruits and vegetables – certain signs of well-being, vigour, fertility, and the continuity of life. The final words of the film – "sex, of course, but also of life" – remind the viewers that fathers' deaths, including that of the iconic Martin Luther King Jr, are tragic but can lead to renewal. They also remind the viewer that the age-old axiom that men are only interested in sex has been reconstructed to focus on participating in the cycle of life. This film expands *Smoke Signal*'s search to form a strong friendship and reconcile with a dead father. It shows a triumph of love, family, and community over the problems of personal failure, family breakdown, and mortality; and a postmodern masculinity of expression and overt affection in action.

SIDEWAYS: IR/RESPONSIBLE POSTMODERN MASCULINITY OF CAMARADERIE

If *Smoke Signals*, *Brokeback Mountain*, and *Elizabethtown* are road movies about how young men construct new masculinities, learn how to bond with their friends, and (in two instances) repair the wounds of their failed relationships with their fathers, Alexander Payne's *Sideways* shows how buddies crossing into middle age handle their lives, loves, and families through two very different masculinities: one an increasingly responsible postmodern masculinity of camaraderie; and one traditionally hegemonic. In this film, the forty-something male leads, Miles (Paul Giamatti) and his old college buddy Jack (Thomas Haden Church) handle neither their own friendship nor their relationships with others well, but that is the charm of the narrative, which Roger Ebert calls "lovable."[51] Miles, an English teacher and would-be writer, has had his marriage end in divorce and, while his ex has started another family, he has not been able to accept the divorce or move on, becoming morose, depressed, uncommunicative, and even belligerent. His friend Jack, a small-time actor in soap operas and commercials, has had a series of meaningless relationships over the years, and, despite having finally found a woman he wants to marry, cannot quit his sexual philandering. Consequently, on this prenuptial bachelor week gifted by Miles, Jack deliberately jeopardizes his wedding plans by pursuing a last sexual fling. There is no father in this film, though there is a mother whom Miles visits (and steals money from) on his way to pick up Jack. As with so many of the other relationships in this book, there is something both tender and manipulative about this mother-son dynamic. Perhaps the absent father is a clear sign that the men have not really grown up and entered society in a clear and responsible way. Contrary to Katie Mills's view that these are men with "a little too much autonomy and mobility in their unhappy lives,"[52] these are men who are stuck in a groove and move in circles.

Despite their personal idiosyncrasies, their seeming inability to transform themselves, and the resulting complications, the road trip that takes these middle-aged men north from San Diego through Los Angeles into the vineyards of the Santa Ynez Valley near Santa Barbara is about friendship, love, and growing responsibility to the larger community. It is "full of beautiful and painful things" – as Miles's friend Maya (Virginia Madsen) says of his failed novel. Despite its wide popularity among movie goers who even want to follow the same wine route, critics have not been altogether kind to this movie. Orgeron comments that, "with its premarital chaos and tidily ironic marital ending," it "blatantly descends ... from the happily hokey road-elopement films" "that begin with the illusion of institutional escape only to find the outlaws themselves re-absorbed, surrounded by in-laws."[53]

Wanting the best for his friend, covering the costs of the bachelors' holiday, and supplying the battered red Saab convertible,

Miles provides a certain, though flawed, moral compass for the film. Unable to move beyond the divorce from his wife Vicky (perhaps because he had an affair that broke up the marriage), "officially depressed for two years," and tending to go "on the dark side," he still manages to climb out of his slough of despondency to celebrate with Jack and to visit his mother on the way to the vineyards. He plans special dinners, buys special wines, and arranges first-rate golfing to ensure that this is a festive occasion to cement their friendship. Though he has a more reflective and dark personality than his priapic friend Jack, he wants to be a good friend and do the right thing. Jack, who shares neither Miles's interests nor his knowledge of great wine, wants "a week to get crazy" – happy to drink anything, sleep with anyone, and, not incidentally, arrange for Miles to get laid as a way of lifting him out of his depression. He also depends on his friend to bail him out of his sexual misadventures. It is this dilemma that made this romantic comedy such a hit: these likeable men of opposing Apollonian and Dionysian personalities and highly disparate masculinities are flawed, compulsive, dysfunctional, and entertaining in different ways, but also compassionate and funny.

Miles's choice of wines and vineyards, as well as his drinking, provide a key to his friendship, compulsions, and masculinity. He has brought along great wine for this celebration and, knowing which varietals and years are especially good, plans to buy more as he moves through the vineyards. In Miles's quest for the perfect pinot noir, this film pays tribute to knowledgeable drinking and fine dining, the development of the wine industry in this area, and the beauty of the California landscape – the appreciation of landscape being a staple feature of buddy road films, as seen in *Easy Rider*, *Brokeback Mountain*, and *Elizabethtown*. Miles's love of the grape, however, has a negative dimension as well: it is not just a passion but also a compulsion. Given his limited salary, he spends more on wine than he should and consequently is financially pressed. As well, when he is emotionally down, lamenting his failure in relationships and writing, he drinks more that he should, blurring his vision and blunting his ability to deal with himself and others.

What Miles especially has not been able to foresee in arranging this week is that at the very first dinner in a restaurant where his old acquaintance Maya works, Jack will immediately take up with her friend Stephanie (Sandra Oh), never telling either of the young women that he is to be married the following Saturday. Conflicted between his developing relationship with Maya and his loyalty to Jack, Miles fails to take responsibility for the obvious problems of Jack's affair. When the relationship has gone much too far and Jack has made promises he never intends to keep, Miles lets it slip to Maya that Jack is to be married, precipitating a crisis for everyone. Stephanie feels betrayed by Jack's sexual and emotional exploitation of her and breaks his nose with her motorcycle helmet, and Maya feels betrayed by Miles's failure to tell her of Jack's immoral behaviour and immediately breaks with him. What was to be a bachelor celebration turns into a premarital disaster. Miles's quiescent postmodern masculinity turns out to be as deeply flawed as Jack's hegemonic masculinity, because neither of them has taken the kind of personal responsibility and care for others that they should.

The red Saab convertible that carried the men to the vineyards and new relationships, however, also helps to solve the problems raised in these relationships, cementing the camaraderie between the men, ensuring that Jack will marry his fiancée, and finally returning Miles to Maya. The thematic role of the car is emphasized in the opening shot of the film, when Miles rushes out of his apartment to keep his car from being impounded after he has drunk too much in a wine tasting the night before and left it in a no-parking zone. Following that, the car is highlighted taking Miles and Jack (whom he picks up in Los Angeles) to the vineyards and again helping Jack to escape when a cuckolded and outraged husband chases him after his brief affair with another restaurant employee. As with the trucks in *Brokeback Mountain*, this car becomes an alibi when Jack suggests they crash it so that his fiancée will feel compassion for him instead of outrage, and the wedding can go ahead as planned. Finally, the car becomes redemptive when, some time after Jack's wedding, Miles drives the Saab back to the Santa Ynez Valley, when Maya leaves a call for him that suggests she has reached a new understanding and that the relationship might resume. The car initially solidifies the friendship of the two, opens up numerous possibilities for them, then assures their personal happiness, and finally secures legitimate family relationships (the wedding) and social harmony (suggested by Miles's engaging smiles with Jack at the wedding and reconciliation with Vicky and her acceptance of her new life following the wedding). Such a wedding is a typical ending for social romances, but here the car and the road add a new, engaging, and playful postmodern feature, not suggesting that any of the happiness is deserved, but also not suggesting that either Miles or Jack should be punished because of their questionable behaviour. Jack learns nothing from this pre-nuptial week, and his hegemonic masculinity stays firmly in place. Miles, however, may have learned responsibility, so his postmodern masculinity will survive and help him to form better relationships in the future.

BROKEN FLOWERS: POSTMODERN MASCULINITY OF RELATIVITY

Broken Flowers, *About Schmidt*, and *The Straight Story* are also about men on the road, but these are all late middle-aged and elderly, who in the past had jobs and careers, but now seek new meaning. These are not buddy films, but instead are solo road movies about having adventures and trying to rescue meaning alone. To a great extent, buddy road films concern the initial stages of putting life together through the assistance of other people, but solo or loner road films are, at least in the case of older men, about having gone through and lost youthful connectedness and marital happiness and/or responsibility, and now having to construct meaning independently. Don Johnston (Bill Murray) of *Broken Flowers* has sold his computer firm and is pushed to discover whether he has a son. Warren Schmidt of *About Schmidt*, who has retired from the insurance business and unexpectedly lost his wife, sets out in his oversized Winnebago RV to disrupt his daughter's wedding because he dislikes the groom and wants to protect his daughter. *The Straight Story*'s Alvin Straight, reduced to walking with canes and with no car or driver's licence, drives through two states on a lawn tractor to repair his relationship with his brother (who has had a stroke) because it is the only personally noble way to get there. Not one of these is a tragic road trip with "hopeless and lamentable mobility," but the characters do go through serious tests as they pursue their personal goals, continue to construct their masculinities, struggle to build or rebuild family relationships, and consolidate relationships with friends and community. All of these films develop around the theme of a repair to the wounds in family relationships, but more generally between fathers and children or between siblings.

Jim Jarmusch's *Broken Flowers*, which Orgeron thinks represents a new "screen relevance" for the road movie,[54] is the story of a sedentary, passive, and lonely late-middle-aged bachelor who, upon receiving a letter on pink stationery telling him that he may have an almost-19-year-old son on his way to see him, accedes to his neighbour's request to set out on a trip to see whether this is a hoax or whether one of a handful of ex-girlfriends really has given him a child. In this way, the narrative addresses the father's perspective (instead of the son's, as discussed above) in the enduring controversy of father-son relationships. Through the dialogue and photography, this road movie subtly exposes Don Johnston's reclusive character, though, as with Miles and Jack in *Sideways*, he is little wiser at the conclusion of the journey than at the beginning. Contrary to what Orgeron believes of this film, it does not "begin with the illusion of institutional escape" and end with the protagonist absorbed into society, "surrounded by in-laws";[55] Johnston enjoys no escape and is just as alone at the end as at the beginning.

Don's masculinity has clearly been hegemonic but leads to dysfunctionality. As part of his masculine identity, he has been a successful businessman, though he has never wanted to be saddled with responsible friendships, love, or children. After selling his firm, he seems unable to function at home or in society, for his work may have been his total identity. In his retirement he only watches television and is disconnected from the rest of humanity, including the girlfriends who are said to have passed through his life. The opportunity to find out whether he has a son could remediate his masculinity and lead to new options, but he is half-hearted about it. Though he seems to have abandoned a hegemonic masculinity, this new passivity is a failed, not a reconstituted, postmodern identity.

Don's neighbour, Winston (Jeffrey Wright), sees that Don's masculinity is in crisis and tries to serve as an agent of change by prompting him to set out to find out whether he has a son and, if so, who the mother might be. Don would not have set out on the road trip had not Winston taken the lead role, insisting that he be given the list of Don's relevant old girlfriends, looking up their addresses on the web, creating an itinerary, and booking flights, car rentals, and hotel rooms even before Don agrees to the adventure. Winston seems to undertake the demands of this task without compromising his good relationship with his wife or children. His organizational skills, family commitment, and care for Don provide a good model of masculinity for Don, but have too little impact.

The road is everywhere present as reality and trope in Don's intended journey to discovery and remediated masculinity, but, without destination or conclusion, it has the air of contrivance and artificiality. His hypothetical son supposedly has taken a road trip to find Don, and Don takes a road trip – in both airplanes and cars – to locate his former girlfriends and find whether this son is real, but this trip seems as false as Don's own masculinity. He first flies to various cities and then rents cars, but none of the airports are given specific names or locations, and, while we do have images of airport lounges and bus transfers to car-rental offices, the focus is on the women surrounding Don rather than the places. The highway, too, is as empty and vacant as it is full and present. Don passes miles of countryside and numerous houses in cities and suburbs, but no specific cities are mentioned and there are no distinguishing signs to mark particular streets or to identify features of the landscape, and the various houses – the small unkempt yellow house, the cookie-cutter suburban mansion, the new-age animal clinic, and the down-and-out country house – seem at once individually recognizable and stereotypical. Although in reality they were all filmed in New York and New Jersey, the film seems to suggest they were much further apart, and yet gives no sense of particularity or "presence." This postmodern landscape and Don's road trip promise fullness but deliver emptiness in the same way that Don's reputed sexuality and masculinity promise fullness (a son, among other things) but deliver passivity and emptiness.

As Don follows his journey, he cannot reconstitute his masculinity and identity because he remains trapped in passivity. Arguably, a powerful hegemonic masculinity would be an improvement over his present neutered state, because it would indicate energy, action, and assertiveness, but he has none of those traditional characteristics or the redeeming qualities of a new, engaged, postmodern masculinity. As a male, Don is a cipher, a zero, in the same way that there is no message to be gained from the pink letter or discovery from the search. This is form without substance and a signifier of masculinity without any signified.

And so we have it – Don does not find out what the hints might tell him; he does not discover whether one of his former lovers has mothered his son; he does not know whether Sherry or Winston has put him up to this search; the places in the journey are never identified; and, consequently, the viewer has no more certainty than Don about the meaning of any of these things. Don's postmodern masculinity of relativity is constructed without identity and meaning, and

Broken Flowers is built on inconclusive randomness, uncertainty, and ambiguity. In this context, Laderman's comments about Jim Jarmusch's first road movie, *Stranger than Paradise*, apply: "Lumbering with ironic urbanite 'attitude' and ennui, the aimless purpose of the film's journey is revealed in the stationary scenes as well as the driving scenes. Stability in the film is so exaggerated it becomes an excessive caricature, the extreme opposite of movement and motivation, an 'emptiness' in the mise en scène, a void that only mobility can fill. Yet mobility too will be 'empty,' unfulfilling, a rearticulation of nonmovement."[56]

Despite the emptiness, paucity of meaning, ennui, and masculinity of relativity, the road trip and the film itself ironically make a profound statement about the inability to discover absolute meaning, about uncertainty in information, the tantalizing unknowability of life, and, ultimately, the paradoxical need for action and mobility. In this respect, it is a very special kind of solo road movie and comic romance. Don is returned to his home, no wiser than he was at the outset, but also none the worse. He has got off his duff and out of his house; he has reconnected with old girlfriends; and, consequently, he has had an opportunity to reprise his life – whether or not he takes advantage of that opportunity. He has fulfilled the requirements of his quest without gaining greater understanding, but his connection with past lovers and present friends creates the potential for a more engaged life, though not actualized. This combination of postmodern romance, masculinity, and the road is a lesson for the viewer, if not the character.

ABOUT SCHMIDT: INTERCONNECTED POSTMODERN MASCULINITY OF GENEROSITY

Alexander Payne's *About Schmidt* is much less playful and much more serious than *Broken Flowers* in exploring masculinity and the lessons the road can teach older men. It is, as Manohla Dargis argues, "perfectly pitched between comedy and tragedy, hope and despair," and "comes far closer than many movies to expressing the way many of us live – someplace between consuming self-absorption and insistently demanding otherness."[57] In this solo road film, the 66-year-old Warren Schmidt (Jack Nicholson) has just retired from his position as assistant vice-president at Woodman's Insurance in Omaha, Nebraska, when Helen (June Squibb), his wife of 42 years, dies just short of the wedding date of their daughter Jeannie (Hope Davis) to Randall Hertzel (Dermot Mulroney), a waterbed salesman whom Warren dislikes and regards as socially inferior. Schmidt's nearly simultaneous retirement, wife's death, and daughter's wedding create a crisis of existential masculinist proportions for Warren, compounded by his discovery that Helen had an affair with his best friend Ray (Len Cariou) some 25 years earlier.

What Warren discovers is that, as Mills notes, there is a huge gap between image and reality and that, as with Don Johnston in *Broken Flowers*, the structure of his hegemonic masculinity has come undone.[58] He no longer has a job to provide focus or financial compensation. His marriage is over and has been shown to rest partly on false foundations. His friendship with Ray has been compromised with the revelation of infidelity. In addition, he can no longer control his daughter's life. A job, marriage, children, and male friendship are all important constituents of traditional hegemonic masculinity, and, while their demise gives Schmidt an opportunity to transform masculinities and identities, that is a hard task.

Consequently, Warren's setting out on the road is more intensely about loss than the six other male-centred buddy and solo road films, but, in common with the young males of *Smoke Signals* and *Elizabethtown*, this loss is not articulated or recuperated until the end of the film. In the concluding moment of remorse that is tantamount to self-annihilation, Warren cries about his loss and the lack of connectedness and meaning in life, but he also cries because of a letter and picture he receives from Ndugu, a young Tanzanian boy he is supporting, to whom he writes throughout the film and who finally reminds him of the importance of reaching out to others.

Warren comes to this growing realization that he might have a role to play as a result of his road trip in an oversized Winnebago Adventurer RV. This is not Drew's sporty car in *Elizabethtown* or Miles's aging Saab in *Sideways;* it has none of the sexual connotations of the pick-up trucks in *Brokeback Mountain* or fierce independence of Arnold Joseph's truck in *Smoke Signals*; nor is it the bus of *Smoke Signals* signifying community. This RV signifies purposeless retirement and abandoned masculinity – partly a reprise of David Howard in Albert Brooks' *Lost in America* (1985), who takes to the road in a Winnebago after being passed over for a promotion. What Warren finally discovers, then, must be regarded with that signification in mind.

Warren and Helen had planned together to drive this van to their daughter's wedding in Denver, but Warren sets out on his road trip in anger after confronting his friend Ray about love letters that his wife left behind. He wants to drive immediately to see his daughter, but she puts a stop to that, so he takes the more typically circuitous route of road movies that retraces the protagonists' youth while providing social commentary on national issues. His first stops reflect his intention to rediscover parts of his youth, both the Nebraska house where he grew up and his university in Lawrence, Kansas. He then visits certain spots in other Nebraska towns that connect to him geographically and historically: antique shops in Cozad, Buffalo Bill Cody's house in North Platte, and the Custer County Museum in Broken Bow. These very specifically identified places establish networks of historical and communal connection and meaning in the construction of his original masculinity. These are not the uncertain and ambiguous locations of *Broken Flowers*, but very specific places that yield meaning for Warren and the viewing audience about the difficult but redemptive movement to, and settling of, the West.

When he arrives in Denver, Warren stays with his future son-in-law's mother, Roberta Hertzel (Kathy Bates), though his intention is to stop the wedding and prevent the development of these networks of relationships. However, because of his daughter's specific warning and Roberta's help while he has a bad back that immobilizes him two days before the wedding, he does take part, tolerating the ceremony, praising the strengths of his daughter's new family, and ending his speech at the wedding banquet with "I am very pleased." As a result of letting his daughter go and experiencing her happiness and approval, he is able to part amicably, though he is undoubtedly lonely as a result.

In returning from Denver to Omaha, he drives straight through, except for a stop at the archway monument over the freeway in Kearney, Nebraska, that commemorates the old wagon trail, highlighting the road, a sense of community, and a historical purpose as well. It is in Omaha that he has to assimilate the lessons he has just learned on the road and create a new masculinity and identity. This is where Ndugu comes in. Ndugu has been the silent witness throughout the film: as Warren writes to him, reading his letters to the viewing audience, he pours his heart out to this boy, who, until the end, does not reply. When he does communicate in a letter penned by a Sister of the Sacred Heart (he himself is illiterate) and includes his own naïve-style picture of an older man and a small boy holding hands under a blue sky, Warren dissolves into tears partly in grief over a phase of his life clearly ended but also with knowledge that he has touched, and been touched by, someone across the globe. Over space (the highway and the world) and time (the duration of his life and Nebraska culture), he has discovered interconnectedness, communication, and purpose – a new inter-cultural postmodern masculinity. These are important discoveries for someone who has lost all meaning. He now has the understand-ing and the means to connect with others through his relationship with Ndugu – should he choose to follow that route. He has man-aged to repair the wound between himself and his daughter, and this new father-adopted son bond can open the floodgates to a new interconnected postmodern masculinity of sharing and generos-ity. The end of this film is consequently more positive than that of *Broken Flowers*, because his masculinity and identity are in the pro-cess of remediation.

STRAIGHT STORY: POSTMODERN MASCULINITY OF SELF-REDEMPTION AND FAMILY SOLIDARITY

In David Lynch's *The Straight Story*, the last of these seven buddy or solo films of men on the road, and arguably the most heart-warming, the 73-year-old Alvin Straight (Richard Farnsworth) of Laurens, Iowa, sets out at a snail's pace on a lawn tractor to visit his stroke-afflicted 75-year-old brother Lyle (Harry Dean Stanton) in Mt Zion, Wisconsin, a several-hundred-mile journey across two states. This "blind and lame" "old geezer," as Alvin calls himself, goes on this six-week, late summer and early autumnal odyssey to mend his rela-tionship with Lyle, and this is the only way that he can manage the trip: he gets around slowly on two canes because of bad hips; he has limited vision because of diabetes, so he cannot have a driver's license or a car; and he does not trust bus drivers. But he must mend the wound in his soul and family as so many fathers and "brothers" have done in other recent road films. To mend that wound, he has to travel slowly and deliberately, much as Whitman recommended in "Song of the Open Road" (see Slethaug in chapter 1) to avoid the pitfalls of speed that cause chaos on the road and that almost do in Alvin himself when the technology fails in his tractor as he roars out of control down a hill towards an assembled group of people.

This astonishing narrative, based on a true story, begins with one of David Lynch's trademarks – grotesques in decayed surroundings. Alvin himself first appears as a bearded old man with a bad haircut lying helpless on the kitchen floor of a run-down frame-house while a fat neighbour (Jane Galloway Heitz) with sunglasses lies outside on a lounge chair; his seemingly simple daughter Rosie (Sissy Spacek), who has a speech impairment, can do little more than make bird houses; and his male companions in Laurens who peer at him are, like Alvin, mostly unattractive old men who appear to have outlived their usefulness. This is hardly a positive community identity or personal masculinity. As with Don in *Broken Flowers* and Warren in *About Schmidt*, it seems more about loss than the desire or ability to reconfigure.

But, as in all of Lynch's films, reality is never what it seems. Alvin is a canny man, whose shabby appearance and deep reserve belie his ability to bargain hard and show good sense, wisdom, and deep compassion. Similarly, Rose, though autistic, is quite capable of managing her life and the house, and his friends in Laurens look out for him and each other with respect and friendly attachment. The opening impression of weakness and grotesqueness is dead wrong, and everyone has to learn respect and affection for these people, as they did in similar circumstances in *Grapes of Wrath*, the film that Laderman thinks is behind this one.[59] These are individuals in the family and community who have compassion and straightforward values.

As Alvin sets out going northward instead of the conventional westward (and, therefore, precluding any sense of hegemony or domination), the spectators in the film itself and in the theatre seats share a similar reaction: driving an old lawn tractor and pulling a heavy trailer – a "pile of junk" as the pregnant runaway calls it – the foolhardy Alvin is not likely to make it beyond the edge of town. And he does not on the first try, but then he negotiates with the John Deere salesman for a newer lawn tractor, and his abilities begin to shine – as they do in some ten separate encounters on the road. He bargains with the twin tractor repairmen when the transmission fails, negotiating the price from $250 to $180; a "stubborn man," he pays his way at every mile of the journey, not accepting handouts from anyone; he is always friendly, waving to everyone along the route, willing to listen and talk to those he meets, and allowing them to show "kindness to a stranger"; he shows deep compassion and understanding to a woman who has hit her fourteenth deer in seven weeks and gives good advice to the pregnant girl running away from home; but he also hints at the struggles he has had throughout his life – losing seven of his fourteen children – and the pain he has caused – inadvertently killing a fellow soldier on the battlefields of France and, through drink, setting off the "Cain and Abel" confrontation with his brother Lyle that has kept them apart for ten years.

None of these experiences and confessions characterize a traditional hegemonic masculinity: he knows he has wronged his brother – his best friend – and wants to repair that; he is not a selfish or self-centred man but is compassionate at all times; he is not controlled by work; while he does have a sense of independence and pride, he subordinates those to helping others along the way; and he speaks eloquently about the pain of losing his children and causing harm to a fellow soldier in France. In short, he opens up completely and discloses secrets that he has hidden for many years. His slow-moving and self-reflective road trip to see his brother Lyle is consequently his ongoing journey in constructing a postmodern masculinity of openness and generosity.

Laderman finds that this postmodern, defamiliarized road "synthesizes conformist trends with revitalized rebellion"; Orgeron finds it a postmodern "space of reunion, not rebellion; a space of community and communication, not of solitude and silence"; and Mills sees it as a space for "quiet revelation."[60] I agree with those summations. Alvin, who says "I've been a traveller most of my life," shows the lessons in humanity that he has learned on the road and that he can share with others. Getting to his brother's house and reconciling their differences before he dies may be a personal quest in fulfilling a family obligation, but the journey becomes a collective sharing of experience with those he meets and a self-redemptive act in constructing identity and masculinity. In journeying down the highway, seeing the ripening corn, reddening autumn leaves, and carefully cultivated farms, he is careful and respectful of others; he willingly shares his food and coffee; and he has timely words of advice to everyone about personal endurance and the strength of family unity, which he gives almost as parables. The landscape he travels through is independent of his past life, but it prompts him to reflect on that life, nevertheless.[61] As well, when he sits outdoors and looks at the stars glittering in the sky (reminiscent of John Merrick in Lynch's 1980 film, The Elephant Man), it is not so much that he enjoys the solitude, reflects on the past, or identifies with nature, but that he senses a spiritual dimension to life.

What Lynch has done that is so touching (but never maudlin) is to show a man at the end of his life who, in setting out on a solo road journey, believes that he must still accomplish something purposeful and good, and maintains a "naïve" belief in the deep connections among human beings, nature, and spirituality. Alvin is not just a geezer on the road but a man who has come to understand himself and his masculinity, accept his limitations with humility, show his abiding love for "Rose darlin'" and, by extension, the rest of his family, and share life with his close companions and the world beyond in a clear-sighted, ethical, humane, and optimistic way.

The journey of life is no less a struggle for Alvin than for the youthful to middle-aged buddies (Victor Joseph and Thomas Builds-the-Fire, Ennis Del Mar and Jack Twist, Drew Baylor and Clare Coleburn, and Miles and Jack) or for the other middle-aged and older men on the road (Don Johnston and Warren Schmidt) who have had to make their way alone, but the correspondence of self, society, and soul seems to be so much more integrated, articulated, and profound. Human imperfection and limitations have all been factored in but have made the steel stronger instead of tragically brittle.

Paradoxically, then, it is not necessarily in youth that the experience of the road is sharper and the wonder of the starlit sky more intense, as Paul Theroux would have it in "Remember the Cicadas and the Stars," but perhaps in old age when priorities are established and when the need to repair the wounds and come to terms with self, family, society, and nation is more keenly felt. In any case, the road is not of necessity the place where the counterculture must flourish and the dominant society fall, and where disillusionment and tragedy strike; it can be the place where projects of emancipation and reconstruction are carried out, perceptions heightened, values confirmed, postmodern masculinities defined and reified, and "civic discourses" highlighted.[62]

Transamerica: Queer Cinema in the Middle of the Road

GINA MARCHETTI

Sexual minorities, the road, and the cinema share a long, complex, multifaceted history in American popular culture. Facing the constraints of the heterosexual norm or threats of violence at home, some LGBT people have found themselves on the road throughout American history as explorers, adventurers, prospectors, trappers, hobos, itinerant merchants or performers, hitchhikers, truckers, drifters, or cowboys. In rural America, the road provides the anonymity of the "closet" – an ability to move on to avoid stigma, to encounter others in similar circumstances (gay or straight) with a "past," and, perhaps, find fellowship on the way. If America has always had a romance with the road as part of its pioneer heritage, queer America shares that same romance as a backdrop for a journey of escape, self-discovery, awakening, transcendence, and, occasionally, romantic love. However, the road divides the landscape into two halves, and the "dark" side of the road for straight America – the horrors of delinquency, banditry, and deviance – can be the hopeful side of the road for queer America looking for freedom, tolerance, and acceptance outside the constraints of "settled" heterosexuality.[1]

On the road, the cowboy stands as the contested icon of American sexual borders. The furor surrounding Ang Lee's *Brokeback Mountain* (2005), for example, exposes facts about the history of the American West that many would like to suppress – including the truth that some men chose to be cowboys because they were homosexual, many cowboy "partners" were homosexual, and the openly gay rodeo circuit dates back to the mid-1970s. The cowboy has always been a conflicted figure in American popular culture – civilized and savage, violent and honourable, independent and the archetypal "buddy," perpetually on the road and forever dreaming of settling down on a little ranch of his own. Away from the company of women, shy around the opposite sex, inept at heterosexual romance, the cowboy's studied machismo and homosocial lifestyle fail to belie homoeroticism.

Given that in the Hollywood Western many cowboys would rather kiss their horse (if not each other) than the girl, the gay romance with the cowboy goes back a long way. In fact, the cowboy has long been out of the closet in popular culture. Andy Warhol's *Lonesome Cowboys* (1968) documents the queer allure of the cowboy, and John Schlesinger's *Midnight Cowboy* (1969) makes the link between gay street life and the cowboy icon perfectly clear. When the naïve would-be street hustler, Joe Buck (Jon Voight), looks into the mirror, he sees a macho Paul Newman from *Hud* (1963) as an object of lust for older women, but Rico 'Ratso' Rizzo (Dustin Hoffman) and the rest of the street life of New York see a gay hustler dressed as a cowboy to drum up business. Eventually, Joe's (platonic) love for Ratso leads him to accept this role up to a point in order to finance a road trip to Florida for his ailing tubercular buddy. The road, the cowboy, and the queer come together in a string of films, including *Johnny Guitar* (1954), *The Ballad of Little Jo* (1993), and *Even Cowgirls Get the Blues* (1993). Consider Gus Van Sant's *My Own Private Idaho* (1991), which features Scott (Keanu Reeves) as a "Homo on the Range" coming to life as a gay cowboy image on a magazine cover, and Mike (River Phoenix) getting a blowjob to the strains of a cowboy lullaby. Trans-gendered Brandon Teena (Hilary Swank) wears a cowboy hat while on the road in Kimberly Peirce's *Boys Don't Cry* (1999). Moreover, when hustler J.D. (Brad Pitt) appears wearing his cowboy hat in *Thelma and Louise* (1991), he could be coming off the set of Andy Warhol's *Lonesome Cowboys*.[2]

Outlaws on the road take on a queer cowboy quality as well. The outlaw Clyde Barrow, of course, was homosexual, but this metamorphosed into impotence in the film version *Bonnie and Clyde* (1967).[3] Even as the cowboy drifts into the background as a figure, the road continues to provide a framework for the queer cinematic imagination. *Vanishing Point* (1971), for example, features gay hitchhikers, and Steve McLean's *Postcards from America* (1994), based on the autobiographical writings of David Wojnarowicz, deals with the life of a gay hustler on the road. In the same vein as *Thelma and Louise* and *Leaving Normal* (1992), *Boys on the Side* (1995) adds to the female-bonding road narrative by including a lesbian character. The ranks of New Queer Cinema boast films by Gregg Araki such as *The Living End* (1992)[4] and *The Doom Generation* (1995), as well as *My Own Private Idaho*. Wong Kar-wai's *Happy Together* (1997) features a gay couple from Hong Kong on the road in Argentina, and the Mexican road trip film Alfonso Cuaron's *Y Tu Mama Tambien* (2001) also has a queer aspect. In "Driving into the 'Dustless Highway' of Queer Cinema," Daniel Mudie Cunningham notes:

> The "movability" of queer is often expressed in queer cinema through the recurring motif of the road. The idea that queer moves across things is evocative because in some queer films, its subjects don't inhabit any one specific place for too long. Instead, such characters keep moving across the landscape, forever passing *through* and *between* places, identities, things. For example, some of the most notable films of the New Queer Cinema were road movies about young, free-floating characters who hustle their way through life.[5]

Even road movies without any LGBT characters have been open to queer interpretations. The quintessential "queer" road movie is, of course, *The Wizard of Oz* (1939), and many gay fans have identified with Dorothy (Judy Garland) on the yellow brick road and elevated the film to the highest ranks within the camp classics canon.[6] As Robert Lang points out in *Masculine Interests*: "Almost every mainstream road movie in which two men travel together ... contains at least one scene that turns on homosexual anxiety and the taboo of same-sex attraction."[7] However, even though the road movie often touts its homophobic suppression of homoeroticism, *Transamerica* can still send up "queer readings" of mainstream films by featuring a scene in which the *Lord of the Rings* is retold as a gay epic.

In addition to *Boys Don't Cry*[8] mentioned above, transvestites and transsexuals take to the road in films such as *To Wong Foo Thanks for Everything! Julie Newmar* (1995), come from abroad in *Hedwig and the Angry Inch* (2001), and tour the outback in the Australian feature *The Adventures of Priscilla, Queen of the Desert* (1994). Transvestite actress Divine has been on the road in films such as John Water's *Female Trouble* (1974) and Paul Bartel's *Lust in the Dust* (1985). What Chris Straayer has termed the "temporary transvestite"[9] film often features cross-dressers on the run (if not always on the road) in films such as *Some Like It Hot* (1959) or the more recent version *Connie and Carla* (2004)[10] with two women who take a page from *Victor Victoria* (1982) and disguise themselves as drag queens to hide from mobsters. Sexual outlaws, gender-benders, carnival hermaphrodite "freaks," and a range of sexual minorities find themselves on the road or at the side of the road in films as diverse as *Freaks* (1932), *Lolita* (1962, 1997), and *Psycho* (1960, 1998).

Transamerica takes bits and pieces from this cinematic legacy and positions itself between the other two major "road movies" of 2005, so that this story of a pre-operative transsexual on the road with the son fathered years before finds itself in conversation with the paternity issues at the heart of *Broken Flowers* and the politics of queer identity underlying the love story of *Brokeback Mountain* (see Slethaug, chapter 8).

First-time director, Duncan Tucker, who also wrote the screenplay, bases the film on Katherine Connella, Tucker's roommate, who describes herself as "inter-sex." Working with a character who knows "both sides of the road" in the sex-gender landscape of America, Tucker crafted *Transamerica* to fit squarely within the road movie genre. In fact, it provides a road map of the form.[11] However, it is a particular type of road movie in which the protagonists find themselves on the road inadvertently, and, rather than going in search of America or on a journey of self discovery, they learn about themselves and their country by chance. In this case, pre-operative transsexual Bree (formerly Stanley) – played by *Desperate Housewives* regular Felicity Huffman – cannot get the green light for her final operation from her analyst until she reconciles herself to the fact she fathered a child, Toby (Kevin Zegers), and takes some sort of responsibility for the past. She flies from Los Angeles to New York, bails Toby out, and concocts a plan to reunite him with his stepfather in Kentucky. They share their first meal in a diner, and the road trip begins in a dilapidated wreck that one of Toby's gay street hustler pals sells to Bree with the promise she can resell it in Los Angeles at a profit. Dreaming of a Hollywood career in porn films, Toby accepts Bree's masquerade as a missionary trying to "save" a wayward boy – not suspecting Bree is his father, but assuming "the older woman" has romance with a younger man as an ulterior motive.

In this case, *Transamerica* takes a page from *Midnight Cowboy* and *My Own Private Idaho*, among other films, and puts a male hustler on the road, while Bree joins the ranks of transsexuals on the cinematic highway. Like *Planes, Trains, and Automobiles* (1987) and many other road trip comedies, Bree and Toby form a mismatched pair constantly at odds. Although both belong to sexual minorities, neither understands the other. Bree finds Toby's lifestyle – drug use, sex for sale, unhygienic living conditions – unacceptable. Toby has trouble coming to terms with Bree's failure to tell him she has a penis; he condemns a pre-operative transsexual's decision to "pass" as a woman as tantamount to lying. Although each has flirtations along the road (Bree with Native American Calvin Many Goats [Graham Greene] and Toby with a hitchhiker and an underage girl Taylor [Stella Maeve], as well as picking up a john at a roadhouse for some ready cash), neither has a serious love interest. The plot revolves around their relationship as parent and child, how that dyad fits into the larger family structure, and how Toby and Bree's status as members of sexual minorities puts them at odds with traditional notions of the American family.

The American road provides the backdrop for the reconstitution of the family after the death of the patriarchal norm. However, Toby and Bree do not find the journey easy. Rather, Toby's "need" to find his father and Bree's "need" to be a woman conflict, and they fit uneasily into their roles as parent and child. Their lack of mutual understanding finds its parallel in their poor "fit" within the American landscape. Both city dwellers find themselves out of their element in the American heartland, and, as in many "fish out of water" road movies, they are strangers not only to each other and to those they encounter on the road, but to family and friends they visit along their route, as well as to America itself – homeland, heartland, motherland, fatherland, and chamber of horrors rolled into a single landscape that takes them from New York to Los Angeles.

For the queer traveller, the road may promise freedom, but it also threatens destruction. For Bree, it means constant worry about her gender "status" as somewhere between male and female, and, for Toby, it represents the dangers faced by any hustler who may run afoul of the police or the wrong john on the road. Although not particularly "violent" and played as comedy/melodrama, the potential for violence haunts *Transamerica* – occasionally erupting – and the cruelty of Brandon Teena's rape and murder in Nebraska and Matthew Shepard's death, strung up by the side of the road in Wyoming, shadow this film.

BORDERS

Road movies tend to be about borders. As David Laderman points out in *Driving Visions*: "the genre of the road movie explores the 'borders' (the status quo conventions) of American society." Often these borders mark racial differences, and Laderman goes on to note: "a certain exoticism regarding race pervades many road movies."[12] The road cuts through the landscape and divides it in two. Like the wrong side of the tracks, it is easy to come from the wrong side of the highway – in terms of class, race, ethnicity, nationality, religion, or any number of other identity markers that indicate a hierarchy of relative power/powerlessness within America.

LGBT individuals find themselves on that "wrong" side of the sex-gender divide, and their identities become intermingled with other minorities. As Jennifer Esposito points out,[13] queer characters on the road in films like *Boys Don't Cry* act out their identities in relation to the border, and, in *Transamerica*, both Toby and Bree constantly "test" their identities against a white, Christian, American middle-class mainstream. After the road trip is over, they seem to have come to an understanding of how they "fit" within a reconfigured American home – father/mother and son next to the Christmas tree in sunny Los Angeles – however, the contradictions at the heart of that image remain raw as Dolly Parton sings "Travelin' Thru" over the closing credits.

From the outset, Bree's gender identity is played off against her racial and class identity. "Over-dressed" in her prim suit, she stands out as she lines up for the bus with the markedly lower-class, immigrant bus patrons, who must be well off the radar of the average working-class or lower-middle class Californian who can at least afford a motorcycle or used car. While the copy of a book on "black" Africa she puts in her purse indicates something at odds with her "pretty in pink" feminine whiteness, the fact that she lines up to take the bus only makes sense when the voice-over reveals that every cent she has goes into her plan to become a woman. Everything that does not contribute to that plan has been stripped away, and she's left with a cinderblock bungalow, no car, and the necessity of working two jobs to finance her operation. Later, when the middle-class comfort of her parents' home comes into view in the mise-en-scene, the drop in her class standing due to the expense of her gender reassignment surgery becomes salient.

With "world" music playing on the soundtrack, books on Africa on hand, and a job working in a Mexican restaurant, Bree embraces the Third World.[14] As she reveals later on the road, her study of anthropology in college led her to realize that Native American, African, and other non-European cultures recognize and occasionally "honour" individuals who defy male-female gender classifications as "two soul people." However, she keeps her own understanding of the racial divide in America on this plane, and she does not move from "two soul people" and a romantic conception of Native American culture into the facts of imperialism, racism, and W.E.B. Du Bois's "double consciousness." Although she suffers the same stigma as racial minorities who attempt to "pass" in the white world and she sees herself as having a "female" soul in a male body, she does not interrogate the construction of her "new" body as white. Given this, Bree creates her feminine self with make-up, colours, and style more suited to a debutante from 1950s white Middle America than to a new woman of the multicultural turn of the new millennium. Hiding the facts of paternity from Toby, Bree constructs an uptight, conservative, Christian missionary as her "cover." Half-Jewish and half-male, Bree passes as a Christian missionary to distance herself from her son, and it is difficult to pin down how much of the character comes from this masquerade and how much Bree is meant to be genuinely naïve about drugs, hustlers, gay male subcultures, the community of transsexuals, and her own identity in a sexual minority.

Part of the road trip for Bree (as planned by her analyst) involves her coming to terms with the fact that no operation can erase the past, that she was a man, and that must be part of her identity as a woman. As comfortable as she seems with racial/ethnic minorities, she has difficulty coming to terms with sexual minorities, of which she is a part. The narrative reinforces this, so that presumably heterosexual people of colour support her and white sexual minorities threaten her in various ways. Even when an African-American child "reads" her and asks whether she is male or female, Bree seems more threatened by the thought of her own inability to pass than by the child's innocent curiosity. As Bree travels across America, she seems most comfortable with African-Americans, Native Americans, and Hispanics, while she is constantly under threat from whites.

However, since the film opens after Stanley has become Bree, whether the proprietors, fellow workers, and customers at Papi's Kitchen supported her transformation or whether she took on the job after she had already begun to present herself as Bree remains moot. Still, her analyst Margaret, played by Cuban-American Elizabeth Pena, brings with her a tacit acceptance of transsexuality coupled with an insistent need to support paternal responsibilities. Although Bree describes her/Stanley's encounter with Toby's mother as "tragically lesbian," she accepts her analyst's order to go to New York to see Toby. Bree never considers other options (changing analysts, asking for a second opinion), but accepts Margaret's values and feelings about paternity, albeit reluctantly, as her own.

"LORD TAKE AWAY THESE CHAINS"

Taking up the ruse of being a missionary from the "Church of the Potential Father," Bree also absorbs an American Christian heritage sometimes at odds with her half-Jewish/transsexual identity. She embodies a wide array of debates inside and outside American Christianity. These range from the proper way to handle homosexual, pedophilic Catholic priests, to the right of openly gay clergy to become church leaders, to debates as to whether LGBT believers are "abominations" doomed to hellfire. As Dolly Parton's song indicates, Bree is a "pilgrim" on the road to potential salvation, and Dolly Parton, as Chris Holmlund points out in her discussion of "Dolly dialectics," provides an important bridge here: "The ability to engage audiences interested in 'divine guidance' and audiences attuned to 'queer speak' via 'straight talk' entails a balancing act that Dolly manages better than most: few other media personalities can please both right-wing fundamentalists and drag queens."[15] Dolly Parton's theme song for the film was nominated for an Oscar, indicating the regard Parton enjoys in Hollywood and underscoring her ability to appeal to various members of the audience who may have diametrically opposed attitudes toward religion, sexuality, and "family values." *Transamerica* attempts a similar balancing act.

In the film, even Toby questions a transsexual's "right" to church membership. In one of the more emotional scenes in *Transamerica*, Bree answers back to Toby that "even though my body is a work in progress, there is nothing wrong with my soul," and she compares her death as a man and resurrection as a woman to the story of Jesus. She continues: "Jesus made me this way for a reason, so I could die and be reborn like he was." Later, after the operation, Bree compares her pain not to Jesus on the cross but, rather, to medieval

heretics impaled on stakes. Given the practice of burning "sodom-
ites" as "faggots" in the Middle Ages, the latter comparison may
be more to the point in expressing not only her physical pain but
also the pain of her abandonment by America (represented by her
alienation from her son). However, Bree continues to clutch her "I'm
Proud to Be a Christian" cap as she cries on her analyst's shoulder.

Many oppressed and marginalized Americans seek solace in the
Judeo-Christian tradition. The African-American church's pleas for
freedom from bondage, the Catholic Hispanics' faith in redemption,
and the appeal of Bible Belt values to working-class people testify to
the importance of Christianity in pleas for economic, racial, and ethnic justice. Although uncomfortable in bowing her head to say grace
to maintain her cover with Toby, Bree claims this tradition forcefully
and weds it to her feelings of solidarity with other disadvantaged
minority groups. Although Bree's sister, Sydney (Carrie Preston),
"outs" the family as Jewish when she adds her own Hebrew prayer
to the dinner gathering at a restaurant in Arizona, Bree still "keeps
the faith" as a Christian and/or a Jew. After all, she may identify
with Jesus persecuted on the cross, or with the return of the Prodigal
Son, but she also has been in exile, literally wandering in the desert,
like Moses and the Israelites. While established churches (Christian,
Jewish, or otherwise), racial/ethnic minorities, and the white working classes may not always be accepting of sexual minorities (in this
case, transsexuals) and active, open, virulent homophobia is, sadly,
not uncommon, *Transamerica*'s fantasy, mirroring Bree's own belief
in an America free from prejudice of all sorts, of a nation of "family
values" reconstituted in a world without hate, remains compelling
– as indicated by critics and by box-office returns – and appealing.

The American road includes sympathetic minorities and abusive representatives of the mainstream, and Bree and Toby encounter both on their journey. In Kentucky, the horror of Toby's abusive
stepfather is offset by the warmth of his African-American neighbour. Although blind to the fact that Toby has been abused, as well
as to the fact that the hair in Bree's nose may point to an incomplete
transformation of a man into a woman, the kindly woman tries to
reunite Toby with his stepfather and take care of the errant hair with
electrolysis.

Even before the Civil War, a Northerner or any "stranger"
going South signalled trouble. Although set along the Chattooga
River, which runs in the Carolinas, John Boorman/James Dickey's

Deliverance (1972) represents a cinematic standard for inbred, homo-sexual mountain men that also taints the Tennessee/Kentucky/Ozark/Appalachian region. The mountain men who force Bobby (Ned Beatty) to "squeal like a pig" while he is being raped, have created a template for psychotic hillbillies who enjoy sodomy that Toby's stepfather fits quite well. As Bree and Toby travel among Confederate flags and mountain men with long beards, they feel less comfortable in their own "skins." Sitting around a campfire, Toby fashions himself as part Native American through the father he imagines himself to have – a spiritual understanding that he claims is an "Indian thing."

Of course, within the road movie genre, the "campfire scene" marks a dramatic turning point in which previously unknown aspects of a character's identity come to (fire) light: George Hanson/Jack Nicholson getting high and talking about civil rights with Wyatt/Peter Fonda and Billy/Dennis Hopper in *Easy Rider* (1969); and Mike/River Phoenix declaring his love for Scott/Keanu Reeves in *My Own Private Idaho*, for example.[16] Given Bree sees part of her own identity as a transsexual linked to the Native American concept of "two soul people," this does make some sort of sense poetically if not genetically. Given the abusive nature of his white Southern step-father, it makes dramatic sense for Toby to dream of a Noble Indian as his "real" father, rather than the woman sitting next to him by the fire. However, the fact that Toby purchases a "Redskins" baseball cap to show his ethnic pride shows how clueless he really is about Native America.

The South and the West often serve in popular culture as the well-spring of American xenophobia, and only the presence of racial minorities saves the region from complete degeneracy. However, the romantic encounter with the racial "Other" on the road often fails to go beyond the surface. Both the nurturing "Black Mammy" and the sage "Noble Savage" make appearances in *Transamerica* to set the white travellers on the "right" road. Like other road movies, *Transamerica* makes ample use of popular conceptions of the fron-tier West and the Gothic horrors of the South. The West promises hope, frontier values softened by a renewed reverence for Native American culture, and room for alternative lifestyles and counter-cultures. Like the Hippie commune and family ranch in *Easy Rider*, *Transamerica*'s West offers the nonconformist open spaces and room to breathe away from judgmental eyes.

In addition to being saved by the good graces of a Native American Good Samaritan, Bree and Toby find a warm welcome at a party celebrating the successful gender reassignment surgery of a transsexual in Texas. Although the closeted Bree feels uncomfortable within her own subcultural milieu, Toby accepts the transsexual partygoers as "nice." However, like Ratso (Dustin Hoffman) and Joe Buck (John Voight) who never quite fit in at the Factory party in *Midnight Cowboy*, among the ranks of Warhol regulars like Viva, Taylor Mead, Ultra Violet, and Paul Morrissey, Toby and Bree find themselves on the outside, and they prefer to retire to their guestrooms rather than stay and enjoy the hostess's rendition of "Home on the Range."

COWBOYS AND INDIANS

After Toby discovers Bree's penis, he again turns to his fantasy of Native America to come to terms with sexual trauma. He asks to stop at Sammy's Wigwam, a kitsch roadside souvenir shop selling Indian arrowheads and other bric-a-brac, and he coerces Bree into picking up a hitchhiker who looks like a descendant of the Hippies on the commune in *Easy Rider*. The young vagabond claims to be a vegan and a peyote shaman (making an oblique reference to the Native American shaman from another road movie, Oliver Stone's *Natural Born Killers*, 1994). While the drifter ingratiates himself with Bree by saying that being a transsexual is a "highly evolved state of being," he is really just a white punk scam artist who takes the opportunity of a skinny dip with Toby at a waterhole to steal Bree's car. His Native American credentials as a "shaman" and his Hippie credentials as a "vegan" fall by the wayside as it rolls away in a cloud of dust.

Oddly, although he never questioned the "peyote shaman's" authenticity, Toby has trouble coming to terms with Native American Calvin (Navajo/Zuni), who works as a rancher and wears a cowboy hat. The white appropriation of "Indian-ness" seems "natural," while Calvin needs to justify to Toby his cowboy hat (better at keeping the sun out of his eyes than a feather headdress) and his very existence on his own land. Calvin Many Goats' presence brings *Transamerica* back into the realm of the Western, and borders between whites and Natives as well as between gays and straights become more apparent. *Transamerica* joins Calvin to the road for a short while, conjuring up films like Jonathan Wacks' *Pow Wow Highway* (1989) or Chris Eyre's *Smoke Signals* (1998) in which Native Americans take to the road and pose questions of identity with a different significance from those in the white mainstream road film.

Calvin does try to help Toby come to grips with his identity, however, by giving him a cowboy hat in exchange for the "Redskins" cap, assuring him that "now you look like a warrior," and claiming to see "some Cherokee" in him – stating that the Cherokee are a "proud" people. Seeing the Cherokee in Toby, Calvin may also see the Trail of Tears, the forced evacuation of the Cherokee to Oklahoma in 1838, or the legacy of Will Rogers, America's most famous Cherokee cowboy. As a Navajo, he may also sympathize with the Trail of Tears because of the Long Walk of the Navajo in 1863, which also removed them forcibly from ancestral lands. However, Calvin shares his claim to America, in spite of this legacy of racism and prejudice, with the gift of the cowboy hat – an emblem of frontier imperialism that he refashions into a war bonnet.

If Calvin is mistaken when he sees Toby as Cherokee, he may be less mistaken when he sees Bree as a woman. Schooled in anthropology and impersonating a Christian missionary, Bree is still taken aback by Calvin's moniker as evidence of Protestant missions to the American West. However, Calvin asks few questions about Bree and simply accepts her and seems pleased by her flirtations. Although Toby hints that Bree "has secrets," Calvin remains unconcerned and frets, rather, over his own "secrets" (jail time, failed relationships). Although not as open about Calvin's attraction to a transsexual as the suitor of Bernadette (Terence Stamp) who jilts his Filipina wife to pursue one of "Les Girls" in *The Adventures of Priscilla, Queen of the Desert*, the possibility remains open, since Bree decides to take Calvin's phone number for future reference, without mentioning her upcoming operation. Focusing on paternity and its obligations, *Transamerica* shies away from the ethics of pre- and post-operative transsexual "passing." Toby disapproves of "passing" as a "lie," but Bree only craves acceptance without questions. Perhaps, as Calvin plays "Beautiful Dreamer" on the guitar for Bree at his ranch, her dream of a contemporary Native American accepting a "two soul" person comes to mind.

FUCKING THE FATHER

Two scenes of violence involving fathers punctuate *Transamerica* and frame the narrative within the parameters of "acceptable" and "unacceptable" behaviour for sexual minorities. Two sides of the road divide the sexual landscape with the "natural" acceptance of difference on one side (linked to African-Americans, Hispanics, and Native Americans) and abuse, abandonment, and "unnatural" horror on the other (linked to the Gothic South and to the white, dysfunctional suburban family). In both scenes, Toby puts on a performance in which he apparently attempts to seduce his stepfather/biological father. In the first instance, he uses this performance to re-enact dramatically his abuse in order to prove his case. In the second, he attempts to show his loyalty to Bree to counter the overtures being made to him by her mother/his grandmother, Elizabeth (Fionnula Flanagan).

In a reworking of the Oedipus myth, the shock of potential father-son incest underlies each scene. Like Mike in *My Own Private Idaho*, Toby has been the victim of a dysfunctional family. In this case, Toby's mother has been involved with two queer men (one abusive and a pedophile, the other trans-gendered and unable to "commit"), and she has been driven to suicide and consigned to a faded photo in the mise-en-scene. While hustler Mike goes in search of his mother who abandoned him, Toby goes in search of his father, and, although he has a photo of Stanley, he never sees his father in Bree. Toby has gone from being abandoned, abused, and unloved to being loved too well, and it is dramatically understandable that the attentions lavished on him by both Bree and Elizabeth should be misinterpreted.

As in Tsai Ming-Liang's *The River* (1997), father and son end up in bed together due to a case of mistaken identity (also after a father-son road trip), but also due to the assumption of the heterosexual norm. While Tsai lets the scene play out, Tucker steps back in order to highlight the differences between Bree and Toby's stepfather. While the stepfather's abuse drove Toby away, Bree has come back into Toby's life to try to atone for Stanley's abandonment. Of course, Toby does not understand the battle between Bree and Elizabeth for his affection. Throughout the film, Bree has refused the label of "mother" when strangers assume Toby is her son. However, reunited with her suburban family, Bree gradually comes to relish

Tony's filial attentions. While the rest of the family ostracizes Bree, Toby gallantly pulls out the chair to help her take a seat. In front of Elizabeth, Bree welcomes the compliment when someone observes Toby's polite treatment of his mother.

If Elizabeth has "lost" a son, she seems determined to hang onto her grandson. Murray (Burt Young), Bree's father, and sister Sydney sit by the sidelines and watch this play out. No one dares tell Toby the truth about his place in the family. Like the son in *The River*, Toby only finds out the "truth" about his father when he finds himself naked in bed with him. Offering sex and marriage, Toby's advances are stopped cold with a kiss, and Bree asks Toby to take a good look at his father in the photograph with his mother. Finally, Toby "sees" his father in Bree and lashes out. When Toby reveals his stepfather's abuse in Kentucky, it is the older man who becomes violent, and Toby runs away. In this scene, the violence comes full circle when Toby beats his biological father and again runs away. Elizabeth and Sydney come out to help Bree, and the women of the family (Bree now included) regroup after Toby's outburst.

After Toby runs away, other plot elements seem to come full circle as well. Bree is able to "come out" in public by claiming to be Toby's father to the policewoman with whom she files a missing person's report. The officer has no discernable reaction to Bree's claims of paternity, and Bree seems to have reconciled herself to the fact that she will always be, at some level, Stanley. Finally reconciled, Murray, Elizabeth, and Sydney see Bree off as the airport shuttle picks her up to take her back to Los Angeles and to the gender reassignment surgery.

As in many road movies, at the end of the road, Bree does return home; in fact, she returns twice – to her mother, father, and sister in Arizona out of desperation and to her little bungalow in Los Angeles. After her surgery, she begins to enjoy her new body – luxuriating in the bath and striding out from the kitchen of the Mexican restaurant where she works with a more confident step. As in *The Wizard of Oz*, the road has transformed the heroine and brought her home.

During the Christmas season, Toby reappears on Bree's doorstep. Hair bleached blond to fit into a porn industry in love with "surfers," Toby has moved up a notch in the sex industry. Although his days may be numbered because of a question about his ability to "perform" even after taking Viagra, Toby still seems proud to show Bree the flyer for his porn video debut. She grudgingly accepts this, as he accepts the small Christmas tree on her table even though they are "Jewish" in Toby's eyes. Bree returns Calvin's hat to Toby and reminds him to keep his feet off the furniture. Gestures of reconciliation and the exercise of parental authority draw them together at the film's close. The gift of a cowboy hat by a Native American and the confirmation of the Judeo-Christian ethos with a Christmas tree affirm their place within the American "melting pot" as members of sexual minorities within a country of racial, ethnic, religious, and other minorities. As Katie Mills notes, *Transamerica* and road movies like it use "the ready narratological structure of the road genre to represent rebellion as well as the collective longing for transformation of a minority community."[17]

Road movies end in death, the settled life, or a new journey, and *Transamerica*, like some other films in the genre, ends with all three. The final "death" of Stanley, the settling of Bree and Toby into their little home "out West" in the "promised land" at the end of the road, and the new journey of a new type of family reconfigured as outside the heterosexual norm. Bree and Toby have crossed sexual, gender, religious, ethnic, racial, and class borders. They have drawn in elements of Hispanic, Native American, Jewish, Christian, working class, and African-American culture into their own "melting pot" bungalow. However, there is also submission to a white, middle-class, patriarchal ideal in Toby's bleached blonde hair in a cowboy hat and the still prim Bree decorating her home with a Christmas tree. Bree is not her father or her mother or Toby's stepfather, but she maintains her role as "parent." Toby is no longer abused or incarcerated, but he has not managed to escape from a capitalist system in which he needs to use his sexuality to get cash to survive while maintaining the illusion of his Hollywood dream of fame and fortune.

QUEER AS CORRECTIVE – OR, WHY WE ALL NEED TO TRAVEL ON THE QUEER HIGHWAY

As *Transamerica* opens up and attempts to reconcile fundamental contradictions at the heart of American society between gay/straight, male/female, middle/working class, white/non-white, native/foreign, rural/urban, urban/suburban, and nomadic/settled, the question remains as to whether or not this journey has corrected any of the imbalances of power fundamental to those contradictions. Has "saving" Toby from the excesses of an abusive stepfather, an uncaring juvenile justice system, and life on the streets of New York saved America from the excesses of a dysfunctional state or the pathology of the patriarchal family? Has Bree's operation "saved" her from heterosexism or the stigma associated with transsexuals? Have Toby and Bree been able to apply a queer corrective to the American family? Have they saved it as an institution based on Judeo-Christian values cleansed of homophobia? Has the film reconciled straight America with queer culture?

Transamerica opens the queer highway to gay and straight audiences, and even the casting of Felicity Huffman rather than a transsexual actress brings the film closer to a viewing public more familiar with television's *Desperate Housewives* than with the New Queer Cinema. This strategy seems in keeping with other recent films that have opened the queer road to the mainstream multiplex viewer. Speaking of *Brokeback Mountain*, for example, Ang Lee observes: "It's a good gay film for people because it's in the middle of the road. I don't squeeze the characters into gay cinema. I think that's what's good ... or not so good. I always try my best when I do a film that feels genuine to me. I put myself in the middle to try to make cinema work."[18] At the end of *Transamerica*, Bree and Toby also end up in the "middle of the road." Their journey has been treated with sympathy and humour. They represent no "radical" challenge to the racial, ethnic, or class hierarchy. Bree "enjoys being a girl," and she crafts a type of femininity that offers little challenge to the sex-gender status quo,[19] and Toby fits easily into a cash economy that offers no challenge to the marginalization of gay men within the larger society.

Bree and Toby cling to the cowboy hat, the Christmas tree, and the prim little bungalow with rose-coloured curtains as icons of an America into which they need to be absorbed. Family affection wins out at the end, and Bree's family in Arizona and son in California seem settled into this order. With only loose ties to working-class ethnics, Native Americans, and LGBT communities, they are cocooned within their own "middle of the road" dyad in a sexual borderland between the First and Third Worlds. However, at a time when LGBT communities in America agitate for equal rights and the ability to live free from fear, *Transamerica*'s middle of the road may offer a much needed rest stop on the highway to a more enduring critique of heterosexual and patriarchal norms in America.

10

Fools on the American Road: "Gimpel the Fool," *The Frisco Kid*, and *Forrest Gump*

WENDY ZIERLER

Over the past decade, a number of film critics have undertaken the task of defining the main thematic features of the road film genre. Most of these critics link the road film to the Western and the masculine ethos of the American frontier, with the open road symbolizing such notions as rugged individualism, freedom, weightlessness, mobility, equal access, and self-transformation.[1] According to Shari Roberts, American geography and history are as significant in the road film as in the Western, "so that the image of the white dotted line becomes a visual shorthand indicating a new start, endless possibility, and equal possibility – the American dream."[2] In contrast to the Western, however, the road movie tends to question the very idea of the American dream: "The road stands in for the frontier but instead of symbolizing a romanticized America in which the American dream will come true, it simply asks over and over as each mile marker is passed, what does America mean today? Are dreams even possible?"[3]

Other critics such as Timothy Corrigan and David Laderman view the road film in relation to the journey or quest motif in Western culture, as a descendant of such epic and picaresque narratives as Homer's *Odyssey*, Cervantes' *Don Quixote*, and Voltaire's *Candide*. What distinguishes the road film from these prior works, however, is its valorization of mechanized travel, particularly the automobile. According to Corrigan, the road movie is very much a "postwar phenomenon," a form that reflects a breakdown in the traditional family unit, where characters (almost always male, usually buddies) leave their domestic surroundings and set out on a mechanized quest. "Cars and motorcycles," writes Corrigan, "represent a mechanized extension of the body, through which the body could move faster and faster than ever before."[4] According to David Laderman, the infatuation with driving that is emblematic of the road film reflects a "modernist sensibility, which celebrates technology as a liberating force that can lead us into the future."[5] As part of this preoccupation with speed, Laderman identifies within the genre a concern for what it means "to exceed the boundaries, to transgress the limits of American society."[6] More often than not, however, these mechanized quests prove unsuccessful, as in the 1960s classic, *Easy Rider*, with its tagline: "A man went looking for America and couldn't find it anywhere!" Speed and technology notwithstanding, these journeys often come to a dead-end, with little wisdom or understanding having been achieved (See Slethaug, chapter 1).[7] In an even more recent study, Katie Mills observes that by the end of the 1970s, the dead-ends on the road force the travellers onto a temporal rather than a spatial highway. "Instead of stories about people on the road," she argues, "cinematic travel in the 1980s" – as exemplified by such blockbuster films as Robert Zemeckis's *Back to the Future* (1985) – "goes backwards in time. The subliminal message in the 1980s was, if you don't like the present – don't rebel, rewind!"[8]

Nowadays, in America, can one really escape or achieve weightlessness on the road? Is there an open road left? There is something terribly naïve, terribly foolish, about the very idea. What then, if you send a fool on this foolish journey? If the road film is a generic descendant of both the Western and the picaresque, and if saintly, foolish picaros, such as Don Quixote and Candide are part of this generic genealogy, what images of the journeying fool can be culled from American road movies? To what extent do films of fools on the road support or undermine prior understandings of the road genre and its meanings? Do American road-film fools reinforce or discredit the notion of rugged American individualism, of aggressive masculinity, and a desire to escape "civilization, law and domesticity" or exceed the boundaries of American culture? Do the filmic adventures of fools on the road serve a satirical function, mocking the presumptions and pretensions of American society, or do they, in keeping with the innocence and goodness of their protagonists, recuperate or reinvigorate a naïve version of the American dream?

In this chapter I attempt to answer these questions by examining two films about fools on the American road, *The Frisco Kid* (1979, directed by Robert Aldrich) and *Forrest Gump* (1994, directed by Robert Zemeckis), neither of which figure in any of the recent studies of the road film genre, and thus provide an opportunity to expand the boundaries of the road canon. Against the grain of many road stories and films that celebrate the liberating potential of speed and motorized mobility, both of these films offer a more naïve, less mechanized experiential map of the American road. *The Frisco Kid*, set in the 1850s during the era of American railway expansion, tells the story of a young rabbi named Avram Belinsky, who is sent from Poland to America to serve a congregation in San Francisco. The film follows his bumbling journey across the country (by coach, by rail, by horse, and on foot), in which he partners up with a cowboy named Tommy, a much savvier rider on the American road, and charts what each of them learns along the way. *Forrest Gump*, the Academy Award winner for Best Picture in 1994, is the story of an "idiot" named Forrest Gump, who learns, from a very young age, how to hit the road running in order to escape ridicule and abuse. Forrest's road-running paradoxically leads him to a college football career, to Vietnam, where he earns a Congressional Medal of Honor, to China where he becomes a ping-pong champion, to the sea, where he becomes a shrimp boat captain and a successful entrepreneur, and across the US, where he earns fame as a cross-country runner and cult hero. Like many other road-movie comedies, both films feature foolish or gullible protagonists who are paired up with seemingly savvier buddies over the course of the journey, which takes them across various landscapes and acquaints them with many of the current events, personalities, and developments of their day.[9] Their conflicting attitudes are highlighted and contrasted to comic effect, with the supposed savant eventually coming to admire the paradoxical, abiding wisdom of the fool.[10]

More than that: both feature protagonists who might be identified as divine or holy fools, whose ideas and actions are "abnormal in that they are opposed to, or conflict with the customs and conventions of his society and culture. In consequence, [their] logic and thoughts proceed from different premises and values, and [their] conclusions and judgments are opposed to the conventional wisdom."[11] In this sense, Forrest Gump can be likened to Sal Paradise, the holy fool of Jack Kerouac's *On the Road*. As Mark Richardson observes, "[i]n *On the Road* as in *Forrest Gump*" – and I would argue, in *Frisco Kid*, as well – "we are invited to admire a faithful, forward-looking hero and discouraged ever from regarding his faith and goodwill as mere gullibility, which we could never respect."[12] In contrast to Kerouac's novel, however, the emphasis in both *Frisco Kid* and *Forrest Gump* on non-mechanized as opposed to mechanized travel underscores the simultaneously traditional and counter-cultural/non-conventional roles of these travelling protagonists. In both films, the journey involves development, change, and growth, as well as the reassertion of certain traditional or God-centred values that add a circular dimension – a doing as well as an undoing – to the linear journey across the country.

THE FOOL IN MODERN JEWISH LITERATURE

To be sure, the representation of the (holy) fool has a long history in Eastern and Western literature. While Enid Welsford begins her history of buffoons, clowns, court fools, poet fools, and harlequins in second-century Greece, the specific type of the holy fool is often linked in "fool scholarship" to St Paul's teaching in 1 Corinthians 4:10 that the Christian is a fool in the eyes of the world.[13] As Paul N. Siegel notes,

> [the] idiot was regarded in the Middle Ages and in the Renaissance as being under the special protection of God. He was also often regarded as an "innocent" or a "natural,' a child of nature who lived without thought of the past or the future and was consequently happier than the supposedly wise man."[14]

In Voltaire's *Candide*, the credulity and optimism of the fool become the target of satire; the sufferings endured by foolish Candide also provide an occasion to critique the folly and cruelty of humanity. In much of this literature, the whole question of who is wise and who is foolish is very much thrown into question, the purported fool often emerging as a preferred alternative to the corrupt cleverness of the "wise."

In Jewish literature, the cultural matrix from which *The Frisco Kid* emerges, the fool plays a distinctive role. I would like to consider the special career of the fool in Jewish culture, not only because of the unabashedly Jewish sensibility of *The Frisco Kid*, but also because of its relevance to the representation of the fool in *Forrest Gump*, as I explain later. The earliest origins of the notion of the holy fool in Jewish literature, and the reputed source for Paul's

New Testament evocation of the holy fool, are in the Hebrew Bible. As Sandra Billington notes, there are two Hebrew words for fool: "One, *tam*, means the innocent fool, who has no regard for material rewards. The other comes from the root *ksl*, and contains the willful, evil meanings of folly ... St Paul meant the first. The mode of [his] thinking is Hebrew-Aramaic; it arouses pleasant associations of completeness and integrity."[15]

Elsewhere in post-biblical Jewish literature, the fool is commonly referred to as the "schlemiel," literally, *shlomi-el*, meaning my well-being is God, as in "God watches over fools" (Psalms 116:6). *The American Heritage Dictionary of the English Language* (Fourth Edition, 2000) defines schlemiel as a "bungler or a dolt," but Jewish literary tradition portrays him much more lovingly. According to Sanford Pinsker, for a Jewish Diaspora community often persecuted and powerless, Jewish humour about the schlemiel constituted an important cultural strategy of self-mockery. Indeed, the schlemiel served as a kind of metaphorical stand-in for the Eastern-European shtetl Jew:

> In the face of world's injustice [sic] – and, at times, even God's – the shtetl Jew solidly maintained his innocence ... At the same time, however, they [shtetl Jews] also saw the schlemiel's ineptitude in socioeconomic matters as an extended metaphor of their own ... Because he was a character of ineptitude, a bumbling misrepresenter of reality, his comic victimhood helped to sustain those who were only partially schlemiels.[16]

In addition to providing comic relief from the woes of shtetl life, the schlemiel or Jewish simpleton figures prominently in Jewish literary representations of the modern conflict between reason and faith. A good example of this is "A Story about a Clever Man and a Simple Man" (*a mayse mit a hokhm un a tam*), (1805), by the Hasidic master, Nachman of Bratzlav (1772–1810). The story tells of a clever boy and a simple boy who grow up as neighbours. The *hokhm* (clever man) goes out on the road, travels from place to place, achieves success in every city and in every endeavour, yet is never satisfied, finding fault with each of his achievements; the *tam* (simple man), a poor shoemaker, stays home but is happy with his lot. The King of the land hears about these two young men, who, having grown up next to one another, have nevertheless developed such different abilities and dispositions; curious about how this happened, he invites them both to his palace. The simple cobbler immediately responds to the King's invitation, travels to the palace, and the King, tired of the intrigue and corruption of his current governor, appoints the simple man in his stead. In contrast, the clever man responds skeptically, doubts the King's existence, and rejects his invitation. As a result, a role reversal occurs, with the simple man ascending to prominence while the clever man, so wracked by doubt and dissatisfaction, becomes wholly incapable of any positive action or feeling. For Rabbi Nachman, who was worried about the negative spiritual effects of both European rationalism and rigidly traditional forms of Talmud study, this story upholds the value of faith in the face of stultifying intellectualism and empiricism.[17]

In this story, the clever man rather than the simple man is the true denizen of the road; until the King beckons him to the palace, the simple man is perfectly happy to live within the confines of his native village. In part, it is a question of purpose. When the clever man travels the road, he does so restlessly, skeptically. Thus, he gains little in the way of satisfaction or spiritual wisdom. When the simple man travels, he does so with the purpose of meeting the King – a barely veiled metaphor for meeting God – and as a result, gains wisdom, as indicated by the end of the story, where the supposedly simple man reprimands the wandering "clever man" for failing to receive "the grace of simplicity."[18] As Ruth Wisse notes, "the story puts the clever and simple men to a basic pragmatic test, the criteria of which are worldly success, happiness and healthy psychic survival. The simple man is not a natural saint; in fact his reliance on faith seems no more than a compensation for his lack of a power to reason. Nevertheless, and whatever its origins, his trust brings him the trust of others and enables him to take full advantage of opportunities."[19] As we will see in the ensuing film discussion, the personalities and careers of both Avram Belinsky and Forrest Gump follow this model.

The best known modern American Jewish tale of a "*tam*" is I.B. Singer's "*Gimpel tam*" (published in Yiddish in 1945), a story about a fabulously gullible baker who is repeatedly tricked by his community and cheated on by his wife, yet somehow, in the face of all of this, maintains his faith both in human beings and in God. The title of Singer's Yiddish story is commonly translated as "Gimpel the Fool," which does not quite capture the many meanings of the

Hebrew/Yiddish word "*tam*," and consequently, the many meanings of this suggestive, ambiguous story. The word *tam* variably means simple (as in a simpleton), complete or unblemished (as in the many Biblical uses of this word to describe animals brought as rituals sacrifices), mild (as in Genesis 25:27, where the patriarch Jacob is described as an *ish tam*, a mild man, a dweller in tents), or blameless (as in the description of Job as *tam veyashar*, as a blameless, upright man, Job 1:1), epithets that all fit Singer's hero, in varying degrees. When Gimpel consults with the rabbi about how he is being treated by the townspeople, the rabbi advises that "it is better to be a fool all your days than for one hour to be evil. You are not a fool. They are the fools. For he who causes his neighbor to feel shame loses Paradise himself."[20] Though foolishly credulous, Gimpel is ethically blameless. That is, until his wife confesses her unfaithfulness and an evil spirit seizes him, telling him that there is no such thing as God and urging him to harm all those who have deceived him by urinating into the dough for the next day's bread. Gimpel is ultimately prevented from executing this spiteful plan by his dead wife Elka, who appears to him in a dream, and scolds him for betraying his nature as a *tam*. "Because I was false, was everything else false too? ... I'm paying for it all, Gimpel. They spare you nothing here."[21] So shaken is Gimpel by all of this that he resolves that he must leave his native village and go out on the road, becoming a kind of archetypal Jewish wanderer/sage: "I wandered over the land, and good people did not neglect me. After many years I became old and white; I heard a great deal, many lies and falsehoods, but the longer I lived the more I understood that there were really no lies. Whatever doesn't really happen is dreamed at night."[22]

To be sure, Gimpel's "wise" assertions are dubious pronouncements. Given the post-Holocaust publication date of the story, his credulity and faith strike the reader as both visionary and preposterous. Who, before the death camps, could ever imagine such horrors coming to pass, and yet, here they are in the historical record! Who in their right mind would believe in God after all of this, and yet, is the alternative such an appealing and exalted option? The ambiguity of the end of the story is crucial to its power and to our mixed assessment of Gimpel's character. On the one hand, his goodness and faithfulness seem to be held up as a model to which to aspire; on the other hand, Gimpel is a gullible idiot, a dupe and a dolt, who couldn't possibly stand for the Jewish people let alone any average, functioning human being. The example of Gimpel can be marshal-led to make a very conservative, reactionary argument that what this morally benighted world needs now is not intellectualism or sophis-tication or cleverness, but the steadfast belief and constancy of a Gimpel, for tomorrow we shall die. By contrast, Gimpel's story also reads as a subversive tale against believing overmuch and accepting whole-cloth any doctrine or dogma. In taking to the road, Gimpel is both a reactionary and a revolutionary, a keeper of the system and one who explodes all systems as imaginary and false. As read-ers, we become interpretive wanderers, straying from one interpreta-tion to another in an effort to arrive at an ever-elusive hermeneutic conclusion.

AVRAM THE *TAM*: THE FOOL ON THE ROAD IN *THE FRISCO KID*

As a work of popular culture, *The Frisco Kid* is not such a relentlessly ambiguous work of art as Singer's story. Nevertheless, it shares many important features with Singer's master-tale. According to Jewish-American writer and Nobel Laureate Saul Bellow, what makes a story characteristically Jewish is a curious co-mingling of "laugh-ter and trembling."[23] "*Gimpel tam*," first translated into English by Saul Bellow, certainly evinces this mixture of comedy and tragedy. *The Frisco Kid* tilts decidedly in the direction of the comic, but is not without references to the tragedy of Jewish history. The suffering, wandering Jew of this film is a young rabbi named Avram Belinsky (Gene Wilder), who has just graduated from the rabbinical academy at the bottom of his class. Like Gimpel, Avram is an object of wide scorn in his Yeshiva community; when the teachers at the rabbinical academy meet to decide on the question of whether to send Avram to assume a rabbinical post in America, all of them, with the excep-tion of the Rosh Yeshiva (head of the academy) and his child assist-ant, object to the idea of "sending such a fool to America with the Indians." Knowing what he knows about Avram, why does the Rosh Yeshiva decide, against the advice of his colleagues, to dispatch him across the Atlantic? Like the Rabbi in Singer's story, is this Rosh Yeshiva aware that Avram – whose name recalls the biblical Abram, first immigrant to the Promised Land – possesses gifts that might be appreciated in the New World more than in his native Poland? Avram has already managed to learn English, no doubt a distraction from his rabbinical studies. Does the Rosh Yeshiva perhaps recognize that Avram is precisely the right kind of fool to undertake and succeed in this journey?

One thing is clear: the wise rabbis in the rabbinical academy, all Yiddish speakers and Torah scholars, are no better suited than Avram to immigrate to America; even the Rosh Yeshiva, who speaks English, thinks that San Francisco is next to New York, presenting himself as something of a dolt when it comes to American geography. If, as Sanford Pinsker argues, the schlemiel acts as a stand-in for the shtetl Jew, Avram is an exaggerated representation of Jewish-immigrant-everyman, a fool in the context of the New World, with its different mores and language, its vast territory, and its strange peoples. His rabbinical training, the very opposite of a rugged life on the road, would seem to doom him to failure; much of the comedy in the film derives from the incongruity of seeing a rabbi involved in cowboy/American road-traveller physicality. His unexpected triumph becomes emblematic, however, of American Jewish immigrant success. Ironically, what enables his triumph is his foolish unwillingness to compromise his religious principles. In contrast to many other earlier accounts of the Jewish immigrant assimilation, Avram's story (anachronistically) exudes cultural confidence born out of the discovery and celebration in the late 1970s and 1980s of ethnicity and hyphenated identities.

Avram's journey across the American Promised Land begins in Philadelphia – in Avram's immigrant idiom, "the city where all the brothers love each other." Things get off to a bad start when Avram misses his boat to San Francisco and becomes ready prey for two crooked brothers, whom he pays to give him a stagecoach ride to San Francisco, but who repay him by beating him up, stealing his money and the ornament for the Torah scroll he is bringing to San Francisco, and throwing him off the coach. As they pummel Avram, the brothers laugh hysterically, a moment (as in Singer's "Gimpel the Fool," when the townspeople constantly amuse themselves at Gimpel's expense) that reveals their moral turpitude. Avram's abuse at the hands of the brothers from the city of brotherly love, birthplace of the Constitution, calls to mind the European history of Jewish persecution and casts the notion of American exceptionalism in an ironic light. If this is what happens to a Jewish immigrant on the American road, then America is no better than Europe, where time and again, Jews have been beaten, robbed, and murdered, their holy places and ritual objects destroyed or desecrated. But all is not lost. One by one, Avram begins to retrieve his possessions. Misfortune gives way to comedy, when after having struggled to put on his boots, Avram finally retrieves his socks. And when he finds the Torah scroll that had been thrown off the coach with his clothes, he strokes and kisses the little Torah like a baby or a doll, a moment of almost childlike piety and ecstasy.

Indeed, if Avram's first brush with the American road seems to recapitulate the story of Jewish victimization, his experiences immediately thereafter greatly alter the European script. Walking despondently along the road, Avram suddenly sees a group of bearded men with long coats, Pennsylvania Dutch Christians whom he mistakes for a band of Hasidim. Crying out "Landsman" (countrymen), he runs over and begins to speak in a torrent of Yiddish; when he realizes these men do not understand him, he spots a cross on one of their Bibles and swoons. Underlying the comedy of mistaken identity in this scene is a serious point about the possibilities for Jewish and Christian cooperation in America. Falling into the hands of pious Christians is a frightening proposition for the European Jew, but here in America, the Amish treat Avram with kindness and respect and even give him money so that he can resume his journey. Avram's encounter later on in the film with a group of Catholic monks reinforces the idea that in terms of Jewish-Christian relations, America is in fact a New World.

Avram's nature as a *tam*, then, his gullibility, his susceptibility to misunderstandings, his simple faith in people and his naïve generosity of spirit, make him a target for hardship but also allow him to be open to the wonders and possibilities of the American road. As he leaves the Amish community and sets out across the frontier, he naively proclaims that America is a wonderful country. Riding on a train, he emerges from the bathroom to find all the passengers with their arms folded over their heads; they have just been victims of a hold-up, but Avram simple-mindedly assumes that their hands are on their heads because they're playing Simple Simon, a game a child had taught him earlier in the ride. In need of more money to make his journey, Avram gets a job working on the railroad, alongside a Chinese man and a Mexican, whose foot he repeatedly hits, albeit unintentionally, with a sledgehammer. Avram is an exasperatingly inept railroad worker, but because of his kindness, faithfulness, and good intentions, even Paco, the injured Mexican, regrets that

Avram decides to leave the work detail and proceed on his journey to San Francisco.

Equally inept at riding, hunting, and fishing, Avram luckily meets up with a man named Tommy who teaches him to how to survive on the road. Naïf that he is, Avram has no sense of Tommy's occupation – he is the same man who robbed the train when Avram was in the bathroom. Unwittingly, Avram becomes an accessory to a bank robbery and the target of a posse. At this juncture, one might expect Avram to shed some of his *Gimpel tam*-like traits and do his best to emulate Tommy so as to save himself. Instead, this event precipitates an even greater assertion of "foolish" Jewish values on Avram's part as he refuses to violate the Sabbath in order to make a smooth getaway. As the sun sets, they manage to escape, but only very narrowly. Brought to the brink, Avram makes it clear that religious obligation comes first; Tommy – doubting Thomas rather than *tam* (see John 20:24–9) – thinks he's a "crazy bastard."

Later, when pursued by Indians, Avram's Torah falls off his horse and he insists on going back to retrieve it, leading to their capture by the Indians. In a scene very reminiscent of past stories of public burnings of Jews in punishment for their continued adherence to Jewish law, Avram agrees to submit himself to fire rather than to forsake the Torah; the chief is so moved by Avram's religious devotion that he has him lifted off the flames. Ironically, then, it is Avram's seemingly insane willingness to die for his religion that saves him and Tommy. According to Patricia Erens, "*The Frisco Kid* is one of the few films to seriously question the difference between Jewish and American values, finding neither inherently superior."[24] Indeed, this is one of the moments in the film where Jewish values are lauded, where "simple" faith triumphs over pragmatism.

Even so, the dangers of the road persist. When Avram and Tommy finally reach the California coast and stop to take a swim in the ocean, they are ambushed on a beach by the Philadelphia brothers. Earlier, they had met up with the brothers at a saloon, and Tommy (as if to repent for implicating Avram in a robbery) had helped Avram retrieve the Torah ornament and his stolen money. The brothers now have guns and are intent on getting their revenge; when one of the brothers grabs the Torah scroll and throws it into the fire, the assault once again takes on an anti-Semitic quality. In response, Avram runs to extract the Torah from the fire, completely oblivious to the danger to his own life. Only after saving the Torah does Avram concern himself with the gun battle, and even then it takes a great deal to get him to act. When Tommy is injured and disarmed and one the brothers is about to grab a fallen gun and shoot them both, Avram finally grabs a gun and shoots their assailant dead.

Avram's killing of the outlaw precipitates a crisis of faith and vocation, not unlike Gimpel's; until this point, despite his association with the outlaw Tommy, he has remained steadfast in his determination to reach San Francisco and pursue his rabbinate despite the other influences and mores that threaten to lead him astray. The act of murder, albeit in self-defence, unmoors Avram and throws his journey off course. In his mind, he is no longer fit to assume the duties of the rabbi. The surviving Philadelphia brother catches up with Avram in San Francisco and tries to challenge him to a showdown like a real cowboy. In Singer's story, Gimpel is on the verge of doing evil when he reaffirms his good, believing nature. Likewise, it is at the showdown, when faced with the option of embracing the violence of the frontier, that Avram rediscovers his rabbinic vocation and asserts his own brand of wisdom. Refusing to undertake any more violent action, he invokes, instead, the example of the biblical Abram (still not renamed Abraham), as seen in Genesis 13. Abram immigrates to Canaan with his nephew Lot, but when tensions develop between his shepherds and those of Lot, Abraham declares that this is a large enough country: you go your way and I'll go mine.[25] Refusing to shoot anyone, Avram Belinsky resolves the tension between him and his outlaw adversary by deciding that he'll keep San Francisco; the outlaw can have the rest of America. Avram's road journey thus concludes with a re-affirmation of (Jewish) law and order – albeit, only in the city of San Francisco, where he, the rabbi, presides!

The rabbi fool thus plays the dual role of sheriff and cleric. Unlike Singer's Gimpel, who is married off to Elka, a prostitute, by his jeering townspeople in a would-be ritual to ward off cholera, Avram makes a healthy, proper match with the daughter of the president of his congregation. He does not, however, marry Sara Mindel, the daughter whose name recalls the biblical Sarah and who had been promised to him (while he was still in Poland) according to the conventions of arranged marriages; instead, he marries Rosalie, the daughter he falls in love with upon arriving in San Francisco, proving that if he has not embraced all of the ways and freedoms of America, he has at least accepted the American prerogative of choosing his own wife.

The ending of this film, then, is far more optimistic and affirmative than the ending of Singer's haunting story; in contrast to the ending of Singer's "Gimpel the Fool," where the fool continues to wander as if perpetually, the end of *The Frisco Kid* brings an end to Avram's journey; in Avram Belinsky's America, the fool can become a respectable sage by virtue of his prior wanderings across America. San Francisco is the Promised City; he can settle down and make his mark on his new community.

FORREST GIMPEL GUMP

Though not a Jewish film, *Forrest Gump*, the runaway hit of 1994, is a cousin both to *The Frisco Kid* and to Singer's "Gimpel the Fool" in its mixture of comedy and tragedy, representation of the "wise" or sainted fool, and road thematics. The Winston Groom novel that serves as the basis of the film begins as Singer's story does ("I am Gimpel the Fool. I don't think myself a fool") with the first-person narrator both declaring and repudiating his identity as an idiot: "I been an idiot since I was born. My IQ is near 70, which qualifies me, so they say. Probly, tho, I'm closer to bein an imbecile or maybe even a moron, but personally, I'd rather think of myself as like a *halfwit*, or something – and not no idiot."[26] In the film, this simultaneous acceptance and rejection of the mantle of the fool finds expression in Forrest's constant repetition of the phrase "Stupid is as stupid does." Blameless goodness, constancy, and faithfulness are traits shared by all three of these characters – Gimpel, Avram, and Forrest – descendants of the biblical *tam* and St Paul's fool in the eyes of the world. Their virtues reveal the fickleness and malevolence of others. In setting out upon the road, all three are transformed to some degree and yet strengthened in their core traits. Gimpel's love for his departed wife intensifies as does his faith in the lies that constitute his world; Avram's Jewish convictions are tested and his rabbinic vocation is reaffirmed; and Forrest – rich, accomplished, decorated, and travelled – maintains just about everything about himself: his devotion to his mother and to Jenny (as well as to Bubba and Lieutenant Dan), even his style of dress and his crew-cut. Only once, during his cross-country running trip back and forth across America (four times) does he ever let his hair grow, but more about that later.

Despite their intellectual limitations, all three of these holy fools on the road achieve a large measure of material success. As in the

Rabbi Nachman story about the clever man and the simple man, *Forrest Gump* seems not only to value kind-hearted constancy and simplicity but also to link it causally with stupendous wealth and achievement. According to Dave Kehr's reading, Forrest survives and succeeds in the film precisely "because he isn't very smart":

> He reacts, he runs, he remains magnificently blank, allowing those around him to read whatever they want into him (as do the crowds he attracts to his late guru phase, running aimlessly across the country). He is the feather presented in Zemeckis's magical opening, buffeted by the breeze, carried along by fate and luck ... But while this is a lovely image (and certainly one of the most sublime creations of modern special effects technology), it is not a comforting or a complacent one. Only by going along, by surrendering your will and identity, by refusing to see the horror around you, can you make it in America. Those near Forrest who try to stand up, to register a protest or to alter their fate, are soon struck down. Ambition is fatal: Jenny wants to become famous as a singer. Bubba wants to succeed as a businessman. But it's Forrest who achieves both fame and success, by the purest of chance, while Bubba and Jenny die pointless, early deaths, victims of war and disease respectively.[27]

Kehr makes a convincing argument. The film does appear to valourize Forrest's tolerant love and unconditional constancy over the political perfidies, violence, and ideological struggles of the recent American past. Kehr is right to call attention to the potential meaning of the feather sequences at the beginning and end of the film as representative of Forrest's role as a passive, unreflective participant in his own destiny. It is my argument, however, that to interpret the feather sequence, and consequently the entire film, along these lines is to fail to recognize the ambiguity of both. In my earlier discussion of the ending of Singer's "Gimpel the Fool," I stressed that in trying to assess the meaning and resultant wisdom of Gimpel's wanderings on the road, we, as readers become interpretive wanderers, drifting from one interpretation to another and then back again. I'd like to suggest that the feather sequence, and indeed, much of the substance of this film, hermeneutically buffets us as "readers," carrying us up and along its interpretive road, sliding off a shoulder of one interpretation and onto the sidewalk of another. There are moments, as when Forrest picks up the feather that has fallen by his feet and places it securely into his copy of Curious George, when we feel as though we have arrived at a correct and cogent response to this film. Recognizing the way it applauds Forrest's simplicity, we conclude, as does critic Thomas B. Beyers, that this is an aggressively conservative, Reagan-era film. According to Beyers's scathing critique, *Forrest Gump*

1) distorts and flattens out history
2) fantasizes idiotically about racial reconciliation (through Forrest's relationship with Bubba and his family and his "role" in the experience of desegregation), but in reality co-opts black aspiration for the cause of white entrepreneurship
3) erases feminism (it is one of the only movements important to this period that is not represented in the film) and yet elevates Forrest as a sensitive new-age husband and father
4) punishes political opposition (the anti-war movement) and countercultural experimentation to death, as evidenced so clearly in the death of Jenny to HIV.[28]

But just as we feel we have trapped the meaning of this film between the pages of our interpretive/critical "book," we become skeptical about our own cleverness and curious about other potential interpretations. We consider this film's popularity and wonder: is it fair to dismiss and deny the power that Forrest's goodness and constancy have had on all these viewers? When Bubba/Forrest's mother dies and he encapsulates his feelings of despair with the words "And that's all I have to say about that," do we not sense great wisdom in his verbal restraint? When Forrest watches Jenny throw stones at her father's old house and says, "some times there just aren't enough rocks," do we really feel that we, in our sophistication, could say it any better?

At other times we disdain Forrest's cluelessness. When Forrest names his shrimp boat *Jenny* and hopes "that whatever she is doing is making her happy" and at that very moment a drug-addled Jenny is on the verge of hurling herself over the edge of a balcony, we are reminded that Forrest is just a fool. We find it difficult to take seriously the idea that he, with his IQ of 70, his unthinking meteoric speed, and his accidental fortune, stands for us, that he is our highest exemplar of good American values and the enduring truth of the

American dream. Does it not make more sense, as Maurice Yacowar suggests, to view *Forrest Gump* as a "satire of the mythical powers of the 'common man'" rather than its apotheosis?[29]

What I'm arguing, by way of all of this interpretive waffling, is that *Forrest Gump* is best understood as an ambiguous text, one that admits contradictory interpretations simultaneously. More specifically, I'd like to suggest that the ambiguity or polyphony of the film is expressed over and over again in its many references and representations of the road.

I mentioned earlier that in road movies, the road is often presented as weightless, fast, automated, transforming. In this film, the feather sequence notwithstanding, this road mythology is in large part rejected. Road imagery proliferates in this film, as in *The Frisco Kid*, but despite his late twentieth-century context, Forrest is never associated with an automobile. On several occasions in the film, Forrest boards buses, but contrary to the idea of bus/train travel as fast, free, accessible, and democratic (see Slethaug, chapter 8), these bus journeys are never unencumbered or unfettered for Forrest. The first time he rides a school bus as a child, no one, with the exception of one child at the back, the abused, impoverished Jenny, agrees to sit next to him. The second time he boards a bus (as a soldier in the US Army) only Bubba, Forrest's black counterpart, agrees to have Forrest share his seat. At the end of the film, Forrest waits for a bus, and it is in this waiting, rather than in boarding the bus, that his story unfolds. Forrest never does get on that bus. Instead, he runs the few blocks to Jenny's apartment, reinforcing the film's association of Forrest with a simpler, non-mechanized form of road travel.

Forrest's distance from the mechanized American road casts a shadow on the idea of American mobility. The road motif plays a significant role in Forrest's Vietnam experiences, but again, with a satirical result. The army may advertise itself as a context where you can "Be all that you can be," but, in the case of Forrest's buddy Bubba, a young man obsessed with the entrepreneurial dream of being a shrimp-boat captain, all that he can be is dead. Many of the Vietnam scenes in the film take place along roads, and although the trip to Vietnam has expanded the road map of Forrest's life, the roads on this map are filled with hidden mines and buried traps. According to the logic of its road imagery, one of the ostensible messages of *Forrest Gump* is the end of the American dream, the closing down of its roads, the impossibility or the futility of efforts toward self-transformation (see Attinello, chapter 6) – that is, according to one possible interpretation.

For while buses in this film don't promise a meaningful or transformative ride (see, for example, the scene where Jenny joins her abusive boyfriend in boarding a bus back from Washington, DC to Berkeley, a moment where it is clear she is on the road to absolutely nowhere), and while unchanging Forrest represents the very opposite of the Jack Kerouac hipster on the road, the film is built around images of Forrest running down various roads, each time with spectacular success. From the beginning of the film, that post-war period of the 1950s-early 1960s in which the American road became inextricably connected to the car, Forrest's road experience is defined in direct opposition to machines, in general, and the automobile, in particular. The first time Jenny exhorts Forrest to run away from his tormentors (Run, Forrest, Run!), he bursts out of the restraints of his braces (symbolic of the very idea of limited physical mobility) and outruns his bike-riding pursuers, even though they have the advantage of wheels and gears. Fast forward a number of years, and now a teen-aged Forrest manages to outrun the same bullies who now chase him in a truck. Forrest's ability to command the road on foot simultaneously deflates and re-inflates the ideological wheels of American freedom and mobility.

The same mixed message emerges when one attempts to chart the course of Forrest's various journeys. On the one hand, Forrest's running reinforces the idea of the linear journey, as seen in Avram's journey from the eastern port of Philadelphia to the western coast of San Francisco. When properly directed, Forrest knows how to run a straight line, from Jenny or from his shrimp boat named Jenny all the way home to his (ailing) Mama, or from one end of the football field to another. On the other hand, Forrest often seems to be running in circles, as represented linguistically by the circular/repetitious structure of Jenny's exhortation ("Run, Forrest, Run!"). In Vietnam, he achieves distinction as a soldier not because he knows how to run in a straight line and get from point A to point B, but because he runs back and forth, doubling back to save his friend Bubba. Bubba dies, of course, but Forrest manages to save Lieutenant Dan, a victory born of speed and mobility that is tempered by the amputation of Lieutenant Dan's legs. Forrest achieves fame as a ping-pong player, taking him further east on the Asian road, to China. Once again, note that ping-pong is a game of back and forth.

"It used to be," Forrest says, reflecting on his running prowess, "I ran to get where I was going; I never thought it would take me anywhere." The tautological quality to this statement encapsulates the ambiguous workings of road imagery and directionality in this film. We refer to the artist ultimately responsible for creating a film as a director, but, ironically and very artfully, in this film Robert Zemeckis achieves multi-directionality. If one attempts to parse the meaning of Forrest's road journey, one arrives at once in different places. The road for Forrest is a means of escape and also the way back to Greenbow. It is a path to success, and yet he gives it all up to be a gardener (referencing Voltaire's foolish Candide, and the message of "cultivate thy garden," as well as Jerzy Kosinski's novel *Being There* and Hal Ashby's film of the same name, and his fool-hero, Chance the Gardener).

Perhaps the most deliberately ambiguous road sequence in the film is the set of scenes in which Forrest sets out on a four-year stint of cross-country running. Once again, Forrest doesn't seem to think very deeply about why he is doing what he is doing. In the absence of an articulated position, various Americans elevate him (like Kosinski's Chance the Gardener) to the level of spiritual guru and assign their own meanings to his running. Their over-cleverness about why Forrest runs becomes an occasion of satire, mocking American pretensions to understanding as well as the yawning, spiritual void that their embrace of Forrest's running seems to fill, albeit temporarily. But is that the only way to understand this sequence?

Forrest himself supplies two possible interpretations: on the one hand, he says that he just feels like running; on the other, he invokes the wisdom of his mother and says that he is running to put his past behind him. But are either of these interpretations correct, in some absolute, unimpeachable way? After all, he only began running after the shock of Jenny's departure, a moment in the film that corresponds to the devastating deathbed confessions of Gimpel's wife, Elka. He feels like running because he has experienced a great shock and loss that he feels ill-equipped to bear standing still. As for the claim that he is running to put the past behind him, Forrest never really achieves that, for all of his roads lead back to home and to his past – to his mother and to Jenny. The back and forth quality of this cross-country journey suggests, on a geographical level, that Forrest's running is not really about leaving the past (point A) to arrive at the future (point B), but about a literal mixing of the two.

During this running sequence, Forrest changes – at least, he seems to change. For the first time, he lets hair and beard grow; he begins to look like a hippy, like one of Jenny's Berkeley friends. In the Southwest of the United States, a visual setting evocative of the Western and the American frontier, he sees rock formations, and sunsets, and natural wonders that have deep impact. But when he is tired of running, he simply stops, cuts his hair, and puts his old clothes back on. Before we know it, he is back in the American South, in pursuit of his long-lost Jenny. And so, as in the case of the elusive feather, we have yet another visual sequence that doubles back on itself, another quest for meaning that returns us to where we began.

CONCLUSIONS

What generalization can be made then about the representation of fools on the non-mechanized road as seen in these two movies? In large measure, these films depart from the established conventions. Avram and Forrest's experiences on the road are ultimately less about "weightless life" than about responsibility and (religious) obligation, less about the pursuit of freedom than about the pursuit of love, friendship, and/or the will of God. According to David Laderman, road films generally communicate the sense of the road as outside of and opposed to mainstream urban culture.[30] In these two films, however, the road often leads to or ends up in the city and in community. Both films include elements of adventure as well as domesticity, the road serving as a way out as well as a way back home. If the typical road film celebrates the connection between freedom (an essential tenet of American life) and the road, these films critique certain kinds of wanton freedom (lawless aggression, hedonism, theft, and murder) and uphold other forms (the freedom to make money and pursue happiness, to move around the country and associate across social and racial borders, and to care for those you love). In a suggestive essay about pre-war road movies, Bennet Shaber writes about the use of Biblical motifs in the road genre, especially that of Exodus and the wandering in Sinai, and discusses how these Biblical resonances elevate the significance of the road journey to a metaphorical, indeed, metaphysical level. According to Shaber, in these early films of the road, "the road metaphor oscillates between abandonment and promise, desperation and a new resourcefulness."[31] *Forrest* and *Frisco* each employ this wilderness imagery, in varying measures, but with a comic cast, portraying their protagonists as both clowns and holy seers, as fools as well as desert visionaries, whose vision blurs as well as sharpens as their journey progresses. *Frisco*'s Avram ultimately reaffirms his Jewish commitments and finds a way to reconcile this religious "foolishness" with the immigrant demands and new-world rigours of the American road, both in and out of the city. The meaning of Forrest Gump's journey, like that of his literary predecessor, Gimpel, is harder to pin down. If there is an engine that drives *Forrest Gump*, it is the engine of interpretation, as we the viewers, cast about for new ways to understand not only the meaning of the American road but also the idea of wisdom itself.

Generically Mobile: The Projection of Protocol from the Road Movie to Virtual Reality and Video Games

MICHAEL TRUSCELLO

Control is not discipline. You do not control people with a highway. But by making highways, you multiply the means of control.

Gilles Deleuze

We don't need a map to keep this show on the road.

The Muppet Movie (1979)

In the tradition of Harold Innis and James Carey, Jeremy Packer explores the historical relationship between transportation and communication. For Packer, this relationship is a "political rationality" that attempts to consolidate and expand "the possibilities of liberal governance."[1] Specifically, Packer analyzes "how driving behavior and the mobility it creates have been dually represented, on the one hand, as having great potential and, on the other, as a serious threat to social order."[2] His analysis follows a trajectory familiar to Foucauldian governmentality literature, which posits neo-liberal governance as something that "depends not simply on legal compliance, but also on the production of subjects whose freedoms and responsibilities necessitate their investment and belief in popular truth. In simple terms," Packer writes, "following the law is not necessarily as important as being safe."[3] The discourse of safety unites transportation and communication in the neo-liberal governing order. In this context Packer argues, "Struggles over mobility and access thus need to be examined in both the virtual and material realms."[4]

A central component in the production of subjects who prize "freedom that accords with the expansive demands of culture and

economy," or freedom that produces governability, is popular culture, specifically, according to Toby Miller, "the concept of genre."[5]
For Miller, genre is "simultaneously textual, economic, and social,"
and "these concepts and their parental human sciences are technologies of governance, systems of ordering conduct."[6]

In what follows I argue for one form of "struggle" over "mobility
and access" in "both the virtual and material realms," by examining the genre of the road movie (and, I argue, its generic cousin the
virtual reality movie) in terms of Alexander Galloway's notion of
protocol. The concept of protocol returns the focus of genre analyses to the material technical delimitations of automobility and its
attendant offers of psychic freedom (see Ford, chapter 7 in this book,
for another examination of genre, the reality television road trip).

In her book, *The Road Story and the Rebel: Moving Through
Film, Fiction, and Television*, Katie Mills employs the term "automobility" to represent the perceived autonomy and mobility of identity construction in the road movie genre.[7] Mills's treatment of the
genre echoes a common articulation of where form meets content
in the once-prototypical American story: "The driving force of road
stories is questions about autonomy, mobility, and identity, whether
that identity be threatened or expanded by being on the road. The
road genre offers a pop cultural forum for imagining a fluid self and
new genres of relating with others."[8] Given the emphasis on autonomy and mobility in much road movie scholarship, it is surprising
how many theorists define the genre in terms of the affordances of
vehicles and not the constraints of the road. This tends to be the
case, even though in road stories "the concept of liberty is most con-
sistently defined as freedom of movement" and not form of movement.[9] Automotive movement is generally only as free as the road
permits. Never mind the off-road fantasies of various truck and SUV
commercials; or, rather, mind them as indications of just how powerful is the desire to contravene the rules of the road. Mills's reading of
the road movie does not capture the reactionary quality of the genre,
in part, I suspect, because of the absence of a proper discussion in
the road movie literature of how the road determines the aesthetic
and narrative boundaries of the genre. A broader definition of automobility must be considered, to account for the central tension of
the genre, a tension that several road movie theorists frame as a kind
of limitation to the freedom of the road, sometimes even a fatalism
related to the road trip. The limitations or affordances of the road

movie narrative return attention to the materiality of the road, often ignored by road movie theorists in favour of the apparent freedom of movement.

THE PARADOXES OF AUTOMOBILITY

John Urry's use of the term automobility incorporates elements similar to Mills's usage, but expands the definition to recognize that "what is key is not the 'car' as such but the system of [these] fluid interconnections" among vehicles, roads, and various extensions of this ecology.[10] Automobility, for Urry, "can be conceptualized as a self-organizing autopoetic, non-linear system that spreads world-wide, and includes cars, car-drivers, roads, petroleum supplies and many novel objects, technologies and signs."[11] This definition foregrounds the systemic materiality of the road over the ephemeral desire for freedom. Considered aesthetically, this definition of automobility puts the "road" back into the road movie. Its essential component is the paradoxical observation that "automobility is thus a system that *coerces* people into an intense *flexibility*."[12] The "paradox in the promise of automobility," as Cotten Seiler calls it (chapter 4 in this volume), actually has a surprisingly extensive history in American writing about cars, but Seiler believes automobility must be considered a greater force than Urry's system of "fluid interconnections": "More than merely a set of policies or attitudes cohering around cars and roads," Seiler writes, "automobility comprises a 'multilinear ensemble' of commodities, bodies of knowledge, laws, techniques, institutions, environments, nodes of capital, sensibilities, and modes of perception" (Seiler, chapter 4). Seiler invokes Foucault's notion of the *dispositive*, or *apparatus*, to capture the expansion of governmentality that followed the paving of America. "Automobility – in particular that of the elevated, limited access highway of the postwar era," Seiler charges in *The Republic of Drivers*, "provided a quotidian performance of both autonomous self-direction *and* acquiescence to systemic parameters. To drive, in other words, was to live motion without change."[13] "To live motion without change" aptly captures the self-deluding equation of movement with liberation – often either overtly or implicitly incorporated into road movie analyses – and, more broadly, the workings of Foucault's disciplinary society. The phrase "to live motion without change" also defines the experience of the audience for a road movie, something not lost on Devin Orgeron, who calls the motion of the road movie a "seductive illusion."[14]

The paradox of automobility expressed by Urry, Seiler, and others – driving as a freedom born of coercion, the road as built environment or "substrate" for liberal society (Seiler, chapter 4) – parallels Alexander Galloway's notion of *protocol*, a form of control based on technicity.[15] Galloway compares the distributed networks of the interstate highway and the Internet, both systems that achieve openness through voluntary submission to technical protocols (the TCP/IP protocols of the Internet, or the lane markings, signs, and other affordances of highway travel). To enjoy freedom of movement on the interstate highway, one must observe the technical parameters of the road; similarly, to enjoy the freedom of communication between computers on the Internet, those computers must speak the same language, observe the same technical protocols. Galloway's work provides this essay with a theoretical conjunction between the road movie and virtual reality films, which also depict motion as something achieved by stasis; both genres exhibit freedom as a function of technicity.

For the road movie, the voluntary submission to parameters of protocological control helps explain the central generic tension with reference to the material circumscription of the road rather than to the vehicles that travel upon it. Most theorists of road movies have focused almost exclusively on the vehicles in these films. David Laderman, for example, sees the road movie as a specifically "modernist" genre, driven, as it were, by the mechanization of movement and the modernist romanticization of technology.[16] He does not mention *The Wizard of Oz* in his introduction, for example, presumably because Dorothy does not drive a car; "traveling in a motorized vehicle is what Road Movie characters do," writes Laderman.[17] While Laderman admits, "More significant than the proliferation of the automobile as stylized commodity is the construction of the *actual* interstate highway system," his discussion of the road movie focuses solely on motorized vehicles and the act of driving.[18]

Together, road movies and virtual reality films are expressions of what I will call *foregrounding the apparatus*. The *apparatus* is a term that recognizes the paradoxical freedom of distributed networks, a freedom derived from the coercion of technological delimitations; the genres in question typically *show* or *foreground* the apparatus that produces reactionary forms of governmentality. A protocological reading of these genres can begin to articulate the constraints of technicity, in the form of a road movie such as *The Wizard of Oz* (1939), or in the form of a virtual reality film such as TRON (1982) and its sequel, TRON: *Legacy* (2010). Typically, films that foreground technically restrictive freedom appear during the emergence of new forms of protocols. The meditative and pivotal quality of the Yellow Brick Road in *The Wizard of Oz*, for example, captures the emergence of newly surfaced roads across America, before the period of ubiquitous automobility. TRON transforms the Yellow Brick Road into the circuitous control of the post-industrial society, at the birth of personal computers and networked computing. The contradictions of highway and cyberspace protocol are better understood in terms of Galloway's central insight: "The founding principle of the Net is control, not freedom. *Control has existed from the beginning.* Perhaps it is a different type of control than we are used to seeing. It is a type of control based on openness, inclusion, universalism, and flexibility. It is control borne from high degrees of technical organization (protocol), not this or that limitation on individual freedom or decision making (fascism)."[19] On the protocological road, the buoyant refrain "follow the Yellow Brick Road" becomes less the jubilant expression of deliverance from self-imposed exile and more the controlled imperative of industrialized wandering. Or, as Cotten Seiler states, "in these moments of danger that threatened capitalist-liberal hegemony by destabilizing its narrative of selfhood, automobility performed a crucial restorative role by giving that selfhood a vital form conducive to the existing arrangement of power."[20]

THE CENTRAL TENSION OF THE ROAD MOVIE

Theorists of the road movie are particularly attuned to this dynamic – a contradictory impulse, an overbearing sense of control in the emancipatory structure of networked abandon – and characterize this central tension as everything from a classical ontological trope of movement versus stasis, to a figure for the act of interpretation and its inherent ambiguities. Steven Cohan and Ina Rae Hark argue that the road movie "sets the liberation of the road against the oppression of hegemonic norms," projecting "American Western mythology onto the landscape traversed and bound by the nation's highways."[21] Typically, one half of this dialectic – the "liberation of the road," and not the ways in which the liberation is "bound by the nation's highways" – is foregrounded as the more salient feature of the road movie; but always the liberation of the road is "bound," the outlaw posture always curbed and directed by the asphalt and markings on which it flees. David Laderman describes the road movie dynamic as "a *tension* between rebellion and conformity."

> That is, just as the Road Movie's machine is always present in its garden, so too more broadly the Road Movie's overt concern with rebellion against traditional social norms is consistently undermined, diluted, or at least haunted by the very conservative cultural codes the genre so desperately takes flight from.[22]

In generic terms, Laderman poses this qualified form of cultural critique as a "distinctively modernist staging of a rather classical, perhaps timeless and universal struggle between two primal drives: the dynamic and the static."[23] Devin Orgeron echoes this sentiment, arguing that road movies "extend a longstanding cinematic tradition that posits a hopeless and lamentable mobility in an effort to eulogize or find *stability*."[24] Orgeron's dichotomy of mobility and stability is informed by a reactionary nostalgia, "a desire to roll history back, to return to a pre-technological, mythically innocent moment."[25] However, the contradictory impulses of the road movie, according to Laderman, are "confined by the conventional road-blocks of classical genre film," whereas Orgeron sees the generic contradictions as emanating from a "desire to both admire *and* critique American mythologies in a distinctly European dialect."[26] "The genre [of the road movie] has always been inherently schizoid," claims Michael Atkinson, "offsetting our mad romance with the internal combustion engine, upholstery, tailfins and endless asphalt with a seemingly unpreventable collapse into failure and pain."[27] For Stuart C. Aitken and Christopher Lee Lukinbeal, the central tension of the road movie exists at the hysterical "edge of self-identity, being simultaneously motionless (holding onto the seat of one's identity) and in motion (transcending social/spatial scales and annihilating space and time)," a psychoanalytic expression of the road movie paradox.[28] For Christopher Morris, road movie quests are "not only futile but repetitive" because they "anticipate" and dramatize "paralysis and redundancy in reading"; Morris sees road movie reflexivity as analogous with the Derridean "act of reading."[29] The genre itself is elusive and full of contradiction because the road is a figure "for reading itself."[30] The liberation of the road, then, is "bound" by the impossibility of the journey, just as meaning through interpretation is bound by interpretive aporias: "the road journey repudiates the idea of arrival at something worthwhile; redundant endings vitiate beginnings."[31] Finally, Corey K. Creekmur reminds us, "Every American who knows 'there's no place like home' – the mantra of America's most famous Road Movie – also remembers that 'you can't go home again.'"[32] Folk wisdom frames the freedom of the road trip as redundant, futile and, upon return home, somewhat tragic.

Whether a classical trope, a generic limitation, a hermeneutic blindside, or a slice of American common sense, the central tension in the road movie – and, as I argue, in the virtual reality movie – expresses an emancipation based on movement and speed and dislocation that is always constrained, redundant, or perhaps inadvisable. The road should be a path to freedom, these films want to believe, just as computers conjoined by common languages should embody a form of communicative autonomy. But as Alexander Galloway demonstrates, distributed networks such as the highways and the Internet only achieve autonomous postures through the imposition of a reactionary protocol, a set of procedures that enable data transmission between computers or traffic passage between destinations, "a distributed management system that allows control to exist within a heterogeneous material milieu."[33] To illustrate computer protocol, Galloway uses the analogy of the highway system:

> Many different combinations of roads are available to a person driving from point A to point B. However, en route one is compelled to stop at red lights, stay between the white lines, follow a reasonably direct path, and so on. These conventional rules that govern the set of possible behavior patterns within a heterogeneous system are what computer scientists call protocol. Thus, protocol is a technique for achieving voluntary regulation within a contingent environment.[34]

For the Internet, protocol is constructed on the basis of what are called RFC (Request for Comment) documents. These documents are compiled by experts, and contain rules and recommendations for technical standards. On the basis of these standards, open communication is possible on the Internet; that is, the communicative freedom engendered by computers on the Internet is a product of submission to reactionary technical standards. Galloway returns to the analogy of the road to explain the functioning of computer protocols, which delimit control in an otherwise open and decentralized system (whether Internet or interstate highway): while "signage and police compel [the] driver to slow down ... Bumps, on the other hand, create a physical system of organization. They materially force the driver to acquiesce."[35] "Bumps," the exemplar of protocological control in this example, shape voluntary submission in a distinctly different fashion from the coercion of police surveillance.

COLD WAR FEARS AND DISTRIBUTED NETWORKS

Both the interstate highway and the Internet emerged during the Cold War for the purposes of facilitating increased mobility and communication in the event of a nuclear war; that is, in both cases the spectre of war was the impetus for subjecting a greater portion of the populace to "high degrees of technical organization" in the service of open transportation and communication.[36] To forward the case for a federally funded interstate highway, the highway lobby tapped into a popular perception among ordinary Americans that Russia wanted to "rule the world," and that a nuclear attack was imminent.[37] In addition, "Eisenhower's appointment of a general to head the advisory committee made plain the connection between highways, national defense, and the fear Americans had about their security."[38] Eisenhower's own experience during and after the Second World War convinced him that railroad lines were much easier for invading armies to disrupt, but a highway, such as the autobahn he witnessed in Germany after the war, "proved a harder target."[39] (See also Skidmore, chapter 2). Despite Eisenhower's conviction, and the popular sentiment of the American public, the interstate highway was arguably not necessary for improved national defence:

> Even though about 80 percent of war materials in World War II had been moved by rail, the alleged strategic need for an interstate system for national defense became the main argument of the highway lobby. In 1956 the official name of the system became the National System of Interstate and Defense Highways. National defense was the major justification for increasing the federal share of funding from the 60–40 ratio in the 1944 Federal Aid Highway Act to 90–10 in the 1956 Interstate Highway

Act and for permitting federal funds from general tax revenues as well as special user taxes to be used for building the system. St. Clair and Leavitt both demonstrate convincingly that, contrary to the contention of the Road Gang, the Interstate System was never essential to national defense.[40]

The highway that ushered in a new automotive culture was couched in militaristic provenance but characterized by a different form of control from traditional hierarchical military authority. Instead this was a protocological road, a technicity wrapped in the flag but managed by a distributed and voluntary regulatory mode. Americans who desired freedom in the form of automobility – and their government, which desired military advantage in the form of distributed networks – had to accept the rules of the road. At the turn of the twentieth century, only 7 per cent of American roads were surfaced, and from 1900 to 1929 the number of registered automobiles in America increased from eight thousand to 23.1 million (See also Skidmore, chapter 2).[41] An automobile culture existed, and even flourished among the middle class in the 1920s, but it was not until after the passing of the Interstate Highway Act in 1956 that the automobile also became a pastime of working-class Americans.[42] Following the passage of the Interstate Highway Act, Flink notes, "Motor vehicle registrations in the United States consequently more than doubled, from 49.2 million in 1950 to 108.4 million in 1970."[43] This period witnessed some of the most famous road movies, such as *Catch Us If You Can* (1965), *Bonnie and Clyde* (1967), *Weekend* (1968), *Easy Rider* (1969), and *Five Easy Pieces* (1970). While the films themselves often embodied the outlaw spirit and the countercultural disaffection of the 1960s, the newly paved and marked interstate roads on which escape from societal conformity was made possible were the product of state-sanctioned technological regulations. The fatalism expressed in many of these films reflected the dawning awareness of the counterculture's overall failure to transform American society, so eloquently and forcefully depicted in Hunter S. Thompson's road reportage, *Fear and Loathing in Las Vegas*, later turned into a film directed by Terry Gilliam (1998). But at least part of the fatalism was derived from the material circumscription of the road as another form of control. Critics who focus on the liberating quality of the roads optimistically foreground desire over material constraint: movement attempts to supersede technological control. But the birth of the interstate highway offered another form of voluntary submission to technical control, only two evenly demarcated trajectories, only two directions for individuation. The limitations of this material reality made the highways cause for lamentation as much as celebration. As Thompson wrote, "Old elephants limp off to the hills to die; old Americans go out to the highway and drive themselves to death with huge cars."[44]

THE WIZARD OF OZ AND CENTRIFUGAL SPACE

The most famous American road movie precedes the period of interstate highway expansion and does not feature an automobile. *The Wizard of Oz* features a bicycle, a horse-drawn carriage, a hot air balloon, and a flying broomstick, but no car, and so there is no evidence of a modernist sensibility; thus, according to Laderman's criteria, this is not a "road" movie. (See also Slethaug, chapter 1 and Zierler, chapter 10 for non-mechanized road films.) The movie opens with Dorothy following a dirt road back to her family's Depression-era Kansas farm. Later, Miss Gulch arrives with her bicycle on the dirt road. After Miss Gulch takes Toto and rides away, he escapes and he too follows the road, this time back to Dorothy's room. The next invocation of a road is the Technicolor phantasm of the Yellow Brick Road, which, unlike any other interlocking meshwork of paved roads, has a beginning, a point of origin. As if to punctuate the emerging voluntary submission to the technicity of the surfaced road, Dorothy begins her journey by walking along the spiralling origin of the Yellow Brick Road, instead of simply walking (or skipping) directly to where the road expands and exits Munchkinland. The sing-song directive to "follow the Yellow Brick Road" is the transformative moment in *The Wizard of Oz*, one of the great departures in the history of American leaving, and a recognition, at the dawning of widespread surfaced roads, that the impoverished tracks of dirt in front of Dorothy's Kansas farm are the sepia-toned engravings of the past and not the vibrant gold-bricked prosperity of the future. That is, this movie is more about the coming of (surfaced) roads than any other American road movie.

Arriving as it did at the tail end of the Great Depression, *The Wizard of Oz* captures the longing to escape the desperate conditions of the Depression, and simultaneously captures the lack of automobility for most of the people attempting this escape. Many people hit the road during the 1930s "simply because there were no jobs or because their families were disintegrating around them."[45] This car-less exodus produced the ultimate irony of the period: "in a world where so many took to the road, so few had any real mobility."[46] Dorothy's experience embodies this contradiction. By imagining her trip to Oz, Dorothy leaves without moving. Her paradox exemplifies the "fantasy culture of the 1930s," which "is all about movement, not the desperate simulation of movement we find in the road stories but movement that suggests genuine freedom."[47] The road symbolized a "thrust toward the future" in Depression-era culture, even without the mobility of an automobile.[48]

Some have suggested that Oz is an allegory of Franklin Roosevelt's New Deal, an idea promoted by *The Wizard of Oz* lyricist E.Y. Harburg, a dedicated socialist, in an interview with *The Washington Post* just before his death.[49] Dorothy escapes the dust bowl of Depression-era Kansas, but amidst the many perils of the land of Oz, such as the fascist threat of the Wicked Witch, the Yellow Brick Road leads assuredly to the Emerald City and the New Deal antidotes to Depression-era misery, with the Wizard himself "a good-natured satire of Franklin Roosevelt."[50] The "movement" of this road movie imbues the Yellow Brick Road with futurity, the promise of mobility and purpose without the mechanized means to establish "a sense of transcending the boundaries of scale."[51] In later road movies speed effects the disappearance of the road itself, and gives the impression that the central tension of the road movie is something immaterial: genre, classical trope, the act of reading. The sense of transcendence engendered by speed is, ultimately, as Aitken and Lukinbeal argue, "only a sense ... a psychic freedom that offers emancipation but, in actuality, practices emasculation."[52] Perhaps this is why Dorothy's dream does not proffer the same disillusionment as many post-1956 road movies – the feeling that, once the tires stop spinning, so too does the emancipatory buzz. Dorothy's song and dance on the Yellow Brick Road never escapes the material technicity of passage, and everyone she meets in Oz, whether friend (the Scarecrow, the Tin Man, the Cowardly Lion) or foe (the flying monkeys), engages her on or just off the road, a fantastic manifestation of America's burgeoning road ecology.

The great irony of *The Wizard of Oz* is Dorothy's conflicting desire both to find "a place where there isn't any trouble," while she is in Kansas, and, later, while in Oz, "to get out of Oz altogether"; Pamela

Robertson calls this "the Road Movie's contradiction between the desire for home and away" and Salman Rushdie describes it as "the purity of an archetype ... the human dream of *leaving*, a dream at least as powerful as its countervailing dream of roots."[53] Dorothy wants to be nowhere and somewhere simultaneously. In addition to being an archetypal desire, her hysterical and hyperbolic inclination to leave in spatially expansive terms ("a place where there isn't any trouble," "over the rainbow," "out of Oz altogether") is only constricted by the protocological space of the road. While Dorothy's expansive gestures are certainly the product of an adolescent penchant for exaggeration, they also reflect the changing complexion of Depression-era America as its growing road system enabled its citizens to imagine a more broadly striated America, in which hope and futurity were spatially arranged.

From the moment Dorothy begins her journey on the Yellow Brick Road and its originary spiral, she is tracing the outward movement of what Edward Dimendberg calls "centrifugal space."[54] Centrifugal space is a "determinant feature of the built environment of modernity," and "largely defines the geographic arrangement of the United States after 1930." The highway, with its propensity for speed and sprawl, "may well be the preeminent centrifugal space of the twentieth century," replacing the centripetal navigation of the street and the railroad in pre-1930s cinema.[55] As Dorothy prances away from the munchkins and the smoking carnage of the Witch of the East, she first walks in a spiralling motion, then heads for the centrifugal space of Oz with gathering speed, before stopping to wave goodbye to the munchkins. The next we see of Dorothy she has reached a crossroads. The efferent road becomes a multitudinous assemblage. Eventually, Dorothy and friends will enter the metropolis of the Emerald City, whose skyline resembles that of New York City. Dorothy travels from the dirt roads of Kansas, an engineering nowhere, to the sparkling modernity of somewhere, in Emerald City. Instead of a romanticized modernity that celebrates "technology as a liberating force that can lead us into the future," Emerald City offers a vision of technology as a form of cunning magic, and the purveyor of progress is a charlatan.[56] Unlike Laderman's road movie, *The Wizard of Oz* does not follow a mechanized escape from "choking industrialized stability" but instead echoes another classic theme of American film, the "portrait of hicks from the sticks arriving at the metropolis."[57] This trajectory of events in *The Wizard of*

Oz is a consequence of the film depicting the burgeoning promise of roads prior to the ubiquitous ownership of cars, a brief moment in American car culture during which centrifugal space outstripped a pervasive capacity for sense-distorting velocity, and the proto-cological road was imposing technical control only on a relatively small and middle-to-upper class segment of the population. Consider that the major transformation in American roads during the twentieth century was not quantitative but qualitative: "The U.S. road system has less than doubled in length since 1900. What has changed is the quality and capacity of that system."[58] The Yellow Brick Road is a reminder of the qualitative material transformation of America's roads. By the end of the 1950s centrifugal space had thoroughly transformed American social life, and by the end of the 1970s the protocological road entered the American imaginary not as a golden-bricked futurity but as an asphalt scar of misshapen and abusive social planning.

WILD AT HEART AND PAVED ON TOP

By 1980, Flink reports, "some 87.2 percent of American households owned one or more motor vehicles, 51.5 percent owned more than one, and fully 95 percent of domestic sales were for replacement."[59] Road movies acquired a distinctively fatalistic tone in the 1960s and 1970s, and by the 1980s and 1990s, with almost every American household in possession of a motor vehicle, the fatalism of the outlaw journey frequently turned into ironic deadpan or postmodern pastiche. As Michael Atkinson writes, "lately, everybody is packing into the nearest stolen roadster, slapping an Elvis tape into the stereo and leaving their ruined lives behind."[60] The critical consensus for years has been that the road movie became exhausted by the same postmodern aesthetics that proclaimed the "end" of everything. Atkinson expressed this consensus most famously in his review of the genre for *Sight and Sound*:

> Today, there's little frontier to speak of and little hope of national rediscovery, and the movies confirm the generational sense of Generation-X defeatism by transforming the travelled landscape into a bricolage of cinematic tropes – especially the omnipres-ent stench of burnt gunpowder and smoking bodies – and by being, with or without a helpful dollop of irony, unabashed Road

Movies. Characters hit the road less for any concrete, plot-driven reason than because they've seen a lot of movies and that's what you do. Objectively speaking, what could be more of a dead end?[61]

Clearly an epochal cultural discourse that one might categorize as postmodern did influence the road movie genre, the material circumscription, and the central tension of the protocological road. But by the 1980s a form of technicity experienced by the vast majority of Americans more centrally informed the aesthetic of the road. More frustrating than the loss of a frontier – which, let's face it, disappeared the moment dirt trails were covered in asphalt – is the repeated experience of voluntary submission to technical control. Consider the quotidian experience of commuting to work as a measure of this repeated submission to technicity. About 15 per cent of workers commuted across county lines in 1960; by 1980, about 20 per cent of workers commuted; and by 2000, more than 25 per cent, over 34 million workers, commuted.[62] The expansion of centrifugal space in the postmodern era is matched by the proliferation and banality of car-bound duties.

Typical of the road movie in this postmodern era is David Lynch's *Wild at Heart* (1990), in which *The Wizard of Oz* acts as an archetypal icon of Pop Art self-fashioning, and the road trip is a journey into what Atkinson calls "the ragged outskirts of pop culture."[63] In *Wild at Heart*, the paradoxical push-and-pull of the road found in Oz becomes an emblem of the futility of desire, couched in the cultural pastiche of Sailor and Lula. Sailor and Lula play the parts of desperate outlaws on the lam, but their experience of the road is so completely hemmed in by four decades of centrifugal space that actions reverberate only as unconscious evocations of pop culture iconography, perhaps best illustrated by Sailor's rehearsed declaration that his snakeskin jacket is a "symbol of [his] individuality and [his] belief in personal freedom." Like Dorothy, Sailor and Lula did not have to leave in order to arrive at their destination; the destination was always a function of self-invention. Lynch explains the frequent allusions to *The Wizard of Oz* in *Wild at Heart* – "with Marietta's picture disappearing at the end; when Bobby Peru is with Lula and she clicks the heels of her red shoes together; the Good Fairy at the end" – as an expression of a central tension in *The Wizard of Oz*: "There's a certain amount of fear in the picture," he says, "as well as things to dream about. So it seems truthful in some way."[64] The "truth" of

The Wizard of Oz is synonymous with how Galloway defines protocol: "protocol appeals to the body ... it always operates at the level of desire, at the level of 'what we want.'"[65] With those "bumps" in the road, Galloway says, "the driver wants to drive more slowly." For Lynch, desire is the bump in the road, the constraint that produces voluntary social organization, even if it is an organization that is "wild at heart and weird on top." If the road movie lost some of its idealistic and naturalistic verve in the 1980s and 1990s, it is most likely because hitting the road became less of a conscious departure and more of an unconscious necessity. Protocological technologies recurred with habitual frequency. In *Wild at Heart*, the Yellow Brick Road is depicted as the striation of the Symbolic Order it always was, America looking at itself in a mirror after a long and strange love affair with the automobile.

TRON AND THE VIRTUAL OTHER

Films that depict the protocological road, films that *foreground the apparatus*, often appear at the emergence of a new form of protocol. *The Wizard of Oz* appears before interstate highway expansion but captures the emergence of centrifugal space in distributed networks. The virtual reality movie is similarly "protocological," in that its central tension derives from an increasing social organization at the level of computational rules. The distributed networks of the Internet, like the interstate highways, were born of Cold War logic but protocological instantiation. Regarding the different sources for the development of packet-switching technology in the late 1950s – the forerunner of the ARPANET and later the Internet – RAND engineer Paul Baran's proposal for the necessity of "survivable communications" in the event of a nuclear war led him to formulate "distributed communications."[66] Even if part of the communications system were downed by war, messages could be re-routed to arrive at their destinations. The now-familiar history of networked computing eventually merged with another technological trend that began in earnest in the late 1970s and early 1980s: personal computing. "By 1984 personal computer sales [in the United States] accounted for more revenue than IDC's large, medium-sized, or small computer market segments, with shipments of 9.7 million personal computers for a total revenue of some $17 billion, bringing the installed base in 1984 to 23 million machines."[67] If by 1980 the hegemonic protocological road were the interstate, the emerging protocological road was that of the inter-twining personal computer user and networked computing.

The dream-state metaphorics of Oz find their late twentieth-century counterpart in the technocultural discourse of virtual reality films such as TRON (1982), TRON: Legacy (2010), Brainstorm (1983), The Thirteenth Floor (1999), eXistenz (1999), and The Matrix trilogy (1999, 2003, 2003). The mechanization of transportation cedes to the computerization of mobility, and the circuit is the road on which code rides. The vehicular extension of the body is replaced by the digital doppelganger, an elecTRONic Other that acts and is acted upon by the discursive forces of the mode of information. In films such as TRON and The Matrix, the quest for liberation from the panoptic power of the code is achieved by the ability of the hero to transform the virtual environment from an authoritarian one to a protocological one; however, like the road movie quest, this journey is haunted and ultimately contained by the paradoxical freedom of technical regulation. This central tension, depicted in The Wizard of Oz as the journey Dorothy takes while being motionless, occurs in the virtual reality film in the form of the often seated protagonist who ports with a computer by being plugged in or, in the case of TRON, interpellated by an extension of the computer.

In TRON, which appeared at the height of video-arcade-game popularity, the Oz-like centralized authority is the Master Control Program (MCP), an oppressive artificial intelligence that controls the virtual world of the film. Hacker Kevin Flynn is trying to access a file being hidden by the MCP when he is literally transported into the computer, in a scene reminiscent of Dorothy's tornado vortex to the Land of Oz. Virtual reality films often feature some form of kaleidoscopic flux that represents the transition from real world to virtual world; the visual precursor for these trippy transformations is the psychedelic monolith sequence from 2001: A Space Odyssey (1968), but thematically The Wizard of Oz and its famous tornado-to-Technicolor transition is the primary cinematic referent for the beginning of many virtual reality journeys. Devin Orgeron suggests "changes in film stocks and a general consciousness about the effect of the 'material' of the cinema on the efficacy of the journey have become fundamental icons of the road genre," citing examples such as Wild at Heart, Thelma and Louise (1991), and Natural Born Killers (1994).[68] If Dorothy's famous declaration that she's "not in Kansas anymore" is the line that separates Depression-era dirt roads from surfaced roads, then the digital vortex that often represents real-to-VR transitions is visual shorthand for the same thing in post-industrial aesthetics. When Flynn tries to hack into the MCP in the real world, the MCP warns that he will "have to put [Flynn] in the game grid" to "see what [he] is made of." The transition from real world to "game grid" is depicted at first as like looking into a kaleidoscope, which then turns into a vortex. This ends with a digital image of a circuit board, which transforms into a digitized globe and is hovered over as in the *2001* sequence, until the camera peers into one of the I/O towers and Flynn is deposited in VR form. From the drab colours of the real world, Flynn transforms into the neon articulations of the virtual reality world, an effect achieved by "backlit animation," a visual differentiation of ontologies similar to *The Wizard of Oz*'s use of Technicolor.

Flynn's database search is depicted as a literal war between the libertarian forces of Flynn's "users" and the panoptic power of the MCP's "programs." As in *The Wizard of Oz*, characters from the real world have their virtual counterparts. The programs created by Flynn and other users are portrayed in the virtual world by the same actors who portray their users. The journey to the MCP across the striated paths of the circuits includes virtual cars, tanks, and planes. These vehicles must follow the geometric striations of the digital world. Cars drive along grid-like digital planes. Some of the flying machines travel along beams of light. For a user like Flynn, the beams can be redirected, and, at one point in the film, Flynn redirects a beam to avoid colliding with an enemy ship. On another occasion, Flynn creates a flying machine called a Recognizer from the digital detritus of his environment, a manipulation of virtual space of which only Users are capable; Neo's manipulation of time/space in *The Matrix*, both in the "bullet time" sequence and at the end when confronting the Agents, offers a later exemplar of the same phenomenon. The goal of Flynn's quest while he is "in" the computer is to make accessible a file that betrays the duplicity of his former employer. In the process, Flynn hacks the MCP and disables its dictatorial control over the system. At the end of the film, the I/O towers of the virtual world light up, signalling that the system is now open and communicating with other networks. *TRON* ends, that is, with the triumph of computer protocols, of "survivable communication," the openness of digital communication made possible by submission to reactionary regulations.

As a subset of the science-fiction genre, VR films (often categorized as cyberpunk) foreground mobility as a narrative "structuring device."[69] The immensely popular Matrix films gave us a "representation of movement that has not previously been possible."[70] And yet the same dynamic or central tension that haunts the road movie can be found in the VR movie. As Cranny-Francis says of *The Matrix*, "the impossible bodily movement of *The Matrix* enacts the perceived (conceptual) freedom of post-industrial information societies, while also signifying its dependence on the technologies it deploys – the immobile body of the operator jacked into the machine."[71] The information society practice of Web interface "navigation" elicits a similar practice of imagining movement while stationary. TRON, *The Matrix*, and other VR movies participate in this assemblage of popular culture and neo-liberal practices.

CONCLUSION: NO MAP REQUIRED

Perhaps TRON is also an appropriate exemplar of the protocological road because it features an actual road race, albeit a digital approximation without dirt, dust, or even a proper road. The "light cycle" race, in which digitized motorcycles criss-cross a matrix while making ninety-degree turns and attempting to enclose or block their opponents with the solidified trace of their passage, foregrounds simultaneously the act of movement and the "high degrees of technical organization" typical of protocol. The light cycles cannot make diagonal movements; they are restricted to perpendicularity. Winning the race involves using the protocological restrictions against your opponent. And still, even within the enclosure of the geometric grid, Flynn finds a way out. The promise of liberation glimpsed in Flynn's escape is rescinded somewhat by the realization that escaping the technical control of protocol only leads to another protocological construct. Mostly, however, the light cycle sequence reminds viewers of the speed that characterizes contemporary road movies, the speed that provides a sense of transcending scale, the speed that momentarily releases identity from technicity even as it fuses the two. Ultimately, there is no escaping the rules of the road, and, as witnessed by the conclusion of TRON, the liberation found in a road movie is a compromised freedom at best, a communicative freedom that owes its potential to reactionary technical standards. Most road movie scholarship focuses intently on the speed of mechanized

transport – cars, trucks, motorcycles – and its delirious phenomeno-
logical effect: the road movie liberates by obliterating, the motor
outpaces the material forms of constraint and frees the body from
itself, as imaginary exile, unconscious invocation of a pop culture
icon, or cyberspace avatar. But whatever the road movie promises,
the reality is that you can only go where protocol will allow. No map
is required.

For many young people, the racing video game has replaced the
road movie and VR film as the defining protocological experience.
Game franchises, such as *Gran Turismo*, *Forza Motorsport*, *Need for
Speed*, *Burnout*, and countless others, have proliferated into multiple
subgenres and remain among the most popular video game franchises.[72] Recent psychological studies suggest a "racing-game effect,"
the notion that playing racing games "can trigger risk-supportive
cognitions and emotions," and thus increase "risk-taking behaviour,
both within and beyond the driving context."[73] Correlations between
the tens of thousands of illegal street-racing incidents in California
alone and playing racing video games have been established.[74] The
study of road movie and VR genre films should consider whether
video games, in their frequent attempts to approach realistic physics
with game play, might be sources of imagining *meta-technical possibilities* for the reactionary technicities of industrial life, hopefully
possibilities more liberating than illegal street racing. Such meta-
technical possibilities, as Jeremy Packer reminds us, should be
aligned with communication and transportation mobilities:

> What I want to call for, then, is a renewed importance placed
> upon the function of transportation as a cultural and com-
> municative practice that defines relationships between the two
> as complicit. The two need to be thought of in the same terms,
> especially with the increasingly mobile capabilities of nearly all
> communications technologies. At the same time, transporta-
> tion and the forms of mobility produced by its various modes
> need to be analyzed as key sites of culture and communication.
> Struggles over mobility and access thus need to be examined in
> both the virtual and the material realms. Many of the debates
> over the control of these networks of mobility follow the same
> logic.[75]

As digital communications become mobile and globally networked, the projection of protocol enters new habits, spaces, and logics. Simultaneously, the depletion of resources globally, especially oil, may foreshadow a generation whose primary experience of the road is in the form of a game.

Notes

INTRODUCTION

1 Seiler, *Republic of Drivers*, 2.
2 Ibid., 34.
3 Primeau, *Romance of the Road*, ix.
4 Lackey, *Roadframes*, ix.
5 Casey, *Textual Vehicles*, 4, 23–4.
6 Orgeron, *Road Movies*, 5–6, 8.
7 Corrigan, *A Cinema without Walls*, 143.
8 Katie Mills, *The Road Story and the Rebel*, 6.

CHAPTER ONE

1 Laderman, *Driving Visions*, passim, and Mills, *The Road Story and the Rebel*, passim.
2 Schaber, "Hitler Can't Keep 'em That Long," 26.
3 Mills, *The Road Story and the Rebel*, 25.
4 Bryson, *Made in America*, 189.
5 Ibid., 190.
6 Ibid.
7 Ibid.
8 Lackey, "Transcendental Motoring," in *Road Frames*, 80–111.
9 Primeau, *Romance of the Road*, 3.
10 Kusmer, *Down and Out*, 13–22.
11 Mills, *The Road Story and the Rebel*, 2. In using this term, Mills does not refer to Whitman but to the road in general.
12 Primeau, *Romance of the Road*, 3.
13 Ibid., 33.

14   Lackey, "Transcendental Motoring," 5–6, 16.

15   Mills, *The Road Story and the Rebel*, 3.

16   Ambrose, "Introduction," in *Undaunted Courage*, 13.

17   Smith, *Virgin Land*, 45.

18   Turner, "The Significance of the Frontier in American History," 83–96. See also Duncan, *Out West*, 375.

19   Madsen, *American Exceptionalism*, 123.

20   Seiler, *Republic of Drivers*, 21.

21   Jefferson, Letter to William Henry Harrison, 1803.

22   Engelhardt, *The End of Victory Culture*, 37. For the Native American approach to this, see Takaki. "The Significance of the Frontier in American History."

23   Hollywood had produced other road films before and during the 1930s with a variety of modes of transportation (see, for instance, *It Happened One Night*, 1934), but *Stagecoach*'s links to the frontier coupled with John Ford's production of *Grapes of Wrath* in the same year established the related importance of the frontier, the West, and the road.

24   Lynn, "Roughing It," 41.

25   Orgeron, *Road Movie*, 39–45, argues that early road films such as Billy Bitzer's *The Elopement* (1903), D.W. Griffith's *They Would Elope* (1909) and *Sunshine Sue* (1910), and Mack Sennett's *An Interrupted Elopement* (1912) were characterized by the chase, domestic rebellion, and the triumph of romance and that these heavily influenced the direction of later road movies.

26   Orgeron, 109, places this cinematic emphasis of Monument Valley on John Ford's *The Searchers* (1956); but, while *The Searchers* certainly reiterates Monument Valley's importance, the foundational images are from *Stagecoach*.

27   Orgeron, *Road Movie*, 48–9. He also argues that the "motion" in motion pictures coincided nicely with the American love of mobility, so that "moving pictures, no matter their simplicity, tell the story of motion," 18.

28   As Gordon points out, within a twenty-year period, horses disappeared from the urban landscape, and the farmland used to raise them quickly became another burden: before the Great Depression, almost one-third of the land in the East was used to raise horses, but, as the demand for horses evaporated, farmers tried unsuccessfully to turn that land to other profitable uses by producing massive amounts of wheat and corn, flooding the markets, lowering the prices, and bringing on the Great Depression more quickly and forcefully. See Gordon, *The Great Game*, 225.

29 Flink, *The Car Culture*, 19.

30 Ibid., 24.

31 Ibid., 38.

32 Flink, "The Three Stages of American Automobile Consciousness," 451.

33 Lackey, "Transcendental Motoring," 4.

34 Route 66 was commissioned in 1926, but not completed until 1928 and even then only one third of the nearly 2,500 miles was paved. Paving was not completed until 1938.

35 See, for example, Laderman, *Driving Visions*, 9.

36 Lackey, "Transcendental Motoring," 26.

37 Casey, *Textual Vehicles*, 78.

38 See Gordon, *The Great Game*, 225ff.

39 Casey, *Textual Vehicles*, 82.

40 Ibid., 7.

41 Mills, *The Road Story and the Rebel*, 41.

42 Primeau, *Romance of the Road*, 37.

43 Laderman, *Driving Visions*, 11.

44 Weinreich, *The Spontaneous Poetics of Jack Kerouac*, 34.

45 Kerouac, *On the Road*, 7.

46 Ibid., 19.

47 Ibid., 22. Also see Ladd, *Autophobia*, 16. He claims that for early automobile "enthusiasts, speed was the key attraction, coupled with the sense of individual mastery that came with driving."

48 Mills, *The Road Story and the Rebel*, 86.

49 Larson, "Free Ways and Straight Roads," 40.

50 Ibid., 38, 53, 54.

51 Holton, "Kerouac among the Fellahin," 78.

52 Grace, *Jack Kerouac and the Literary Imagination*, 80.

53 Kerouac, *On the Road*, 239.

54 Hunt, "An American Education," 27, 36.

55 Weinreich, *The Spontaneous Poetics of Jack Kerouac*, 49.

56 Witzel, *Route 66 Remembered*.

57 Another factor that affected the road during the late 1950s was the Federal-Aid Highway Act, first debated in Congress in 1955 as the National System of Interstate and Defense Highways and finally signed by President Eisenhower on 29 June 1956 as the Interstate Highway System. Though this new system delivered more rapid travel, the literature and film of the road still focused with nostalgia on the byways, or what William Least Heat-Moon called the blue highways rather than the interstate highways, so that, while they could speak of speed and progress, the

culture of delivering it was often based on different rhythms. See *Blue Highways*.

58 Ladd, *Autophobia*, 95ff.

59 Orgeron, *Road Movies*, 102.

60 Cagin and Dray, *Born To Be Wild*, 47.

61 Orgeron, *Road Movies*, 115.

62 Klinger, "The Road to Dystopia," 179–203.

63 Hill, *Easy Rider*, 54.

64 Laderman, *Driving Visions*, (83, 89, 126) claims that this countercultural social rebellion becomes internalized in the 1970s to emotional uncertainty and existential loss in an increasingly "politically conservative" environment.

65 Klinger, "The Road to Dystopia," 179.

66 Ibid.

67 Laderman, *Driving Visions*, 132–3.

68 Ibid., 134.

69 Mills, *The Road Story and the Rebel*, 173, 188.

70 Ibid., 165.

71 Ibid., 163.

72 Laderman, *Driving Visions*, 175.

73 Mills, "Revitalizing the Road Genre," 324.

74 Laderman, *Driving Visions*, 135, 139, 151.

75 See Scott, "Healing Road Trips in Cinematic America," 9.

76 Orgeron calls David Lynch's *The Straight Story* postmodern insofar as it seeks to rebuild the modern family and links the family and the road (167, 169), but he also notes that road movies almost always contain social criticism, suppressed or brought to the fore (156).

77 Primeau, *Romance of the Road*, 100.

78 Hutcheon, *A Poetics of Postmodernism*, 66.

CHAPTER TWO

1 Skidmore, "Uncovering the Northernmost Named Trail," 123; see also Skidmore, "Minnesota and America's Bully Boulevard," 11.

2 Butler, *First Highways of America*, 14.

3 See, e.g., Benavie, *Social Security Under the Gun*; Hiltzik, *The Plot Against Social Security*; and Skidmore, *Securing America's Future*.

4 See McCoy, *The Last of the Fathers*, 92–105.

5 Sadowski, "The Erie Canal," 1; see also the official New York State Canal Corporation website.

6   See Skidmore, *Presidential Performance*, 65–6.
7   Cole, *The Presidency of Andrew Jackson*, 66–7.
8   Remini, *Andrew Jackson*, 145–6.
9   For varying interpretations, see Brown's *Hear that Lonesome Whistle Blow* and Ambrose's popular overview of the construction of the Central Pacific and the Union Pacific, *Nothing Like it in the World*; for a definitive history of the subject, see Bain, *Empire Express*.
10 Skidmore, "Minnesota and America's Bully Boulevard," 11.
11 See Mason, *Making Michigan Move*, 7–9.
12 Skidmore, "Remembering TR," 23–4.
13 Skidmore, "Remembering TR," 23–4.
14 Mason, *Making Michigan Move*, 7, 13.
15 Hornung, *Wheels Across America*, 256.
16 For an excellent history of American roads, see Rose, *History of American Roads*.
17 See Norton, *Fighting Traffic*.
18 Duncan and Burns, *Horatio's Drive*, 3–5.
19 Ibid., 16
20 Ibid., 16–7.
21 Ibid., 117.
22 Ibid., 125.
23 Many excellent works describe the growth of transportation in America, including the development of automobile travel; among the most interesting is Bourne, *Americans on the Move*.
24 Hill, *The Mad Doctor's Drive*.
25 Duncan and Burns, 132.
26 Hokanson, *The Lincoln Highway*, xv.
27 Duncan and Burns, *Horatio's Drive*, 126.
28 Hokanson, *The Lincoln Highway*, xv.
29 Ibid., 103
30 Ibid., 105.
31 Butler, *First Highways*, 115–17.
32 Hokanson's study is the definitive work on the Lincoln Highway.
33 Hokanson, *The Lincoln Highway*, 8.
34 Ibid., 95.
35 Ibid., 3–5.
36 For a rousing account of Post's journey, see Hokanson, *The Lincoln Highway*, 22–30.
37 For the definitive account of this enormous undertaking, see Davies, *American Road*.

38   Davies, *American Road*, 61.

39   Trani and Wilson, *The Presidency of Warren G. Harding*, 87.

40   Ferrell, *The Presidency of Calvin Coolidge*, 95.

41   Ibid., 100.

42   Hokanson, *The Lincoln Highway*, 108–9.

43   Snell, *American Ground Transport*; see also Snell, "The Streetcar Conspiracy."

CHAPTER THREE

1   Ives, *Wayfaring Stranger*.

2   Seeger, *The Incompleat Folksinger*, 146.

3   Leisy, *The Folk Abecedary*, xi.

4   Lomax and Lomax, *American Ballads and Folk Songs*, xxviii.

5   Howard, *Our American Music*, 613.

6   Lomax, *Folk Songs of North America*, xvi.

7   Howard, *Our American Music*, 613.

8   Ibid., 640.

9   Leisy, *The Folk Song Abecedary*, xi.

10   Carney, "Introduction," 3.

11   Orgeron, *Road Movies*, 14–15.

12   Whitman, *Democratic Vistas, and Other Papers*, 66.

13   Chancellor, "What Songs has America?," 81.

14   Howard, *Our American Music*, 633.

15   Sharp, *American-English Folk Songs*.

16   Law, *American balladry from British broadsides*.

17   Lomax, *Folk Songs of North America*, xv.

18   Ibid., xvii.

19   Carney, "North American Music, 11–13.

20   Lomax, *Folk Songs of North America*, 9.

21   Cazden, Haufrecht and Studer, *Folk Songs of the Catskills*, 161–4.

22   *The Traditional Ballad Index*. Fresno: California State University. http://www.csufresno.edu/folklore/BalladIndexDocs.html (accessed July 2010).

23   *Digital Tradition Folk Song Database*, Mudcat Café Music Foundation, Inc., http://mudcat.org/ (accessed July 2010).

24   Carney, "Country Music and the South," 115–36.

25   Lomax, *Folk Songs of North America*, 156.

26   Ibid., 162.

27   Howard, *Our American Music*, 138–42.

28 Lomax, *Folk Songs of North America*, 239.

29 Howard, *Our American Music*, 607.

30 Lomax, *Folk Songs of North America*, 238.

31 Ibid., 449–50.

32 Ibid., 247.

33 Ibid., 457–9.

34 Ibid., 456–7.

35 Ibid., 474–5.

36 Ibid., 475.

37 Ibid., 484.

38 Douglass, *My Bondage and My Freedom*, 279–80.

39 Jones, "Spirituals as Coded Communication." http://ctl.du.edu/spirituals/
    Freedom/coded.cfm (accessed 20 July 2010).

40 Lomax, *Folk Songs of North America*, 75, 85.

41 Ibid., 87–8.

42 Ibid., 396.

43 Lomax and Lomax, *Our Singing Country*, 215–18.

44 Lomax, *Folk Songs of North America*, 112.

45 Ibid., 113.

46 Ibid., 309–10.

47 Ibid., 308.

48 Ibid., 322–3.

49 Ibid., 307.

50 Ibid, 318–19.

51 Ibid., 326.

52 Ibid., 334–5.

53 Ibid., 202.

54 Ibid., 220.

55 Lomax, *Cowboy Songs*, 307–10.

56 Malone, *Singing Cowboys and Musical Mountaineers*, 90.

57 Lomax, "Collector's Notes," *Cowboy Songs*, 5–6 of unnumbered pages.

58 Ibid., 3 of unnumbered pages.

59 Lomax and Lomax, *American Ballads and Folk Songs*, 376–9. See also
    Lomax, *Folk Songs of North America*, 371–2.

60 Lomax and Lomax, *American Ballads and Folk Songs*, 376–9.

61 Lomax, *Folk Songs of North America*, 371.

62 Lomax and Lomax, *American Ballads and Folk Songs*, 379.

63 Lomax, *Folk Songs of North America*, 368.

64 Ibid., 378.

65 Ibid., 381.

66 Ibid., 329.
67 Ibid., 328.
68 Ibid., 337–8.
69 Ibid., 335–6.
70 Lomax, *Cowboy Songs,* 37–8.
71 Lomax, *Folk Songs of North America,* 329.
72 Ibid., 339–40.
73 Ibid., 334–5.
74 Church of Jesus Christ of Latter-Day Saints, *The Pioneer Story,* 2000. http://www.lds.org/gospellibrary/pioneer/pioneerstory.htm (accessed July 2010).
75 Whitman, *Leaves of Grass,* 425.
76 Lomax and Lomax, *Our Singing Country,* 220.
77 Lomax, *Folk Songs of North America,* 415.
78 Sandburg, *The American Songbag,* viii.

CHAPTER FOUR

1 Doctorow, *Ragtime,* 256. Doctorow adapted the character of Walker from Heinrich von Kleist's 1808 novella, "Michael Kohlhaas," which recounted the tale of a sixteenth-century merchant who seeks justice for wrongs suffered at the hands of a Saxon *junker.* The novella documents the tension between the emancipatory forces of modernity – individualism and the "contractual" forms of association, equality under the law, free mobility – and a feudal order based on arbitrary privilege. The lesson Doctorow appears to impart through his retelling of the Michael Kohlhaas story is that, for African-Americans, modernity arrived late, if it arrived at all. See Sterne, "Reconciliation and Alienation," 5–22. Moreover, as Katalin Orbán notes, "(b)oth Kleist's and Doctorow's texts focus, with great ambivalence, on the potential for transcending pervasive difference, for the dissolving of borders and the merging of divisions." Orbán, "Swallowed Futures, Indigestible Pasts," 328.

2 James J. Flink has defined the term automobility as "the combined import of the motor vehicle, the automobile industry and the highway, plus the emotional connotations of this import for Americans." Flink, "The Three Stages of American Automobile Consciousness," 451. For examples of scholarship on black automobility, see Franz, "The Open Road," 131–54; Gilroy, "Driving While Black," 81–104; Preston, *Automobile Age Atlanta*; Foster, "In the Face of 'Jim Crow'," 130–49.

3   On the importance of mobility to modern identity, see Leed, *The Mind of the Traveler*.

4   See Warner, *The Letters of the Republic*, 72. See also Burgett, *Sentimental Bodies*.

5   Fisher, "Democratic Social Space," 64–5.

6   Klinger, "The Road to Dystopia," 188.

7   Mills, *Blackness Visible*, 155.

8   Franz, "The Open Road," 135.

9   Cohen, *At Freedom's Edge*, 13. Regarding the Great Migration, it is important to remember that "no one went north because he simply wanted to ... All were forced north by terror and violence or some form of racist practice." Gibson, "Individualism and Community in Black History and Fiction," 124.

10 Scharff, *Twenty Thousand Roads*, 143. Kenneth L. Karst further notes that "Our civic culture is, among other things, a constant stream of messages encouraging individuals to take action to advance their conditions and those of their families. Blacks living under the Jim Crow system were not insulated from those messages, and yet they were denied the opportunity to act on them." Karst, *Belonging to America*, 67.

11 Wylie, *Tomorrow!*, 272–3.

12 Castells, *The City and the Grassroots*, 311–12.

13 Wiese, *Places of Their Own*, 291.

14 Preston, in his study of early twentieth-century Atlanta, argues that the rise of automobility reinforced segregation by both race and class: whatever the significance of increased individual mobility, car ownership both separated whites from blacks and divided the black community along lines of affluence. "(T)he land-use pattern which automobility brought about in Atlanta ... laid the ground work for the easy exploitation of blacks via the 'separate-but-equal-doctrine ... By 1930 ... racism could be measured by miles and minutes." Preston, *Automobile Age Atlanta*, 111–12.

15 Quoted in Flink, *The Automobile Age*, 131.

16 Quoted in *The Crisis* 1, 1 (November 1910): 8.

17 Gilroy, "Driving While Black," 84.

18 Franz, "The Open Road," 139.

19 See Gould, *For Gold and Glory*.

20 Bontemps, "A Summer Tragedy," 62.

21 Quoted in Franz, "The Open Road," 135.

22 See *African-American Masters*. See also Crouch, *One-Shot Harris*.

23 Himes, *If He Hollers Let Him Go*, 13, 14, 31.

24 Milloy, "Black Highways"; Harris, *South of Haunted Dreams*, 25.

25 Jerome, *The Death of the Automobile*, 14; Lackey, *Roadframes*, 114,
    130.

26 hooks, *Wounds of Passion*, 47.

27 Isaacs, *The New World of Negro Americans*, 16.

28 Editors of *Fortune* and Davenport. *U.S.A.: The Permanent Revolution*.

29 Ibid., 167, 170; Schuyler, "The Phantom American Negro," 52.

30 On the effect of the Cold War on race relations, see Borstelmann, *The
    Cold War and the Color Line*; and Dudziak, *Cold War Civil Rights*.

31 Maisel, "The Negroes Among Us," 106.

32 Eisenhower confined his administration's civil rights objectives "to areas
    of clear federal jurisdiction, greatest international propaganda value, and
    minimum risk of political fallout or domestic unrest." For example, "non-
    discrimination plans for the military resembled more closely the scripting
    of a modern morality play, staged for the benefit of foreign and domestic
    observers rather than benefiting the black serviceman himself." Burk, *The
    Eisenhower Administration and Black Civil Rights*, 23–4.

33 Foremost among these "model Negroes" put on display for their tactical
    value in the Cold War was political scientist Ralph Bunche, whose "status
    proved that American democracy works ... Bunche's success in the 1950s
    Cold War proved that the United States was indeed the land of oppor-
    tunity despite what the Communists said." Henry, *Ralph Bunche*, 4, 160.
    The Department of State sponsored a number of "Goodwill Ambassador"
    tours of African-American speakers, jazz musicians, and dance troupes.
    See Von Eschen, *Satchmo Blows Up the World*.

34 Powell, "The President and the Negro," 61–4. By contrast, Arthur Larson,
    a key White House advisor, concluded in 1968 that "President Eisenhower,
    during his presidential tenure, was neither emotionally nor intellectually in
    favor of combating segregation in general." Quoted in Alexander, *Holding
    the Line*, 119.

35 "Negroes Have Their Own Wall Street Firm," *The Saturday Evening Post*,
    (29 October 1955), 12; Snowden, "They Always Ask Me About Negroes,"
    The Saturday Evening Post (10 March 1956), 32–3, 105–6; USIA press
    release quoted in Skrentny, "The Effect of the Cold War on African-
    American Civil Rights," 248.

36 The liberal dream holds that "The market will provide the mechanism
    that decides which individuals become equal, at what time, and to what
    extent without penalizing anyone for their group identity." Newfield, *The
    Emerson Effect*, 181.

37 Hodgson, *America In Our Time*, 76. A hybrid of classical and progressive
    liberalism, the vital centre consensus remained rooted in a vision of the

market as producing "a natural harmony of interests," yet was amenable to Keynesian regulation of that market by the state. See Schlesinger, *The Vital Center*.

38 Washington, "The Atlanta Exposition Address," 88.

39 Powell, "The President and the Negro," 61.

40 Maisel, "The Negroes Among Us," 104.

41 Frazier, *Black Bourgeoisie*, 186.

42 "St. Alban's: New York Community is Home for More Celebrities than Any Other U.S. Residential Area," *Ebony*, September 1951, 34, cited in Wiese, *Places of Their Own*, 148.

43 Belasco, "Motivatin' With Chuck Berry and Frederick Jackson Turner," 266.

44 Gilroy, "Driving While Black," 90.

45 Hoover, "Let's Say Something Good About Ourselves," 41. The piece was an excerpt from Hoover's essay, "Saying Something Good About Ourselves," published in *U.S. News and World Report* six months earlier.

46 Granger, "Last of Pioneers."

47 "Democracy Defined At Moscow" (editorial), *The Crisis* (April 1947): 105.

48 hooks, *Wounds of Passion*, 48.

49 The Chesnutt and Mamie Garvin Fields anecdotes are quoted in Foster, "In the Face of 'Jim Crow'," 143, 141. Leslie Perry of the NAACP cited the Mallard murder in his statement before Congress's Antilynching and Protection of Civil Rights Hearings. Subcommittee of the Committee on the Judiciary, House of Representatives, 81st Congress, 1st and 2d Sessions, June 1949; January 1950. Washington, DC: US Government Printing Office, 1950.

50 Cohen, *A Consumer's Republic*, 188.

51 The reconciliation of these values is particularly fraught for African-Americans. As Loren Schweninger has argued, antebellum free blacks "created a type of individualism recognizable to whites but also consistent with their particular history of moving from slavery to freedom." Schweninger, "From Assertiveness to Individualism," 129.

52 *The Negro Motorist Green Book*, 1938, 1940, 1941.

53 Eulogy for Billy Butler by Marion Cumbo, St Joseph's Church, 23 March 1981. William H. Butler Papers, Box 1, Schomburg Center, NYPL.

54 "Billy Butler to Publish Travel Guide," *Pittsburgh Courier*, 5 April 1947; "Musician and Guide to His Bedeviled Race," *New York Post*, 5 August 1947; Granger, "Last of Pioneers," William H. Butler Papers, Box 1, Schomburg Center, NYPL.

55 Mabel A. Roane, Administrative Secretary of the Negro Actors Guild, *Travelguide*, 1947.

56 1895 Cleveland *Gazette* column, quoted in Henry Louis Gates, "The Trope of a New Negro and the Reconstruction of the Image of the Black," 136.

57 I borrow this term from Frazier's 1957 polemic *Black Bourgeoisie*. Andrew Wiese documents the near-doubling of the national African-American population in census-defined suburbs between 1940 and 1960. See *Places of Their Own*, 110–42. On the leisure opportunities available to affluent African-Americans earlier in the century, see Foster, "In the Face of 'Jim Crow.'"

58 *The Negro Motorist Green Book* (1937). The guidebook ran from 1937 to 1959, though I could find no physical record of its publication from 1942 to 1946. Green also acknowledged Jewish travel guides to a restricted America as an inspiration.

59 Others profiled in either the "Travelguide Salutes" or "People (or Things) You Should Know About" sections during the periodical's eleven years included Philippa Duke Schuyler, W.C. Handy, Ralph Bunche, Roy Campanella, Radio Corporation of America, Mollie Moon, William R. Hudgins, Philip Morris & Co., CBS, Schenley Industries, Justice Harold A. Stevens, Randolph A. Wallace, and the United Negro College Fund.

60 See Cohen, *A Consumer's Republic*, 166–91.

61 Among these others, most of which appeared after *Green Book* and *Travelguide*, were *Go: Guide to Pleasant Motoring, Hackley & Harrison's Hotel and Apartment Guide for Colored*, and *The Afro-American's Travel Guide* (published today as *The African-American Travel Guide*).

62 These covers featured both professional "sepia" models and African-American women of note, such as Rachel Robinson (Jackie's wife) and Elaine Robinson (wife of Bill). The layouts were often done by James Drake, art director for the Pittsburgh *Courier*.

63 Letter from Dickinson, North Dakota, in "Replies from Our Correspondents," *The Negro Motorist Green Book* (1948), 5.

64 Cartwright, "A Thought From a Friend."

65 *The Negro Motorist Green Book* (1948), 1.

66 *Travelguide* (1955), 5.

67 Hutchinson further notes that "You didn't need the 'Green Book' to travel through the South. You knew that you couldn't eat in a roadside cafe or stay overnight in a roadside motel. The book was primarily for travel in the North and the West." Earl Hutchinson, Sr, with Earl Ofari Hutchinson, *A Colored Man's Journey Through 20th-Century Segregated America*, 87.

68 Scharff, *Twenty Thousand Roads,* 143.

69 Raper, *Preface to Peasantry,* 174–5; Kirby, "Black and White in the Rural South." Both Raper and Kirby are quoted in Lesseig, *Automobility,* 112–14.

70 Himes, *The Quality of Hurt,* 123.

71 See Mohl, "Planned Destruction," 226–45; Bullard et al., eds., *Highway Robbery*; Sugrue, *The Origins of the Urban Crisis*; and Connerly, "From Racial Zoning to Community Empowerment," 99–114.

72 Lewis, *Divided Highways,* 270–1.

73 Scharff, *Twenty Thousand Roads,* 140.

74 See Ritzer, *The McDonaldization of Society.*

75 Newfield, *The Emerson Effect,* 218.

CHAPTER FIVE

1 Van Elteren, "The Subculture of the Beats," 77.

2 Johnson (Glassman), *Minor Characters,* 136.

3 Grace and Johnson, *Breaking the Rule of Cool,* 3.

4 Lynell, George, "Muses of a Revolution," *Los Angeles Times.* (25 November 1996):1.

5 Kerouac and Johnson (Glassman), *Door Wide Open.* His friend, Neil Cassady, was even more susceptible to women, as he records the influence of the real Patricia Lague and a teacher on a bus. See Moore, ed., *Neal Cassady: Collected Letters,* 18–19.

6 McNally, *Desolate Angel,* 257. This is true, too, of sidekick Dean Moriarty (Cassady).

7 Kerouac, *On the Road,* 76.

8 Grace, "A White Man in Love," 43. Grace points out that *Maggie Cassidy* (1953) reflects Kerouac's high-school sweetheart Mary Carney; *The Subterraneans* (1953) makes use of his "brief intense relationship" with Alene Lee, who became Mardou Fox in the novel; and *Tristessa* (1955–56) is based on Esperanzo Tercerero, a morphine addict that Kerouac knew – and on Billie Holliday, Ava Gardner, and Louise Rainer.

9 Grace, "A White Man," 57.

10 McNally, *Desolate Angel,* 4–7 and 11. Mamere's relationship with her third child, Jean (later Jack) would become problematic and close, especially after she lost her first-born, and he lost his much admired older brother (he would later also lose his older sister). Above all, Jean/ Jack lost the happy innocence of his early childhood, and he failed to mature in his sexual attitudes, so his biographer Dennis McNally implies: "Sexuality above all could not stand comparison with Gerard," and "rather than

becoming either a prude or a degenerate," Jack "hung suspended between the ethical boundaries, fascinated by the perverse as well as the holy."

11 McNally, *Desolate Angel*, 78.

12 Brinkley, ed. *Windblown World*, 31 (the italics are Kerouac's). Later in the journals, he records his mother's disapproval of his friends, "a bad influence on me" (Brinkley, 49). Joyce Johnson Glassman also recorded Mamere's disapproval of her dishwashing skills. In Charters, *Kerouac*, 305. Eventually Kerouac moved Mamere to Florida, where, joined by sister Nin, he completed his life, sad, drunk, and separated from friends, but connected to his mother, to whom he spoke on the morning of his death. In McNally, *Desolate Angel*, 342.

13 McNally, *Desolate Angel*, 14.

14 Ibid., 15.

15 Ibid., 169.

16 Ibid., 196.

17 Brinkley, *Windblown World*, 57.

18 Ibid., 29.

19 Ibid., 76.

20 There were Sarah Yokley and Adele Morales, who would later marry Norman Mailer, and the eignteen-year-old Beverly Ann Gordon, whom he found "proud, poised, dark, *serious,* lovely." Other female friends, most of whom showed up in Kerouac's work, included Joan Burroughs, wife of William, whose life ended in a bizarre William Tell experiment gone wrong (Brinkley, *Windblown World*, 75); Vicki Russell, who shows up as Rosie in *The Town and the City;* Bea Franco, a Chicagoan who joined Kerouac's travels in 1947; and the aforementioned Mardou Fox who "bedazzled" Kerouac and whose exotic (she was half American Indian) beauty he used in *The Subterraneans*. McNally, *Desolate Angel*, 102, 157, and 172–3.

21 McNally, *Desolate Angel*, 114. Gordon inspires much introspection by Kerouac in his journal. Here he meditates on why he finds her so attractive: "She has all the amazing qualities of womanhood: a low voice, a statuesque figure, dark, midnight eyes, moonlight skin – and youth, the grace of a little girl – And *consciousness* and *sadness* and *simplicity* ... just ripe for six babies" (Brinkley, *Windblown World*, 75).

22 Charters, *Kerouac*, 331.

23 McNally, *Desolate Angel*, 212–13.

24 Charters, *Kerouac*, 243.

25 McNally, *Desolate Angel*, 72. The end of the Edie Parker story appears to be as strange as its beginning. After *On the Road* caused Kerouac to

become world famous, Parker "begged to go on the European tour for the road book" (McNally, *Desolate Angel*, 231), an offer he turned down. Although she appears not to have made much of a mark on Kerouac's life, he transformed her into Judie Smith in *The Town and the City*.

26 McNally, *Desolate Angel*, 131–5.

27 When Kerouac left Haverty for an affair with Carolyn Cassady and failed to acknowledge paternity or supply child care for the child Joan expected when they parted, Joan pursued her rights. After Kerouac became famous (Jan, born in 1952, was then about 10), Joan succeeded in extracting a small agreement for support, but not his acknowledgment of fatherhood.

28 Jan Kerouac saw her father on only two recorded occasions (Knight, ed., *Women of the Beat Generation*, 309), but she talked to him often, and she knew Ginsberg well. That, too, was a disappointing link with her father. Included in the posthumous 1998 reprint of *Trainsong*, Jan Kerouac's 1988 memoir, are transcripts of interviews with her. In one, a 1996 interview with Diane Jones, Jan said, "I would like to challenge Allen Ginsberg to announce publicly why it is that he is not helping Jack Kerouac's daughter at all, even though I've known him for forty years and I was so close to him (Jan Kerouac, *Trainsong*, 234–5).

29 Jan Kerouac, *Trainsong*, 218.

30 Knight, ed., *Women of the Beat Generation*. Knight quotes Jan Kerouac: "So shame on the shaman. Daddy don't live in dat New York City no more … Daddy don't live nowhere, no more. And so time passes, passes by, passes over, passes away and through and pass the butter please," 318.

31 Jan Kerouac, *Trainsong*, 217.

32 Ibid., 234.

33 Johnson, "Mapping Women Writers," 33.

34 Ibid., 32.

35 See Ronna Johnson's discussion of "self-inscription" in the memoirs included in Grace and Johnson. Many works, says Johnson, achieve "a retrospective, transgressive reconstruction in which they can be figured as subjects." These include the amalgamation of the domestic and the hipster concerns – the cultural concerns with the household concerns; the paradoxical embodiment of "domestic femininity" with the "rebellious antidomestic Beat discourse"; the "spin on the buddy road tale" of the pregnant woman. She concludes that "using the memoir form, which is not the genre privileged by the male Beat writers, allows the women to tell their own Beat tales outside their colonization by Beat literature, without conforming to the norms that compromise or elide them" ("Mapping Women Writers," 32–8).

36 Johnson, "Mapping Women Writers," 32.

37 These include Lita Hornick, chief patron of *Kulchur*; Gloria Schoffel, later McDarrah, a sometime editor; Cynthia Robinson, who sold "Beat and Hipster Fortune Cookies" at poetry readings; Mary Nichols, the Swarthmore graduate in whose apartment "the Beat generation was practically founded." See McDarrah and McDarrah. *Kerouac and Friends*, 188.

38 These include Carolyn Cassady and the doomed Joan Haverty Kerouac; the Holocaust survivor Ruth Weiss, the sexually adventurous Diane di Prima, and the talented and scholarly Anne Waldman; and truly groundbreaking and brave women like Jane Bowles and Josephine Miles.

39 Grace and Johnson, *Breaking the Rule of Cool*, 3.

40 Waldman, "Introduction" to Knight's *Women of the Beat Generation*.

41 Kashner, *When I Was Cool*, 141. Another indication of di Prima's importance to the men and women of the Beat Generation is that she is the only woman to appear in the fourteen essays in Robert Bennett's book on teaching the Beat Generation. Bennett says that di Prima "reinterprets the Beat counterculture ... by focusing on how women actively participated in and helped create the Beat revolution instead of just passively standing around and washing the dishes." See Bennett, "Introduction: Teaching the Beat Generation to Generation X," 14. Today Diane di Prima's website begins with a quotation from Allen Ginsberg that she is "a learned humorous bohemian, classically educated and twentieth-century radical" http://dianediprima.com.

42 Di Prima did help Kashner with his literary goals, but, in the book written fifty years after that meeting, Kashner says that he wishes he had asked her about sex: "The Beats seemed to know something I would never know about sex," he said. "They were like Houdinis, slipping out of padlocked trunks thrown into the river. They always managed to get out and away" (Kashner, *When I was Cool*, 172).

43 Ronna Johnson, in "Mapping Women Writers," 36–7, calls the book "salacious," but finds that it both fits and contradicts hipster expectations.

44 di Prima, *Recollections of My Life as a Woman*, 26.

45 Ibid., 74.

46 Ibid., 78.

47 Grace and Johnson, *Breaking the Rule of Cool*, 89.

48 Ibid., 97.

49 Waldman, ed., *The Beat Book*, 139.

50 Ibid., 133.

51 Ibid., 123. These di Prima selections from Anne Waldman's collection are representatively exceptional. Even the frontispiece/invocation

from Kerouac's *Road* places the emphasis on the masculinity of the Beat Generation writers: In the hefty collection DiPrima is one of only a few women: Lenore Kandel, Jeanie Skerl, Carolyn Cassady, Ann Charters, Anne Waldman herself, and Joanne Kryger. Among Waldman's selectons the male writers' female representations range widely: Kerouac's Maggie; Amiri Baraka's praying daughter in his famous poem; Ginsberg's aging, unlovely but wonderfully left-wing mother in "Kaddish"; and a few others. Most selections, however, are remarkably free of any women.

52 Di Prima, *Recollections of My Life as a Woman*, 109.

53 Ibid., 114.

54 Di Prima, *Memoirs of a Beatnik*, 127.

55 Di Prima, *Recollections of My Life as a Woman*, 15.

56 Ibid., 3.

57 Ibid., 77.

58 Ibid., 26–7.

59 In a moderately celebratory review, Bill Zavatsky says of her *Collected Poems 1956–1975* that they have "effectively graphed her journey." See *New York Times* (17 October 1976). By contrast, Barbara Grizzuti Harrison says "she leaves us in an opaque world, murky and undecipherable, a slag heap of incoherent, disjointed impressions." See *New York Times* (6 May 2001).

60 Grace and Johnson, *Breaking the Rule of Cool*, 87.

61 Ibid., 222.

62 Cassady, *Off the Road*, 3.

63 Ibid., 1.

64 Ibid., 20.

65 Ibid., 29.

66 Ibid, 12.

67 Ibid, 25.

68 Cassady, *Collected Letters: 1944–1967*, 178.

69 Ibid., 179.

70 Cassady, *Off the Road*, 181.

71 Ibid., 69.

72 Ibid., 137–8. More problematic are the collected letters edited by Dave Moore, for which Carolyn Cassady wrote the introduction and which she presumably read before publication. They present at least a sampling of Cassady's relationships with women: Mary Ann Freeland (10); Patricia Lague (18–19); first wife Lu Ann Henderson; Diana Hanson; Natalie Jackson; and others. However, the letters also make clear that Cassady loved his wife. Early on (November 1947) he wrote to Jack, "My

conviction that Carolyn was enough is, I find, correct – so don't worry about your boy Neal, he's found what he wants and in her is attaining greater satisfaction than he had ever known" (Cassady, *Collected Letters*, 59).

73 Knight, *Women of the Beat Generation*, 57 ff.

74 Ezard, "Auction of Kerouc Manuscript 'blasphemy.'"

75 Cassady, *Off the Road*, 103, 111–15.

76 Ibid., 281.

77 Ibid., 287.

78 Henry Miller, as interpreted by Carolyn Cassady, is particularly interesting. He was, she reports, "only mildly interested in Jack's spontaneous prose style," but he took the meeting time to give the writer's beautiful young wife a quick course in world literature, beginning with the Greeks. Ever open-minded, Carolyn says, "This charming, cultured, genial gentleman didn't fit my preconceived image at all" (Cassady, *Off the Road*, 328).

79 Ibid., 144.

80 Ibid., 187.

81 Ibid., 188.

82 Ibid., 168.

83 Ibid., 184.

84 Ibid., 187.

85 Ibid., 196.

86 The obituary was terse: "Neal Cassady, 43, of San Francisco, a former railroad conductor and long associate of prominent members of the beatnik and hippy generations, has died here [in San Miguel]. See Cassady, *Off the Road*, 196. When he died, Neal Cassady was on a quest for one more woman. His last letter was to Janice Brown: "I love you, hurry up I can't wait much longer." See Cassady, *Letters*, 466.

87 Cassady, *Off the Road*, 422.

88 Grace and Johnson, *Breaking the Rule of Cool*, 109.

89 Bremser, *Troia*.

90 Grace and Johnson, *Breaking the Rule of Cool*, 265.

91 Bremser, *Troia*, 17.

92 Ibid., 31.

93 Ibid., 40,

94 Grace and Johnson, *Breaking the Rule of Cool*, 114.

95 Ibid., 111.

96 Ibid., 114–5.

97 Bremser, *Troia*, 11.

98 McNally, *Desolate Angel*, 134.

99 Grace and Johnson, *Breaking the Rule of Cool*, 115.

100 It is striking, therefore, that although Bremser/Frazer credits Kerouac as a primary inspiration and although her work was published well before McNally's *Desolate Angel*, her name does not appear in it – or in most books on the Beat Generation. However, Bremser notes appreciatively Allen Ginsberg's encouragement when his return from India coincided with her circulation of *Troia*. Ginsberg did more: he invited Bremser to live and work on his New York farm after she left her husband and made the transition to graduate school and a whole new career. She was also included in Ann Charters *The Portable Beat Reader*, the publication that provided an opportunity – which Bremser spurned – to read from her book. Nor did she participate in the roundtable arranged by Charters to celebrate the publication of Brenda Knight's book. See Grace and Johnson, *Breaking the Rule of Cool*, 130.

101 Bremser, *Troia*, 124.

102 Jones, *How I Became Hettie Jones*, 106.

103 Ibid., 112–13.

104 Ibid., 210–18. *Time* magazine talked about the couple in 1960. Hettie Cohen Jones was listed as Mrs Leroy [sic] Jones, and, one year later in an anthology of new writers, the collection bragged that there were stories by Burroughs, Creeley, Kerouac, and LeRoi Jones: "a new Negro writer" (Jones, *How I Became Hettie Jones*, 205).

105 Ibid., 38.

106 Ibid., 13.

107 Ibid., 41.

108 Ibid., 42.

109 Ibid., 48.

110 Norman Podhorez's "The Know Nothing Bohemians" would challenge Jones and Ralph Ellison, Stanley Edgar Hyman, Frank O'Hara, and Denise Levertov; Jones, *How I Became Hettie Jones*, 56.

111 Grace and Johnson, *Breaking the Rule of Cool*, 175.

112 Di Prima, *Recollections*, 170.

113 Ibid., 222.

114 McNally, *Desolate Angel*, 69–72.

115 Johnson (Glassman), *Minor Characters*, 20.

116 Johnson (Glassman), *Come and Join the Dance*, 134.

117 Johnson (Glassman), *Minor Characters*, 32.

118 Ibid., 77–8.

119 Ibid., 117.

120 Ibid., 65.

121 Johnson, "Introduction," in Kerouac and Johnson, *Door Wide Open*, xvi.

122 Johnson, *Minor Characters*, 130.

123 Ibid., 131.

124 There are other dividends. For example, Jack enclosed a nearly porno-graphic sixteen-line poem on a woman writer he mentioned in novels as well, Emily Dickinson. It begins "Sweet Emily Dickinson/ Who played with your hair?" In fact, the whole book places these writers in the main-stream of American literature. Kerouac and Johnson, *Door Wide Open*, 87.

125 Ibid., 47.

126 Ibid., 44.

127 Johnson, *Minor Characters*, 136.

128 Johnson, "Introduction," *Door Wide Open*, xxv.

129 Ibid., xiii.

130 Ibid., xx.

131 Ibid., xviii.

132 Kerouac and Johnson, *Door Wide Open*, 51.

133 Ibid., 11.

134 Ibid., 21.

135 Ibid., 79–85.

136 Ibid., 105.

137 Johnson, *Door Wide Open*, 41.

138 Johnson, *Minor Characters*, 185.

139 Kerouac and Johnson, *Door Wide Open*, 66.

140 Ibid., 67–8.

141 Johnson, *Minor Characters*, 189.

142 Ibid., 240.

143 Kerouac and Johnson, *Door Wide Open*, 158.

144 McNally, *Desolate Angel*, 329.

145 Kerouac and Johnson, *Door Wide Open*, 173.

146 Johnson, *Missing Men: A Memoir*, 236.

147 Johnson, "Introduction," *Door Wide Open*, xv.

148 Charters, *Kerouac: A Biography*, 288.

149 Charters, "Panel Discussion," 611–32.

150 Ibid., 624.

151 Ibid., 627.

152 Johnson, *Minor Characters*, 187.

153 Ibid., xiv.

154 Grace and Johnson, *Breaking the Rule of Cool*, 119.

CHAPTER SIX

1 Roberts, "Western Meets Eastwood," 45.

2 Kimmel, "Masculinity as Homophobia," 29–30.

3 Klinger, "The Road to Dystopia," 181.

4 Gann, *American Music in the Twentieth Century*, 344.

5 Their first large-scale stage work, *The Way of How*, Dresher (1981), already included Dresher's wide range of live and studio sampling techniques, which was arrestingly experimental in the 1980s in conjunction with the new technology of the time. Although much of the music is gentler and more "classical" than the later stage works, the texts already involve dense "sound poetry" techniques (notably verbal fragmentation and transformation through puns and related sounds, including processes that seem to refer to dreams or to early computer processes) that were favourites with Eckert, and reappear in the more meditative sections of *Slow Fire. Was Are/Will Be* (1983–85) in Dresher, *Dark Blue Circumstance*, uses the more assertive electric guitar sounds and overlapped live samples that appear in *Slow Fire*; Eckert's text already has the latter work's combination of the immediate and the conceptual, complete with its temporal and/or hallucinatory alterations. After *Slow Fire, Shelf Life*, Dresher and Eckert, (1987), a stage work created with the Margaret Jenkins Dance Company, had even more in common with *Slow Fire*, despite Eckert taking a more musical than dramatic role. The strong masculine tone and ideas are familiar from *Slow Fire*, although the whole is more abstract and oblique, as the theatrical foreground is occupied by dancers. The music uses a similar contrast between gutsy, energetic rhythms and dreamlike, shimmering "memory" sections – although those gutsy rhythms also develop into slow quasi-country "licks" that suggest the score for a Western film. Even the plot, partially reflecting Eckert's Midwestern background, is more assertively connected to the Western, speaking of trucks, highways, and the Road, in addition to including more characters and relationships (women, friends, etc.). This is especially perceptible because this later work foregrounds Eckert's writing and his formal techniques, with many passages spoken or shouted rather than sung.

6 I am grateful to Paul Dresher for these materials and for our helpful discussions.

7 This last image recalls Theweleit's *Male Fantasies*, a disturbing analysis of proto-Fascist popular culture, where a recurrent female image is the woman on horseback with a gun; Theweleit shows how such images are

created by military men who are especially enraged by the threatening power of women and racial minorities.

8 Anderson, "From the Air."

CHAPTER SEVEN

1 Primeau, *Romance of the Road*, 13.
2 More about this particular series is available in Mills, *The Road Story and the Rebel*, 82–3.
3 Ibid., passim.
4 Ibid., 187.
5 Ibid., 219.
6 Wee, "Selling Teen Culture, 95.
7 Mills, *The Road Story and the Rebel*, 219.
8 Ibid., 219–20.
9 Cullum, "Review of *The Simple Life 2: Road Trip*."
10 Osgerby, "So Who's Got Time," 82.
11 Ibid., 83.
12 Ibid.
13 Douglas, *Where the Girls Are*.
14 Stanley, "Yes, They're Sleazy."
15 Lewis, *Cracking Up*.
16 Ibid., 7.
17 Ibid., 20.
18 Stanley, "Yes, They're Sleazy."

CHAPTER EIGHT

1 Theroux, "Remember the Cicadas and the Stars?", 6.
2 Ibid.
3 Ibid.
4 Whitman, "Song of the Open Road," 149–59. For convenience, the poem's section and lines are cited in the text.
5 Lackey, *Roadframes*, 131.
6 Gitlin, *The Whole World Is Watching*, 202. Gitlin notes the "edgy, apocalyptic popular culture" of *Easy Rider* and other films of the period.
7 Orgeron, *Road Movies*, 2.
8 Laderman, *Driving Visions*, 67.

9 Mills, *The Road Story and the Rebel*, 188.

10 Ibid., 2.

11 Laderman, *Driving Visions*, 132; Natoli and Hutcheon, "Introduction," vii–xiv.

12 Hutcheon. *A Poetics of Postmodernism*, 23.

13 Van den Abbeele, *Travel as Metaphor*, xxvi.

14 Roberts, "Western Meets Eastwood," 47.

15 Laderman, *Driving Visions*, 21; Cohan and Hark, "Introduction," 3; Corrigan, *A Cinema Without Walls*, 143; Roberts, "Western Meets Eastwood," 45, 61.

16 Carden, "Adventures in Auto-Eroticism," 79.

17 Aitken and Lukinbeal, "Disassociated Masculinities and Geographies of the Road," 351.

18 Pease, "Introduction: Men, Masculinities, and Feminism," 1.

19 See Mills, *The Road Story and the Rebel*, 177.

20 Orgeron, *Road Movies*, 166; Laderman, *Driving Visions*, 132.

21 Cohan and Hark, "Introduction," 5.

22 Kimmel, "Masculinity as Homophobia," 29–30.

23 Dolgin, "Men's Friendships," 106.

24 Cohen, "Men as Friends," 98.

25 Swain, "Covert Intimacy," 131.

26 Morgan, "The Feminist Man's Manifesto," 436.

27 Pease, "Introduction," 1.

28 Levant, "Toward the Reconstruction of Masculinity," 232.

29 Reeser, *Masculinities in Theory*, 14.

30 Gutterman, "Postmodernism and the Interrogation of Masculinity," 220.

31 Kimmel, *Manhood in America*, 291ff.

32 Willis, "Race on the Road," 287.

33 Cohen, "Just Because They're Men," 1.

34 Brittan, *Masculinity and Power*, 25, 29.

35 Levant, "Toward the Reconstruction of Masculinity," 243.

36 Leland, *Why Kerouac Matters*, 74.

37 Roberts, "Western Meets Eastwood," 45, 48–9, 55.

38 Mills, *The Road Story and the Rebel*, 25, 189.

39 Alexie, *The Lone Ranger and Tonto*.

40 Slethaug, "Hurricanes and Fires," 136. Laderman, *Driving Visions*, 233.

41 Kerouac, *On the Road*, 291; Alexie, *Smoke Signals*, 147–9.

42 Laderman, *Driving Visions*, 219. See also Lackey, *Roadframes*, 94 and Mills, *The Road Story and the Rebel*, 85–109, 130.

43 Ebert, "*Brokeback Mountain.*"

44 Lang, "*My Own Private Idaho,*" 330–48.

45 See, for instance, the Starpulse.com entertainment poll of 9 September 2008. http://www.starpulse.com/news/index.php/2008/09/09/brokeback_mountain_tops_gay_movie_poll

46 Amy Andre thinks it important not to call this a gay cowboy film because the characters are clearly bisexual and wonders why critics are so uncomfortable calling the men bisexual. See Andre, "Opinion."

47 Bell, "Cowboy Love," 165. Little, "Embodiment and Rural Masculinity," 188.

48 Dargis, Review of *Brokeback Mountain*.

49 See Sachs, "Foreword."

50 Retzloff, "Cars and Bars," 243–4.

51 Ebert, "*Sideways.*"

52 Mills, *The Road Story and the Rebel*, 201.

53 Orgeron, *Road Movies*, 230n3.

54 Ibid., 8.

55 Ibid., 230n3.

56 Laderman, *Driving Visions*, 145.

57 Dargis. Review of *About Schmidt*.

58 Mills, *The Road Story and the Rebel*, 201.

59 Laderman, *Driving Visions*, 236. The way Lynch sets up this encounter precisely follows John Ford's lesson on the Joad family in *Grapes of Wrath*. First, Ford depicted the family grotesquely: Grandpa and Grandma Joad as foolish, inarticulate old country people with no table manners or social graces; Ma Joad as a heavy-set, weathered share-cropper's wife who could not possibly centre her family, keep them together, or facilitate the move to California; and the rest as naïve country hicks – the embodiment of the stereotypes that native Californians despised. The proposed road trip in an old jalopy piled high with people and junk is presented as an exercise in futility. Ford, however, displaced that grotesqueness by fostering deep affection and respect for this courageous family forced to abandon their Oklahoma home and livelihood and seek another far removed by means of a hazardous but necessary trip on Route 66.

60 Laderman, *Driving Visions*, 235; Orgeron, *Road Movies*, 166; Mills, *The Road Story and the Rebel*, 202.

61 Kreider and Content, "The Straight Story," 26–33.

62 Mills, *The Road Story and the Rebel*, 203.

CHAPTER NINE

1 There is a long-standing body of literature on the topic of homoeroticism and the American road; for just one example, see Fielder, "Come Back to the Raft Ag'in Huck Honey!", 142–51.

2 For a discussion of the relationship between the Western and the road movie, see Roberts, "Western Meets Eastwood," 45–69.

3 See Moriel, "Erasure and Taboo," 148–76.

4 For a discussion of *The Living End*, see Mills, "Revitalizing the Road Genre," 307–29.

5 Cunningham, "Driving into the 'Dustless Highway.'"

6 Doty, *Flaming Classics*.

7 Lang, *Masculine Interests*, 247. See also Lang, "*My Own Private Idaho*," 330–48.

8 For a compelling discussion of the "transgendered look" in this film, see Halberstam, *In a Queer Time and Place*.

9 Straayer, *Deviant Eyes, Deviant Bodies*.

10 I am grateful to Nicholas Wong for bringing this film to my attention.

11 For more on the background of the film and its relationship to the road movie genre, see Gagne, "*Transamerica*," 56–7; Williams, "My Father, the Heroine," 42–3, 78.

12 Laderman, *Driving Visions*, 2, 21.

13 Esposito, "The Performance of White Masculinity in *Boys Don't Cry*," 229–41.

14 For a discussion of race and queer sexuality within the road movie genre, see Willis, "Race on the Road: Crossover Dreams," 287–306.

15 Holmlund, *Impossible Bodies*, 164.

16 For more on the campfire and homoeroticism in *My Own Private Idaho*, see Laderman, *Driving Visions*.

17 Mills, *The Road Story and the Rebel*, 197.

18 Franklin, "Interview: Ang Lee."

19 For a discussion of the political contradictions of drag, see Butler, *Bodies That Matter*.

CHAPTER TEN

1 Cohan and Hark, "Introduction," 1.

2 Roberts, "Western Meets Eastwood," 52.

3 Ibid.

4 Corrigan, *A Cinema without Walls*, 146.

5 Laderman, *Driving Visions*, 4–5.

6 Ibid., 2.

7 Mills, *The Road Story and the Rebel*, 160.

8 Ibid.

9 For a brief discussion of the road movie comedy see Laderman, *Driving Visions*, 132–3 and 161–6.

10 See, for example, *Planes, Trains, and Automobiles* (1987), where a successful businessman, played by Steve Martin, finds himself forced to travel and endure a series of trials with a garrulous, backward, and lonely travelling salesman played by John Candy, whose basic decency the Steve Martin figure eventually begins to appreciate, so much so that he invites him home for Thanksgiving dinner. Though not typically billed as a comedy, *Rain Man* (1988) features a similar travelling pair: a street smart businessman (Charlie Babbitt) and his idiot-savant brother (Raymond Babbitt); by the end of the journey, Charlie learns to appreciate Raymond's genius or wisdom.

11 Schutz, *Political Humor from Aristophanes to Sam Earvin*, 81.

12 Richardson, "Peasant Dreams," 209.

13 See Welsford, *The Fool*, and Billington, *A Social History of the Fool*, 16.

14 All this can be contrasted with professional buffoons, clowns, court jesters, and court fools, such as those featured in the plays of Shakespeare. According to Siegel, "[t]he court jester was either a feeble-minded person who evoked amusement by his inaneness or his antics. He might also be someone who pretended to be a fool and used his assumed folly as a license for his wit." See Siegel, "Gimpel and the Archteype of the Wise Fool," 159.

15 Billington, *A Social History of the Fool*, 16.

16 Pinsker, *The Schlemiel as Metaphor*, 18–19.

17 Wisse, *The Schlemiel as Modern Hero*, 21.

18 Buber, *The Tales of Rabbi Nachman*, 94.

19 Wisse, *The Schlemiel as Modern Hero*, 21.

20 Singer, "Gimpel the Fool," 4.

21 Ibid., 13.

22 Ibid., 14

23 Bellow, "On Jewish Storytelling," 16–17.

24 Erens, *The Jew in American Cinema*, 337.

25 See Genesis 13:5–9.

26 Singer, "Gimpel the Fool," 1; Groom, *Forrest Gump*, 1.

27 Kehr, "Who Framed Forrest?" 50–1.

28 Beyers, "History Re-Membered," 419–44.

29 Yacowar, "Forrest Gump," 671.
30 Laderman, *Driving Visions*, 10.
31 Schaber, "Hitler Can't Keep 'em that Long," 26.

CHAPTER ELEVEN

1   Packer. *Mobility Without Mayhem*, 81.
2   Ibid., 3.
3   Ibid., 109–10.
4   Ibid., 186.
5   Ibid., 140: Miller, *Technologies of Truth*, 13.
6   Miller, *Technologies of Truth*, 13.
7   Mills, *The Road Story and the Rebel*, 3.
8   Ibid., 12.
9   Ibid., 26.
10 Urry, "The 'System' of Automobility," 26.
11 Ibid., 27.
12 Ibid., 28. Italics in original.
13 Seiler, *Republic of Drivers*, 104.
14 Orgeron, *Road Movies*, 104.
15 Galloway, *Protocol*.
16 Laderman, *Driving Visions*, 4–5.
17 Ibid., 17.
18 Ibid., 38. Italics in original.
19 Galloway, *Protocol*, 142. Italics in original.
20 Seiler, *Republic of Drivers*, 3.
21 Cohan and Hark, "Introduction," 1.
22 Laderman, *Driving Visions*, 19–20. Italics in original.
23 Ibid., 37.
24 Orgeron, *Road Movies*, 2. Italics in original.
25 Ibid., 31.
26 Laderman, *Driving Visions*, 42; Orgeron, *Road Movies*, 4. Italics in original.
27 Atkinson, "Crossing the Frontiers," 16.
28 Aitken and Lukinbeal, "Disassociated Masculinities," 358.
29 Morris, "The Reflexivity of the Road Film," 25, 26.
30 Ibid, 26.
31 Ibid., 27.
32 Creekmur, "On the Run and On the Road," 91.
33 Galloway, *Protocol*, 8.

34 Ibid., 7.

35 Ibid., 241.

36 Ibid., 38. For a discussion of the historical development of roads in America, see Skidmore, chapter 2 in this book.

37 Lewis, *Divided Highways*, 107.

38 Ibid.

39 Ibid., 90.

40 Flink, *The Automobile Age*, 371.

41 Ibid., 5; Seiler, *Republic of Drivers*, 36.

42 Flink, *The Automobile Age*, 158.

43 Ibid., 359.

44 Thompson, *Fear and Loathing in Las Vegas*, 18.

45 Dickstein, "Depression Culture," 232.

46 Ibid., 237.

47 Ibid., 238.

48 Ibid., 239.

49 MacDonnell, "The Emerald City was the New Deal," 71–2.

50 Ibid., 75.

51 Aitken and Lukinbeal, "Disassociated Masculinities," 353.

52 Ibid., 353.

53 Robertson, "Home and Away," 271; Rushdie, *The Wizard of Oz*, 23. Italics in original.

54 Dimendberg, "The Will to Motorization," 92.

55 Ibid., 93.

56 Laderman, *Driving Visions*, 4–5,

57 Ibid., 8; Rushdie, *The Wizard of Oz*, 50,

58 Forman et al., *Road Ecology*, 27.

59 Flink, *The Automobile Age*, 359.

60 Atkinson, "Crossing the Frontiers," 14.

61 Ibid., 17.

62 Pisarski, "Commuting in America."

63 Atkinson, "Crossing the Frontiers," 17.

64 Rodley, *Lynch on Lynch*, 194.

65 Galloway, *Protocol*, 241.

66 Abbate, "Cold War and White Heat," 353.

67 Steinmueller, "The U.S. Software Industry," 34.

68 Orgeron, *Road Movies*, 125.

69 Cranny-Francis, "Moving *The Matrix*," 101.

70 Ibid., 111.

71 Ibid., 112.

72 See http://en.wikipedia.org/wiki/Racing_video_game#List_of_racing_
    game_ sub-genres and http://en.wikipedia.org/wiki/List_of_best-selling_
    video_game_franchises.
73 Fischer et al., "The Racing-Game Effect," 1,397.
74 Ibid., 1,396.
75 Packer, *Mobility Without Mayhem*, 185–6.

Works Cited

ARTICLES AND BOOKS

Abbate, Janet. "Cold War and White Heat: The Origins and Meanings of Packet Switching." In *The Social Shaping of Technology*, 2nd ed. Donald McKenzie and Janet Wajcman, eds. Buckingham: Open University Press, 1999. 351–71.

African-American Masters: Highlights from the Smithsonian American Art Museum. Gwen Everett, ed. New York: Harry N. Abrams, 2003.

The Afro-American's Travel Guide. (Published today as *The African-American Travel Guide.*)

Aitken, Stuart C. and Christopher Lee Lukinbeal. "Disassociated Masculinities and Geographies of the Road." In *The Road Movie Book.* Steven Cohan and Ina Rae Hark, eds, London and New York: Routledge, 1997. 349–70.

Alexander, Charles C. *Holding the Line: The Eisenhower Era. 1952–1961.* Bloomington: Indiana University Press, 1976.

Alexie, Sherman. *The Lone Ranger and Tonto Fistfight in Heaven.* New York: HarperPerennial, 1993. Reissued with two new stories by Grove Atlantic Press, 2003.

– *Smoke Signals: A Screenplay.* New York: Miramax Books, 1998.

Allentuck, Marcia, ed. *The Achievement of Isaac Bashevis Singer.* Carbondale and Edwardsville: Southern Illinois University Press, 1969.

Ambrose, Stephen E. *Nothing Like It in the World: The Men Who Built the Transcontinental Railroad, 1863–1869.* New York: Simon and Schuster, 2000.

– *Undaunted Courage: Meriwether Lewis, Thomas Jefferson, and the Opening of the American West.* New York: Simon & Schuster, 1996 and 2003.

Anderson, Laurie, "From the Air," *Big Science* [CD]. Burbank, CA: Warner Brothers, 1982.

Andre, Amy. "Opinion: Bisexual Cowboys in Love." National Sexuality Resource Center (NSCR): 16 December 2005. http://nsrc.sfsu.edu/article/opinion_bisexual_cowboys_love. Retrieved 2010-03-24.

Atkinson, Michael. "Crossing the Frontiers." *Sight and Sound*, 4:1 (January 1994): 14–17.

Bain, David Haward. *Empire Express: Building the First Transcontinental Railroad*. New York: Penguin, 1999.

Bauman, John F., Roger Biles, and Kristin M. Szylvian, eds. *Tenements to the Taylor Homes*. University Park: Pennsylvania State University Press, 2000.

Beemyn, Brett, ed. *Creating a Place for Ourselves: Lesbian, Gay, and Bisexual Community Histories*. London: Routledge, 1997.

Belasco, Warren. "Motivatin' With Chuck Berry and Frederick Jackson Turner." In *The Automobile and American Culture*. David L. Lewis and Laurence Goldstein, eds. Ann Arbor: University of Michigan Press, 1980.

Bell, David. "Cowboy Love." In *Country Boys: Masculinity and Rural Life*. Hugh Campbell, Michael Mayerfeld Bell, and Margaret Finney, eds. University Park: the Pennsylvania State University Press, 2006. 163–80.

Bellow, Saul. "On Jewish Storytelling." In *What Is Jewish Literature?* Hana Wirth Nesher, ed. Philadelphia: Jewish Publication Society, 1994.

Benavie, Arthur. *Social Security Under the Gun*. New York: Palgrave, 2003.

Bennett, Robert. "Introduction: Teaching the Beat Generation to Generation X." In *The Beat Generation: Critical Essays*. Kostos Myrsiades, ed. New York: Peter Lang, 2001. 1–20.

Beyers, Thomas B. "History Re-Membered: *Forrest Gump*, Postfeminist Masculinity, and the Burial of the Counterculture." *Modern Fiction Studies* 42:2 (1996): 419–44.

Billington, Sandra. *A Social History of the Fool*. New York: St. Martin's Press, 1984.

"Billy Butler to Publish Travel Guide." *Pittsburgh Courier*. 5 April 1947.

Bloom, Harold. *Jack Kerouac's ON THE ROAD: Bloom's Modern Critical Interpretations*. Philadelphia: Chelsea House Publishers, 2004.

Bontemps, Arna. "A Summer Tragedy." In Langston Hughes, ed., *The Best Short Stories by Black Writers*. Boston: Little, Brown, 1967.

Borstelmann, Thomas. *The Cold War and the Color Line: American Race Relations in the Global Arena*. Cambridge: Harvard University Press, 2001.

Bourne, Russell. *Americans on the Move: A History of Waterways, Railways, and Highways.* Golden, Colorado: Fulcrum Publishers, in cooperation with the Library of Congress, 1995.

Bremser, Bonnie. *Troia: Mexican Memoirs.* New York: Creton Press, Ltd, 1969.

Brinkley, Douglas, ed. *Windblown World: The Journals of Jack Kerouac: 1947–1954.* New York: Viking, 2004.

Brittan, Arthur. *Masculinity and Power.* Oxford: Basil Blackwell Ltd, 1989.

Brod, Harry and Michael Kaufman, eds. *Theorizing Masculinities.* Thousand Oaks: Sage Publications, 1994.

Brown, Dee. *Hear that Lonesome Whistle Blow: The Epic Story of the Transcontinental Railroads.* New York: Henry Holt, 1977.

Bryson, Bill. *Made in America.* London: Black Swan, 1994.

Buber, Martin. *The Tales of Rabbi Nachman.* Atlantic Highlands, NJ: Humanities Press International, 1988.

Bullard, Robert D. et al., eds. *Highway Robbery: Transportation Racism & New Routes to Equity.* Cambridge, MA: South End Press, 2004.

Burgett, Bruce. *Sentimental Bodies: Sex, Gender, and Citizenship in the Early Republic.* Princeton: Princeton University Press, 1998.

Burk, Robert. *The Eisenhower Administration and Black Civil Rights.* Knoxville: University of Tennessee Press, 1984.

Butler, John L. *First Highways of America.* Iola, Wisconsin: Krause Publications, 1994.

Butler, Judith. *Bodies That Matter: On the Discursive Limits of "Sex."* New York: Routledge, 1993.

Cagin, Seth and Philip Dray. *Born To Be Wild: Hollywood and the Sixties Generation.* Boca Raton, FL: Coyote Books, 1994.

Campbell, Hugh, Michael Mayerfeld Bell, and Margaret Finney, eds. *Country Boys: Masculinity and Rural Life.* University Park: Pennsylvania State University Press, 2006.

Carden, Mary Paniccia. "'Adventures in Auto-Eroticism': Economies of Traveling Masculinity in *On the Road* and *the First Third.*" In *What's Your Road, Man? Critical Essays on Jack Kerouac's On the Road.* Hilary Holladay and Robert Holton, eds. Carbondale: Southern Illinois University Press, 2009. 77–98.

Carl, Robert. "Paul Dresher: *Slow Fire*" [CD review]. *Fanfare* (November/December) 1994.

Carney, George O. "Country Music and the South." In *The Sounds of People and Places: a Geography of American Folk and Popular Music.*

George O. Carney, ed. Lanham: Rowman & Littlefield Publishers, Inc., 1994. 115–36.

– "Introduction." In *The Sounds of People and Places*. George O. Carney, ed. Lanham: Rowman & Littlefield Publishers, Inc., 1994.

– "North American Music: A Historic-Geographic Overview." In *The Sounds of People and Places*. George O. Carney, ed. Lanham: Rowman and Littlefield Publishers, Inc., 1994. 11–13.

– Ed. *The Sounds of People and Places*. Lanham: Rowman and Littlefield Publishers, Inc., 1994.

Cartwright, Marguerite. "A Thought From a Friend." *Travelguide* (1947).

Casey, Roger N. *Textual Vehicles: the Automobile in American Literature*. New York and London: Garland Publishing, Inc., 1997.

Cassady, Carolyn. "Introduction." In *Neal Cassady: Collected Letters: 1944–1967*. Dave Moore, ed. New York: Penguin Books, 2004.

– *Off the Road: My Years with Cassady, Kerouac, and Ginsberg*. New York: William Morrow, 1990.

Cassady, Neal. *Neal Cassady: Collected Letters: 1944–1967*. Dave Moore, ed. New York: Penguin Books, 2004.

Castells, Manuel. *The City and the Grassroots*. Berkeley: University of California Press, 1983.

Cazden, Norman, Herbert Haufrecht, and Norman Studer. *Folk Songs of the Catskills*. Albany: State University of New York Press, 1982. 161–4.

Chancellor, Paul G. "What Songs Has America?" *The English Journal* (National Council of the Teachers of English) 33.2 (February 1944): 81–8.

Charters, Ann, ed. *Beat Down to Your Soul: What Was the Beat Generation?* New York: Penguin, 2001.

– *Kerouac: A Biography*. San Francisco: Straight Arrow Books, 1973.

– "Panel Discussion with Women Writers of the Beat Generation." (1996). In *Beat Down to Your Soul: What Was the Beat Generation?* New York: Penguin, 2001, 611–32.

Church of Jesus Christ of Latter-Day Saints. *The Pioneer Story*, 2000. http://www.lds.org/gospellibrary/pioneer/pioneerstory.htm (accessed July 2010).

Cohan, Steven and Ina Rae Hark. "Introduction." In *The Road Movie Book*. Routledge: London and New York, 1997. 1–16.

–, eds. *The Road Movie Book*. Routledge: London and New York, 1997.

Cohen, Lizabeth. *A Consumer's Republic: The Politics of Mass Consumption in Postwar America*. New York: Knopf, 2003.

Cohen, Theodore. "Just Because They're Men." In *Men and Masculinity: A Text Reader*. Theodore F. Cohen. ed. Australia: Wadsworth, 2001.

– "Men as Friends." In *Men and Masculinity: a Text Reader*. Theodore F. Cohen, ed. Australia: Wadsworth, 2001.

– ed. *Men and Masculinity: a Text Reader*. Australia: Wadsworth, 2001.

Cohen, William. *At Freedom's Edge: Black Mobility and the Southern White Quest for Racial Control, 1861–1915*. Baton Rouge: Louisiana State University Press, 1991.

Cole, Donald B. *The Presidency of Andrew Jackson*. Lawrence: University Press of Kansas, 1993.

Connerly, Charles E., "From Racial Zoning to Community Empowerment: The Interstate Highway System and the African-American Community in Birmingham, Alabama." *Journal of Planning Education and Research* 22, 2 (2002): 99–114.

Corrigan, Timothy. *A Cinema Without Walls: Movies and Culture after Vietnam*. New Brunswick, NJ: Rutgers University Press, 1991.

Cranny-Francis, Anne. "Moving *The Matrix*: Kinesic Excess and Postindustrial Being." In *The Matrix Trilogy: Cyberpunk Reloaded*. Stacy Gillis, ed. London, UK: Wallflower Press, 2005. 101–13.

Creekmur, Corey K. "On the Run and On the Road: Fame and the Outlaw Couple in American Cinema." In *The Road Movie Book*. Steven Cohan and Ina Rae Hark. eds. London and New York: Routledge, 1997. 90–112.

The Crisis 1, 1 (November 1910).

Crouch, Stanley. *One-Shot Harris: The Photographs of Teenie Harris*. New York: Harry N. Abrams, 2002.

Cullum, Judge Brett. "Review of *The Simple Life 2: Road Trip*." www. thejuryroom.com, 22 December 2004.

Cunningham, Daniel Mudie. "Driving into the 'Dustless Highway' of Queer Cinema." *Film Journal* 5 (2003). http://www.thefilmjournal.com/issue5/highway.html

Curry, Richard O. and Laurence B. Goodheart, eds. *American Chameleon: Individualism in Trans-National Context*. Kent, Ohio: The Kent State University Press, 1991.

Dargis, Manohla. Review of *About Schmidt. Los Angeles Times*. 13 December 2002. http://www.calendarlive.com/movies/reviews/cl-et-dargis13dec13,0,6488114.story

– Review of *Brokeback Mountain. New York Times*. 18 December 2005.

Davies, Pete. *American Road: The Story of an Epic Transcontinental Journey at the Dawn of the Motor Age*. New York: Henry Holt, 2002.

Davis, Glyn and Kay Dickinson, eds. *Teen TV: Genre, Consumption and Identity*. London: British Film Institute Publishing, 2004.

"Democracy Defined At Moscow." (editorial) *The Crisis* (April 1947): 105.

Dickstein, Morris. "Depression Culture: the Dream of Mobility." In *Radical Revisions: Rereading 1930s Culture*. Bill Mullen and Sherry Linkon, eds. Chicago: University of Illinois Press, 1996. 225–41.

Digital Tradition Folk Song Database, Mudcat Café Music Foundation, Inc., 2010. http://dev.mudcat.org/ (accessed July 2010).

Dimendberg, Edward. "The Will to Motorization: Cinema, Highways, and Modernity." *October* 73 (Summer 1995): 91–137.

Di Prima, Diane. *Memoirs of a Beatnik*. San Francisco: Last Gasp of San Francisco, 1969 (Rpt. Olympic Press, 1988.)

– *Recollections of My Life as a Woman*. New York: Viking Penguin, 2001.

Doctorow, E. L. *Ragtime*. New York: Penguin Press, 1974.

Dolgin, Kim. "Men's Friendships: Mismeasured, Demeaned, and Misunderstood." In *Men and Masculinity: a Text Reader*. Theodore F. Cohen, ed. Australia: Wadsworth, 2001.

Doty, Alexander. *Flaming Classics: Queering the Film Canon*. New York: Routledge, 2000.

Douglas, Susan J. *Where the Girls Are: Growing Up Female with the Mass Media*. New York: Three Rivers Press/Random House, 1994.

Douglass, Frederick. *My Bondage and My Freedom*. New York: Miller, Orton, & Mulligan, 1855.

Dreiser, Theodore. *A Hoosier Holiday*. Bloomington: Indiana University Press, 1997.

Dresher, Paul. *Casa Vecchia* [CD]. Boulder, CO: Starkland, 1995.

– *Dark Blue Circumstance* [audio cassette]. Berkeley, CA: Minmax Music, 1987. [N.B.: different contents from the CD of the same name.]

– *Dark Blue Circumstance* [CD]. San Francisco: New Albion Records, 1993.

– Paul Dresher Ensemble. http://www.dresherensemble.org/.

– *The Way of How* [audio cassette]. Berkeley, CA: Minmax Music, 1981.

Dresher, Paul and Rinde Eckert. *Power Failure* [CD]. Berkeley, CA: Minmax Music, [n.d.].

– *Shelf Life* [audio cassette]. Berkeley, CA: Minmax Music, 1987.

– *Slow Fire*: Paul Dresher Ensemble with Rinde Eckert [CD]. San Francisco: Minmax Music/Paul Dresher Ensemble, 1992.

– *Slow Fire*: Paul Dresher Ensemble with Rinde Eckert [videotape]. San Francisco: Target Videos, 1986.

- *Slow Fire*: Paul Dresher Ensemble with Rinde Eckert, the Complete Electric Opera in Two Acts Recorded in Performance at Theater Artaud [audio cassette]. Berkeley, CA: Minmax Music, 1988.

Dresher, Paul, Rinde Eckert, et al. *Pioneer* [CD]. Berkeley, CA: Minmax Music, 1990.

Dudziak, Mary L. *Cold War Civil Rights: Race and the Image of American Democracy*. Princeton: Princeton University Press, 2001.

Duncan, Dayton. *Out West: American Journey along the Lewis and Clark Trail*. New York: Penguin, 1988.

Duncan, Dayton and Ken Burns. *Horatio's Drive: America's First Road Trip*. New York: Alfred A. Knopf, 2003.

Ebert, Roger. "*Brokeback Mountain*." *Chicago Sun Times*. 16 December 2005. http://rogerebert.suntimes.com/apps/pbcs.dll/article?AID=/20051215/REVIEWS/51019006/1023

- "*Sideways*." *Chicago Sun Times*. 29 October 2004. http://rogerebert.suntimes.com/apps/pbcs.dll/article?AID=/20041028/REVIEWS/40922017/1023

Eckert, Rinde. [Website.] http://www.rindeeckert.com/

Editors of *Fortune* and R.W. Davenport. *U.S.A.: The Permanent Revolution*. New York: Prentice-Hall, 1951.

Engelhardt, Tom. *The End of Victory Culture: Cold War America and the Disillusioning of a Generation*. New York: HarperCollins, 1995.

Erens, Patricia. *The Jew in American Cinema*. Bloomington, Indiana: Indiana University Press, 1984.

Esposito, Jennifer. "The Performance of White Masculinity in *Boys Don't Cry*: Identity, Desire, (Mis)Recognition," *Cultural Studies – Critical Methodologies* 3, 2 (2003): 229–41.

"Eulogy for Billy Butler by Marion Cumbo." St Joseph's Church, 23 March 1981. William H. Butler Papers, Box 1, Schomburg Center, New York Public Library.

Ezard, John. "Auction of Kerouac Manuscript 'Blasphemy.'" *The Guardian*, 5 April 2001.

Faris, John T. *Roaming America's Highways*. New York: Farrar and Rhinehart, 1931.

Ferrell, Robert H. *The Presidency of Calvin Coolidge*. Lawrence: University Press of Kansas, 1998.

Fielder, Leslie. "Come Back to the Raft Ag'in Huck Honey!" *An End to Innocence: Essays on Culture and Politics*. Boston: Beacon Press, 1955.

Fischer, Peter, Tobias Greitemeyer, Thomas Morton, Andreas Kastenmuller, Tom Postmes, Dieter Frey, Jorg Kubitzki, and Jorg Odenwalder.

"The Racing-Game Effect: Why Do Video Racing Games Increase Risk-Taking Inclinations?" *Personality and Social Psychology Bulletin* 35 (2009): 1,395–409.

Fisher, Philip. "Democratic Social Space: Whitman, Melville, and the Promise of American Transparency." *Representations* 24 (1988).

Flink, James J. *The Automobile Age*. Cambridge, MA: MIT Press, 1988, 2001.

– *The Car Culture*. Cambridge, MA: MIT Press, 1975.

– "The Three Stages of American Automobile Consciousness," *American Quarterly* 24 (1972).

Forbes, Robert Pierce. *The Missouri Compromise and Its Aftermath: Slavery and the Meaning of America*. Chapel Hill: University of North Carolina Press, 2007.

Forman, Richard T.T., Daniel Sperling, John A. Bissonette, Anthony P. Clevenger, Carol D. Cutshall, Virginia H. Dale, Lenore Fahrig, Robert France, Charles R. Goldman, Kevin Heanue, Julia A. Jones, Frederick J. Swanson, Thomas Turrentine, Thomas C. Winter. *Road Ecology: Science and Solutions*. Washington: Island Press, 2003.

Foster, Mark S. "In the Face of 'Jim Crow': Prosperous Blacks and Vacations, Travel and Outdoor Leisure, 1890–1945." *The Journal of Negro History* 84, 2 (Spring 1999): 130–49.

Franklin, Garth. "Interview with Ang Lee." 7 December 2005. *Dark Horizons, http://www.darkhorizons.com/news05/brokeback2.php*

Franklin, John Hope and Isidore Starr, eds. *The Negro in Twentieth Century America: A Reader on the Struggle for Civil Rights*. New York: Vintage Books, 1967.

Franz, Kathleen. "The Open Road: Automobility and Racial Uplift in the Interwar Years." In *Technology and the African-American Experience*. Bruce Sinclair, ed. Cambridge, MA: The MIT Press, 2004, 131–54.

Frazier, E. Franklin, *Black Bourgeoisie: The Rise of a New Middle Class*. New York: The Free Press, 1957.

Friedman, Lester D., ed. *Arthur Penn's BONNIE AND CLYDE*. Cambridge, UK: Cambridge University Press, 2000.

Gagne, Nicole V. "*Transamerica*." *Cineaste* 31, 3 (Summer 2006): 56–7.

Galloway, Alexander R. *Protocol: How Control Exists After Decentralization*. Cambridge, MA: MIT Press, 2004.

Gann, Kyle. *American Music in the Twentieth Century*. New York: Schirmer Books, 1997.

Gates, Henry Louis. "The Trope of a New Negro and the Reconstruction of the Image of the Black." *Representations* 24 (1988).

Gibson, Donald R. "Individualism and Community in Black History and Fiction." *Black American Literature Forum*. 11, 4 (Winter 1977).

Gillis, Stacy, ed. *The Matrix Trilogy: Cyberpunk Reloaded*. London, UK: Wallflower Press, 2005.

Gilroy, Paul. "Driving While Black." In *Car Cultures*. Daniel Miller, ed., Oxford and New York: Berg, 2001, 81–104.

Gitlin, Todd. *The Whole World Is Watching: Mass Media in the Making and Unmaking of the New Left*. Berkeley: University of California Press, 1980.

Gordon, John Steele. *The Great Game: The Emergence of Wall Street as a World Power 1653–2000*. New York: Scribner, 1999.

Gould, Todd. *For Gold and Glory: Charlie Wiggins and the African-American Racing Car Circuit*. Bloomington: Indiana University Press, 2002.

Grace, Nancy McCampbell. *Jack Kerouac and the Literary Imagination*. London: Palgrave Macmillan, 2007.

– "A White Man in Love: A Study of Race, Gender, Class, and Ethnicity in Jack Kerouac's *Maggie Cassidy, The Subterraneans, and Tristessa*." *College Literature* 22, 1 (2000): 39–60.

Grace, Nancy McCampbell and Ronna C. Johnson, *Breaking the Rule of Cool: Interviewing and Reading Women Beat Writers*. Jackson: University of Mississippi Press, 2004.

Granger, Lester B. "Last of Pioneers." Publication unknown. William H. Butler Papers, Box 1, Schomburg Center for Research in Black Culture. New York Public Library.

Greenstein, Fred. *The Hidden-Hand Presidency: Eisenhower as Leader*. Baltimore, MD: Basic Books, 1982.

Groom, Winston. *Forrest Gump*. New York: Pocket Books, 1986.

Gutterman, David S. "Postmodernism and the Interrogation of Masculinity." In *Theorizing Masculinities*. Harry Brod and Michael Kaufman, eds. Thousand Oaks: Sage Publications, 1994. 219–38.

Halberstam, Judith. *In a Queer Time and Place: Transgender Bodies, Subcultural Lives*. New York: New York University Press, 2005.

Harris, Eddy. *South of Haunted Dreams: A Ride Through Slavery's Old Backyard*. New York: Simon & Schuster, 1993.

Heat-Moon, William Least. *Blue Highways: A Journey into America*. Boston: Back Bay Books (Little, Brown and Co.), 1999.

Henry, Charles P. *Ralph Bunche: Model Negro or American Other*. New York: New York University Press, 1999.

Hill, Lee. *Easy Rider.* London: British Film Institute Publishing, 1996.

Hill, Ralph Nading. *The Mad Doctor's Drive.* Brattleboro, Vermont: Stephen Greene Press, 1964.

Hiltzik, Michael. *The Plot Against Social Security.* New York: Harper Collins, 2005.

Himes, Chester. *If He Hollers Let Him Go.* New York: Thunder's Mouth Press, 1986.

- *The Quality of Hurt.* New York: Paragon House, 1990.

Hodgson, Godfrey. *America In Our Time.* New York: Vintage Books, 1976.

Hokanson, Drake. *The Lincoln Highway: Main Street Across America.* Iowa City: University of Iowa Press, 1988.

Holladay, Hilary and Robert Holton, eds. *What's Your Road, Man? Critical Essays on Jack Kerouac's On the Road.* Carbondale: Southern Illinois University Press, 2009.

Holmlund, Chris. *Impossible Bodies: Femininity and Masculinity at the Movies.* London: Routledge, 2002.

Holton, Robert. "Kerouac among the Fellahin: *On the Road* to the Postmodern." In Harold Bloom, *Jack Kerouac's ON THE ROAD: Bloom's Modern Critical Interpretations.* Philadelphia: Chelsea House Publishers, 2004. 77–92.

hooks, bell. *Wounds of Passion: A Writing Life.* New York: Owl Books, 1999.

Hoover, Herbert. "Let's Say Something Good About Ourselves. *Reader's Digest*, February 1956.

Hornung, Clarence P. *Wheels Across America.* New York: A.S. Barnes & Co., 1959.

Howard, John Tasker. *Our American Music: Three Hundred Years of It.* New York: Thomas Y. Crowell Company, 1954.

Hunt, Tim. "An American Education." In Harold Bloom, *Jack Kerouac's ON THE ROAD: Bloom's Modern Critical Interpretations.* Philadelphia: Chelsea House Publishers, 2004. 27–75.

Hurwitt, Robert. "Twenty years later, intense *Slow Fire* burns bright again" [performance review]. *San Francisco Chronicle*, 16 March 2007.

Hutcheon, Linda. *A Poetics of Postmodernism: History, Theory, Fiction.* New York and London: Routledge, 1988.

Hutchinson, Earl, Sr with Earl Ofari Hutchinson, *A Colored Man's Journey Through 20th Century Segregated America.* Los Angeles: Middle Passage Press, 2000.

Isaacs, Harold R. *The New World of Negro Americans.* New York: Viking, 1963.

Ives, Burl. *Wayfaring Stranger*. New York: Whittlesey House, 1948.

Jefferson, Thomas. Letter to William Henry Harrison, 1803. Downloaded
    1 May 2010. http://courses.missouristate.edu/ftmiller/Documents/
    jeffindianpolicy.htm

Jerome, John. *The Death of the Automobile: The Fatal Effect of the
    Golden Era, 1955–1970*. New York: W.W. Norton, 1972.

Johnson, Joyce (Glassman). *Come and Join the Dance*. New York:
    Atheneum, 1962.

– "Introduction," Jack Kerouac and Joyce Johnson. In *Door Wide Open:
    A Beat Love Affair in Letters, 1957–1958*. New York: Viking, 2000.

– *Minor Characters: A Young Woman's Coming of Age in the Beat Orbit
    of Jack Kerouac*. 1983. Rpt. New York: Anchor Book 1994.

– *Missing Men: A Memoir*. New York: Viking, 2004.

Johnson, Ronna C. "Mapping Women Writers of the Beat Generation."
    In *Breaking the Rule of Cool: Interviewing and Reading Women Beat
    Writers*. Nancy M. Grace and Ronna C. Johnson, eds. Jackson: Univer-
    sity of Mississippi Press, 2004. 5–41.

Jones, Arthur C. "Spirituals as Coded Communication." In *Sweet Chariot:
    The Story of the Spirituals*. The Spirituals Project at the University of
    Denver, 2004. http://ctl.du.edu/spirituals/Freedom/coded.cfm (accessed
    2010–20–July).

Jones, Hettie. *How I Became Hettie Jones*. New York: Grove Press, 1990.

Karst, Kenneth L. *Belonging to America*. New Haven: Yale University
    Press, 1989.

Kashner, Sam. *When I Was Cool: My Life at the Jack Kerouac School: A
    Memoir*. New York: Harper Collins, 2004.

Kehr, Dave. "Who Framed Forrest?" *Film Comment* 31, 2 (March–April
    1995): 45–51.

Kerouac, Jack. *On the Road*. 1955. Rpt. London: Penguin, 1999.

Kerouac, Jack and Joyce Johnson. *Door Wide Open: A Beat Love Affair in
    Letters, 1957–1958*. New York: Viking, 2000.

Kerouac, Jan. *Trainsong*. 1988. Rpt. New York: Thunder's Mouth Press,
    1998.

Kimmel, Michael. *Manhood in America: a Cultural History*. New York:
    Free Press, 1996.

– "Masculinity as Homophobia: Fear, Shame, and Silence in the Con-
    struction of Gender Identity." In *Men and Masculinity: a Text Reader*.
    Theodore F. Cohen, ed. Australia: Wadsworth, 2001.

Kirby, Jack Temple. "Black and White in the Rural South, 1915–1954,"
    Agricultural History 58 (July 1984).

Klinger, Barbara. "The Road to Dystopia: Landscaping the Nation in *Easy Rider.*" In *The Road Movie Book.* Stevan Cohan and Ina Rae Hark, eds., London and New York: Routledge, 1997.

Knight, Brenda, ed. *Women of the Beat Generation: The Writers, Artists and Muses at the Heart of a Revolution.* Berkeley: Conari Press, 1996.

Kosman, Joshua. "Dresher, Eckert Sizzle in Now-Complete *Slow Fire*" [performance review]. *San Francisco Chronicle,* 26 February 1988.

Kreider, Tim and Rob Content. "The Straight Story." *Film Quarterly* 54, 1 (Fall 2000): 26–33.

Kusmer, Kenneth L. *Down and Out, On the Road: The Homeless in American History.* Oxford: Oxford University Press, 2002.

Lackey, Kris. *Roadframes: The American Highway Narrative.* Lincoln: University of Nebraska Press, 1997.

Ladd, Brian. *Autophobia: Love and Hate in the Automotive Age.* Chicago and London: University of Chicago Press, 2008.

Laderman, David. *Driving Visions: Exploring the Road Movie.* Austin: University of Texas Press, 2002.

Lang, Robert. *Masculine Interests: Homoereotics in Hollywood Film.* New York: Columbia University Press, 2002.

– "*My Own Private Idaho* and the New Queer Road Movies." In *The Road Movie Book.* Steven Cohan and Ina Rae Hark, eds. London and New York: Routledge, 1997. 330–48.

Larson, Lars Erik. "Free Ways and Straight Roads: the Interstates of Sal Paradise and 1950s America." In *What's Your Road, Man? Critical Essays on Jack Kerouac's On the Road.* Hilary Holladay and Robert Holton, eds. Carbondale: Southern Illinois University Press, 2009. 35–59.

Law, George Malcolm. *American balladry from British broadsides: a guide for students and collectors of traditional song.* Philadelphia: American Folklore Society, 1957.

Leed, Eric. *The Mind of the Traveler.* New York: Basic Books, 1991.

Leisy, James F. *The Folk Song Abecedary.* New York: Bonanza Books, 1966.

Leland, John. *Why Kerouac Matters: the Lessons of On the Road.* New York: Viking, 2007.

Lesseig, Cory. *Automobility: Social Changes in the American South, 1909–1939.* New York: Routledge, 2001.

Levant, Ron. "Toward the Reconstruction of Masculinity." In *A New Psychology of Men.* Ronald F. Levant and William S. Pollack, eds. New York: Basic Books, 1995. 229–51.

Levant, Ronald F. and William S. Pollack, eds. *A New Psychology of Men.* New York: Basic Books, 1995.

Lewis, David L. and Laurence Goldstein, eds. *The Automobile and American Culture*. Ann Arbor: University of Michigan Press, 1980.

Lewis, Paul. *Cracking Up: American Humor in a Time of Conflict*. Chicago: University of Chicago Press, 2006.

Lewis, Tom. *Divided Highways: Building the Interstate Highways, Transforming American Life*. New York: Penguin, 1997.

Little, Jo. "Embodiment and Rural Masculinity." In *Country Boys: Masculinity and Rural Life*. Hugh Campbell, Michael Mayerfeld Bell, and Margaret Finney, eds. University Park: Pennsylvania State University Press, 2006. 183–201.

Lomax, Alan. *Folk Songs of North America*. Garden City: Doubleday & Company, Inc., 1960.

Lomax, John A. *Cowboy Songs: and Other Frontier Ballads*. New York: Macmillan Company, 1918.

Lomax, John and Alan Lomax. *American Ballads and Folk Songs*. New York: The Macmillan Company, 1934.

– *Our Singing Country: Folk Songs and Ballads*. New York and Mineola: Macmillan Company and Dover Publications, 1941 and 2000.

Lynell, George. "Muses of a Revolution; They Were Wives, Lovers, Writers and Observers Of the Beat Generation. But Their Contributions Were Mostly Overlooked." *Los Angeles Times*. 25 Nov. 1996. [Home Edition], 1.

Lynn, Kenneth S. "Roughing It." In *Mark Twain: A Collection of Critical Essays*. Henry Nash Smith, ed. Englewood Cliffs, NJ: Prentice-Hall, 1963. 40–6.

MacDonnell, Francis. "'The Emerald City Was the New Deal': E.Y. Harburg and *The Wonderful Wizard of Oz*." *Journal of American Culture* 13 (Winter 1990): 71–5.

Mackey, Steve and Rinde Eckert. *Ravenshead, the Complete Opera in Two Acts* [CD]. Berkeley, CA: Minmax Music, 2000.

Madsen, Deborah L. *American Exceptionalism*. Jackson: University Press of Mississippi, 1998.

Maisel, Albert Q. "The Negroes Among Us," *Reader's Digest*, September 1955.

Malone, Bill C. *Singing Cowboys and Musical Mountaineers: Southern Culture and the Roots of Country Music*. Athens: University of Georgia Press, 1993.

Mason, Philip P. *Making Michigan Move: A History of Michigan Highways and of the Michigan Department of Transportation*, Lansing: Michigan Department of Transportation, 1992.

McCoy, Drew R., *The Last of the Fathers: James Madison and the Republican Legacy.* Cambridge, MA: Harvard University Press, 1989.

McDarrah, Fred W. and Timothy S. McDarrah. *Kerouac and Friends: A Beat Generation Album.* New York: Thunder Mouth Press, 2002.

McKenzie, Donald and Janet Wajcman, eds. *The Social Shaping of Technology.* 2nd ed. Buckingham: Open University Press, 1999.

McNally, Dennis. *Desolate Angel: A Biography: Jack Kerouac, the Beat Generation and America.* New York: Random House, 1979.

Miller, Daniel, ed. *Car Cultures.* Oxford and New York: Berg, 2001.

– ed. *Technology and the African-American Experience.* Cambridge, MA: MIT Press, 2004.

Miller, Toby. *Technologies of Truth: Cultural Citizenship and the Popular Media.* Minneapolis: University of Minnesota Press, 1998.

Milloy, Courtland. "Black Highways: Thirty Years Ago in the South, We Didn't Dare Stop." *Washington Post*, 21 June 1987.

Mills, Charles W. *Blackness Visible: Essays on Philosophy and Race.* Ithaca: Cornell University Press, 1998.

Mills, Katie. "Revitalizing the Road Genre: *The Living End* as an AIDS Road Film." In *The Road Movie Book.* Steven Cohan and Ina Rae Hark, eds. London and New York: Routledge, 1997. 307–29.

– *The Road Story and the Rebel: Moving Through Film, Fiction, and Television.* Carbondale: Southern Illinois University Press, 2006.

Mohl, Raymond A. "Planned Destruction: The Interstates and Central City Housing." *From Tenements to the Taylor Homes.* John F. Bauman, Roger Biles, and Kristin M. Szylvian, eds. University Park: Pennsylvania State University Press, 2000. 226–45.

Moore, Dave, ed. *Neal Cassady: Collected Letters: 1944–1967.* New York: Penguin Books 2004.

Morgan, Jon. "The Feminist Man's Manifesto." In *Men and Masculinity: a Text Reader.* Theodore F. Cohen, ed. Australia: Wadsworth, 2001.

Moriel, Liora. "Erasure and Taboo: A Queer Reading of *Bonnie and Clyde*." In *Arthur Penn's BONNIE AND CLYDE.* Lester D. Friedman, ed. Cambridge, UK: Cambridge University Press, 2000. 148–76.

Morris, Christopher. "The Reflexivity of the Road Film." *Film Criticism* 28, 1 (Fall 2003): 24–52.

Mowery, D. C., ed. *The International Computer Software Industry: A Comparative Study of Industry Evolution and Structure.* Oxford, UK: Oxford University Press, 1996.

Mullen, Bill and Sherry Linkon, eds. *Radical Revisions: Rereading 1930s Culture.* Chicago: University of Illinois Press, 1996.

"Musician and Guide to His Bedeviled Race." *New York Post.* 5 August 1947.

Myrsiades, Kostos, ed. *The Beat Generation: Critical Essays.* New York: Peter Lang, 2001.

Natoli, Joseph and Linda Hutcheon. "Introduction." *A Postmodern Reader.* Joseph Natoli and Linda Hutcheon, eds. Albany: State University of New York Press, 1993. vii–xiv.

– eds. *A Postmodern Reader.* Albany: State University of New York Press, 1993.

The Negro Motorist Green Book. New York: Victor H. Green & Co., 1937–1959.

"Negroes Have Their Own Wall Street Firm." *The Saturday Evening Post.* 29 October 1955.

Newfield, Christopher. *The Emerson Effect: Individualism and Submission in American Life.* Chicago: University of Chicago Press, 1996.

Norton, Peter. *Fighting Traffic: The Dawn of the Motor Age in the American City.* Cambridge, MA: MIT Press, 2008.

Orbán, Katalin. "Swallowed Futures, Indigestible Pasts: Post-Apocalyptic Narratives of Rights in Kleist and Doctorow." *Comparative American Studies* 1, 3 (2003).

Orgeron, Devin. *Road Movies: From Muybridge and Méliès to Lynch and Kiarostami.* New York: Palgrave Macmillan, 2008.

Osgerby, Bill. "'So Who's Got Time for Adults!': Femininity, Consumption, and the Development of Teen TV-from *Gidget* to *Buffy*." In *Teen TV: Genre, Consumption and Identity.* Glyn Davis and Kay Dickinson, eds. London: British Film Institute Publishing, 2004.

Packer, Jeremy. *Mobility Without Mayhem: Cars, Safety, and Citizenship.* Durham, NC: Duke University Press, 2008.

Pease, Bob. "Introduction: Men, Masculinities, and Feminism." In *Recreating Men: Postmodern Masculinity Politics.* London: Sage Publications, 2000.

Pinchbeck, Daniel. "The Children of the Beats." *New York Times Magazine,* 5 November 1995. Rpt in Ann Charters, *Beat Down to Your Soul: What Was the Beat Generation?* (New York: Penguin 2001). 462–79.

Pinsker, Sanford. *The Schlemiel as Metaphor: Studies in Yiddish and American Jewish Fiction.* Carbondale and Edwardsville: Southern Illinois University Press, 1991.

Pisarski, Alan E. "Commuting in America." *Issues in Science and Technology Online.* Winter 2007. http://www.issues.org/23.2/realnumbers.html. Downloaded: July 23, 2009.

Powell, Adam Clayton. "The President and the Negro." *Reader's Digest*, October 1954.

Preston, Howard L. *Automobile Age Atlanta: The Making of a Southern Metropolis, 1900–1935*. Athens: University of Georgia Press, 1979.

Primeau, Ronald. *Romance of the Road: the Literature of the American Highway*. Bowling Green, OH: Bowling Green State University Popular Press, 1996.

Raper, Arthur F. *Preface to Peasantry: A Tale of Two Black Belt Counties*. Chapel Hill: University of North Carolina Press, 1936.

Reeser, Todd W. *Masculinities in Theory*. Chichester, UK: Wiley-Blackwell, 2010.

Remini, Robert V. *Andrew Jackson*. New York: Harper Perennial, 1999.

Retzloff, Tim. "Cars and Bars: Assembling Gay Men in Postwar Flint, Michigan." In *Creating a Place for Ourselves: Lesbian, Gay, and Bisexual Community Histories*. Brett Beemyn, ed. London: Routledge, 1997. 226–52.

Richardson, Mark. "Peasant Dreams: Reading *On the Road*." In *Jack Kerouac's* On the Road. Harold Bloom, ed. Philadelphia: Chelsea House Publishers, 2004.

Ritzer, George. *The McDonaldization of Society*. Thousand Oaks, California: Pine Forge Press, 2004.

Roberts, Shari. "Western Meets Eastwood: Genre and Gender on the Road." In *The Road Movie Book*. Steven Cohan and Ina Rae Hark, eds. London and New York: Routledge, 1997. 45–69.

Robertson, Pamela. "Home and Away: Friends of Dorothy on the Road in Oz." in *The Road Movie Book*. Steven Cohan and Ina Rae Hark, eds. London and New York: Routledge, 1997. 271–86.

Rodley, Chris. *Lynch on Lynch*. 2nd ed. London: Faber and Faber, 2005.

Rose, Albert C. *History of American Roads: From Frontier Trails to Super-highways*, New York: Crown Publishers, 1976.

Rushdie, Salman. *The Wizard of Oz*. London: British Film Institute, 1992.

Sachs, Carolyn. "Foreword." In *Country Boys: Masculinity and Rural Life*. Hugh Campbell, Michael Mayerfeld Bell, and Margaret Finney, eds. University Park: Pennsylvania State University Press, 2006.

Sadowski, Frank E., Jr, "The Erie Canal: 'Clinton's Big Ditch'," http://www.eriecanal.org.

Sandburg, Carl. *The American Songbag*. New York: Harcourt, Brace & Company, 1927.

Sanders, Linda. "Blown Wiring" [performance review of *Slow Fire*]. *Village Voice*, 1 July 1988.

Schaber, Bennet. "'Hitler Can't Keep 'em That Long': The Road, the People." In *The Road Movie Book*. Steven Cohan and Ina Rae Hark, eds. London and New York: Routledge, 1997. 17–44.

Scharff, Virginia. *Twenty Thousand Roads: Women, Movement, and the West*. Berkeley: University of California Press, 2003.

Schlesinger, Arthur M. *The Vital Center: The Politics of Freedom*. Boston: Houghton Mifflin, 1949.

Schutz, Charles E. *Political Humor from Aristophanes to Sam Earvin*. Rutherford, NJ: Fairleigh Dickinson University Press, 1977.

Schuyler, George. "The Phantom American Negro." *Reader's Digest*. July 1951.

Schweninger, Loren. "From Assertiveness to Individualism: The Difficult Path from Slavery to Freedom." In *American Chameleon: Individualism in Trans-National Context*. Richard O. Curry and Laurence B. Goodheart, eds., Kent, OH: The Kent State University Press, 1991.

Scott, A. O. "Healing Road Trips in Cinematic America." *International Herald Tribune*. Tuesday, 25 October 2005: 9.

Seeger, Pete. *The Incompleat Folksinger*. Lincoln: University of Nebraska Press, 1992.

Seiler, Cotten. *Republic of Drivers: A Cultural History of Automobility in America*. Chicago: University of Chicago Press, 2008.

Sharp, Cecil James. *American-English Folk Songs from the Southern Appalachian Mountains*. New York: G. Schirmer, Inc., 1918.

Siegel, Paul N. "Gimpel and the Archteype of the Wise Fool." In *The Achievement of Isaac Bashevis Singer*. Marcia Allentuck, ed. Carbondale and Edwardsville: Southern Illinois University Press, 1969.

Singer, Isaac Bashevis. "Gimpel the Fool." In *The Collected Stories*. New York: Farrar, Strauss and Giroux, 1982.

Skidmore, Max J. "Minnesota and America's Bully Boulevard," *Journal of American and Comparative Cultures* 23, 1 (Spring 2000).

– *Moose Crossing: Portland to Portland on the Theodore Roosevelt International Highway*. Lanhane, MD: Hamilton Books, 2007.

– *Presidential Performance: A Comprehensive Review*. Jefferson, North Carolina: McFarland Publishing, 2004.

– "Remembering TR: North Dakota and the Theodore Roosevelt International Highway." *North Dakota History* 67, 1 (2000).

– *Securing America's Future*. Lanham, Maryland: Rowman and Littlefield, 2008.

– "Uncovering the Northernmost Named Trail: The Theodore Roosevelt International Highway." *Popular Culture Review* 13, 1 (January 2002).

Skrentny, John David. "The Effect of the Cold War on African-American Civil Rights: America and the World Audience, 1945–1968." *Theory and Society* 27, 2 (1998).

Slethaug, Gordon E. "Hurricanes and Fires: Chaotics in Sherman Alexie's *Smoke Signals* and *The Lone Ranger and Tonto Fistfight in Heaven.*" *Literature/Film Quarterly* 31, 2 (2003): 130–40.

Slow Fire. Act II script with Dresher live-performance instructions in red ink [photocopy]. Unpublished, 1986.

Slow Fire. Dresher/Eckert. Original two-act version (not final version); Recorded Nov. 1986, Seattle, WA [DVD]. Unpublished, 1986.

Slow Fire. Libretto typescript. Act II, Dresher performing script. Unpublished, 1988.

Slow Fire. Libretto by Rinde Eckert [photocopy]. Unpublished, 1992.

Slow Fire. Paul Dresher Ensemble with Rinde Eckert, Live at the Cowell Theater, June 1992 [videotape]. Unpublished, 1992.

Slow Fire. Score: various untitled drafts, versions and sections, handwritten and printed out. Unpublished, 1986 and 1988.

Smith, Henry Nash, ed. *Mark Twain: A Collection of Critical Essays*. Englewood Cliffs, NJ: Prentice-Hall, 1963.

– *Virgin Land: The American West As Symbol and Myth*. Boston: Harvard University Press, 1978.

Snell, Bradford. *American Ground Transport*. Part 4A of Hearings on S1167, The Industrial Reorganization Act, Subcommittee on Antitrust and Monopoly, Committee on the Judiciary, US Senate, 93rd Congress, 2nd Session, Washington: GPO, 1974.

– "The Streetcar Conspiracy: How General Motors Deliberately Destroyed Public Transit. *New Electric Railway Journal* (Autumn 1995).

Snowden, Frank M. "They Always Ask Me About Negroes." *The Saturday Evening Post*, 10 March 1956.

"St. Alban's: New York Community is Home for More Celebrities than Any Other U.S. Residential Area." *Ebony*. September 1951, 34.

Stanley, Alessandra. "Yes, They're Sleazy, but Not Originals." *New York Times/International Herald Tribune*. 19 August 2010.

Steinbeck, John. *Grapes of Wrath*. New York: Viking, 1939.

– *Travels with Charley: In Search of America*. New York: Penguin, 1962.

Steinmueller, W. Edward. "The U.S. Software Industry: An Analysis and Interpretive History," in *The International Computer Software Industry: A Comparative Study of Industry Evolution and Structure*. D.C. Mowery, ed. Oxford, UK: Oxford University Press, 1996. 15–52.

Sterne, Richard. "Reconciliation and Alienation in Kleist's 'Michael Kohlhaas' and Doctorow's *Ragtime*," *Legal Studies Forum* 12, 1 (1988): 5–22.

Straayer, Chris. *Deviant Eyes, Deviant Bodies*. New York: Columbia University Press, 1996.

Sugrue, Thomas J., *The Origins of the Urban Crisis: Race and Inequality in Postwar Detroit*. Princeton: Princeton University Press, 1996.

Swain, Scott. "Covert Intimacy: Closeness in Men's Friendships." In *Men and Masculinity: a Text Reader*. Theodore F. Cohen, ed. Australia: Wadsworth, 2001.

Takaki, Ronald. "The Significance of the Frontier in American History: An Indian Perspective." In *A Larger Memory: A History of Our Diversity, With Voices*. Boston, New York, and London: Little, Brown & Co., 1998.

Theroux, Paul. "Remember the Cicadas and the Stars?" *International Herald Tribune*. Wednesday, 3 January 2007. 6.

Theweleit, Klaus. *Male Fantasies* (two volumes; translated from the 1977–78 *Männerphantasien*). Minneapolis: University of Minnesota, 1987–89.

Thompson, Hunter S. *Fear and Loathing in Las Vegas*. 2nd ed. New York: Vintage Books, 1998.

Trani, Eugene P. and David L. Wilson. *The Presidency of Warren G. Harding*. Lawrence: University Press of Kansas, 1977.

Travelguide. Mabel A. Roane, Administrative Secretary of the Negro Actors Guild, 1947.

Turner, Frederick Jackson. "The Significance of the Frontier in American History." *The American Studies Anthology*. Richard P. Horwitz, ed. Wilmighton, DE: Scholarly Resources, 2001. 83–96.

Urry, John. "The 'System' of Automobility." *Theory, Culture & Society* 21, 4/5 (2004): 25–39.

Van den Abbeele, Georges. *Travel as Metaphor: From Montaigne to Rousseau*. Minneapolis: University of Minnesota Press, 1992.

Van Elteren, Mel. "The Subculture of the Beats: A Sociological Revisit." *Journal of American Culture* 22, 3 (Fall 1999): 71–99.

Von Eschen, Penny M. *Satchmo Blows Up the World: Jazz, Race, and Empire in the Cold War*. Cambridge, MA: Harvard University Press, 2004.

Waldman, Anne, ed. *The Beat Book: Poems and Fiction of the Beat Generation*. Foreword by Allen Ginsberg. Boston: Shambhala Publications, Inc., 1996.

– "Foreword." In *Women of the Beat Generation: The Writers, Artists and Muses at the Heart of a Revolution*. Brenda Knight, ed. Berkeley: Conari Press, 1996. ix–xii.

Warner, Michael. *The Letters of the Republic: Publication and the Public Sphere in Eighteenth-Century America*. Cambridge, MA: Harvard University Press, 1990.

Washington, Booker T. "The Atlanta Exposition Address." In *The Negro in Twentieth Century America: A Reader on the Struggle for Civil Rights*. John Hope Franklin and Isidore Starr, eds. New York: Vintage Books, 1967.

Wee, Valerie, "Selling Teen Culture: How American Multimedia Conglomeration Reshaped Teen Television in the 1990s." In *Teen TV: Genre, Consumption and Identity*. Glyn Davis and Kay Dickinson, eds. London: British Film Institute Publishing, 2004.

Weinreich, Regina. *The Spontaneous Poetics of Jack Kerouac: a Study of the Fiction*. Carbondale and Edwardsville: University of Southern Illinois Press, 1987.

Welsford, Enid. *The Fool: His Social and Literary History*. Gloucester, MA: Peter Smith, 1966.

Whitman, Walt. "Backward Glance O'er Travel'd Roads." In *Leaves of Grass*. Philadelphia: David McKay, Publisher, 1891–2. 425.

– *Democratic Vistas, and Other Papers*. London: Walter Scott, 1888.

– "Song of the Open Road." *Leaves of Grass: Comprehensive Reader's Edition*. Harold W. Blodgett and Sculley Bradley, eds. New York: W.W. Norton & Co., 1965. 149–59.

Wiese, Andrew. *Places of Their Own: African American Suburbanization in the Twentieth Century*. Chicago: University of Chicago Press, 2004.

Williams, Linda Ruth. "My Father, the Heroine." *Sight & Sound* 16, 4 (April 2006): 42–3, 78.

Willis, Sharon. "Race on the Road: Crossover Dreams." In *The Road Movie Book*. Steven Cohan and Ina Rae Hark, eds. London and New York: Routledge, 1997. 287–306.

Wisse, Ruth. *The Schlemiel as Modern Hero*. Chicago: University of Chicago Press, 1971.

Witzel, Michael Karl. *Route 66 Remembered*. St. Paul, MN: Motorbooks International, 2003.

Wolfe, Tom. *The Electric Kool-Aid Acid Test*. New York: Farrar, Straus & Giroux, 1968.

Wylie, Philip. *Tomorrow!* New York: Rinehart & Company, 1954.

Yacowar, Maurice. "Forrest Gump; Rejecting Ideology." *Queen's Quarterly* 101, 3 (Fall 1994): 669–82.

Zavatsky, Bill. Review of *Selected Poems 1956–1975* by Diane di Prima. *New York Times*: 17 October 1976.

FILMS

2001: A Space Odyssey. Dir. Stanley Kubrick. 1968.

About Schmidt. Dir. Alexander Payne. 2002.

The Adventures of Priscilla, Queen of the Desert. Dir. Stephan Elliott. 1994.

Alice Doesn't Live Here Anymore. Dir. Martin Scorsese. 1974.

Back to the Future. Dir. Robert Zemeckis. 1985.

The Ballad of Little Jo. Dir. Maggie Greenwald. 1993.

Being There. Dir. Hal Ashby. 1979.

Bonnie and Clyde. Dir. Arthur Penn. 1967.

Boys Don't Cry. Dir. Kimberly Peirce. 1999.

Boys on the Side. Dir. Herbert Ross. 1995.

Brainstorm. Dir. Douglas Trumbull. 1983.

Brokeback Mountain. Dir. Ang Lee. 2005.

Broken Flowers. Dir. Jim Jarmusch. 2005.

Butch Cassidy and the Sundance Kid. Dir. George Roy Hill. 1969.

Catch Us If You Can. Dir. John Boorman. 1965.

City Slickers. Dir. Ron Underwood. 1991.

Connie and Carla. Dir. Michael Lembeck. 2004.

Deliverance. Dir. Blake Edwards. 1972.

Detour. Dir. Edgar G. Ulmer. 1945.

The Doom Generation. Dir. Gregg Araki. 1995.

Drugstore Cowboy. Dir. Gus Van Sant. 1989.

Easy Rider. Dir. Dennis Hopper. 1969.

The Elephant Man. Dir. David Lynch. 1980.

Elizabethtown. Dir. Cameron Crowe. 2005.

The Elopement. Dir. G. W. (Billy) Bitzer. 1903.

Even Cowgirls Get the Blues. Dir. Gus Van Sant. 1993.

eXistenz. Dir. David Cronenberg. 1999.

Fear and Loathing in Las Vegas. Dir. Terry Gilliam. 1998.

Female Trouble. Dir. John Water. 1974.

Five Easy Pieces. Dir. Bob Rafelson. 1970.

Forrest Gump. Dir. Robert Zemeckis. 1994.

Freaks. Dir. Tod Browning. 1932.

The Frisco Kid. Dir. Robert Aldrich. 1979.

Get on the Bus. Dir. Spike Lee. 1996.

Grapes of Wrath. Dir. John Ford. 1940.

Happy Together. Dir. Wong Kar-Wai. 1997.

Harold and Kumar Go to the White Castle. Dir. Danny Leiner. 2004.

Hedwig and the Angry Inch. Dir. John Cameron Mitchell. 2001.

Henry and June. Dir. Philip Kaufman. 1990.

Hud. Dir. Martin Ritt. 1963.

I Love Lucy's Zany Road Trip: California Here We Come. Dir. William Asher. 1951.

An Interrupted Elopement. Dir. Mack Sennett. 1912.

It Happened One Night. Dir. Frank Capra. 1934.

Johnny Guitar. Dir. Nicholas Ray. 1954.

Leaving Normal. Dir. Edward Zwick. 1992.

The Living End. Dir. Gregg Araki. 1992.

Lolita. Dir. Stanley Kubrick. 1962.

Lolita. Dir. Adrian Lyne. 1997.

Lonesome Cowboys. Andy Warhol. 1968.

The Long, Long Trailer. Dir. Vincente Minnelli. 1954.

Lord of the Rings trilogy (*The Fellowship of the Ring* [2001], *The Two Towers* [2002], and *The Return of the King* [2003]). Dir. Peter Jackson.

Lost in America. Dir. Albert Brooks. 1985.

Lust in the Dust. Dir. Paul Bartel. 1985.

The Matrix trilogy. (*The Matrix* [1999], *The Matrix Reloaded* [2003], *The Matrix Revolutions* [2003]). Dirs. Andy and Larry Wachowski.

Midnight Cowboy. Dir. John Schlesinger. 1969.

My America, Or, Honk If You Love Buddha. Dir. Renee Tajima-Pena. 1997.

My Man Godfrey. Dir. Gregory La Cava. 1936.

My Own Private Idaho. Dir. Gus Van Sant. 1991.

Natural Born Killers. Dir. Oliver Stone. 1994.

Planes, Trains, and Automobiles. Dir. John Hughes. 1987.

Postcards from America. Dir. Steve McLean. 1994.

Pow Wow Highway. Dir. Jonathan Wacks. 1989.

Psycho. Dir. Alfred Hitchcock. 1960.

Psycho. Dir. Gus Van Sant. 1998.

Rain Man. Dir. Barry Levinson. 1988.

The Rain People. Dir. Francis Ford Coppola. 1969.

Raising Arizona. Dir. Joel Coen. 1987.

The River. Dir. Tsai Ming-Ling. 1997.

Scorpio Rising. Dir. Kenneth Anger. 1963.

The Searchers. Dir. John Ford. 1956.

Sideways. Dir. Alexander Payne. 2004.

Smoke Signals. Dir. Chris Eyre. 1998.

Some Like It Hot. Dir. Billy Wilder. 1959.

Stagecoach. Dir. John Ford. 1939.

The Straight Story. Dir. David Lynch. 1999.

Stranger than Paradise. Jim Jarmusch. 1984.

Sugarland Express. Dir. Steven Spielberg. 1974.

Sunshine Sue. Dir. D. W. Griffith. 1910.

Thelma and Louise. Dir. Ridley Scott. 1991.

They Live By Night. Dir. Nicholas Ray. 1948.

They Would Elope. Dir. D.W.G. Griffith. 1909.

The Thirteenth Floor. Dir. Josef Rusnak. 1999.

To Wong Foo Thanks for Everything, Julie Newmar. Dir. Beeban Kidron. 1995.

The Tramp. Dir. Charles Chaplin. 1915.

Transamerica. Dir. Duncan Tucker. 2006.

TRON. Dir. Steven Lisberger. 1982.

TRON: Legacy. Dir. Joseph Kosinski. 2010.

Vanishing Point. Dir. Richard C. Sarafian. 1971.

Victor Victoria. Dir. Blake Edwards. 1982.

Weekend. Dir. Jean-Luc Godard. 1968.

When Harry Met Sally. Dir. Rob Reiner. 1989.

Wild Angels. Dir. Roger Corman. 1966.

Wild At Heart. Dir. David Lynch. 1990.

The Wild One. Dir. Laslo Benedek. 1953.

Wizard of Oz. Dir. Victor Fleming. 1939.

Y Tu Mama Tambien. Dir. Alfonso Cuaron. 2001.

GAMES

Burnout

Forza Motorsport

Gran Turismo

Need for Speed

TELEVISION SERIES

Alias (2001–2006)

Alice (1976–1985)

The Amazing Race (2001–)

America's Next Top Model (2003–)

Beverly Hills 90210 (1990–2000)

Buffy: The Vampire Slayer (1997–2003)

Caroline in the City (1995–1999)

Commander in Chief (2005–2006)

Desperate Housewives (2004–)

Family Ties (1982–1989)

Felicity (1998–2002)

The Fugitive (1963–1967)

The Ghost Whisperer (2005–2010)

The Girls Next Door (2005–)

Grey's Anatomy (2005–)

Green Acres (1965–1971)

Have Gun – Will Travel (1957–1963)

Heroes (2006–2010)

I Love Lucy (1951–1957)

Jersey Shore (2009–)

Keeping Up with the Kardashians (2007–)

The Kendra Show (2009–)

Kung Fu (1972–1975)

Lost in Space (1965–1968)

Maverick (1957–1962)

Moesha (1996–2001)

On the Road with Charles Kuralt (1967–1992)

One Day at a Time (1975–1984)

The Partridge Family (1970–1974)

Private Practice (2007–)

Rawhide (1959–1966)

Real Housewives (2006–)

The Real World (1992–)

Road Rules (1995–2007)

Route 66 (1960–1964)

Sex in the City (1998–2004)

The Simple Life (2003)

The Simple Life 2: Road Trip (2004)

Sister, Sister (1994–1999)

Star Trek (1966–1969)

Survivor (2000–)

Then Came Bronson (1969–1970)
Three for the Road (1975–1976)
The Time Tunnel (1966–1967)
Tru Calling (2003–2005)
The View (2001–)
Wagon Train (1957–1965)
The West Wing (1999–2006)

Contributors

PAUL ATTINELLO is senior lecturer at the International Centre for Music Studies at Newcastle University; he has taught at the University of Hong Kong and UCLA. He has published in *Contemporary Music Review, Radical Musicology*, the *Journal of Musicological Research, Musik-Konzepte, Musica/Realtá*, the revised *New Grove*, and in essay collections and reference works, including the groundbreaking *Queering the Pitch: The New Lesbian & Gay Musicology*. He is co-editor of collections on reinterpreting the Darmstadt avant-garde and on music in *Buffy the Vampire Slayer*. Current projects include a monograph on music about AIDS and a collection on contemporary composer Gerhard Stäbler.

STACILEE FORD is an honorary associate lecturer in the Department of History and the American Studies program at the University of Hong Kong. Her scholarship focuses on women's and gender history, transnational American studies, and US cultural history. She is the author of *Troubling American Women: Narratives of Gender and Nation*, and *Mabel Cheung Yeun-Ting's An Autumn's Tale*. She has lived in Hong Kong since 1993.

ELEANOR ELSON HEGINBOTHAM, professor emerita of English at Concordia University St. Paul (MN), was inspired to return to the brave, trailblazing writers in her chapter when, as a senior Fulbright fellow in the University of Hong Kong, she taught under the chairmanship of Gordon Slethaug. Having also taught in Liberia, Vietnam, and Indonesia, she was aware of the global interest in America's Beat writers, including women. Usually, however, her focus is on Emily Dickinson, on whom she has published widely, including a 2002 volume on Dickinson's "Fascicles." She continues to teach and write in the Washington, DC, area.

SUSAN KUYPER, an independent scholar and international teacher of music, has taught at the Harbour School in Hong Kong and the Hong Kong International School and has guest lectured on the globalization of music and the road at the University of Hong Kong. She has also taught ESL at the National University of Singapore and the Des Moines Area Community College. She presently teaches music privately and with the Central College Music Connection.

GINA MARCHETTI teaches in the Department of Comparative Literature, School of Humanities, at the University of Hong Kong. Her books include *Romance and the "Yellow Peril": Race, Sex and Discursive Strategies in Hollywood Fiction* (University of California, 1993); *Andrew Lau and Alan Mak's INFERNAL AFFAIRS – The Trilogy* (Hong Kong: Hong Kong University Press, 2007); *From Tian'anmen to Times Square: Transnational China and the Chinese Diaspora on Global Screens* (Philadelphia: Temple University Press, 2006); and *The Chinese Diaspora on American Screens: Race, Sex, and Cinema* (Philadelphia: Temple University Press, 2012).

COTTEN SEILER is associate professor and chair of the American Studies Department at Dickinson College in Carlisle, Pennsylvania. His teaching and research interests include US cultural and intellectual history, popular culture, and social and political theory. His work on automobility and US history has appeared in a number of international journals, and in his book *Republic of Drivers: A Cultural History of Automobility in America* (Chicago, 2008). His current research project examines expressions of "sameness" across a range of political and racial thought in the late twentieth-century United States. He is also associate editor of *Transfers: Interdisciplinary Journal of Mobility Studies*.

MAX J. SKIDMORE (PhD, Minnesota) is Curators professor of political science, and Thomas Jefferson fellow, at the University of Missouri-Kansas City. Recent books include *Securing America's Future* (2008); *Moose Crossing: Portland to Portland on the Theodore Roosevelt International Highway* (2007); *Politics and Language* (with Andrew Cline, 2007); *After the White House: Former*

Presidents as Private Citizens (2004); *Presidential Performance* (2004); *Social Security and Its Enemies* (1999; *Legacy to the World: A Study of America's Political Ideas* (2008). He has been distinguished Fulbright lecturer (India), senior Fulbright scholar (University of Hong Kong),and edits the peer-reviewed journal, *Poverty and Public Policy*.

GORDON SLETHAUG has taught at universities in Canada, China, Denmark, Hong Kong, and the United States, and draws from these experiences in his teaching and writing. He is currently professor at the University of Waterloo, where he teaches and researches contemporary American culture, film, and literature; globalization and communications; and international education. He is also honorary professor in Arts at the University of Hong Kong and has recently been visiting professor of English Studies at the University of Southern Denmark, where he was also senior Fulbright professor. He has co-authored *Understanding John Barth* and co-edited *International Education and the Chinese Learner*. He is the sole author of: *The Play of the Double in Postmodern American Fiction*; *Beautiful Chaos: Chaos Theory and Metachaotics in Recent American Fiction*; and *Teaching Abroad: The Cross-Cultural Classroom and International Education*.

MICHAEL TRUSCELLO is an assistant professor in English and General Education at Mount Royal University in Calgary, Alberta. His research includes post-anarchism, technology studies, and materialist cultural studies. His recent publications include contributions to *A Decade of Dark Humor: How Comedy, Irony, and Satire Shaped Post-9/11 America* from University Press of Mississippi; *Post-Anarchism: A Reader* from Pluto Press; and *Transgressions 2.0: Media, Culture, and the Politics of a Digital Age* from Continuum Press. He is also the director of the 2011 documentary film, *Capitalism Is The Crisis: Radical Politics in the Age of Austerity* (www. capitalismisthecrisis.net).

WENDY ZIERLER is associate professor of feminist studies and modern Jewish literature at Hebrew Union College in New York. Prior to joining HUC-JIR she was a research fellow in the English Department of the University of Hong Kong, where she co-taught a course on the Road in American Culture. She received her PhD and her MA from Princeton University, and is currently working on an MFA in Fiction Writing from Sarah Lawrence College. She is the author of *And Rachel Stole the Idols: The Emergence of Hebrew Women's Writing* (2004) and co-editor of the *Collected Writings of Hava Shapiro* (Hebrew, Resling Press, 2008), forthcoming in English from Wayne State University Press in 2013.

Index